JIMMY CONNORS SAVED MY LIFE

JIMMY CONNORS
SAVED MY LIFE

JOEL DRUCKER

Introduction by Mary Carillo

SPORT CLASSIC BOOKS

Published in the United States of America by Sport Media Publishing Inc., Wilmington, Delaware, and simultaneously in Canada.

For information about permission to reproduce selections from this book, please write to:
Permissions
Sport Media Publishing, Inc.,
21 Carlaw Ave.,
Toronto, Ontario, Canada, M4M 2R6
www.sportclassicbooks.com

Cover design: Paul Hodgson / pHd
Cover Photograph: Jimmy Connors, The SPORT Collection;
  Bedroom, Constance Giamo, The Image Bank

Back Cover Photograph: Author collection
Interior design: Greg Oliver
This book is set in Bembo.

ISBN: 0-9731443-8-6

Library of Congress Cataloging-in-Publication Data

Drucker, Joel.
  Jimmy Connors saved my life / Joel Drucker ; introduction by Mary Carillo.
    p. cm.
  Includes bibliographical references and index.
  ISBN 0-9731443-8-6 (hardcover)
  1. Connors, Jimmy, 1952- 2. Tennis players—United States—Biography.
3. Drucker, Joel. I. Title.
GV994.C66D78 2004
796.342'092--dc22

                              2004011315

  Printed in Canada

To Joan, always

ACKNOWLEDGEMENTS

Writers, like tennis players, regard themselves as hardcore soloists. But even someone as defiantly solitary as Jimmy Connors has admitted at least a few helped him along the way. In my case, many:

● Dave Engelberg, Mike Anderson, Jeff Williams, present at the creation
● Steve Flink, courtside colleague past, present, future
● David Shields, a writer who knows all about hitting for the lines
● Charlie Hoeveler and Allen Fox, who helped me see even when I wasn't ready to see
● S.L. Price, Bruce Jenkins and Nancy Price all knew I'd die if I didn't write it
● Mary Carillo, graced with a first-rate mind and an even bigger heart
● Trey Waltke, generous and as insightful as they come at grappling with how this game seeps into our souls
● Mark Preston, Dan Weinberg, Peter Bodo, Randy Walker, for support and insight
● Al Young, the first to encourage me to write about Connors
● Tom Schaub, as vital to my formative writing days as Segura was to Connors
● On the research front, two places were exceptionally helpful. At CBS, Laura Ouziel, Lon Samuelson and Bob Mansbach graciously rounded up tapes. At the International Tennis Hall of Fame, Mark Stenning, Mark Young, Ken Yellis and Kat Anderson opened up their archives and provided much assistance
● Peter Sawyer, my agent, who instantly grasped the concept
● At SPORTClassic Books, Jim O'Leary and Mike Simpson were everything a writer wants: thoughtful and attentive, pointed and mindful
● My parents, Alan and Erna; and brother, Ken, who of course lived through so much of this
● Most of all, to my wife, Joan Edwards, who never stopped believing in me

Intertviews

Over the last 20 years, as I've scraped barnacles off of Connors' massive hull, dozens in tennis provided insights and anecdotes. These below have been exceptionally helpful:

Vijay Amritraj, Jimmy Arias, Arthur Ashe, Glenn Bassett, Ray Benton, Ed Berman, Ron Berman, Bjorn Borg, Vic Braden, Stan Canter, Paul Cohen, Jimmy Connors, Donald Dell, Kent DeMars, Phil Dent, Eddie Dibbs, Cliff Drysdale, Richard Evans, Robert Evans, Chris Evert, Ken Flach, Tom Gorman, Brian Gottfried, Jim Grabb, Frank Hammond, Jeff Heely, John Heller, Doug Henderson, Luke Jensen, Bill Johns, Bob Kramer, Jack Kramer, Lornie Kuhle, Rod Laver, John Lloyd, Clarence Mabry, Barry MacKay, John McEnroe, Bob McKinley, Ilie Nastase, John Newcombe, John Powless, Mel Purcell, Dennis Ralston, Raul Ramirez, Pancho Segura, Leif Shiras, Steve Stefanki, Dick Stockton, Roscoe Tanner, Tony Trabert, Erik van Dillen, Guillermo Vilas, Mark Winters

CONTENTS

Introduction
by Mary Carillo

Whether you like the son of a bitch or you hate him, the fact is that Jimmy Connors is the most important tennis player of the last 50 years. Not the best or the most talented or the one with the most big titles, or any of that. All Jimmy Connors did was show up at the sport and blow open its doors, blow down its sides, blow off its roof. He changed the way the game was played by the pros, perceived by the fans and produced by television networks. He made it bigger, more exciting, more vulgar, and in all those ways, I suppose he made it more American. He made tennis matter.

I was a kid weaned on Rod Laver, Ken Rosewall, classy, understated Australians sporting all-white tennis outfits amid the splendor of the grass courts of nearby Forest Hills, New York. But I was lucky enough to get introduced early to the changing tide of tennis practically in my own backyard. I was born and raised in Douglaston, Queens, a few blocks away from another fellow who'd change the sport of tennis in his time—John McEnroe. We practiced at the famous Port Washington Tennis Academy, where another homegrown phenom a few years older than us, Vitas Gerulaitis, played his tennis. Vitas had a flamboyant personality, rock star looks—and a great game. Everyone I knew wanted to be like him and be around him.

I tell you this about Vitas because it eventually brings me to a point about Jimmy Connors. At the top of the tennis mountain—that is, the very top—there are only so many goodies to be had, and with these guys all vying for them, friendships among those guys were rare. Borg and McEnroe got along fine, but Guillermo Vilas was a bit of a loner, so Vitas had to draw him into the mix. Gerulaitis was good friends with all his rivals from those heady tennis boom days of the '70s—Bjorn Borg, Vilas, McEnroe, and Connors. Believe me, only Vitas had the right mix of oncourt performance and offcourt panache to pull that off.

As Connors was the first to tell anyone, he was very much his own man, and while he tried to generate hatred for Borg and Vilas, they mostly responded with their rackets. Try as Jimmy could, it was hard to make his rivalries with these guys get overly personal.

But McEnroe-Connors was a clash, like something out of a Japanese horror movie—two highstrung, combative lefthanders jousting to be America's best. Having known and played with McEnroe since early puberty, I admit I was deeply loyal to John, even as I admired the quality of Connors' tennis. But believe me, except for a few odd times in their long history together, these two couldn't stand each other. This was no media-manufactured hate-fest. Their matches were like one of those disasters where you put your hands over your face but couldn't help but stare through your fingers. And they also played some of the best all-court points you'll ever see.

Yet even though Connors was always a loner—much more even than McEnroe—I was constantly struck by his affection and loyalty to Vitas. In the '80s, after his playing days were over, Vitas, always a lover of the good life, was becoming a drug addict. I watched as he struggled and lost the battle of his addiction, and I watched as some friends tried to help, some made it worse, and some just left. But with Vitas, Jimmy was every bit as dogged a friend as he was a competitor. Connors had always hated drugs, despised how Vitas could play so fast and loose with his body, his mind and the law. As Vitas descended into his own private hell, Jimmy was there for him. He told Vitas in no uncertain terms that he had to quit all of it. Connors told Vitas that he would welcome him as a traveling hitting partner, even though by then Vitas wasn't able to give Jimmy or anyone else much of a practice. Connors was throwing Vitas a lifeline, pure and simple, and, at least for a while, Vitas took hold of it. The Gerulaitis family adored Jimmy for it. And when Vitas died, the grief-stricken Connors was among the eulogists and spoke candidly and lovingly about his friend. I will never forget Jimmy's loyalty and kindness. Nor will I forget another rare moment: Connors and McEnroe hugging one another at the funeral.

Considering Connors was so frugal with his friendships, what I liked about him most of all was the way he made all of us watching him part of his act. He drew you in right from the jump and had the uncanny ability to make you feel as though you could, merely as a spectator, conspire with him to win the match he was playing. Unlike McEnroe, who wanted everyone to shut the hell up, to make linesman go away and opponents slink off the court, Connors wanted to create a grand collusion of every possible element. Jimmy was well aware that plenty of people came to see him lose. He used that as fuel too. He used everything.

Connors was once asked what it would take for people to like him. He answered that he'd have to get older and he'd have to start losing. He was right, of course. It was at this time, during the '80s, when I truly got to appreciate Jimmy Connors, because I was announcing his matches by then. His semifinal run at the 1991 U.S. Open is still the greatest thing I've ever been a part of, and if my career peaked back then, so be it. By then Jimmy was 39 years old, years away from his dominance, and he'd very nearly lost in the first round. He brought so much to New York and left every bit of it out there on the court, and as a tennis announcer all I had to do was get the hell out of his way. He got me at that U.S. Open, me and so many others who were either confirmed Connors bashers, McEnroe aficionados, Borg lovers or rock-ribbed purists who longed for the good old days at Forest Hills. I thought that nothing short of a deathbed conversion could change people's minds about Jimmy Connors. I was wrong. Jimmy willed himself to greatness at that U.S. Open and willed us all to love him for it once and for all. Then he picked up his rackets and went home to California.

There's another tenacious California lefty with a will as great as Connors' and the singular ability to explain Jimmy and his legacy, and he is the author of this book. In the same way that Gay Talese brought insight and a keen, sharp eye to such complicated American icons as Frank Sinatra and Joe DiMaggio, Joel Drucker explores Jimmy Connors. Joel grew up on Jimmy, was formed and transformed by the young Connors, the champion Connors, Connors as colleague and friend, Connors as he left the sport. Jimmy Connors is so many things. Joel carefully teases them apart, studies them all, then weaves them together again. No one I know has spent more time watching his matches, thinking about the man, analyzing his actions and words, comparing and contrasting himself to the legend, obsessing over the bigger picture that Jimmy Connors takes him to. Simply put, Joel had to write this story. As an old friend and admirer of Joel, I know that for sure; it's a purging, this book. As you will see, Joel is everywhere in these pages, as fascinating and gutsy a journey as the one taken by Jimmy. Few people I know are willing to reach deep into their inner lives and so beautifully and power-fully express what they find. In this book Joel Drucker goes to where Jimmy Connors leads him—then goes even further by himself.

Connors will be surprised by what he finds out—about himself, about his far-reaching powers, and especially about the author. So will you.

Epigraph

People don't get it. They think that because tennis is played at these clubs that it's a rich man's sport. But it doesn't take more than a racket and a heart to play this game. That's the great thing about a sport like tennis. It's a great test of democracy in action. Me and you, man, in the arena. Just me and you, baby. Doesn't matter how much money you have, or who your dad is, or if you went to Harvard, or Yale, or whatever. Just me and you.

—Pancho Segura, Hall of Famer and
former coach of Jimmy Connors

Prologue:
One-Way
Love Story

Besides, why should we be cowed by the name of Action? 'Tis a trick of the
senses,—no more. We know that the ancestor of every action is a thought . . .
To think is to act. —Ralph Waldo Emerson

Jimmy Connors saved my life. With a snarl and a grunt and a back-hand and a squeaky pair of shoes, he saved me—from, what? Predictability. Mediocrity. Irony. Unhappiness.

Connors saved me by legitimizing a sissy sport and making me a part of it. He saved me because he showed me how to turn thought into action. He saved me because he simultaneously let me lose my head and keep it when those around me were losing theirs. He saved me because he was, as the saintly Arthur Ashe put it, "my favorite asshole." He saved me because he inspired me to play better tennis and apply that intensity to love and work. He saved me because he didn't care about anyone but himself, because at heart he's a greedy, narcissistic, paranoid, tenacious, predatory, sensate creature—qualities that triggered my own visceral desires and lofty ambitions.

Why did I need Connors to succeed? After all, long before Connors entered my life, I was raised with those specifically American and Jewish notions of exceptionalism. On Halloween night, 1965, when I was five years old, my father pinned cotton balls on a towel worn over a jacket, concocted a glittery magic wand for my left hand and fancied a paper crown with the words "Old King Joel" on it. From birth, my older brother Ken and I were photographed and celebrated as extensively as the Kennedys. We were the stars of our family, the shining, entertaining, brilliant children of an upper middle-class couple.

Great accomplishments were our destiny. Of course in a Jewish, urban

family, these deeds would be achieved more with the mind than the
body. Sports was for dumb jocks. The best careers for us verbal types were
as writers, scholars, thinkers. Ken and I were programmed that way. "How
old are those children?" goes the joke. "The lawyer's two and the doctor
is three." How does a man as vulgar as Connors fit into that environment? What would he know of my parents' coffee table and its
omnipresent Sunday *New York Times*? Like most athletes, he likely believes
"book smart" is synonymous with "less smart." Body and mind, heart
and head, thought and action—how to unify? The great tennis player
Jack Kramer dropped out of college because he didn't want to read about
kings. He wanted to meet them. Connors would love this notion, too,
particularly since he too saw himself as a king. But Jack and Jimmy,
wouldn't you have more to talk about if you knew about them too?

Ken and I occupied a different world than that of the jock. Ours
was a family where brains trumped brawn. A snowy winter's evening in
1968. I'm seven and have just been given the gift of a globe. It's one of
those new ones where you screw a lightbulb into Antarctica, flick a
switch with your thumb and the whole planet becomes illuminated. Ken
and I plug it in and trace our fingers over the entire landscape. Then
we quiz each other on state capitals.

I admit it's rather puzzling and even disgusting that I, the bookish,
friendly winner of sportsmanship awards and a dutiful second son, find
myself so smitten with someone as crude as Jimmy Connors. It helped
to learn, though, that Connors was also a dutiful second son.

Yet if not for Connors, what would I be? It was Jimbo's world of
action, not mine of contemplation, which pointed me to visualize success
in different ways. Connors inspired me to be something other than a
Beverly Hills lawyer, Madison Avenue hack or Wall Street financier—
all viable, easily-attainable career routes for a child of my streets. Connors
showed another avenue. Connors showed that the middle of life's court
was nothing. It was the lines where you wanted to live. Connors showed
me how to will myself into a sport I loved (even as I resisted its advances).
Connors showed me it was worth pursuing passion. Jimbo and me. It's
a twisted, one-way love story, fueled by my quest for transcendence
and the illusion of friendship.

Had all gone as I'd hoped, you'd be reading Connors' sanctioned biography, filled with his insights on how his mother Gloria and grandmother
Bertha made him a champion, how he won eight Grand Slam singles
titles and what made his rivalries with Pancho Gonzalez, Bjorn Borg,
John McEnroe and Andre Agassi so compelling.

For Connors was probably the most important player in tennis history.

The first champion to start his professional career in the Open Era, Connors was at the head of the line when tennis made its transition in the 1970s from a lily-white parlor game played at elite clubs to today's Technicolor, multi-million-dollar pro sport contested in massive stadiums and viewed on national television. As both protagonist and antagonist, catalyst and influence, villain and hero, no one more than Connors personified the notion that a tennis player was more than a skilled athlete, but a superstar, a cultural icon with crossover appeal.

What helped him most, of course, was that he'd emphatically delivered the goods from the get-go. In his first full year as a pro, Connors won six titles. Within two years, he reached the top—and finished five straight campaigns ranked number one on the ATP Computer, a mark only broken by Pete Sampras 20 years later. Connors was also ranked in the top three from 1973-85, a record of top-tier excellence likely never to be matched. Ditto for his Open-era achievement of 109 tournament victories.

There was a point when I felt my life's mission was to be Connors' appointed biographer. The journey stretched back to childhood trips to the presidential mansions of Roosevelt and Truman, nights spent devouring tales of Kennedy, Koufax and King, college courses studying the craft of narrative, history and biography. My ambition culminated with a rarely-seen side of Connors.

It was Monday, August 27, 1990, the first day of the U.S. Open. For two decades, this was a time of action for Connors, the day when he geared up to play the tournament he loved more than any other and where, as the world knew, he played his finest tennis. But Connors had not played a match since injuring his wrist in February. Instead he spent hours pounding his feet on a StairMaster—and contemplating his next move.

Concerned about Connors' possible retirement, I wrote an article for *World Tennis*. Titled "Play It Again, Jimmy," the story explained my personal connection to Jimbo, a heartfelt affinity I believed stretched to everyone in the sport. "Jimmy Connors' true gift," I wrote, "is his will to survive." The story included my photo and the caption: "A portrait of the author as a Connors fan," a pleasing allusion to the great writer James Joyce's classic, *A Portrait of the Artist as a Young Man*.

Eager to see Connors ride into the sunset, I made plans to attend the Open, taking time off from my full-time job at a public relations firm. A week before the Open, Connors' name was placed in the draw. Arriving in New York the day before the tournament was played, I was devastated to learn he pulled out.

Dissipated energy lurks through the first afternoon of the U.S. Open. Unlike Wimbledon, where the defending men's champ strides onto Centre Court in front of a full stadium at precisely 1:00 p.m., the U.S. Open starts with little fanfare and an underfilled stadium. It's easy to feel dazed and even bored in anticipation of greater players and bigger moments.

With Connors gone, my attention drifted. As I sat in the press section, I stared out into the sun-baked Louis Armstrong Stadium where Connors had waged so many campaigns. The TV commentator Mary Carillo looked my way. We'd only met once three years before, so I was surprised when she said, "You're the guy from the Connors story. That was a good piece." I thanked her and replied, "Too bad he's not here." Carillo responded, "Ah, Jimmy."

Then in the media cafeteria, I ate next to Arthur Ashe. A year prior, he and I had a three-hour dinner and interview, during which he explained to me how difficult it was for Connors to make the transition out of tennis. Now, both of us aware that Jimmy wasn't playing, Ashe chuckled. "Connors," he said. "Connors. Doesn't know whether he wants to come or go. Connors."

Still distraught at Connors' absence, I strolled the grounds, glimpsed a few matches and headed into the players' lounge. At 3:00 p.m., I pondered a return trip to Manhattan.

And then I saw him.

They say luck is the residue of hard work. Many of my face-to-face encounters with Connors had occurred less amid grand public celebrations and more during private moments in odd places. But this wasn't the hallway of a dingy arena. It was the U.S. Open, Jimmy Connors' personal pulpit. Shaking my hand, he said without any prodding, "That was a hell of an article. My mom loved it too."

He was wearing tennis clothes, hoping to practice as much as his wrist would tolerate. It was odd to see Connors at the Open, as if he were a high school grad cruising the old parking lot. He invited me to join him for a late lunch and introduced me to his older brother, Johnny, and a group from his hometown that Johnny had brought for the day.

Connors was uncharacteristically subdued. So often at this venue he'd keyed himself up for battle, building up the "tiger juices" nurtured by his mother. Now the lion looked at winter. The sunny day turned dark. A rainstorm washed out Connors' hitting session. He scarcely paid attention to his brother and the Belleville troupe. Then he asked me a question I'd waited eight years to hear.

"Son," he said, "have you ever written a book?"

The image that came to mind was one of Connors moving in on a short ball to his backhand. I was primed to attack.

"No, but if I wrote one about you it would be the best book ever written about tennis."

"Well—"

Right then, one of Connors' many tennis cronies, Vitas Gerulaitis, approached. Topic derailed.

At any moment, I was ready for Connors to utter some comment like "Nice seeing you" or "We'll see ya," or "Gotta get to work." The last thing I wanted was to overstay my welcome.

The dispatching never came. As I walked the grounds of Flushing Meadows alongside Connors, I witnessed a magnet. Connors attracted greetings from various media, agents, equipment company reps, players and more. He glanced at a TV screen where John McEnroe was playing. "Oh, it's him," said Connors. He shook his head in dismay at Andre Agassi, who in those days came on court adjusting his hair, earrings and clothes. "That boy sure creates a lot of clutter for himself," said Connors. There was a friendly interaction with the prominent journalist John Feinstein. Connors jokingly introduced me to him as "a guy who knows a thing or two about tennis." In all these interactions, Connors was less athlete and more like an exiled CEO at a trade show. He was a source of revenue for so many of these people—and they in turn built a world that made him rich too. He too knew that commerce was one thing, and tennis was another. When another player asked Connors his thoughts on the current USTA president, Connors scoffed. "All these guys want is a plaque with their name on it, as if they ever did anything," he said. "Tell you what. How 'bout I pay $200, give them a plaque and they can go away?"

Then came a more emotional encounter with Pancho Segura. Arguably the greatest tactical mind in tennis history, Segura was responsible for turning Connors from a tenacious teenager into a court-savvy champion. But the Connors family purged Segura at an unwise time. There'd been occasional reunions, but it was never quite the same between these two. In spite of Connors' cruelty, the big-hearted Segura had never stopped adoring Connors.

"Jimbo!"

"Pancho!"

They hugged. Segura and Connors had each attacked the sport with so much emotion, conspired in the alchemy of competition that's deeper than words, rode their mutual intensity all the way to the top. Though the younger man would no doubt cry deeply at the older man's death, never did Connors give Segura the praise he deserved.

"Your coach," I said as we left Segura.

"*Former* coach," said Connors.

We marched on. The skies cleared, the courts dried, then another blast of rain. Connors joked with a frequent sparring partner, Aaron Krickstein, about the money "Kricker" owed him from a card game. By 8:00 p.m. the courts were dry again. On Court 24, 150 yards away from the Louis Armstrong Stadium where Connors had won three titles, Connors prepared for a practice session with Carl Chang (Michael's older brother, a fine college player). Connors' wrist required wrapping. He politely asked if I'd mind twisting a thin piece of gauze around it. "There, there, a little more," he said. "Thank you."

A crowd of no more than 75-100 people watched as Connors scampered all over the court for a brisk hour. We headed back to the locker. He got a brief massage, put on a new T-shirt and reconnected with Johnny Connors, bodyguard Bill Lelly and the rest of Johnny's group.

Four of us were crammed into the back seat of a taxi. Beads of sweat glistened on Connors' face. As he turned back to glance at the Louis Armstrong Stadium, Connors said to me, "If I ever get back there, that place is going to rock and roll."

"If" was never more conditional in the life of Jimmy Connors. A year hence, people who wouldn't know a tennis racket from a croquet mallet knew all about Jimmy Connors thanks to his sentimental run to the semifinals. But now, for the first time in his career, he left the U.S. Open without playing a single match.

The book remained the elephant in the room. I wasn't stupid enough to bring it up. It was Connors who made the move. "We could be a good team," he said. "You're on the outside of tennis and want to get in. I'm on the inside and want to get out. Here's the first line of the book: 'This will set the record straight.'"

I wanted nothing more than a massive New York traffic jam. But we zipped our way into Manhattan. The cab headed north on Park Avenue towards Connors' hotel. Just before arrival, he made his final request.

"Here's what I want you to do," he said. "You write down how you'd tell my story and why you're the best one to tell it. As soon as you're through, you call me, find out where I am, and fax it to me. Now get to work."

Two days later, Connors still hanging out in the players' lounge at the U.S. Open, he spotted me and asked, "How's the work going, son?"

Son? I'll admit that long after I've emotionally divorced myself from Connors as any sort of friend (?), I still love the blarney-spewing, paternal flavor of him calling me that.

Connors was never more a man to me than during this period of potential collaboration. His tennis fate threatened, he was forced to contemplate mortality in ways he never had. I held hopes that our book would be introspective, as refreshing and clean as Connors' game. Diving into his life would help me better understand and explain this misunderstood sport. "What is this, a tennis match?" Pittsburgh Steelers linebacker Jack Lambert once yelled mid-game. If you only knew, Jack, I thought, if you only knew. But Connors knew, and if he told, the world would know too.

At the beginning of Anne Rice's *Interview with the Vampire*, an enterprising writer dares ask a vampire if he'd recount the story of his life. Charmed by the writer's nerve, the subject agrees. "Admirably fair," says the vampire. "I would like to tell you the story of my life, then. I would like to do that very much." Connors had been tennis' premier vampire. No one in the sport's history rose from the depths more frequently to bite his opponents in the neck. No one bit more people, sucked more blood and so enjoyed its taste than Connors. Over the course of meals and drinks and interviews, I'd thought he'd issue his confessional to me, so in turn I could taste every drop of that blood. "You know me as well as any writer," he once told me. He led me to believe he cared.

If I'd taken lessons from your mother, I asked him, what would I have learned? We were walking across the lawns of Pebble Beach. It was a long way from his birthplace, East St. Louis. Pausing, Connors' brown-green eyes narrowed. He turned away, stared at the ocean, then turned back and leaned a foot closer to me. "Son," he declared, "you would have learned *the game*."

It didn't happen. Connors demurred. I became just another opponent, challenging him not with a racket like John McEnroe or Bjorn Borg but with something more dangerous: curiosity. No doubt I was wrong to expect anything less from a man who so viscerally exemplified the meaning of tennis. In a sport so solitary, even the classiest champions are fueled by ample paranoia. The Connors of 1990 was a jock contemplating life as man, a tennis version of Douglas MacArthur staring out at the long shadows in the twilight of his epoch. *Old soldiers never die, they just fade away.* The Connors who scrapped and screamed his way to the '91 Open semis emerged a child reborn, amped up for Madison Avenue like George C. Scott taking Patton to Branson, Missouri, for a one-man show. Call it "Give 'Em Hell, Jimbo," complete with all the headlines prematurely announcing his defeat.

"Do you really think," a Connors hitting partner asked me, "that even Jimmy knows what makes him tick? And if he did, it might be too horrifying for him to talk about, much less see in print. This sport, man, it can eat you alive."

A few preliminary notions on this tennis thing. You think you know it, don't you? Friendly swatting? Leisure activity? Parlor game for the rich? Sport of kings? Guess again. "People just don't understand," went one of Connors' trademark phrases, "that it's a goddamn war out there." Because it wasn't clear if he was referring strictly to tennis, Connors raised the ante. He vividly proved what makes tennis such a hot, passionate and lonely sport. As his mother told him after he'd surrendered a lead versus her, even the person who loves you most will hit the ball down your throat if you don't take care of business.

Kill or be killed. No one more than Connors brought this tennis principle to life. Though its great champions always knew how brutal tennis was, not until Connors leaped into the Technicolor Open Era did millions see tennis' essential combat with their own eyes. Tennis is cockfighting for civilized people. Tennis is a dance where you're trying to trip your partner. Tennis is physical chess. Tennis is boxing with rackets. Tennis is a sport where white lines and polite rituals bracket combat. Tennis is the ultimate embodiment of democracy, where an individual is either in retreat or on the warpath. Tennis is a language, a culture, a romance, a passion, a partnership, a joust. Connors proved this more than anyone. He was tennis' Elvis, its first rock 'n' roll folk antihero whose resilience eventually and invariably made him beloved.

If tennis was to thrive as a sport, it needed the kind of definition and resonance only a Connors biography could provide. What am I saying? It still needs it. Recently Lenny Fox, a chiropractor, offered his advice for recovery from an injury. "You could play a casual game of tennis if you wanted," he suggested.

My eyes narrowed into slits, much the same way Connors' did whenever he glared down a big server on break point.

"Lenny, you play basketball, right?"

He nodded.

"Do you ever play *casual* basketball?"

Lenny admitted he'd never thought this way about tennis.

But I was never going to play tennis as well as Jimmy Connors. From the crib, Connors was fed tennis balls. I was programmed to be a student, a hyper-charged brain trapped inside a sports-loving soul. Thanks to Connors, moments arrived when body and mind joined forces. Connors' manner seeped into my sensibilities as the best way to turn contemplation into movement, private desire into public headlines. Majoring in history at Berkeley, I learned how the historian is no mere critic, no solitary observer. The historian paints the broadest possible canvas. He draws on a spectrum of ideas and breathes meaning into a world in search of definition. And the point of great ideas, said Ralph Waldo Emerson, is to put them into action. It was also Emerson who said, "There is properly no history. There is only biography." The biography of Jimmy Connors was my intended vehicle. By defining him, I would redefine my beloved tennis. A subculture would be raised. And I would soar, a teller of the tales of a sporting king.

It didn't quite happen that way. How dare I admonish Connors for not telling his story? Certainly he has the right to take tennis' secrets to his grave. "Everything I could give was on that court," Connors said at the 2003 U.S. Open. "I left DNA out there." Dare I ask for more?

Yes.

Connors made me demand more from life, and so in turn, I demand more from him. His story, I was convinced, was one that I knew more about than anyone on the planet, and that the final step would be to hear it from Connors himself. Connors, too, knew how much blood I wanted to suck, and perhaps that commingling of fluids scared him, made him more eager to occupy myth than truth. Or, borrowing the line from Jack Nicholson, he might say, you can't handle the truth. I can, Jimmy, yes I can, for you see, when you bit me long ago, you also gave me the power to rise up at night and plunge my own teeth into the neck of a subject. For what more is a biographer than another kind of vampire, sucking every last drop of blood? For more than 20 years, I have been in pursuit of Connors, constantly looking for ways to see both the tapestry and threads of his story.

So I'm not Connors' authorized biographer, nor his ghost, nor even, probably, his friend (I'm told by many he has none, and I believe it). None of that loss stops me from continuing to obsess over Connors, tennis and the way he unleashed the sport and saved me from potential mediocrity; or, at least, ironic midlife alienation. As Billie Jean King put it, "Jimmy Connors will never find himself at the age of 50 sitting in an airport lounge wondering, 'What if?'"

King's comment echoes every time I meet a lawyer, accountant or salesman who laments the dreary arc his life has taken. When I ponder my own ambitions, it's not a courtroom or boardroom that enters my mind. I see Connors. I see him chasing down a forehand, striking it deep crosscourt, rocking his opponent on his heels and going from defense to offense like no one else in tennis history. I'm seeing someone redirect a point, a game, a set, a match, a career, a self. As the German philosopher of history, Hegel, wrote, "I only know an object in so far as I know myself and my own determination through it, for whatever I am is also an object of my consciousness, and I am not just this, that or the other, but only what I know myself to be. I know my object, and I know myself; the two are inseparable."

I'm leaving my DNA in here.

1

Counterpuncher

Few sports are as fair as tennis. You can't blame a coach who won't play you, the point guard who doesn't pass you the ball when you're open, the infielder who blows your no-hitter, the judges who don't award you enough points. As Jimmy Connors once said, "I loved that I always had my destiny in my own hands."

Yet unlike such individual sports as golf or track and field events, tennis players do not evaluate performance by personal measures of performance. Success for a tennis player is gauged in a much baser manner: victories over others. The best way an ambitious tennis player can track progress is to beat someone he's never beaten. For the young Connors, it was at first, of all people, his mother. Later it was Ilie Nastase. For John McEnroe, it was Connors and Bjorn Borg. It's really that simple.

For me, 13 years old in the summer of 1973, the player up the food chain was my older brother, Ken, 17. Hardly a day went by that I was not reminded of my place in the birth order. In one of my earliest pictures, taken on September 21, 1960, just three months after my birth, Ken holds me in his lap. I resemble an oversized Butterball turkey. Ken looks a bit bemused, but also rather pleased with his holdings. Though it's unclear what the diaper-wrapped package in his hands means to him, he seems aware that he's clearly the senior partner.

Talking years later with psychologists, studying the lives of great men, I'd learn that the first-born is considered the trailblazer, the one who struts onto a blank canvas and instantly paints with broad, ambitious strokes. Were the first-born a tennis player, he'd opt to serve first and try to hit winners from the get-go. If you've got the weapons, all-time great Jack Kramer used to say, just lay 'em out on the table and dare the other guy to beat you.

For most of my childhood, Ken played this lead role to perfection. Over a seven-year period, we moved five times, back and forth between New York City, St. Louis and Connecticut before finally settling in West Los Angeles in 1970. At each stop, Ken made friends instantly. He was an adept schmoozer and good athlete. The year we attended Tony Trabert Tennis Camp together, a fellow camper's attractive older sister arrived for a visit. It was Candice Bergen. Ken was at the head of the line of teenagers chatting her up.

I was the opposite—withdrawn, cerebral, deliberate, much more drawn to talk and thought than visceral action. The summer of 1964, when I was four and Ken was eight, we were living in Chesterfield, a St. Louis suburb. The subdivision we lived in had a large communal swimming pool. Each day, Ken promptly dove into the deep end, immediately splashing and yelling. Nervous about entering the water, I spent hours on the laps of housewives, querying them about their cars. Occasionally I'd dip a toe into the shallow end.

Our father, Alan, was an executive in the jewelry business. He and our mother, Erna, had for a time thought Ken would be their only child. But one summer, after they'd seen another couple obsess over the machinations of their precious little boy, they realized one child was too few. In this sense, my conception and childhood was a form of resistance to a notion my parents found utterly unacceptable: the pushy Jewish parent who stage-manages every minute of the prized offspring's life. The notion of parental intrusion—and its needy companion, the immature child—was abhorrent. Instead, we were raised to be independent and cultivated young adults. Trips to museums, plays, movies and libraries took precedence. Autonomy was paramount. My mother was incredulous when I told her how a friend's mother marched into a school principal's offices and demanded her son be upgraded to the honors track.

As the older brother, Ken enjoyed being my boss and hero. Who wouldn't want a constituency? All paths I walked were ones he'd trod on before. I liked it that way, relished the knowledge that my older brother mastered the ropes before I dared climb them. When I was in second grade, Ken read a story to our class that he'd written and illustrated. The audience cheered. I beamed with pride over my brother's charisma. The summer I turned 11 and Ken was 15, we attended sleepaway camp for the first time. So prominent was Ken as a camp leader—captaining his team to victory in the "Color War" competition—that he opted to spend an extra two weeks away.

I wanted nothing more than to head home, sleep in my own bed, watch reruns of "Bewitched" and catch up on back issues of *The Sporting*

News. The afternoon Ken returned, I couldn't help but hover around him as if he was a celebrity. I'd bought him a copy of the Rolling Stones' album, *Sticky Fingers*, for his birthday, and as the sounds of "Wild Horses" rang through his room, I wanted to connect. "What do you want?" he asked. But we both knew. He was the leader and I was the follower.

During this time, I'd started reading about politics. As the child of New York Jewish liberals, I invariably found myself smitten with the Kennedys. The John-Bobby relationship struck a chord. "Robert F. Kennedy," wrote Theodore White in *The Making of the President: 1964*, "who loved his brother more than he loved himself, saw John F. Kennedy, even while alive, as more than a person—as the flag of a cause."

My place in the birth order was so clear. I'll never forget a term I heard to describe Jimmy Connors shortly after I'd first heard of him. Even 30 years later, I savor the term as if it were a delicious cut of sirloin. Jimmy Connors was a counterpuncher. The counterpuncher knows there's someone else in the room vying for the prize. Prior to taking offense, the counterpuncher must rapidly scope out the landscape and determine where he can stake a claim. He takes what his opponent throws and flings it back. Forced to compete in a world created before his arrival, the counterpuncher must establish his own piece of real estate in a crowded environment. Fully aware that there's another person fighting for the same bone, the counterpuncher is on constant alert, primed for defense, opportunistic should offensive openings surface. The counterpuncher thrives on being underestimated, overlooked and not considered powerful enough to compete with the big boys. Bobby Kennedy was a counterpuncher. So was his brother John until the death of his older brother Joe altered the Kennedy fraternal hierarchy. The counterpuncher is life's second sibling. The counterpuncher must think before he can act—even if, as Connors' return of serve demonstrated, cognition must be measured in milliseconds.

Oddly enough, it was the physical world of sports that helped me overcome my reticence and counterpunch my way to success. As the more natural athlete, Ken was quick with his hands and feet, proficient in everything from swimming to basketball to baseball to bicycling. These were all activities where even competence eluded me.

"You've got to be tough," he said. "Don't be a wuss." Later in our teens, Ken showed me his copy of David Halberstam's *The Best and The Brightest*. I relished the description of how Bobby Kennedy evaluated men most of all by how tough they were. But long before that, when I was nine years old, I decided to try out for a football team. Another era, another place, and there would have been community clamoring (particularly among protective Jewish parents) against children playing tackle football. But this was St. Louis 1969, a humble Midwestern city filled with crewcut aerospace executives. My parents never gave football a second thought.

Within weeks, my 65-pound body became a heat-seeking missile. I threw myself at running backs, wide receivers and quarterbacks with abandon. Linebacker—the counterpuncher of the gridiron—was my favorite position. Our team's coaches nicknamed me "The Animal." Discarding my thick black glasses whenever I put on my helmet, I was a nine-year-old nearsighted hunk of fury, a predator chomping at the bit to tear down anything that came my way.

Ken reveled in my success too. For the first time, I was the pioneer. On chilly afternoons in St. Louis autumns, Ken and I played one-on-one football, tackling each other on our lawn. Often we'd wander up the block for backyard scrimmages with Ken's friends. He loved showing me off, particularly when I'd wrestle his buddies to the ground or knock the wind out of their lungs.

One night in the fall of 1969, a teammate's mother drove me home after football practice. Normally when I opened the door to our house I'd hear the sounds of my parents, or the TV. On this night, the only sound I heard was that of my cleats on the floor. I had no idea where Ken and my parents were. It didn't concern me at all.

An hour later, all three entered. Ken was upset. All of 13 years old, he'd surreptitiously planted himself behind the wheel of our '62 Oldsmobile and, on a dare from his friends, started up the car, backed it out the driveway and cruised a couple of blocks—only to bang the car against a homeowner's mailbox. Soon enough, my parents were summoned. "I'm so stupid," Ken cried repeatedly on our dining room table. I'd never seen my older brother so vulnerable.

The incident was soon forgotten. Ken was Bar Mitzvahed three weeks later. At the reception, he and several friends formed a makeshift band and played rock music. I sat in a corner by myself, drinking 7-Ups. I felt less alone because, thanks to football, I'd found a venue all my own. After we moved to Los Angeles a year later, I played another season of football. I was convinced I could be a high school letterman.

And then tennis changed everything. Convinced that everyone in California played tennis, my parents picked up the game in 1971. Southern California's brilliant sunshine made it possible to play tennis year-round. Though our part of West Los Angeles was affluent (if not quite as wealthy as the neighborhoods of Bel Air and Beverly Hills up in the nearby hills), there was no need to join a club. With the game booming in the early '70s, public parks offered an active assortment of lessons, tournaments and players. In large part, tennis was the first child of the fitness boom. There were no aerobics studios. Weightlifting was for body freaks. Instead, a polyglot mix of West LA residents filled the courts, from off-duty cops and screenwriters to schoolteachers, realtors, surfers, divorcees, actors and kids drawn to a sport that for a brief time was considered cool.

Football became irrelevant. At age 12, standing 4 feet, 8 inches tall, did I know that I'd only grow another foot? Maybe there was something else attractive about tennis. In football, I was part of a team, valued as linebacker and lineman, even once praised by name by a coach in a story in the *Los Angeles Times*. But in tennis, I could touch the ball on every point. Here might well be a chance for me to become not just a contributor, but play the role for which I'd been groomed back when I'd donned that king's suit. In tennis, I could be a star.

Even better, tennis was also a perfect sport for my solitary nature. I could walk to a park, hit on a backboard and study opponents without the need for a squad, tryouts or coaches. When Ken and I attended Tony Trabert Tennis Camp in 1972, I most enjoyed practicing serves and hitting against the ball machine. After all, I was barely a beginner. Who wanted to play with me anyway? One day at camp, I asked a player named Mark Binstock if he wanted to hit some. No, he said, you're not good enough. This was a cold introduction to tennis' competitive pecking order. I would remember Binstock.

Ken played with me frequently. Though far better, he liked to dominate me and demonstrate his physical prowess. One of the first times our entire family was on a court, he and our father rocketed forehands back and forth, grinning at each other as the ball flew across the net.

Naturally, I was pensive. I was also lefthanded, which I was told was an advantage in tennis. At first, though, playing lefthanded required an additional step of contemplation. Whenever I took lessons, the instructor gave a command and said, "you lefties, just think the opposite." Simple as this direction seemed, it blunted the sport's instinctual aspects. The upside was that it made me that much more alert.

I became a sponge for information about tennis. I experimented with different rackets, watched tennis on TV and studied everything from history to politics to strategies. Ken was Rival A. Our four-year age gap made a big difference at 12 and 16. Ken's favorite player was Connors' doubles partner, Ilie Nastase, a gifted Romanian with as much flair as anyone in tennis history. After Ken purchased one of the elegant Dunlop Maxply frames that Nastase used, he loved to flick forehand winners, caress deftly-angled volleys and slap serves into corners à la Ilie.

Connors was also a lefty, but far from my favorite player. My heroes were Australians Rod Laver and John Newcombe. Laver was lefthanded, a creative genius who'd proven that southpaws could be versatile, all-court players. It was Laver who advised lefties to build up their back-hands and master topspin. Tony Trabert, the big-time American champ who ran the camp I attended, also made the same recommendation to me. Newcombe was a swashbuckling netrusher, another Aussie whose mustache gave him a macho swagger à la Burt Reynolds. My goal was to have a topspin backhand and learn to serve and volley.

Around our house, though, tennis goals ran a distant third to school and talk of politics. As much as Ken and I enjoyed playing tennis, it was hardly a focal point around our house. There were no delusions that we would do anything more than play high school tennis. No sooner had I picked up a racket at age 12 than I was told by instructors and better players that I'd started too late to pursue any dreams of being a pro or even a college player (in Los Angeles in the early '70s the only tennis schools worth talking about were UCLA and USC, which at that point were so much better than any other college that each could have fielded Davis Cup teams). Moreover, asked my mother, who dared even think about becoming a pro athlete but poor, stupid people? Who'd want to be that uneducated vagabond known as a tennis bum? At best, tennis was a hobby. Our dinner table talk devoted far more energy to the White House than Wimbledon.

Since I agreed with this scheme of priorities, I often found myself more drawn to studying tennis than playing it. For years I'd devoured the sports pages, an interest that extended to dozens of biographies, year-books and magazines devoted to football, baseball and basketball. On library trips, I'd make a beeline towards the section numbered 796 that housed the sports books. At 12, I read Roger Kahn's *The Boys of Summer* and Roger Angell's *The Summer Game* on the same weekend. The only gifts I wanted were sports books. After school one afternoon I took a bus to a row of airline offices in Beverly Hills and researched the possibility of visiting all three sports Hall of Fames in the same summer (mission unsuccessful).

Invariably, I transferred my sports loyalties to tennis. In seventh grade, two months after my first summer at Trabert's camp, I wrote a paper on John McPhee's *Levels of The Game*, the tale of a match between Arthur Ashe and Clark Graebner. McPhee's simple premise—that a player's game reflects his personality—struck me like a lightning bolt.

But at 12, what was my personality? Contemplation seemed so much easier than action. "Hey, guess what?" I asked Ken one December afternoon. "Tomorrow is Julie Heldman's birthday." Heldman was one of the 10 best American women tennis players.

Ken looked at me and paused. "You know," he said, pausing again, "if you spent a little more time playing tennis than reading about it, you might become a good player one day."

He had a point.

By age 13, in addition to glasses, I was wearing braces. Add in the onset of adolescence, and I was scarcely what you'd call physically imposing. But as was the case on the football field, I had an innate competitive gift. Years later I would dub it the disruption gene. It's the instinctual ability to hit the kind of balls that make an opponent feel uncomfortable. Early on as a tennis player, since I knew winning required hitting yet one more ball over the net, I rarely hit too hard. As my game improved, I began taking a few more chances, coming to the net more, experimenting with angles and touch. Now don't get me wrong. Never was I able to become anything more than a reasonably good recreational player. Yet no matter what the level is, I've learned that a talent for taking pace off the ball, at varying speeds and shapes, is a diabolically effective way to unravel an opponent. Being lefthanded also spiced up my mix. In the first tournament I ever played, an opponent who'd just beaten me screamed in my face, "You're a dinker!" This was a horrible putdown, implying that I wasn't playing the game fairly or with proper machismo. Fortunately, the next day I heard Tony Trabert say, "Show me a dinker and I'll show you a room full of trophies."

The upshot was that however low my quality level was, I knew how to compete effectively. While my game was light years removed from Connors' hard-hitting baseline style, we were linked in that we were both lefthanded counterpunchers. Years earlier, the young Connors thought using the new Wilson T-2000—the sport's first significant metal racket—would add more power to his game. Though I knew scarcely anything about Connors at age 12, I followed suit and got a T-2000.

I still had yet to beat Ken. He was stronger, faster and, perhaps most importantly, the one driving us to the courts. Often when I'd start playing better, he'd make a questionable line call. Or he'd decide it was time to go home. Other times, though, he'd be motivational. One afternoon he was leading 6-0, 3-0 and I began moping, thinking about reading the latest issue of *World Tennis* in my bedroom, followed by homework. "What are you, some sort of wuss?" he'd scream. "Are you just going to give up?" The Animal was awakened. I won the next two games and fought hard before Ken won that final set, 6-3. At least on this occasion

I'd earned our frequent reward, Ken treating us to orange soda and onion rings at the nearby Jack In The Box. On the drive home, as the radio blared out music, he'd stagger me with his verbatim knowledge of the lyrics of songs like Simon & Garfunkel's "Mrs. Robinson" and Carly Simon's "You're So Vain."

By the summer of 1973, a year after I'd started the game, I'd taught myself a spin serve and enhanced my netrushing game. I'd won my first tennis tournament that summer, beating everyone in my group of 10 at Tony Trabert Tennis Camp. Tony Trabert saw my match point and congratulated me. Two weeks later I upset the first seed at a local park tournament and reached the semifinals of a regional event at LA's massive facility, Griffith Park.

My brain was still bigger than my game. Eager to hone my attack, I'd read Jack Kramer's advice that forehand approach shots should be hit down the line for two reasons: first, they were aimed at the opponent's backhand, which in those days was usually the weaker side. Second, attacking this way made it easier for the netrusher to cover a passing shot, which from this spot would usually either go back down the line or towards the middle of the court. Kramer's premise was that it was virtually impossible for a player to repeatedly hit sharply-angled backhand passing shots—as difficult as a basketball player making 26-footers from the corner.

But what about lefties hitting forehand approach shots? I took this up with Tony Trabert. Was it better to aim them crosscourt to the backhand—and risk opening up more court? Or should you approach down the line to the forehand? Note that at this time I was a 4-foot, 11-inch 13-year-old who had only become an intermediate. Patting me on the head, no doubt bemused by my question, Tony advised, "Just hit it deep, lefty." Eventually I'd get a more nuanced answer from Connors' coach, but that was years away. The truth was that Trabert's recommendation was all I needed then. Besides, as Ken had advised, shouldn't I just play rather than overthink?

On an exceptionally warm Sunday night in August, Ken drove our family's red 1968 Ford station wagon to Douglas Park in nearby Santa Monica. It was dark, which meant we'd play under lights that cost 25 cents for 30 minutes of play. The people vacating the court before us had time left on their lights, so all we did was shove in one quarter. I whipped out my T-2000 while Ken, mimicking Nastase, gently pinged the heel of his palm against the Dunlop Maxply's strings.

I was a slow starter. The biggest challenge for me was to get my body moving as fast as my brain. Ken usually shot out of the blocks, flicking, moving, darting around the court. Virtually every time we played, he broke my serve immediately.

This night was different. I held my opening service game, bumping a couple of half-volleys into the corners. My backhand was solid, handling several of Ken's forehands. A few times I surprised him with sneak attacks into the net. He covered the court well and forced me into errors. At 3–3 I lunged at a backhand service return that went for a down-the-line winner. Two points later I hit a forehand volley let-cord winner. Breaking serve for 4–3, it was the first time I'd ever taken the lead from Ken this late in a set. I held for 5–3, one game away from the biggest win of my life.

And then the lights went out.

2

Down In The Boondocks

If indeed all action begins with a thought, then the seminal thinker in this story is Gloria Connors. It's hard to call someone so narrowly focused a visionary. Supposedly visionaries are expansive, able to spot phenomena on the horizon undetectable to mere mortals.

There was nothing expansive about Gloria Connors. To many who came in contact with her during her son's career, she was the embodiment of paranoid provincialism, a pushy stage mother only able to see the world through the needs of her beloved Jimbo. Tennis is rife with tales of Gloria holding sponsors, promoters and media hostage for money and time.

Permit another definition of visionary. Visionaries are a peculiar mix of personal desires, disparate skills and fortunate outcomes. Conventional wisdom says they see the future. But perhaps they also so immerse themselves in their own present—absorbed purely in their private passions— that they stir up the frenetic movement required for creation. "The man who writes about himself and his time," said George Bernard Shaw, "is the only man who writes about all people and about all time." And while it's not likely Gloria Connors knew Shaw from Sherlock, she unquestionably knew what it meant to be one of Shaw's most famous characters, that controlling instructor, Professor Henry Higgins from *Pygmalion*. For at heart, Gloria Connors was dedicated not just to the tennis life of her famous son, but to many other students as well.

Head back to 1952. It's been 10 years since Gloria Connors was the number 13-ranked junior tennis player in the United States. A year previously she gave birth to her first son, Johnny. As she carries her second child in her womb, she concurrently clears out land behind her East St. Louis house on 632 N. 68th Street to make room for a tennis court.

She was born Gloria Thompson, the only child of an East St. Louis policeman, Al Thompson, and his wife, Bertha. It was an athletic family. Al was a Gold Gloves boxer. Bertha played tennis. Gloria was made very aware of social strata. East St. Louis lay across the river from the big snooty city, St. Louis. Tennis was one way for Gloria to make a name for herself. Well into the 1990s this schism between affluent St. Louis and those east of the Mississippi continued. Jeff Heely, then in his 40s, was an accomplished athlete from the area who'd served a stint in the Navy. Upon his return to St. Louis, he became a successful executive in finance. A friend suggested he join the prestigious St. Louis Country Club. Heely was asked where he attended high school. When he answered Belleville, the friend pursed his lips and told him it just wasn't going to work out.

The East St. Louis of Gloria Thompson's youth was a miniature version of many other American cities, a mix of blue-collar whites and minorities sifting their way through the economic ups and downs of the first half of the 20th century. It was a period when America shifted from a small-town agrarian economy to urbanized industrialism. This transition was particularly troublesome in such border states as Illinois and Missouri, where long-standing xenophobic attitudes created friction between social classes and races. Early in the 20th century, there were labor struggles in East St. Louis. Blacks migrated from Mississippi and Alabama to take the jobs vacated by striking workers. In the aftermath, an undertone of racial tension seeped through East St. Louis. As one long-standing citizen told me, "It was a nice city before the coloreds got involved."

It's likely policeman Al Thompson was near the frontlines for one of the worst days in the city's history. On July 2, 1917, a race massacre occurred in the streets of East St. Louis that was so destructive its files were kept classified by the U.S. Government until 1986. It's estimated that 40 to 150 African-Americans were killed and that another 6,000 were driven from their homes. Though it's presumptuous to assess the Thompson family's racial attitudes, one can only imagine the psychic impact an event like that had on the entire city, and two decades later, the 12-year reign of East St. Louis' Democratic mayor, one John Connors. If not exactly a city on the brink, the East St. Louis of Gloria Thompson's childhood was far from serene. No doubt this daughter of an ex-boxer turned policeman and a feisty athletic mother rapidly learned how combustible life could be.

Gloria played tennis at Jones Park, an East St. Louis facility she once said was as nice as any country club she'd ever seen. While Bertha was merely a competent recreational player, Gloria became far better, excelling as a junior in the Missouri Valley section of the USLTA. For a time, she played the national circuit of tournaments all around the country that led up to America's most prestigious event, the U.S. Championships at Forest Hills. Since tennis in those days was strictly an amateur sport, there was no prize money. Players stayed at the patrician club members' homes. They competed by day and by night enjoyed elegant dinners and dances. After a few years of this life, a player, man or woman, settled down to domesticity. Players who remember Gloria from those days on the circuit recall a sweet, competitive young lady who was good, but not quite great.

After she stopped competing in the late '40s, she drifted to work as an instructor. Gloria Thompson didn't need tennis to support her. With her delicate features and youthful, athletic appearance, she was an attractive bachelorette. Among those she dated was a top player from upstate in Chicago, Jimmy Evert. Decades later, Evert's daughter, Chris, saw the two at junior tournaments and worried that they might reunite and break up her parents' marriage.

But the person who'd had his eye on Gloria Thompson for a long time was James Connors. Little is known of this man. He was educated at Notre Dame. Upon his return to East St. Louis, he was granted the kind of job classically connected with political patronage. James Connors was in charge of toll collections on the Veterans Bridge, one of four bridges that linked East St. Louis to the bigger, adjacent metropolis. Gloria once said, "he liked being around people in the evenings." As the son of the mayor who'd handed President Harry Truman the keys to the city during the 1948 presidential campaign, "Big Jim" was the classic good old boy, more predisposed to the relaxing qualities of golf and a nice scotch at The Stop Light Restaurant than tennis and a 100-yard walk to the Jones Park water fountain.

One of the first major magazines stories on Jimmy Connors, a 1974 *Sports Illustrated* cover piece, included a photo of Connors with both parents. The writer, Curry Kirkpatrick, was politely steered away from any interviews with the boy's father. The son, always eager to credit his mother, discussed his father with the dispatch of a CEO recalling a terminated employee.

In 1996, I was part of a group of five that played with Connors in a Pro-Am tournament. "So good to be with you, Mr. Connors," said an enthused woman. "I'm not Mr. Connors," he countered. "That was my father. Mister this, sir that, all that formal crap." The disgust in his voice was greater than he'd share for the likes of Ivan Lendl. I had long wondered about Connors' own take on his father's relationship to the tennis (adding "the" prior to "tennis" was a Connors trademark, as if a preface conferred a special respect). "My father," Connors said, then paused longer than usual. "My father, he wasn't around, wasn't around for any of it."

Gloria and James had their first child, Johnny, in 1951. Jimmy was born on September 2, 1952 in East St. Louis. In one of those delicious coincidences that please biographers, his birth coincided with the U.S. National Championships at Forest Hills. That same week, a 17-year-old Australian, Ken Rosewall, made his American debut, reaching the quarterfinals.

Gloria was a dedicated instructor. The history of tennis is filled with tales of ex-players who become teaching professionals. As in basketball, football and baseball, champions tend not to be particularly good at imparting technical knowledge. "Just give it a nudge," was the great Rod Laver's trademark tip, which of course is as valuable as Leonard Bernstein advising an aspiring maestro to give it a twirl.

Most frequently, it's those a step or two down the ladder—the ones who worked much harder just to survive, the ones with first-hand experience absorbing the genius of the champions—who seize upon nuances. Strictly a minimalist, never one to be mistaken for an intellectual, Gloria was an ardent student of tennis.

Before her boys were born, she gave lessons at Jones Park. Like the original piece of dough that's used to make San Francisco's famous sourdough bread, Gloria's instructional style is the nucleus of her son's story. How she taught the game occupies the core of everything that made her son succeed, from technical to emotional to mental.

Understanding her approach requires knowledge of how the game was played during these years. By the late '40s, Jack Kramer had shown the phenomenal success of the serve-and-volley game. Dubbed "The Big Game," Kramer's strategy, developed with strong input from a former automotive engineer, was predicated on the concept of percentage tennis and the application of cumulative pressure. The most important goal was to continually win your service games. From the baseline, went Kramer's thinking, every ball should be hit crosscourt so as to clear the lower part of the net (three feet in the center, it's six inches higher on the sidelines) and travel through the longest portion of the court. More importantly, a player should look for the chance to come to net and force the opponent to try passing shots, which with a man standing at the net for volleys are much harder to execute than baseline-to-baseline shots. Ideally, it was best to charge the net after your serve, always on the first one and usually on the second one too. With the game played mostly on ultra-fast grass, indoor and cement courts, threading the needle with passing shots became even more difficult. Kramer's attack, whether on his serve, return or on a forcing approach shot, rushed opponents into mistakes. It was, in its way, the tennis equivalent of a basketball player constantly charging the lane. The Big Game ushered in a new brand of athleticism in tennis. No longer were players standing languidly in the backcourt thrusting and parrying. The Big Game was in-your-face.

In the spirit of the times, though, it was thought that women didn't have the speed or strength necessary to be ardent netrushers like Kramer. The one major woman netrusher of the '30s, Alice Marble, was believed only able to serve and volley because she was a first-rate athlete who once played baseball in San Francisco with Joe DiMaggio. Accordingly, it was said well into the late '60s that a successful female netrusher played like a man. Conventional wisdom held that women were better off back at the baseline. Many of the other great champions of Gloria's days, those she watched win the tournaments she played such as Pauline Betz, Margaret Osborne du Pont and Sarah Palfrey, were all-court players: competent volleyers, but at heart, more adept from the backcourt.

There was also a man who played baseline tennis who was no doubt much more impressive to the young Gloria. In 1938, Don Budge of Oakland, California, became the first player in tennis history to win all four of the major championships—Australia, France, Wimbledon and the U.S.—in the same calendar year. The feat was dubbed the "Grand Slam." Unquestionably the world's best player in the late '30s, Budge's career was interrupted by World War II, an exile that in many ways heightened his mystique. The Budge Era also coincided with Gloria's coming of age as a player.

Budge struck hard, deep groundstrokes that were exceptionally forceful. His backhand is still often regarded as the best in tennis history. Not until Jimmy Connors arrived in the early '70s was there a male player so able to dictate play from the baseline with strokes that oppressed opponents and kept them pinned in a defensive position. In fact, Kramer built his Big Game in hopes of toppling Budge. Long past Budge's prime, Kramer still considered Budge the most difficult of opponents to attack.

How was Budge able to drive the ball so proficiently? As a child, Budge loved baseball. His backhand mimicked a batter's swing. Working with a notable Berkeley instructor, Tom Stow, who'd studied the mechanics of the golf swing, Budge showed Stow the secrets of his back-hand and, under Stow's guidance, also rebuilt his forehand. Budge and Stow saw that the sources of leverage came from the rotation of shoul-ders, hips and thighs, reinforced by a deep knee bend. This created a compact, all-bodied thrust right through the ball. Budge's technique refuted the recreational player's perception that power was generated by a strong arm and wrist. Execution of this technique required exceptional discipline. Practicing with the devotion of a monk to a shrine, Budge locked in on his swing as devoutly as Ted Williams at bat.

The result was what's referred to in tennis as a "heavy" or "penetrating" ball—a shot that seems effortless but upon arrival on the opponent's racket feels hard as a brick. Added to this was another Budge talent. Typically, a tennis player hits the ball at the peak of its bounce. But because Budge was so well-prepared every time he lined up to strike the ball, and therefore supremely confident in his technique, he hit the ball even earlier, as it rose. Flinging it back to opponents sooner and harder, Budge rushed them mercilessly. Imagine, if you will, one boxer landing punches four seconds apart while his opponent responds in half that time.

While there's no record of Gloria Connors mentioning Don Budge, there's no doubt his game appealed to her on many levels. First, he was the best player in the world throughout her formative years. Second, like a woman, he won primarily from the baseline, where he exerted control of the court and the ball rather than dashing into net. Third, Budge's capacity for hitting on the rise added a high-octane quality to his game. What trio of elements could be more appealing to the driven daughter of a former prizefighter? The whole package came together in Jimmy Connors' hands. Connors later called it, "a woman's game inside a man's body."

Johnny and Jimmy were both exposed to tennis in the crib. As they grew up and played on the backyard court in East St. Louis, each enjoyed the time with their mother and grandmother. It was at once emotional and edifying. As Gloria hit and instructed, her mother, Bertha, nicknamed "Two-Mom" by the boys, scurried around the court, picked up the balls and helped Gloria keep the action going. According to a student, "All the while you were hitting and running, Bertha was giving advice about dedication, about commitment. It's like she was a mini-motivational speaker before those even existed."

The day I'd pressed Connors about what his mother would have taught me, he explained, "Those two weren't just teaching me how to win at tennis. They were teaching me what life was all about." Given their life in East St. Louis and Belleville, given the class resentment and paranoia, given Gloria's mix of xenophobia and paranoia, what kind of life lessons were they? Was it love leavened with combat? Was the tennis court a fortress to be defended against intrusion?

Other instructors across the river emphasized serve-volley tennis.

Earl Buchholz taught his son, Butch, who became one of the world's
top five players by 1960, primarily by virtue of his attacking game.
Another St. Louis instructor, Bill Price, loved the athletic aspects of
Kramer's Big Game. Price was also a great believer in attaining mastery
of spins, a skill he taught by first having his students play table-tennis
so they learned to adjust the face of the racket and create different
effects on the ball. Price's students were known for their swift volleying
skills and shotmaking ability. His prize student, Chuck McKinley, won
Wimbledon in 1963. Chuck's younger brother, Bob, became a childhood rival of Jimmy Connors.

Gloria didn't care for the serve-volley game. Whether it was ignorance
since she was a woman, or her hatred for those St. Louis snobs, she spent
far less time teaching volleys than most instructors of her day. Nor did
she care much for Price's emphasis on spins and shotmaking. Like Don
Budge, she believed the cornerstone of sound strokes was a flat, heavy
ball. But it really wouldn't have mattered if Price taught exactly like
Gloria Connors. He was a rival from across the river, and though he was
no country club patrician, rivals existed to be hated—both stylistically
and personally.

Eschewing technical variations, Gloria emphasized repetition and
intensity. She demanded students hit hundreds of groundstrokes within
inches of the baseline. The racket should be taken straight back and
driven through the ball. "Swing long," she advised. Students were repri-
manded if they flicked their wrist or didn't attack the ball. Even though
Jimmy was lefthanded—and lefties had a long tennis history of imparting
the full spectrum of offbeat spins and paces taught by Price—she too
taught him the same clean and direct way. Jimmy Connors flicking at a
ball is as unlikely as Ernest Hemingway writing a run-on sentence.

Gloria's intensity was relentless. As she gave a lesson one day at Jones
Park, Gloria noticed a player on an adjacent court listening to a transistor
radio. Could you turn that down, she asked. No response. A few minutes
later, Gloria, racquet in hand, walked to the court and banged her frame
down on the radio, shattering it into pieces. The lesson resumed.

Underpinning everything was her extraordinary attention to footwork. The ability to take dozens of little steps gave a player the chance
to make the constant adjustments necessary for an effective swing. This
too required extraordinary discipline. Gloria Connors hated it when
players loped around the court and relied on last-minute movements
with feet, arms and racquet. Ken Flach, later a star on the U.S. Davis Cup
team, worked with her extensively on his return of serve for three years
starting at age 11. As Johnny Connors stood across the court serving one

ball after another, Gloria sat alongside Flach on a stool several feet to his right. A tennis version of Vince Lombardi, she issued one comment after another. The hips turned into the ball too soon. The feet moved too slowly. The head bounced. Finally, she'd say, good job Kenny, that one was good. Flach lived for her occasional compliments.

Layered on top of Gloria's intensity was another factor painfully indigenous to the St. Louis area: humidity. Summers in St. Louis have a swampy quality, an overcoat of suffocation that rises up from the exceptionally sticky deltas of the South. The humidity is uncomfortable, sticky and draining. As the day wears on, it's much easier, at least on a short-term basis, to sprint and whack the ball rather than take dozens of little steps. But Gloria insisted on mastery. Players who worked with her in the '50s, '60s and '70s all independently cite her commands: You've got to be a tiger. You've got to move like a panther out there. Be alert. Be mobile. Be aggressive. Let your footwork intimidate your opponent. Swarm them. Get those tiger juices going. Long into his pro career, Jimmy wore a necklace with the word "Tig" on it.

For Jimmy (and, for a time, Johnny), the lesson started in the car. Gloria and Bertha operated as a pair of motivational crusaders. Even after they'd moved to the more middle-class suburb of Belleville, the notion of social exclusion surfaced. It wasn't so much that the Connorses were poor. They weren't. "Don't let that whole other side of the tracks thing get too blown up," Chris Evert once told me. "Jimmy grew up like most of us in a nice middle-class house." But to Gloria and Bertha, the inherent conflicts of the tennis court infected their sensibilities. Life was polarized between the tight troika and all others. St. Louis' clannish, old-line sensibility, lacking the dynamic qualities of a larger city like Chicago or even the contemporary zest of an automotive center like Detroit, reinforced this sense of limited possibilities—that tennis, and solely tennis, was the way to stick it up the butts of the snooty. Staring out the window of their car, they invariably drove past St. Clair Country Club, a nearby venue that the Connors family hadn't joined. Gloria disparaged rich folks. She told Jimmy that other kids had no respect for him, that you should trust no one on a tennis court. Connors was a fan of rock 'n' roll, though much more in the vein of down-home, rockabilly Americans like Elvis and Buddy Holly than the stylish British Invasion. One of Connors' favorite songs was "Down in The Boondocks,"—"People put me down 'cause that's the side of town I was born in." He loved singing this song while practicing: "Lord have mercy on the boy from down in the boondocks."

On the court, Gloria fed balls into different corners. Jimmy was so little he could only hit his backhand with two hands. While rich kids from country clubs restarted the rally should a ball bounce long, or let the ball go when one went into the doubles alley or beyond, or took it on two bounces when it came short, Gloria demanded her students play and hit every shot from anywhere—all the better to learn how to move and strike confidently from all over the court. Never should the action stop. A junior rival who once joined the Connors family for a practice likened it to a pinball machine.

Bertha reinforced. At a junior event in North Carolina, the players waited out a rain delay inside a gymnasium. Trey Waltke, a talented St. Louis junior three years younger than Jimmy, started hitting delicate touch shots against the wall. Jimmy thought this was a good idea, too, and soon both boys gingerly tapped soft volleys and half-volleys.

From out of nowhere, Bertha surfaced. She stomped her way to Jimmy. Wrenching the racket out of his hands, she yelled, "What are you doing? That's not how you hit the ball! This is how you hit the ball." And with that, she struck it as hard as she could against the wall, shorthop-ping the return and driving one after another. With that she handed the racket back to Jimmy. "That's how you do it," she said. "Now get back to work." As much as tennis might have been considered a "sissy" sport all across America—particularly in rough-and-tumble environments like East St. Louis—once you saw the approach Bertha and Gloria took with Jimmy, you'd never think this again. Tennis wasn't art. It was combat.

There was only one way to play—all-out. If Gloria and Bertha insisted on this from each student, more was expected from their flesh and blood. Whenever Gloria competed, she played to win. After Jimmy squandered a lead and lost to her, she issued a blunt statement: Never let up. See what happens? Even your own mother, the person who loves you more than anyone, will ram the ball down your throat.

Johnny was talented, but by age 14 grew weary of it all. He continued to play, but with none of the urgency that so marked his mother and younger brother. Still, his strokes remained clean, compact, well crafted. As Gloria noted years later, no doubt without any irony or compas-sion, he lacked the guts to become a champion.

The second child took to it like a fish to water. Jimmy got on the court and absorbed every word. Though years later the world celebrated Connors' ability to throw his body into the ball, his physical tumult was possible because his foundation was so precise. Footwork, body turns, the use of his hips and shoulders—the unity of all of these elements is what made Connors so adept at consistently hitting the ball so hard and deep from so many corners of the court. In the history of tennis, he ranks on the highest pedestal, alongside Budge, Ken Rosewall and Andre Agassi, as a player who repeatedly put himself in the best possible position to consistently make a solid swing at the ball and generate supreme direction and power. Were he a baseball player, you'd say he rarely swung at a bad pitch. But in tennis, you can't let one go and take a ball. Your feet must get you into that hitting zone.

Zero in on a summer afternoon in Illinois. It's 79 degrees. The humidity is high. There is no breeze. Prior to walking on the court, the boy jumps rope. The mother stands with a basket. She hits one ball after another. The grandmother picks them up. The mother makes a comment—a hip turn here, a follow-through there, swing long, swing long. The grandmother reinforces it like a church choir. The boy moves, hits, takes in the comment, makes an adjustment. He hits another, then another. More comments. Soon the boy is in the groove. The balls go deep. The mother isn't just feeding now. The two are rallying, engaged and connected by the ball, disconnected by their mutual desire to compromise the other with deep drives into corners. The boy's feet pump like pistons, one small step after another. The way he feels, he could stay on this court for hours.

And then Gloria Connors ends the session.

Whether for 60, 45, 30 or even 15 minutes, she firmly believed in quality over quantity. No one ever left or returned to a tennis court more eager than Jimmy Connors. Even as a pro, his workouts seldom lasted more than an hour. Long before sports science birthed such concepts as interval training or periodization, Gloria Connors had an innate understanding of how to keep her boy from burnout.

She also bent her rules for him. The two-handed backhand was virtually non-existent in tennis during Jimmy's formative years. Gloria and Bertha's plan had always called for him ditching it for the more conventional one-hander. But after a couple of days trying it this way, Bertha weighed in. The boy liked the two-hander and hit it well, so why not let him keep it? Gloria agreed. Soon enough, her boy unleashed one of the finest backhands in the history of the sport.

Off the court, after the tennis was over, the boy was indulged. He and Johnny loved riding go-carts on St. Clair Avenue in East St. Louis. Occasionally, Jimmy played sports like baseball, basketball and football. Other stories cite him riding a pony. School for Connors, he admitted to others and me several times, was mostly something to get through as expediently as possible.

Gloria was not always so attuned to the needs and sensitivities of others young boys who'd walk on the court with her. Richard Waltke,

Trey's father, was a good local player, precisely the competitive standard Gloria wanted Jimmy to joust with as he entered adolescence. A deal was fashioned: Richard played with Jimmy, while Gloria played with the younger Trey. The Connorses and Waltkes often played at such St. Louis venues as the outdoor clay courts of Triple A, a public tennis center inside the city's large Forest Park. In the winter, they played inside the St. Louis Armory, an ultra-slick, wood surface where Jimmy further honed Gloria's directive to strike the ball as early as possible.

Trey Waltke estimates he played 40 matches versus Gloria. None are more vivid to him than the five sets he played with her one excessively humid day at Triple A when he was 10 years old. Gloria won the first four without the loss of a game. Waltke said he'd had enough. No, no, she insisted, we'll play one more set. With Gloria now leading 4-0 in the fifth—she'd won 28 straight games—Waltke won a single game. Two games later, the slaughter was complete. Waltke sat in dazed disbelief. Well, said Gloria afterwards to Richard, we just wanted to see what kind of tiger juices Trey could muster today. We'll see you next week.

Was this a demonstration of Gloria's tough love for a prized student? Or was the tiger marking territory, clearing out via Darwinism any potential threats to the empire she hoped to build for her son? Waltke's desire and talent were obvious even at that age. His father, though not an instructor like Gloria, made a significant commitment to his boy's tennis, driving him all over the country to tournaments.

Waltke did in fact generate the tiger juices Gloria demanded. Within a year, he earned his first—and only—win over Gloria (she subsequently stopped playing him). Soon, Waltke became the third-best 12-and-under player in the country. At about this same time, Jimmy started to beat Richard. The Waltke-Connors alliance was over.

But Gloria did more to push Waltke forward than backward. He enjoyed a 10-year pro career. The first time he played Connors as a pro was in the semifinals of a tournament in the Bahamas in January 1975. Jimbo had just finished 1974 ranked number one in the world. Waltke was in his first pro event. Connors approached the match with the seriousness of a Grand Slam final. It was as merciless as the days when Waltke played Gloria. Jimmy led 6-0, 5-0 when Waltke earned a game. Connors went ballistic, and closed it out a few minutes later. "The guy was number one in the world, way better than me," says Waltke, "but he was going to make me feel every bit of pain." No doubt, as was Jimmy's custom, he called Gloria immediately afterwards and told her of another conquest.

The relationship between Jimmy and Gloria has been psychoanalyzed more than any in the history of tennis. At some level, it is creepy: the maniacal, paranoid mother who drives her child from the crib into a world where he has no say in the matter. She is, to some, the stage mother from hell. Nothing about it seemed hellish to her boy, though. Tennis made him happy and rich. As Connors asked me once, "Why is it OK for Mickey Mantle's dad to teach him baseball but not OK for my mother to teach me tennis?" This question, it should be noted, was precisely what *Sports Illustrated*'s Frank Deford asked in his 1978 story on Connors, "Raised By Women To Conquer Men"—right down to the Mantle comparison. Gloria Connors was indeed a victim of sexism. And I'll admit that while there is much about Gloria's connection to her boy that has made my skin crawl, every time I talked about her with Jimmy or any of her other students, I felt a twinge of jealousy. Many of us spend our whole lives searching for the degree of attention and love Jimmy had every minute of his childhood. He'd lose a match and be told that the guy who beat him was lucky, that it was probably the best win of that kid's life and that Jimmy would kill him the next time they played. In contrast, I was so worried I'd be forgotten that when I sent my parents letters from tennis camp adjacent to my signature I'd add the parenthetical phrase, "your son."

A bigger question: Was the over-the-top love and attention Gloria and Bertha gave to Jimmy conditional? What if he'd said at age four, seven, 12 or 16 that he'd had enough of tennis? What then? Connors says the thought never entered his head. He was too busy concentrating on his tennis. Every time you hit the ball, Gloria Connors taught her students, pray for it to come back so you can hit it again. Young Jimmy devoured this advice. He had the best corner crew you could ask for. Playing a 12s tournament, Connors once blew his nose in between serves. Bertha promptly came oncourt to wipe it. Dare a boy refuse love on any terms? Besides, his results were too good for him to feel discouraged. At eight years old, he won his first tournament in Flora, Illinois. Not only was he rapidly becoming one of the best players in his part of the country, soon he was one of the best in the entire nation.

In the summer of 1963, Jimmy was 10 years old. He, Gloria and Bertha headed to Chattanooga, Tennessee, and the Manker Patten Tennis Club, where over the next four years Jimmy played the National Boys 12 and 14 championships. On hand were a number of children who spent two decades playing Connors through juniors, college and on into the pros: Brian Gottfried, Harold Solomon, Erik van Dillen, Eddie Dibbs, Sandy Mayer, Roscoe Tanner, Dick Stockton.

The motivation for playing junior tennis in the early '60s was very different than what it became within a decade. Tennis then was primarily an amateur sport, with only under-the-table expense money offered to the very best players. Those that did opt to turn pro were barred from playing prestigious events at Wimbledon and Forest Hills, forced instead to barnstorm the world in near-anonymity. The result was a sport divided by itself: the amateurs weren't the best players, and the pros were scarcely visible. Worse yet, both amateurs and pros were itinerant, known to the world as "tennis bums."

Parents of players like Gottfried, Solomon, Mayer and even Connors saw tennis as a means to an end. If a boy became a good enough player, he could play college tennis, tour the world for a few years and maybe, if he was supremely great, even represent the U.S. in Davis Cup play. A 1965 *Tennis Magazine* article on the 12-year-old Connors cited his desire to play Davis Cup (ironic given his later history with this event).

Tennis also brought a middle-class young man in touch with the right kind of people—college coaches, investment banks, good corporations— that led to good jobs and a comfortable lifestyle. As late as the mid-'70s, after Jimmy had become a millionaire, Gloria Connors continued to tell the mother of one of his childhood rivals that he planned to return to college. Never mind that the Connors' single-minded devotion to the sport made Jimmy a rather indifferent student.

With the extrinsic rewards so minimal, with goodies like Davis Cup and a pro career available to a scant few, the intrinsic desire to become the best possible player was high. With tennis hardly popular then, the few who did play were mightily motivated. The game was more of an art than a business, a long-term craft you honed rather than a short-term talent skill you pedaled. "All you would want to be was someone who could win big and be the best," Connors explained to me years later. "Even once money came in, you had to win big to make lots of it."

The seeds of future Grand Slam draws were planted at austere, muggy venues like Manker Patten. The foreboding environment was far removed from the posh clubs many associated with tennis. Gottfried describes it as "a federal penitentiary with tennis courts." The courts lay 25-30 feet deep at the bottom of a large pit. It was precisely the war zone Gloria and Bertha trained their boy for on the playing fields of East St. Louis.

One year at Manker Patten, moments before he was about to play Connors, an opponent looked skywards and saw the menacing figures of Bertha and Gloria. In this man's memory, the two resembled the most intimidating nuns he can remember, complete with knee socks and rubber shoes. The two sat on metal beach chairs and stared intently at the court, Jimmy and the opponent. This boy had been warned of young Connors' reputation for making bad calls. But he also vowed not to request a linesman until Connors actually cheated. Then, just as he pulled his racket out of its cover, before he and Connors set foot on the court, a loud voice growled. It was Gloria. "We hear this guy cheats," she barked. "Do you want me to get a linesman?"

Jimmy declined, but his opponents knew: Connors was armed. And dangerous. A peer, Sandy Mayer, had a father, Alex, who'd played Davis Cup for Yugoslavia and was one of the finest instructors on the East Coast. Against most players, Alex advised his son, when you get a lead it's wise to merely maintain the same level of play. Let the opponent try and raise his game from a losing position, and he will likely press and make even more mistakes. After he'd seen Connors play a couple of matches, Alex made a rare recommendation. This Connors boy is best when he's losing, said Alex. He has extra gears. Therefore, you must take even more chances to beat him.

Though Connors' intensity, two-handed backhand and double-female entourage distinguished him from other juniors, he was merely one in a pack. That first summer at Chattanooga he reached the quarterfinals. In September 1963, a photo of boy and mother appeared in the leading tennis publication of the time, *World Tennis*. Gloria looked sharp with her blonde hair, white skirt and crisp, short-sleeved tennis shirt. The vinyl cover over Jimmy's Dunlop Maxply (the same frame used by that notable lefthander, Rod Laver) was nearly as big as his head. "One of the more delightful parent-child combinations at Chattanooga," read the caption, "was Gloria Thompson Connors and son Jimmy of East St. Louis, Ill."

A year later he lost in the semis to Gottfried. Throughout his mid-teens, Connors ranked among the country's top 10 juniors. Yet few touted him for greatness. Stockton and van Dillen, a year older, were considered more versatile and stronger, as was Gottfried. As much as Connors' fighting skill was admired, there was heavy competition on that front too. Jack Darrah was a Californian who led America's Junior Davis Cup team in the late '60s. In the October 1967 issue of *World Tennis*, Darrah wrote about a feisty teen from St. Louis:

"Although he is smaller than the other boys, he is the most tenacious. He works so hard no one can match him for endurance. He gives his all on every point and still has energy left for the next one. He lacks some of the physical attributes of the other players but he more than makes up for it in his willingness to put everything second to tennis."

The boy Darrah adored was not Jimmy Connors. It was Bobby McKinley. Two years older than Jimmy, McKinley played serve-and-volley, the style most believed turned a boy into a champion. He and Jimmy played frequently in St. Louis. The age and style difference was critical. McKinley estimates they played 18 times in tournaments, Connors never winning. In Tulsa in the spring of '69, Connors led by a set and 4-1 in the second. McKinley changed tactics and beat Jimmy with a variety of drop shots and lobs, a showcase of diversity learned from the instructor Gloria hated, Bill Price. McKinley's strategy also revealed Connors' technical and tactical limitations. As McKinley came off the court, Gloria wagged her finger in his face and declared, you will never beat my boy that way again.

The truth was that both McKinley and Connors were on their way to becoming outstanding players, who in large part helped each other improve. Had Gloria seen this as a collaborative effort, it might have aided her son's social skills and given him the chance to make a few friends. But the die was cast long ago on stifling days in Jones Park. McKinley was one of many enemies. Jimmy had to learn how to bludgeon him on his way to more victories.

Connors' unprecedented skill at hating his opponents was the rocket fuel of his career. Hatred to him was at once socially unacceptable and yet, the more I understood tennis, intellectually understandable. Let the affluent drawn to tennis deceive themselves into thinking of it as an elegant activity. Tennis' true warriors knew it was as much a sport as any other. To win at any competitive endeavor, you must simultaneously respect your opponent enough to acknowledge his particular set of assets—and hate him enough to relish undermining them. To a tennis player, this capacity for one-on-one annihilation is the heart of compe-tition. It's no different than a boxer's desire to inflict pain, only lessened by the skills of a racket over a glove. The intent is the same: to force the other guy to surrender. Applying this physical, mental and emotional force became as second nature to Connors as breathing air. Blend in Gloria's sense of class inferiority, her intensity and first-rate fundamen-tals and you have one hyper-charged adolescent.

But what Jimmy had in motivation he lacked in strength. Thanks to Gloria's training, he hit the ball deep and flat. It wouldn't hurt, though, if he had more power, all the better to turn the tables on those netrushers.

Enter the Wilson T-2000. Until 1967, virtually all tennis rackets were made of wood. In the mid-'60s, former French star Rene Lacoste (the man who also created the alligator shirt) experimented with extruded aluminum to build the first mass-produced metal racket.

Connors saw the T-2000 in its prototype form during a junior tournament. Initially he was drawn to it strictly for its looks. The stain-less steel frame was like nothing anyone had ever seen. He asked the Wilson representative if he could try one once it was available.

Many others tried the new frame too. Billie Jean King won Wimbledon and Forest Hills with it. Clark Graebner, a top-10 American, found it alleviated arm troubles, and posted his best-ever Grand Slam showing to reach the finals at Forest Hills. Another American, Gene Scott, nearly retired, used it and advanced to the Forest Hills semis.

But rapidly, the thrill around the T-2000 dissipated, not just at the world-class level, but also among club players. The frame was uncontrollable. Balls flew off the trampoline-like stringing bed. It was virtually impossible to hit any delicate, flicky touch shots, or impart much spin to the ball.

Then again, floating spins and off-beat wrist flicks were as detestable to Gloria Connors as high-toned St. Louis Protestants. Her boy possessed precisely the disciplined, straight strokes necessary for the racket. After a few months of adjustments, he had it under control.

In the summer of 1968, Connors won his first national singles title, the boys' 16 championships. McKinley won the 18s, which according to *World Tennis* "made it a double victory for coach Bill Price." Gloria, for good reason, must have been livid when she saw Price (who would work with Jimmy over her dead body) credited for her boy's success.

During these formative years, Connors' father was scarcely visible— at least at the tennis events that dominated his youngest son's life. Jimmy's most notable male role model was his grandfather, Al. But how much time could a boy and his grandfather spend together when the youngster's life was devoted to tennis? Studying Jimmy's connection to Al, two items surface. Allegedly, Jimmy was once with Al in a bar when the two saw a man murdered. Second, Al's nickname was "Lonesome Pop," due to all the time he spent by himself while the trio of Gloria, "Two-Mom" Bertha and Jimmy toured the country. A proud Catholic, Gloria never divorced her husband.

Once again, though, Gloria's selfish desires triggered brilliance. She knew her boy needed to become a man. Whether this was desired for the good of his tennis or his emotional maturity is impossible to know. What we do know is that in the mid-'60s, Gloria approached a former colleague from her touring days and asked if he'd work with Jimmy.

Like the Connors family, Pancho Segura took tennis personally. Raised in Ecuador in poverty, he taught himself to play tennis and came to the U.S. in his late teens. Like Connors, Segura was considered too small to be a champion, and used that lack of respect as a motivational tool. Tenacity, a strong work ethic and a keen mind made Segura one of the top touring pros of the '50s. At one point, only the great Pancho Gonzalez could beat him. And also like Connors, Segura owned a formidable, unorthodox shot hit from the right side of his body, a two-handed forehand Jack Kramer considered the best single shot in tennis history. Considered one of the sport's premier strategists, Segura studied and understood the nuances of court positioning, angles, shotmaking and what it took not just to hit balls, but to build points with both enterprise and consistency.

Segura at this time was in his late '40s. In the early '60s, he retired from the pro tour and worked in Southern California as the head pro at the Beverly Hills Tennis Club. One of the most generous coaches in tennis history, he worked with many young players, including Arthur Ashe and Stan Smith. He agreed to take on Jimmy, and work with him for nary a nickel. The only proviso was that the boy move to Southern California.

There was no hesitation. By the fall of 1968, 16-year-old Jimmy, Gloria and Bertha moved to a small apartment in LA's Westwood area less than a mile from UCLA. Johnny and Big Jim remained in Belleville.

The distance from Belleville to Los Angeles was 2,000 miles. Considering the territory the Connors' clan was about to travel, it was more like 2,000 years. The two women had no idea that a tennis revolution was brewing—and that the one who'd be sounding the bugle call was their scrawny boy. Jimmy Connors had gone from wood to metal with his rackets. Now the metal was about to come alive in ways no one could imagine. It was time for Connors and tennis to go electric.

3

Go West

Weather shapes outlook. Weather explains much about the vibrancy of the Mediterranean-based Roman Empire, the austerity of the Scandinavians, the reticence of the British.

A climate of suffocation enveloped the young Jimmy Connors and his tennis game. St. Louis summers were exceptionally humid, stifling at best. Winters were worse. One option was an hour-long drive to the indoor courts of the St. Louis Armory, where court availability was scarce. Often he and Gloria would chisel the ice off outdoor courts.

At the age of 16, as Connors arrived in LA, his game emphasized defending territory over creating opportunities. He ran down anything, banged groundstrokes into corners and kept a point in play all day. But as a boy turns into a man, the goal is less to start points than to end them. In the tradition of the era, the lion's share of Connors' peers—Stockton, van Dillen, Mayer, Tanner, Gottfried, McKinley—had by age 16 become adept netrushers.

Adept as Connors was at responding to an attack, his ability to generate offense at this stage was limited. "He would try to force it from the baseline and miss shots," says Stockton. "He was probably afraid to come to net too much because his volleys weren't good and you could also exploit his overhead." Nor had any of the theatrics that marked his later pro career surfaced. "Sure, he had a temper and would occasionally yell," says Gottfried. "But there wasn't any idea that he was trying to entertain anyone. He was all business."

Connors' constrictive, brass-tacks philosophy was reinforced not just by the weather of his native land, but by Gloria's paranoia. Belleville was a cloistered speck in the Midwest, where working-class whites lived in fear on all sides. The blacks, or "coloreds" as the locals referred

to them, had overrun East St. Louis. Further west, across the river, was
the snobbery of St. Louis. To the north, east and south was an abyss of
Illinois countryside—flat plains, windy afternoons, dusty backwoods
roads, scenes out of *Deliverance*.

Here was the message from Gloria and Two-Mom: Son, everyone is
out to get you. On or off the court, they will kill you. Tennis is your
way to turn them back. Attack the ball early and you'll mop up those
rich kids. You'll shove their country clubs and their rich daddies (as
opposed to Jimmy's absent father) right up their Protestant butts (the
Catholic Gloria was known to concurrently curse and nervously
finger her rosary beads).

Take all this intensity-packed energy and now relocate boy, mother
and grandmother to Los Angeles, where the sun shines year-round and
humidity is non-existent. And not just any part of Los Angeles, but
Beverly Hills. And not just any era, but the late '60s. It's not necessary
here to chronicle American culture during these years, but suffice to
say that Beverly Hills in the late '60s was a place and time gone
Technicolor. Cultural revolutions in fashion, film, music and lifestyles
were in their full glory. Belleville was Sparta, a warrior's boot camp.
Beverly Hills was Athens, a hedonist's delight.

Even stodgy old tennis had changed. In 1968, the sport's leaders jetti-
soned the amateur-professional split. The Open Era began. The sport's
upscale audience attracted the attention of advertisers, which in turn
triggered the injection of more prize money and the beginnings of
national TV coverage. Tennis boomed. In 1970, 10.3 million Americans
played tennis. Four years later, the number more than tripled.

Had Connors arrived in Los Angeles even five years earlier, he would
likely have had to make his name at what for decades was the sport's
Vatican, the Los Angeles Tennis Club (LATC). Located in LA's affluent
Hancock Park neighborhood, since its founding in 1920 the LATC had
spawned more tennis champions than any venue in the world.
Ellsworth Vines, Bobby Riggs, Jack Kramer and Pancho Gonzalez were
just a few of the top players who'd cut their teeth on its 16 cement
courts. The University of Southern California (USC), one of two
supreme college tennis superpowers (UCLA was the other), practiced
there. Any pro who came through LA—Americans like Tony Trabert
and Barry MacKay, Australians Rod Laver and Ken Rosewall, the stars
of lesser tennis nations—made sure to hit at the LATC.

The majordomo was Perry Jones, executive secretary of the Southern
California Tennis Association. A lifelong bachelor whose appetite for
control made him a kindred soul with J. Edgar Hoover, Jones occupied

a small cubbyhole just off the club's center court. From this base at the corner of Cahuenga Boulevard and Clinton Avenue, Jones acted as judge and jury of Southern California tennis. Given the region's dominance of the game, he was as powerful as anyone in the sport. Jones determined the fate of everything from junior memberships to traveling expenses to Davis Cup rosters. He insisted on proper dress, etiquette and sportsmanship. His charges wrote thank-you notes to hosts and patrons. They obeyed his every order, whether it was a decree to vacate a court or a suggestion of who to partner for doubles. In his 80s, decades after Jones' death, Kramer still referred to him as Mister Jones.

Through Jones' prime years—the '30s into the late '60s—tennis predominantly remained an elite sport dominated by white, Anglo-Saxon Protestants. Jews and blacks were not admitted to the LATC. The club annually hosted the Pacific Southwest Championships. Held after the U.S. Nationals at Forest Hills in late September, the "Southwest" was considered the second-most important tournament in the country. For this week, the LATC sold tickets to all. Jones skillfully placed box-seat holders from Jewish-dominated Hollywood in one corner and bluebloods from such towns as Pasadena and San Marino in another. As much as Jones admired the tennis skills of a dark-skinned champion like Pancho Segura—he'd played there frequently—there was no way an Ecuadorian would ever work at a club like the LATC.

Segura's base was five miles to the west. The Beverly Hills Tennis Club (BHTC) was formed in the '30s by Jews as a response, a counterpunch if you will, to the LATC's restrictive admissions policies. The BHTC also had a tennis pedigree, though nowhere as accomplished as LATC. Two of its founders, Fred Perry and Ellsworth Vines, were world champions in the '30s. But with the likes of Charlie Chaplin, Errol Flynn and Groucho Marx on hand, the BHTC was more of a Hollywood playground than a hardcore tennis venue. Within the confines of this small, five-court venue there was a mix of festivities and competition. Marx once popped out of a suitcase prior to a doubles match. His son, Arthur, became a fine player, once beating Kramer in a junior tournament.

The flavors of the two clubs were vastly different. The LATC's membership was understated, dominated by Angelenos who'd earned their wealth in upstanding fields like finance, transportation and real estate. It didn't matter that many of these Angelenos had only become successful a mere generation or two ago. Rapidly the LATC membership took on the attitudes and mores of similar Brahmin tennis venues such as the Newport Casino, Forest Hills' West Side Tennis Club, Philadelphia's Germantown Cricket Club and Boston's Longwood Cricket and Croquet Club. LATC was old money, down-home elitism, subdued conversation and heavily Protestant. To steal from F. Scott Fitzgerald's *The Great Gatsby*, it was strictly East Egg. A blue-collar Catholic like Gloria Connors, her social antennae as fine-tuned as her eye for stroke mechanics, no doubt felt the LATC personified the snobs that pervaded St. Louis. These people looked down their ski-slope noses at hard workers like policeman Al Thompson, his daughter Gloria and her feisty baseliner of a son.

Segura was the perfect teaching pro for a club like the BHTC, which with its nouveau riche Gatsbys was West Egg. Like many of its members, he too was an outsider. "I didn't have any weapons, I didn't have any daddy from Harvard," he says. "I had to try harder to be part of that tennis world. No one but me was looking to help me."

The extra effort that made him a top pro continued when he instructed. Whereas a teaching pro at the LATC typically offered students several clear, thoughtful commands and a series of recommended drills, Segura issued a non-stop barrage of directions, instructions and jokes. The intensity was similar to Gloria's, but the patter was drastically different. Segura was a Borscht Belt routine injected into a great tennis brain. To watch him teach wasn't simply great sport. It was great theater. "Buddy," he'd say, "why don't you take two weeks off— and then quit!"

The mix of sports and entertainment only made sense. The flavor of Hollywood pervaded the BHTC. Not just actors, but directors, producers, writers, agents, attorneys, dentists and doctors who served the stars played there. Perennially hankering for entertainment, BHTC members lived for "action." Usually, this meant placing moderate to large-sized wagers on tennis matches. To be sure, the LATC had a constant flow of "money matches" too. But at the BHTC, money was less important than the ever-present capacity for verbal jousting. "We were Jewish, we liked to banter," says Stan Canter, a movie producer and member who for a short time managed Connors. "Playing for money was only a part of it all. We were really in it for the kibitzing."

As a touring professional, Segura lit up the world. He entertained crowds on every continent with sharp play and keen humor. While Kramer and Gonzalez played the romantic lead roles, Segura was the scene-stealer, the deputy who wins over the crowd. At the BHTC, "Segu" was the sheriff.

It was also, alas, a rather ornamental position. Like anyone who's ever taught tennis, Segura knew that the vast majority of his students were dabblers, mostly bored housewives and bratty children who barely played with any degree of effort or intensity. Much as Pancho tried to help these people appreciate tennis, like any teacher, he hungered for committed students. Whether it was a junior hoping to make his high school team, or the young Ashe and Smith, Segura was drawn to ambition. In this sense, he and Gloria Connors were kindred souls. Their mutual, visceral love of tennis was the common ground that helped her overcome any of her natural prejudices towards the BHTC's disparate mix of races and religions.

Intuition and empathy made Segura a keen appraiser of tennis potential. As he sized up the scrawny teen from Illinois with the pipe-cleaner legs, it wasn't the simplicity of his strokes, or the discipline of his footwork that most struck him. In no way was Segura impressed by Connors' serve. Most lefthanders could at least hit a nifty little slice, but this kid couldn't do that too well. He threw his toss over his head and spun out this bizarre little twist. His volleys—when he hit them—were OK, but there were at least a dozen better within five miles of the BHTC. And the mother? She loved the boy, and unquestionably had instilled him with sound fundamentals. But surely there should be moments when it was best for her to leave the boy alone to the men. And the grandmother too? And where was his father? Better not to ask.

All that was secondary to what Segura saw instantly. What he spotted in Connors would eventually be witnessed, loved and hated by millions. But not yet. On many a warm day in 1969, though, Wimbledon and U.S. champs like Jack Kramer and Tony Trabert, Ted Schroeder and Bobby Riggs, Alex Olmedo and Pancho Gonzalez visited their old friend Segura. As in any sport in any era, when ex-pros converse, the topic was talent. Who was the next great American? Who among these current teens had the goods? The talented van Dillen? The versatile Stockton? The diligent Gottfried? The big-serving Tanner? Rarely was Connors mentioned. To the experts, the classic LATC champions tapped by Perry Jones, the boy from St. Louis was filled with liabilities: short, baseliner, two hands.

Segura's genius was his ability to scratch deeper. Hadn't his own success proven that a surface evaluation meant nothing? He hit with the boy. He watched him play. He saw something so familiar, so obvious, that it stood out clear as a blue sky. It was the same quality that took Segura from Ecuador to Beverly Hills. "Jimbo, Jimbo," he told me a quarter-century after they'd first met. "Others were bigger, others then could hit harder, but Jimbo, he had that one thing that you can't teach: He had desire. He wanted it so bad you could taste his hunger. And he'd do what it took to get there. He wasn't afraid."

Gloria had directed her son's undergraduate career. She'd taken him quite far. Connors was ranked number one in the country in the 16s in 1968, number two his first year in the 18s in '69. She also knew a ranking hardly told the story when there were dozens of Bobby McKinleys out there.

Segura became his graduate advisor. The BHTC's courts were his classroom. His blackboard was a cocktail napkin. On a tiny piece of disposable paper, Segura mapped out a court. He showed Connors the patterns of a point, the way one shot elicited a likely response. No one in tennis history was more prolific at cocktail napkin strategy than Segura. No one devoured Segura's geometry lessons more ravenously than Connors.

Imagine a Tuesday morning during this 1968-'70 period. Connors has shown up at 12:30 at the BHTC from nearby Rexford High, a private school that's permitted him tremendous latitude. Lest you think this revolutionary, Jack Kramer arranged a similar schedule as a teenager.

Connors arrives at Segura's court, and within a few minutes they've started a movement drill. Segura, still formidable enough to compete with virtually anyone, serves wide into the deuce court corner to Connors' backhand. The drill requires Connors to drive deep and cross-court. To do this he must get to the ball extremely early and hit it with abandon. Then Connors moves forward and to his left, into the net area, where Segura strikes a passing shot down the line to Connors' forehand volley. This step alone takes extreme quickness. Jimbo's next move is to firmly punch the volley crosscourt for a winner. If it's not a winner, Segura will draw on several options designed to keep Connors off-balance. He might strike another pass up Jimmy's backhand line. Or, he'll float an off-pace angle low to the forehand volley. Or, he'll loft up a lob, which happens to be one of the best in tennis history. Either way, to succeed at this drill Connors must be constantly on the prowl, primed to move forward. The drill is repeated in the ad court, Segura serving to Connors' forehand. Several dozen points later, Connors pauses. Gloria fetches a Coke. She'd watched every bit of it, and liked what she saw.

When Gloria isn't monitoring Jimmy's tennis, she's paying the bills by working as a hostess at a Beverly Hills restaurant called Nibbler's and giving tennis lessons. Even more than in Belleville, her sense of economic and class injustice is on red alert. Back home, after all, was simply the repressed and understated Midwest, the Connors family just one of many living a middle-class life. Now, riding into flashy Beverly

Hills every day, scrimping so that she can buy her beloved nice pants and shirts, Gloria is truly aware of the gap between her family's modest means and the local swells.

Quick cut to Wednesday afternoon. Segura's arranged a session for Jimbo with the Pancho known throughout the world, the great Gonzalez. Lanky and aloof, rebellious to his core, Gonzalez was probably the first older tennis player who truly impressed the young Connors. Prior to his arrival in LA, Connors was primarily exposed to locals in St. Louis. Though he'd read about and seen many of the touring pros who'd come through town, the transitory nature of these exhibitions, coupled with Gloria's hatred for anyone who stood in her son's way, made it hard for young Jimmy to appreciate another player. Gonzalez was someone he saw in LA several times a week. As champion and competitor, friend and foe, he was the genuine article; precisely the kind of mean, driven son-of-a-bitch Gloria wanted Jimmy to become.

In some ways, Gonzalez was, along with Segura, one of many who acted as surrogate fathers for Connors. Yet any paternalism was subordinated to competition. The last thing anyone dared reveal to Gonzalez was vulnerability. Connors wanted to prove himself to the man who'd been the world's best for so long. On this day, the two played a match. Gonzalez, armed with one of the best serves in tennis history, fired ball after ball into corners. Connors was eager to spit them back down at the older man's feet.

Connors' service return, a shot he'd honed on the slick, indoor wood courts of the St. Louis Armory, became the cornerstone of his game. It was a shot laden with technical and social implications. The return of serve was Connors' best way to turn the tables. Gloria and Segura advised him that a great service return was psychologically devastating. Consider: A big serve like Gonzalez's simply stepped over someone. Granted, Jimmy would have liked one of those, but between his size (barely 5-foot-10 as a pro) and his awkward technique, that likely wasn't in the cards. But if a serve was singularly effective, a return was doubly potent. It took away an opponent's strength and let Jimmy alter the flow from defense to offense. That was precisely the point of the return drill. Segura's full-bodied offense was a logical evolution from Gloria's rock-solid fundamentals. Counterpunching service returns showed up those pretty boys from the snobby clubs. Jimbo would bring 'em down into the boondocks, flip 'em on their backs and show 'em who was boss.

Against a server like Gonzalez, returning well wasn't too easy. Despite the 24-year age gap, Gonzalez remained too strong. He anticipated

Connors' returns and caressed volleys into corners. Though not able to hit as hard as Connors from the baseline, Gonzalez deftly mixed paces and spins. His variety kept Connors off balance enough to frustrate him into errors. It was yet another lesson unavailable in Belleville.

Afterwards, there was conversation. Segura often joined in, particularly since he was considered the only person in tennis able to get the moody Gonzalez to relax. The Panchos regaled Jimmy with tales of the pro tour, insights into active pros like Ken Rosewall and Laver, advice on training, nutrition and even more hedonistic pursuits. These were men, hearty athletes with big-time games and equally robust libidos. Certainly matters of the flesh weren't on Gloria and Two-Mom's agenda.

But for Connors, pleasure always took a back seat to business. One particular topic Gonzalez stressed was racket technology. Like Connors, he too used a metal frame, the Spalding Smasher, and showed Connors how pieces of lead tape added to various points along the head helped generate more power. Gonzalez also shared wisdom about grips and strings. Gloria and Bertha paid attention to these pointers too. The Connors trio trekked to Westwood Sporting Goods near the UCLA campus, where owners Shelby Johns and his son, Bill, strung the rackets for most of LA's top players.

Now it's Friday night. If there's a tournament that weekend, Jimmy's home with Gloria and Two-Mom. Gloria's cooked one of his favorite meals such as chicken fried steak. He'll have a few Cokes and then, perhaps, a brownie. Gloria lays out his clothes for the weekend.

If it's an off-week, Jimmy's headed out for a night on the town with his LA tour guide, Segura's son, Spencer. A fine player, but not in Jimmy's class, Spencer is wise to the ways of the world. He encouraged Jimmy to grow out his short, spiky hair and cultivate what became his trademark Prince Valiant look. He exposed him to local clubs like The Candy Store and saw to it that Jimbo sported sharp velvets and Guccis. Much as all these indulgences weren't to Gloria's liking, she turned her eyes. The boy worked so hard on the court, surely he deserved the occasional splurge. Even on those nights, Connors rarely stayed out too late. There was work to be done. The next morning he planned to jump rope, run a couple of miles and soak up more of Segu's insights. For several years, he took martial arts classes.

Sunday afternoon. Connors relaxes. He plays hit-and-giggle doubles at movie producer Robert Evans' court off Coldwater Canyon. A typical scenario: Evans-Connors versus Spencer and one of Evans' Hollywood cronies. In his book, *The Kid Stays in The Picture*, Evans estimated he and Connors partnered 41 times—and lost them all.

Naturally, there's action, a discreet way for Evans to reward Connors for being his partner—certainly with money but also likely with more sensual delights such as culinary feasts, exotic liquid concoctions and perhaps even a phone number or two of a friendly lady.

Connors also played many singles matches versus Dean Martin Jr., son of the famous singer. "Dino" possessed everything but the one thing Connors owned: a first-rate tennis game. As Connors said to Curry Kirkpatrick in the first *Sports Illustrated* cover story on him in 1974:

> "I just wanted to play tennis. Anyway, the movie stars were coming out there to see me, to play tennis with me. I must have been somebody myself. Here's Dino Martin and rich kids like that hanging around. They get new Ferraris every year, but they aren't responsible people. Never show up on time, forget their friends. Dino wanted to bet me always. He said I had no class, that I'd never get ranked or have my picture on magazine covers. See, he had a famous father and several tons of dough and time on his hands and all the broads. Yet all he wanted to do was to play good tennis. He wanted what I had. So he bet. And if we had kept on playing for money, he probably would have owed me his life."

Dino could afford the loss. What Pancho Segura and Jimmy Connors shared was the lack of a safety net. Dino occupied a socio-economic realm that would catch him if he failed. Though far less affluent, even Spencer was nestled securely. And because life was so cushy, why bother pushing too hard anyway? For Pancho from Ecuador, for Jimmy from Belleville, it was tennis or bust. If not for tennis, I once asked Connors, what would you have done? "Digging ditches," he said. Unlikely as it was that Gloria Connors would let her son become a blue-collar worker, Connors thrived on this imagery. Beverly Hills helped him extend the social alienation Gloria had fostered. It was one thing to counterpunch the moderate affluence of suburban St. Louis. In Beverly Hills, the Connors' encountered the filthy-rich. And, perhaps for the first time, through encounters with those who valued fame every bit as much as money (maybe even more in some cases), the boy realized that tennis might take him further than he, his mother or grandmother dared imagine. To quote again from "Down in the Boondocks:"

> One fine day I'll find a way to move from this old shack/I'll hold my head up like a king/And never, never will look back/Until that morning I'll work and slave.

Work and slave were exactly what he did. With Segura added to the

Gloria and Two-Mom corner crew, with tennis available all day, every day, the only thing bigger than Connors' appetite was his dedication. In the early '80s, sitting with his shirt off at the BHTC for an interview with *Tennis Magazine*'s Peter Bodo, Connors stared into the autumn skies of a Southern California day and reflected on those formative years in Beverly Hills. "My entrée to everything was tennis," he said. "And in my own eyes, I couldn't see it as being just a little tennis. It had to great tennis, top-of-the-pile tennis. So basically in my time here, I just ate, breathed, slept, thought and talked tennis."

As Connors devoured lessons and experiences from Segura, Gonzalez and other fine LA-based players, the basics Gloria built in Belleville came to life, if not quite with the proficiency that made him the world's best by 1974, then certainly with vigor. He learned how to amplify his great groundstrokes. Frequent use of the lob, for example, neutralized netrushers. By forcing them to be on the lookout for a lob, Connors gained a few more inches for his deadly passing shots. From the baseline, Connors' ability to strike the ball with exceptional pace and depth put opponents on the defensive, so why not come to net more and cut off the court? On the serve, Segura helped Connors throw his toss more into the court to generate more power rather than over his head (this would prove a career-long struggle for Connors). Granted, there were dozens of instructors across the country able to pass these tips on to Connors. Would he have listened? It was Gloria's genius to find the very best, mentors like Segura and Gonzalez who were prominent champions and street-smart outsiders.

Connors also absorbed many new ideas off the court. On lawn chairs in Beverly Hills, in conversations with various Hollywood folk, at parties with Spencer, it dawned on him that tennis was not just a sport or a way to put food on the table, but a form of entertainment. Gloria's court was all business. Segu was rigorous too, but with a spirit of fun. Connors began to see that if he could make spectators laugh he might be the one thing he'd never been: one of the boys. Back in St. Louis, when peers like McKinley and Waltke threw a football around between sets, Jimmy was cloistered by his mother. As he blossomed into the country's best junior and escaped the oppressive Midwest for the upbeat West Coast, perhaps there was some breathing room. Perhaps if he learned to make people like him, his Connors gladhandling legacy might nudge its way into his Thompson athleticism.

Yet the competitor in Connors always took priority over the performer. In June 1970, in the finals of the Southern California Junior Sectionals, played at the venerable LATC, Connors beat his doubles partner and BHTC buddy, Bob Kreiss, 6-4, 6-2. Several times early in the match, after Connors felt Kreiss received a bad line call, Jimmy handed the point over to his rival. After a while, he said, "No, I'm sorry, I can't afford to give away any more points today." The truth is that Connors should never have tossed away any points in the first place. Consummate professionals such as Budge, Kramer, Trabert and Segura played with a code: you accepted the calls as they came and moved on with it (the fiery Gonzalez frequently questioned umpires). In no way, wrote a local reporter who covered the match versus Kreiss, was Connors as magnanimous as he feigned. The writer also noted how Connors walked around the court like a bullfighter, complete with scowl and hunched shoulders.

Many years down the road, the security of an unassailable résumé helped Connors strike the mix of blarney and bluster that made him exceptionally popular. But in its nascent form, the Connors act grated. The high-intensity desire of a pubescent momma's boy at Manker Patten was one thing, particularly since Connors wasn't the top dog. The raging ambition of an increasingly dominant teenager in disingenuous pursuit of a few chuckles was not easy to swallow.

Yet there was something more to Connors than just a crude effort to mix competition with entertainment. To watch him play was to sense that what happened on the court was about to become explosive, revelatory, different—that Connors and the audience were about to be tugged into very different emotional territory than they'd witnessed on more peaceful days. Tennis was in the midst of its own change. After years in garden-party isolation, the sport was throwing off its patrician cloak. The notion of tennis no longer as a pastime but as a marketplace, boiling over with money, promotion and television, was about to change everything.

So on a global basis, there was the growth of tennis. On a personal basis, there was the rise of Connors. And all of this occurred against the backdrop of greater shifts in American culture. Connors probably didn't know it then, and rarely admitted that anything other than his mother had ever influenced him, but in his own odd way, in his own mix of provincial breeding and big-time ambition, he was on the cusp of becoming the right man in the right place at the right time. His game tilted towards the edge. His temperament was anti-Establishment. A sport long tethered now unleashed itself on the culture.

In Los Angeles, of course, culture was virtually synonymous with the feel-good entertainment industry. Beneath that glitz lay decay and cynicism. Today's fashion was tomorrow's garbage. More emphatically, thick in the middle of Connors' two high school years in Southern California, there was an increasing attitude that good living was costly. In August 1969, actress Sharon Tate and a group of friends were murdered in her house in Beverly Hills' Benedict Canyon. The victims included a Beverly Hills coffee heiress and a former boyfriend of hers who was a hairdresser to the stars (allegedly the model for the lead character played by Warren Beatty in the 1975 film, *Shampoo*). Tinged with tales of sex and drugs, until the crime was solved three months later, rumors floated through Hollywood that the dead were victims of a lifestyle gone awry. Once it was discovered that Charles Manson and his "family" committed the murders in order to trigger "Helter Skelter" race wars, the trial dominated headlines in Los Angeles in the early '70s. Beverly Hills was a world not just of artifice, but of random crimes and wacky cults. It was light years removed from the heartland pragmatism of Jones Park.

Los Angeles 1970 is the place and time my own story began its parallel jog alongside Connors'. We moved to LA from St. Louis in November 1970. Tennis was non-existent to us, but there was no avoiding what was in the streets and on the news. We lived a mile from Westwood, the UCLA community. Only a block from where Connors' rackets were strung, near my favorite bookstore and movie theater, bald-headed Hare Krishnas chanted daily and handed out pamphlets, the tickets for God the young Elton John referred to in "Tiny Dancer." Nearby Santa Monica had gas stations run by Synanon, an early drug rehab center. Each night, Ken and I watched the news on TV and saw members of Manson's cult praying for their leader. In a West Hollywood studio roughly equidistant between the BHTC and LATC, another Jimbo, Jim Morrison, recorded an album Ken purchased in 1971: The Doors' "LA Woman." As Morrison sang in the title track, "Motel money/murder madness/lets change the mood from glad to sadness." Beneath the sunshine, there was danger. It was all, as Connors said to me 20 years later, "creepy, unreal."

And when those vibrant sounds and senses were wedded to the desires of someone like the adolescent Connors, it didn't always come in such a nice package. "The swashbuckling Connors promises to provide Southern California tennis devotees with many interesting moments and problems over the next few years," said an August 1970 article in *Tennis West*. "In fact, it's questionable whether or not Southern California can survive the antics, explosions and amazing tennis talent contained in this youngster from St. Louis ... Southern California racqueteers beware: THIS IS A NEW BREED OF CAT."

Those who radically change the course of history, wrote the German philosopher of history, Georg Hegel, "are the far-sighted ones: they have discerned what is true in their world and in their age, and have recognized the concept, the next universal to emerge."

Tennis in 1970 continued its transition out of the sleepy amateur days and into the professional era. In September, the same month Perry Jones died, a Jew who ran tobacco giant Philip Morris decided to sponsor the fledgling Virginia Slims circuit. With new fans and sponsors, player expectations changed radically. "We weren't at the mercy of the clubs and the officials anymore," says Billie Jean King. "We were going to compete in the marketplace, and earn an honest living. It was a thrilling time." The piles of money were growing rapidly. Rod Laver, the world's number one player, earned $124,000 in 1969, $201,453 in '70 and $292,717 in '71. African-American Arthur Ashe and All-American Stan Smith emerged as tennis stars with crossover appeal. Each served in the Army, traveled on State Department tours and starred in the Davis Cup. Their credentials, coupled with the sport's growth, made them attractive corporate endorsers.

For an 18-year-old like Connors, about to enter UCLA, it couldn't have been a better time to splash onto the scene. In September 1970, the same month he would start his freshman year at UCLA, he sat around the LATC with his peers, Raul Ramirez and James "Chico" Hagey, on the eve of the Pacific Southwest Open. That June, Ramirez and Hagey lost in the doubles final of the junior sectionals to Connors and Kreiss. Having learned the game in the pre-Open Era, Ramirez and Hagey downplayed their chances of becoming top players. As the three sat alongside the club's pool, they watched the great Australian Roy Emerson practice. At 33, Emerson was in the twilight of his career. Still, he'd won more Grand Slam titles than any man in tennis history, and remained a formidable competitor. Connors was due to play him in the first round. Look at Emmo, Connors told Ramirez and Hagey. He's so cocky, he thinks he's going to beat me tomorrow. Why shouldn't he, said Ramirez, he's Roy Emerson. Well, we'll just have to see about that, said Connors. Old Emmo won't be so happy tomorrow. Ramirez and Hagey were staggered by Connors' confidence.

The next day, Connors came out swinging. Rather rudely, he cheekily sprayed winners all over the court in the warmup rather than let Emerson get prepared. He won the match, 7-6, 6-7, 6-4. An electric current went through an entire generation. Hey, Ramirez suddenly realized, we can all be good. Look what Jimmy's done. Maybe we can do it too. "The world-historical individuals," wrote Hegel, "are those who were the first to formulate the desires of their fellows explicitly."

The less said about Connors' coursework at UCLA in the 1970-'71 school year, the better. Oncourt, he was fanatical. He played number three on the finest college squad in the country. For someone who would years later say, "I sail my ship alone," he was an exemplary teammate. If Connors lost a set, recalls his coach Glenn Bassett, he'd demand the chance to avenge it the next day. Frequently he'd make bets for Cokes, dinners, movie tickets. The entertainer and competitor in Connors merged quite humorously when, after the Muhammad Ali-Joe Frazier fight, Connors wore tassels on his socks, which throughout his career he liked to pull up near his knees.

That year the NCAA Championships were played in South Bend, Indiana on the Notre Dame campus. Bassett remembers how motivated Connors was to play well at his father's alma mater. In the quarterfinals he met Bobby McKinley, now a junior at Trinity. Not since Tulsa two years previously had they played. In the hot Indiana sun, McKinley served at 5-4, 30-30.

Then Connors did something that made him rivaled only by Rod Laver and John McEnroe. Many greats hit clutch shots, but invariably they relied on one or two basic weapons. Gonzalez and Pete Sampras snapped off great serves. Don Budge and Ken Rosewall darted returns. Jack Kramer struck sharp volleys. Having spent 20 years querying Connors' rivals, it's remarkable to hear how many different shots he hit to redirect the momentum of a match.

McKinley played the point in textbook fashion. He served wide to Connors' backhand. Wisely anticipating a return to his backhand volley, McKinley moved forward and knifed it into the far corner— deep and angled. As Bassett, McKinley and McKinley's coach, Clarence Mabry, independently described it, Connors seemed to run the length of a football field to track down the volley. From far back in his own court, Connors ripped a forehand down the line that hit both sideline and baseline. He took the next point too, squared the match at 5-5 and ran it out, 8-6 in the third. It was the only time he'd ever beaten McKinley. The two never played singles again. McKinley retired from the pro tour in 1975, returning to Trinity as head coach. A few days after beating McKinley, Connors became the first freshman to win the NCAA Championships. There were no sightings of Jimmy's father.

By January 1972, in a move that surprised no one, Connors dropped out of UCLA and turned pro. Having taken the fall quarter off, he posted pleasing results. Most notable was his effort at the Southwest, where he beat recently crowned U.S. Open champ Stan Smith before losing in the finals to Gonzalez. At the end of 1971, Connors was ranked seventh among American men and stood head and shoulders above his peers.

The implications of Connors' potential were revolutionary. In the pre-Open Era, excitement around a young teen strictly focused on his long-term potential on-court: Could he become great enough to win Grand Slam events and play Davis Cup? Did the elder patrons and ex-champs who issued these verdicts believe he could be a champion? But in the Open Era, a potential star like Connors wasn't just a prospect, but an instant market, a source of immediate and sustainable revenue and promotional clout. U.S. Davis Cup captain and budding agent Donald Dell wielded power on behalf of Smith and Ashe with everyone from racket companies to tournament directors. Because Connors was younger and riper, he was likely to bear even more fruit. And there was one man who knew precisely how to pluck it.

Bill Riordan was a tennis-loving P.T. Barnum. Wealthy and charming, the lanky Riordan was the kind of fellow of whom it was said, he could sell snow to Eskimos. His teeth resembled a row of corn. His pockets jiggled with coins. His brain constantly tumbled the odds on horse races, stock prices and anything else where one might make a killing. He was a rogue, but unquestionably a likable one, an opportunist with a heart who, like Segura, conducted a fair amount of business on cocktail napkins.

In the tennis world, Riordan commanded a small principality. In the late '50s he got involved in the USLTA's Middle States section as a volunteer. In 1960, Riordan became tournament director of an event in Salisbury, Maryland, with the prosaic name of the Middle Atlantic Indoor Tennis Tournament. Eager for panache and publicity, he renamed it the Salisbury International. In this era when players were paid under the table, Riordan wisely peeled off his share of dollars. One year he awarded a player an $8,000 bonus. Ample hundreds tumbled out to others. As word of his generosity spread, bigger names committed. Soon Riordan added tournaments to his portfolio, usually in cities smaller than Salisbury. When the talented and hotheaded Romanian Ilie Nastase made his first trip to the U.S. in the mid-'60s, he came to a Riordan stop in Macon, Georgia. Riordan, knowing that Nastase had won a $50 bet from a friend for daring to wear polka-dotted pajamas on the court, fined Nastase $50 for violating the dress code. It was the first time a tennis player had ever been fined. Riordan's mission was accomplished: coverage in *The New York Times*.

By the early '70s, the "Riordan Circuit," as it was known, was a loose confederation of tournaments held in unsung venues like Salisbury, Macon, Roanoke, Omaha and Kansas City. Beginning in 1970, the Riordan-run events were folded into a larger circuit known as the Commercial Union Grand Prix. Players earned points at each stop, in pursuit of a year-end bonus pool.

At the same time, a rival circuit flourished. The World Championship Tennis (WCT) tour backed by Lamar Hunt, son of oil baron H.L. Hunt, had the vast majority of the world's top players, including the world's top three in 1970, Rod Laver, Ken Rosewall and John Newcombe.

Anyone who managed a top player commanded tremendous influence in the pro game. Donald Dell negotiated large contracts for Ashe and Smith to play WCT. Whichever circuit landed the top players was rewarded with credibility and box office results. Star power was particularly significant in tennis, where promotional value was heavily attached to individuals rather than cities or teams. WCT became the new tennis establishment, growing so large that by the early '70s its ranks tripled, with three separate groups of players traveling the world.

Without a star—particularly an American star, since that was the home for so many precious sponsors—Riordan's circuit would shrivel. He was exceptionally leery of Dell, who he'd known since Dell's days as a player and aspiring power seeker. Like many people in tennis, Riordan believed Dell wanted to take over the sport, using his clients as pawns for his own personal agenda. Of course, Riordan wanted to do precisely the same thing, and because his circuit lacked the cumulative box office appeal of WCT, he didn't just need any star. He needed a supernova.

Connors was a rookie pro in 1972. He was 19, had never been to Europe and still relied heavily on his mother and grandmother for everything from on-court advice to domestic chores. Agents called constantly. He'd played in several of Riordan's events and, in a Connors rarity, struck up a friendship with the circuit's main star, Nastase. Though Connors recoiled at the concept of being intimidated, he felt uncomfortable about joining WCT. Uncertain which step to take, he visited Riordan in Miami—no doubt the promoter had recently been at the racetrack—and asked his advice.

"If you want to surrender," Riordan told Connors, "all you have to do is pick up the telephone—you can do that in four seconds—they'd be delighted to have you. If you want to be number two in [WCT's] Green Group, or number six in the Chartreuse Group, pick up the phone. But, if you want to become the best-known tennis player in the world, I can't teach you how to hit a backhand, but one thing I know is merchandising. I'll make you the best-known tennis player in the world. With what I know about you, I don't think you are a joiner. I think you have to do your own thing, and I think I'm the guy that can help you do that."

Just as Segura grasped Connors' approach on the court, Riordan clicked into it off the court. Gloria and Bertha were sold too. Catholic and married, Riordan was precisely the kind of man's man able to stroll into any pub in the world and buy a round for all the fellas. He was yet another father figure Jimmy Connors lacked. No way would Connors sign with WCT. Later that year, when a new players' union, the ATP, was formed by a number of WCT stars (with Dell as legal counsel), Connors declined to join. Riordan made noise about his own union that proved an illusion. It was of little concern to Connors. He was Riordan's big fish. WCT and the ATP were The Establishment, haughty, full of themselves and scarcely concerned with Jimbo's welfare. Everything from East St. Louis forward led the Connorses to become anti-Establishment.

Fond of billing Connors as "The One & Only," Riordan keenly massaged the egos of the entire Connors family. Bertha thought Riordan was classy. Jimmy leaned on him for emotional support. And Gloria was given a lesson in media relations she regrettably forgot.

Her education occurred in June 1972, when Connors made his Wimbledon debut. Due to a complicated series of political factors, WCT's 32 players were banned from Wimbledon that year. This gave up-and-comers like Connors a chance to make a big splash. Connors' first-round match versus seventh-seeded Bob Hewitt was scheduled on Centre Court. For many Wimbledon newcomers, this could be daunting. Not for Connors. Despite serving 10 double-faults (triple his typical effort), Connors earned a convincing straight-set win.

But the headlines weren't generated by Connors' backhand. Wimbledon's Centre Court is unquestionably the most intimate of all the Grand Slam venues, orderly and quiet as a cathedral. Throughout the match, Gloria cheered her boy on with cries of "Go, Jimbo!" They were met with silence. The next day, London's papers hammered this noisy American intruder—a female at that—with nasty stories and caricatures.

Riordan took charge. Jimmy was dispatched to practice. Gloria was given instructions. When a local reporter asked her how Jimmy felt about all the negative coverage, Gloria Connors went against type. She laughed and said how much Jimmy teased her about the news stories all through breakfast. Surely there was no dissent in the Connors camp. Connors reached the quarterfinals and lost to Nastase. Notable tennis journalist Richard Evans wrote that, "Not since Lew Hoad and Ken Rosewall … has a teenager made such an impact on his first visit to Wimbledon."

By the end of 1972, Connors won six tournament titles, 75 matches and ranked third among Americans. A year later he won 11 tournaments and finished the year co-ranked number one in the U.S. with Stan Smith. Yet raw numbers hardly told his story.

Once a point started, Connors commanded attention. He played with all-out abandon. No one had ever thrown himself at every ball with such intensity. The quality of his groundstrokes was so good he instantly dispelled notions that he was too small or that his two-handed backhand limited his possibilities. Moreover, his style was new—or, to long-standing followers, it was a throwback to the days when Budge, Perry and Vines won primarily from the baseline. Connors' rallies were longer and more diverse than the dominant serve-volley style of the '50s and '60s. The image of Connors staring down a netrusher was captivating, the quintessential contrast between batter and pitcher. "Winning differently," Kramer called it, adding that, "Jimmy could be a major influence on the American game for years."

Commendable as Connors was as a competitor, it was much harder to appreciate Connors as a person. Where to start? Try the womb. No top male player had ever been so obviously linked to a parent, much less a mother. Since Gloria Connors saw the world strictly through her boy's needs, her talent for diplomacy was negligible. Her narrow view made it difficult to arrange everything from practices to tournament commitments to corporate endorsements.

On the court, Connors engaged in various forms of gamesmanship. Prior to serving, he often bounced the ball many times more than was customary in order to derail the receiver's rhythm. Several opponents, going back to junior days, note that in the warmup Connors hit inordinately high lobs, hence making it hard for the opponent to warm up his overhead. He'd also mock his opponent's form when the player wasn't looking. When he'd miss a shot, Connors would make crude gestures with his finger or wiggle his racket like a phallic symbol. At press conferences, he rarely acknowledged the skill of his opponents. In the locker, he hardly chatted with the other players. In a heavily international sport that prided itself on being somewhat of a globetrotting UN, at once humble and cosmopolitan, Connors was narrow, vulgar and boorish. With his James Cagney-like strut, Connors was the quintessential ugly

American: isolated, ambitious, arrogant, disrespectful of those who'd come before him—and wildly successful. This was a boy who wasn't about to bow to anyone. It vexed the sport's hierarchy. Connors, said Laver, "probably thinks he's the next best thing to 7-Up."

Yet American as Connors was in attitude and manner, he refused to represent his country in team play. Connors' Davis Cup journey couldn't have gotten off to a worse start. After serving as a practice partner for the final round of team play in 1971, he was asked to come to Jamaica in March '72. The Jamaican squad was weak, a perfect chance for the 19-year-old Connors to debut in fairly stress-free circumstances. He was playing well too, having won two tournaments. The three players eligible for the two Davis Cup singles spots were Connors, Tom Gorman and Erik van Dillen. To keep his players sharp, captain Dennis Ralston had them play challenge matches. When van Dillen beat Connors, Ralston announced that van Dillen would play singles—even though his results that year were far worse than Connors'. Meanwhile, word came from LA that "Two-Mom" was sick. Connors, upset about events on and off the court, left Jamaica to see Bertha on her deathbed. He never returned to Jamaica. Two decades later, I said the word "Jamaica" to Connors and he spoke vividly: "That was one fucked week. To have that happen to my grandmother, and then to not even play—can we change the subject?"

Riordan made sure Connors knew that Gorman and van Dillen were close allies of Ralston (both the captain and van Dillen had played for USC, albeit several years apart) and clients of former team leader Dell. Gloria's lifelong warning rang true in the big leagues too: they're out to get you, Jimmy. Bertha, bitter at how Jimmy was treated, demanded on her deathbed that Gloria never let him play Davis Cup.

After Jamaica, at the French Open in June '72, Ralston personally handed airline tickets to Connors and Gorman for the next Davis Cup tie in Mexico City. Having just reached the semis of the doubles in Paris, Connors and Gorman got along well. As they sat in the locker with their tickets to Mexico, Gorman asked Connors what he was planning to do. I don't know, said Connors. His ticket went unused. Since then, he'd resisted all of Ralston's overtures. In the fall of 1973, the opportunistic Riordan told Ralston that Connors was available for the finals versus Australia scheduled for that November. Ralston, loyal to those who'd played all year, declined.

Connors' participation in the lower-quality Riordan circuit also damaged his reputation. A belief surfaced that Connors was kept under wraps. That was indeed true. Riordan loved to market Connors like a prizefighter. Connors built up his reputation versus lesser foes on his way to those big title bouts at Wimbledon and Forest Hills. Connors, politicized by Riordan, polarized by Gloria, enjoyed the chance to build his confidence. "WCT's policy of being committed to 11 tournaments is too much," he said. "That's not the way I was brought up. I was taught not to play myself into the ground and I don't want to burn out at 25." But was he truly putting himself on the line?

There came a time when Jimmy Connors asserted that Riordan used him as a pawn. During these early years, he was a willing chess piece. The ATP boycotted Wimbledon in 1973. At stake was precisely what Connors had argued for when confronted about not playing Davis Cup and WCT: the right of a player to compete when and where he wanted. In the case of the ATP-Wimbledon conflict, the struggle turned on the case of Nikki Pilic, a Yugoslav who had declined to play Davis Cup and then been suspended by the International Lawn Tennis Federation (ILTF). The ATP stood by Pilic at Wimbledon. Of its 82 members, 79 withdrew from the sport's premier tournament.

Since he wasn't an ATP member, Connors played and reached the quarterfinals for the second straight year. He also won the doubles with Nastase, who was one of the three ATP defectors. The Connors-Nastase alliance was punctuated by scatological behavior. Connors, eager to prove he wasn't a momma's boy, used his moments with Nastase to demonstrate machismo. Their doubles matches were ribald. Occasionally it was entertaining, such as when they paraded around the court in mock-British bowler hats and joked with the crowd. Often it was tasteless, particularly when they engaged in mock-homosexual rituals. Connors' connection to Nastase only enhanced the perception that for all the great tennis Connors played, it was not always easy to take him seriously.

Because he raised the stakes so high for himself, throughout his career Connors constantly arrived at moments that were more than invariable passages, but do-or-die crossroads. Either win or head back—to ignominy, or, worse yet, to Belleville. One such juncture occurred at the U.S. Pro Championships in July 1973 at Longwood Cricket and Croquet Club in Boston. Most of the WCT pros were on-hand. Since the boycott had diminished Wimbledon's significance as a competitive event, tournaments like the U.S. Pro took on greater meaning. Having played on the Riordan circuit, Connors was unseeded at Longwood. His first-round opponent: top seed and world number one Stan Smith. On the plane to Boston, Connors repeatedly wrote a short note to himself: Beat the son-of-a-bitch. "If I can't beat Stan in the first round," said Connors, "I don't deserve to play him in the final."

He tore up Smith, 6-3, 6-3. Then he won three more matches to reach the final. There he beat Ashe in a match that wasn't as close as the five-set length made it seem. Said Ashe: "He just kept hitting harder and harder, deeper and deeper. I've played Rosewall and Laver, but I never played anybody who could keep up such tremendous groundstrokes for so long." The wins over Smith and Ashe, along with his quarterfinal victory over Cliff Richey, meant that Connors had beaten the trio of Americans who'd held the country's top ranking since 1968. "I don't think I'm ready for Davis Cup yet," said Connors. The astute journalist Bud Collins begged to differ: "Nobody believed him. I suspect it's just another aspect of the Dell-Riordan rivalry."

Back away from this time, and what emerges is a combat zone. Player and sport are both on fire. The early years of tennis' Open Era were riddled with political intrigue. Agents jockeyed for clients. Associations vied to assert their power. Old tournaments fought to upgrade. New events emerged. A rising star like Connors landed smack in the middle of it. And while stars like Ashe and King used tennis as a vehicle for broader social ideas, Connors made tennis popular simply through his tennis. Several years later, Peter Bodo would write that Connors "looms as the first real 'professional' of the game—meaning a great athlete who was incubated during the transition to the pro game and brought to it the peculiar blend of qualities that distinguishes the ideal pro: pride, personality, talent, a devotion to his craft that borders on monomania and a healthy mercenary instinct. He is what Rod Laver and Ken Rosewall, and all those fellows who threaded their lobs through rafters in smelly gymnasiums on endless one-night stands, spawned when they envisioned pro tennis."

Those who'd directed events and played tennis for so long had merely hoped the Open Era would bring money and leave the culture unchanged. They hadn't reckoned on Connors—this uncivil creature—to barge in on their garden party. But these were the early '70s. It was a time of anti-heroes, of cynicism about institutions and leadership and convention. It was no coincidence that an individual sport boomed in an era where terms like "Do Your Own Thing", "The Me Generation" and "New Age" surfaced. And if tennis was to realize its legacy, and truly touch millions with its essence, Connors was on to something new and different. Understated cool wasn't enough. Tennis was hot. Laver and Rosewall were long past 30. Newcombe was close to the end of his career too, and charismatic as the Australian was, the marketplace demanded an American star. Americans like Ashe and Smith, with wood rackets and calm manners, were Pete Seeger and Woody Guthrie, quietly singing "This Land Is Your Land" on acoustic guitars. Connors was electric, Bob Dylan arriving at the Newport Folk Festival (not far from the tennis Hall of Fame), plugging his guitar into an amplifier and screaming out, "How does it feel, to be on your own?" This boy who couldn't be one of the boys was indeed truly alone.

Tennis for so long had operated under a false pretense. Its small cadre of fans and administrators liked thinking the sport was a sedate lawn party played at humble, elite venues by polished gentleman. Many felt that to win at tennis you simply needed to execute more proficiently: the better man was the one with the better strokes, as if the two competed independent of one another. This assumption helped people cling to the belief that tennis was strictly a gentleman's game.

But its best players always knew the game was more brutal than the elegant settings revealed. Tennis' one-on-one, interactive aspects made it more like boxing. All-time great Bill Tilden, scion of a wealthy Philadelphia family that played at the venerable Germantown Cricket Club, made the case quite clear in his landmark book, *Match Play and The Spin of the Ball*: "I may sound unsporting when I claim that the primary object of tennis is to break up your opponent's game, but it is my honest belief that no man is defeated until his game is crushed, or at least weakened."

Champions like Tilden, Perry, Vines, Budge, Riggs, Kramer, Gonzalez, Trabert, Hoad, Rosewall, Laver and Newcombe knew how to smell and punish weakness. But the sport was so small that they'd labored in obscurity. The cultured, urbane, affluent folks who followed and played tennis regarded it as little more than a genteel, country club activity. Moreover, save for Gonzalez, the champions were so well behaved and restrained that if you watched them you couldn't even tell if they knew the score.

And then along came Connors. Fueled by Gloria, honed by Segura, he stripped the pretense to its bare bones like a vulture over a carcass. Other champions came from backgrounds similar to Connors'. Kramer's father worked for the railroad. Trabert's father took out loans every summer so his boy could play national junior tournaments.

Yet before Connors—and here again, his beloved Gonzalez was an exception—players were eager to gain acceptance among the wealthier patricians who populated tennis. In the pre-Open Era, manners helped propel a young tennis player's career. Good relationships with the affluent could lead to rewards, whether it be the chance to earn an additional few bucks in appearance money, or a referral for a good job, or a plum teaching position at a ritzy club or hotel. Exemplary behavior on and off the court meant the difference between a comfortable life and becoming yet another tennis bum.

But in the Open Era, the rules of the marketplace meant a player was less accountable to the community than to himself. The racket did all the talking necessary. Forget those genteel hosts at the club when you can afford your own hotel room. Lest Jimmy get too close to his opponents, Gloria declined housing during his junior days. As a pro making thousands, he could afford to stay anywhere he wanted.

It was the precisely the independence advocates like Jack Kramer and Billie Jean King craved. Who'd have thought that the person best able to grasp the crude, visceral nature of professionalism would be a counter-punching boy from East St. Louis? Gloria so ardently infused Jimmy with a sense of injustice that he was perfectly primed to compete as a purely solo act in a sport that had changed right under his feet.

During the days when events were played by day in clubs based in elegant suburbs, players would mill around the venue to practice, eat and compete. Nights were spent socializing and cultivating contacts. In the pro era, with more tournaments held at indoor arenas in cities, a marquee player like Connors would have to wait until 7:30 p.m. to play his match. Since these indoor facilities only had a court or two that was booked all day for the tournament, Connors practiced as early as 7:00 a.m. In between, he sat alone in his hotel room. Connors confessed that he didn't even like watching Western movies lest he squander his energy on another conflict. He needed every breath possible for his own. "Listen," said Connors, "people don't understand it's like a war out there. Both guys are hot, thirsty, tired. They want a drink, a rest, anything. One little item can tick off an explosion."

Twenty years later, I sat on a court with Pancho Segura. We had just finished the crosscourt service return and volley drill. He arranged a match for me that afternoon with one his teaching pros, and yelled at me that if my feet didn't move better, I'd be dead. I asked him if this was an echo of how he motivated the young Connors.

"There was a special closeness we had in those days," said Segura. "Before matches, he used to say, 'Coach, do you believe in me?' I said, 'Jimbo, look, what does that guy do better than you? Does he move better than you? Does he hit the ball earlier than you? Does he volley better than you?' Then he'd say, 'No, coach, we're better.' I got Jimmy in a state of hypnosis. He was spellbound."

Soon enough, the whole world would come under that spell.

4

The People
vs. Connors

One morning in September 1974, Jimmy Connors and Chris
Evert inspected a condominium in the apartment building
where I lived. The Brentwood Sycamore was a four-year-old,
50-unit building located in the flatlands of West Los Angeles. Seven
blocks north, up in the hills above Sunset Boulevard, were large homes
with tennis courts and swimming pools. Our neighborhood was a place
for divorcees, singles, UCLA students and lower upper-middle class
families: privileged but prudent. In 1973, my father earned $34,000.

Thirty years later, the notion of the world's two best tennis players
as neighbors seems dazzling. At 14, my only thought was that Connors
was a jerk. Evert was boring. Maybe Connors would help me with my
return of serve.

The real estate agent who showed Connors and Evert the condo
was a no-nonsense British woman named Pat Coles. She too played
tennis, and told my mother and me a couple of stories about the
Connors-Evert romance that she'd garnered from London-based
friends who devoutly read the tabloids. More revealing was Pat's tale of
her follow-up telephone conversation with Connors. As she tried to
gauge his interest, Pat heard a gruff voice in the background.

"Jimmy," barked Gloria, "your sandwich is ready."

Pat and my mother shook their heads in dismay. "Imagine that," said
my mother, "Twenty-two years old and his mother's making his lunch.
What a brat."

I concurred. Connors was rude, obnoxious, unsporting, narrow, a
momma's boy with a chilly fiancée. He was everything I could never
imagine myself being. He personified a term I'd recently heard: stuck-
up little tennis player. The notion of smarmy conceit hung to tennis as

heavily as the perception that it was a sissy sport. Good tennis players were still regarded less as athletes and more like savants such as music prodigies and math geniuses. Tennis players weren't jocks like football, baseball or basketball players. They were wieners. When a high school teammate of mine purchased a letter jacket, he looked as dorky as a quarterback reading poetry.

So on the one hand, tennis fought a rear-guard action against its reputation as a bogus sport. Yet no sooner had the sport blossomed in the '70s than its top player was a twit. No one in all of sports seemed more stuck-up than James Scott Connors. Joe Namath and Muhammad Ali were cocky, but with a wink, a smile and kudos for teammates and fans. Connors was churlish. "I must have been born arrogant," he said, "because I came out of the womb walking that way."

Then again, in September 1974 Connors had every right to feel he had the world by a string. That month he'd put a massive exclamation point on one of the greatest years in tennis history.

It began on the first day of 1974, when Connors won the Australian Open. Granted, well into the '80s, the Australian Open field was extremely shallow. Connors' win the previous summer in Boston was more impressive. Still, Connors had earned his first Grand Slam crown, and as he dominated the Riordan circuit's podunk towns in the first half of 1974, his mystique grew. It wasn't just that he won. It was the way he won. No one turned an opponent's strengths back on him better than Connors. Attack him with pace, and he struck back with even more. While serve-and-volley players like Newcombe or Smith were calm sharpshooters, Connors blasted in every direction.

At Wimbledon, Connors was seeded third. But as was the case when Connors first came to Wimbledon, a woman in his life outshone him. The Connors-Evert romance started at Wimbledon during their debut year, 1972. It was a nifty mesh of sensibilities. Both were Catholic, middle-class children of tennis instructors who'd known each other back in the '40s. Connors and Evert were the top stars of the new generation that surfaced during those tennis boom years of the early '70s. On-court, each legitimized the two-handed backhand. Off-court, each was independent. Connors refused to sign up with WCT or join the ATP. Although far less strident than Connors, Evert hesitated to join the fledgling Virginia Slims circuit that starred the crusading Billie Jean King.

They were insular to the point of annoyance. In a sport where players always traveled solo, Connors and Evert were chaperoned by their mothers. Subsequently, they became the first to travel with entourages of coaches, friends, business handlers and bodyguards, which in turn created an enormous buffer zone between them and their peers. Tricky as their globetrotting tours made it for the two to spend time together, by November 1973, after they'd each won the South African Open, Connors and Evert announced their engagement.

I found them detestable. Connors' conceit went hand-in-hand with Evert's cool. She was the role model for many girls I'd met since I'd picked up a racket: the ultra-focused baseliner who offered perfunctory greetings but scarcely cared about anybody but herself. Billie Jean King was the tomboy, the inclusive one who'd invite everyone—even lesser players like me—to play ball with her. Evert was the Ice Princess, the silent blonde with the scoff. King's game bristled with energy, attacks to the net and bold enterprise. Evert's measured baseline style was as exciting as watching paint dry. Her love for Connors added to my disgust. Supposedly, Connors was a courteous fellow. He opened doors for women, wrote kind notes to Evert and went for hours without uttering a profanity when he was with her. The pretense made me despise him more. Connors clearly knew how to behave properly. Why couldn't he do it on a tennis court?

Connors and Evert each struggled early at Wimbledon. Evert's first-round match versus Lesley Hunt was suspended at 9-all in the third set due to darkness. The next morning, after a hit with Connors, she snapped up two games.

Connors also played a two-day match. In the second round, versus powerful Australian Phil Dent, Connors served at 5-6, love-30 in the fifth set. In the locker room, every male cheered loudly for Dent. A remarkable volley and a fortunate line call on a second serve leveled the game. At 30-30, Dent cracked a crosscourt forehand return so deep to Connors' backhand that Connors was forced to virtually half-volley the ball—which he did, striking an incredible down-the-line winner that hit both lines. Connors won, 10-8.

It was expected that if Connors was to win Wimbledon, he needed to beat at least one of three opponents: the tall netrushers who'd previously won Wimbledon, John Newcombe and Stan Smith, or Nastase, who in those days frequently befuddled Connors. Newcombe, straight-set winner over Connors at Forest Hills the previous summer, dominated WCT in early '74. Smith beat Connors 6-0 in the third set in a grasscourt final just before Wimbledon. These two each fell to Ken Rosewall. Nastase lost to Dick Stockton. Connors reached the finals.

The finals also posed a great opportunity. Rosewall played similarly to Connors. Both built their games on first-rate backhands and nimble all-court play. Like Connors, Rosewall's serve was at best a foil. Pancho Segura had played Rosewall hundreds of times, and advised Connors he should start off the match and rally with Rosewall rather than try to rush points. It worked perfectly. The 39-year-old Rosewall, spry versus Smith and Newcombe, looked very old. Connors beat him handily, 6-1, 6-1, 6-4. "People would never believe it about me," said Connors the next day, "but I almost started to cry yesterday. I looked over at my mother, and thought of how hard she and I had worked to get there. Then I looked at Rosewall, a guy I grew up reading about. Now I'm 22 and I've beaten him and won a championship that he never won. I was really shook."

On the eve of Wimbledon, the odds on a Connors-Evert "Love Double" were 33-1. Evert won too. It was a sensational achievement. At the Wimbledon Ball, as was the custom, the two champions led off the dance, as the band played "The Girl That I Marry."

At 11 a.m. the next morning, Connors celebrated with Riordan in a hotel room at the Inn on the Park. As the two drank champagne and read the newspapers that lay over the room's red carpet, Connors made plans to visit the Playboy Club. "Bill, I'm on Cloud Nine," said Connors. "Kid, don't ever lose that feeling," said Riordan.

The manager also kept his client's head on straight the next week. Landing in New York, Connors felt on top of the world. Riordan arranged a visit, not to a corporation or a nightclub, but to the children's cancer ward of a nearby hospital. Connors was stunned and humbled.

Splendid as life was for Connors in 1974, to his grave he will feel the year was marred. He played World Team Tennis (WTT), the start-up professional tennis league. Because WCT and the ILTF saw the team format as a threat to tournament play, WTT players were banned from the French Open. That year's French Open was won by an ascending teen prodigy, Bjorn Borg. Connors was then better than Borg, most notably when he beat him that summer in the finals of the U.S. Clay Championships on a surface very similar to the one the French was played on. For good reason, Connors believed that if he'd played in Paris he would have come to the U.S. Open with three Grand Slams in his hands—and the chance to become only the third man in tennis history to win all four in a single calendar year.

It's tricky to determine if this would have happened. First was the matter of Connors' chances at the French Open. Though better than Borg, it's not certain if Connors possessed the patience to win seven matches on arduous red clay against a variety of players. Second, a

Connors victorious in Paris might have come to Wimbledon drained—and certainly more hunted. As Connors noted in '74, skipping the French helped him feel refreshed for Wimbledon. Moreover, the expectations on Newcombe, Smith, Nastase and even Borg kept the pressure off Connors. It was part of a pattern that played out his entire career. Connors performed best when he was underestimated, when he was the king forced to enter battle and fight for his throne. "I lived for those opportunities to prove them wrong," he said. He'd started a counterpuncher and would play out the string as a counterpuncher.

Fueled by the canny Riordan, Connors used the ban as yet another reason to fight the tennis establishment. Riordan filed a lawsuit against the ILTF, Commercial Union Grand Prix, Kramer and Dell. Engaging the latter two invariably triggered the ATP's involvement in the lawsuit, if not technically then certainly symbolically. That Connors was ostensibly suing his peers only magnified the rancor between him, virtually all of his opponents and the sport's increasing fan base. It was the logical extension of the attitude of hatred Gloria had infused Connors with since childhood. Only now the frontline wasn't just a small park in St. Louis, a national junior tournament in Chattanooga, or a tennis club in Los Angeles. Kind, noble, understated champions like Kramer and Trabert, Laver and Rosewall, Newcombe and Smith labored for years to bring tennis out from the cold, but it was Connors who brought tennis to the cover with frequency—not just of *Sports Illustrated*, but of *Time*. The game had boomed. Why was its signature star such an asshole? Yet all the bitterness aimed at Connors, wrote Bud Collins in *World Tennis*, "just makes him more ornery and sure of himself."

Connors continued to wear the black hat at the U.S. Open. In the spirit of the decade's many anti-hero movies, the men in white hats crumbled. Laver didn't enter the tournament. Smith lost early. Ashe fell to Newcombe. After he beat Newcombe in the semis, Rosewall again surfaced as the sentimental favorite. Connors remained characteristically truculent. The ATP, Connors told *World Tennis'* Steve Flink on the grounds of Forest Hills, "want to rule the game. They want to tell players what to do and where to play and when to hit good overheads and when to miss them." When Flink mentioned that ATP president Ashe said he'd rather win Forest Hills than Wimbledon, Connors got cranky. "Why would he say that? Because I won Wimbledon?" he asked. "Everybody says what a great title and how great it is to win Wimbledon. Then I win it, and everybody tears it town." Ironically, in future years Connors, thwarted at Wimbledon, claimed the "big finish" at the U.S. Open was the most important part of his tennis year.

Had anyone announced then that Connors and the U.S. Open would eventually be smitten with one another, they would have been laughed out of the West Side Tennis Club. Collins referred to the "Evert-Connors Mafia" which cloistered them from contact with others. "If I'm not with Chrissie around here," said Connors, "then I'm with Pancho or Bill or somebody that's out to help me and look out for me and take care of me, not to hinder me and make everything tough for me. So why be with somebody who makes it tough for you?"

It was hard to believe that fans, peers and sponsors cared to make life "tough." Leave it to Connors to see a private tennis club as a combat zone. No amount of triumph ever helped the Connors clan—and clannish was the apt word—see life as anything but war. "When he was not busy controlling his anger or trying lamely to ingratiate himself," wrote Richard Schickel, "Connors seemed honestly befuddled by the fact that all his victories had failed to win the hearts and minds of the tennis community." But hadn't Gloria always told him that community wanted no part of him? And besides, this was smack dab in the middle of the time when that community was changing in front of Jimbo's very eyes. He in fact helped change it. But he was still reviled.

All the hatred coming from others motivated him to greater heights. You hate me, you really hate me, was the message that seeped through Connors camp. Well, I hate you. I will bury you in that hatred. "No question about who the crowd likes," said CBS' Pat Summerall the day of the final. As Connors noted afterwards, "Not everybody was for Rosewall. There were eight for me." Moments before he walked into the stadium for the finals, Connors turned to Gloria and said, "I think I'm just going to go out there and play tennis."

Rosewall was traditionally a slow starter. Like a doctor, he treated the early stages as a diagnostic. Typically, by the third, he was dropping prescriptions into every corner. Connors barely let him get out his stethoscope. Connors won the first set 6-1. With Rosewall serving at 0-1 in the second, Connors broke him with a vicious four-point sequence: a running forehand down the line, a backhand service return winner, a forehand topspin lob and a crosscourt forehand pass. In 68 minutes, Connors won 6-1, 6-0, 6-1. He treated Rosewall's serve like a creampuff, belting returns that left the Australian severely compromised. Repeatedly, Connors' drives struck the lines, chalk spraying off the grass court. In his red shirt, with his hair flapping, long sideburns and narrow gaze, Connors looked positively Satanic, a tennis devil ushering a beloved angel into oblivion. He admitted afterwards that it was "the best tennis I've ever played in my life, all 22 years of it. I didn't miss a ball." A pleased Gloria gave Segura a congratulatory kiss.

Before Connors faced the press, Riordan offered advice. Riordan had given Jimbo many pre-interview pointers. In Europe, Riordan told Connors to cite names of German poets he had read. Never mind that Connors didn't know Rilke's *Duino Elegies* from Dino Flintstone. It made great copy. With Connors victorious at Wimbledon and Forest Hills, Riordan told him he'd be asked what was next. "The One and Only" was tennis' new boss. He'd finish '74 with 15 titles and a 99-4 match record. Connors was instructed to utter three simple words: Get me Laver.

As I sat in my living room and watched Connors pummel Rosewall, I felt nauseous. Tennis gave me a place to anchor myself. We'd moved so much I'd never felt able to make friends. I was a loner, so unsure of my ability to make friends that one of the reasons I'd dropped out of Hebrew school was that I didn't think I'd have enough people to invite to my Bar Mitzvah.

An individual sport like tennis was perfect for social misfits like me. With tennis it was possible to be independent and make friendships, albeit filtered through the odd lens of competition. I earned a spot on a team in Santa Monica Teen Tennis, a tennis version of Little League baseball. My captains loved me because, unlike Jimmy Connors, I was kind and docile. I'd show up early for practice and play singles or doubles with anyone. Unlike the fiery Connors, I behaved so well I was repeatedly nominated for sportsmanship awards. After losing in the first round of eight straight Southern California junior tournaments, I won a couple of matches at the junior sectionals at the LATC. My parents agreed to pay $15 an hour for private lessons. Though I never thought of myself as becoming a player of note, I dreamed I might find a role for myself in tennis. Attending the Pacific Southwest for the first time, I was smitten when I saw the likes of Ashe, Dell and Smith mill about the grounds, conduct business and interact with fans in their warm-up suits and street clothes. I loved politics, and tennis then so teemed with political intrigue I wondered if perhaps I could find my way into the game that way. Maybe I could be a lawyer like Dell (who'd worked for Bobby Kennedy). Or in the short-term, perhaps a counselor at Tony Trabert's camp. I so wanted tennis to be my community that I was crushed to see the boorish Connors crash around the sport and create such obnoxious commotion.

For while I was in pursuit of something global, sophisticated, heroic and inclusive, Connors wanted none of that. All his life, he'd raged with a sense of exclusion from the heights of tennis. Now that he'd reached the top, he remained in his cocoon, reluctant to use his brilliance for the good of the game. He was so obviously uncomfortable with everything but hitting tennis balls. It put the whole sport on edge. Connors' mix of success and isolation, desire and paranoia, was similar to that other American who made headlines in 1974: Richard Nixon. As Richard Schickel wrote, "By that I mean to say that [Connors] is a narrowly ambitious man, concentrating a furious energy on a narrowly-defined goal—being a winner in his chosen field. To this end, he will sacrifice anything—the graceful presentation of self, the pursuit of pleasure whether it be cultural or merely idle, warm human relations. It accounts for that air of dark suspicion that hangs about him."

Comparing Connors to Nixon damned him to hell in my house. Long before I'd ever seen a tennis racket, talk of politics dominated my family's dinner table. In a Jewish, liberal household of the early '70s, public enemy number one was Richard Milhous Nixon. My parents had loathed him since he'd run a smear campaign for Senate in 1950. In my family's eyes, Nixon's brand of conservatism was based on small-town, xenophobic, stingy values that were also inherently anti-Semitic. He was Tricky Dick, a cheat who vowed we wouldn't have him to kick around anymore but resurrected himself and became President. Like Connors, he surrounded himself with jailkeeper-like handlers. In 1971, I was eligible for the President's Physical Fitness Award. My mother said not to bother competing because she refused to see me bring home a piece of paper that bore Nixon's signature. Like Connors, he lacked class. I'd closely followed the Watergate hearings in the summer of 1973, loved the way the Senate Committee caught Nixon's lackeys in one lie after another. The next summer, of course, the same season of dominance for Connors, Nixon finally got what he deserved—a disgraceful defeat. It was hoped that the same would happen to Connors when he played Laver on February 2, 1975.

I so hated Connors that I recognized his presence in others. Or maybe, just maybe, I sought it out even as I refused to admit that such raw intensity and hatred might be an asset. Mark Binstock, the snobby kid who'd refused to play with me my first summer at Tony Trabert Tennis Camp, played at Barrington Park, the same park where I played. He lived north of Sunset Boulevard in one of those larger houses. His father, Sid, was an overbearing dentist who regaled everyone with tales of Mark's brilliance on and off the court. When I told Sid I wanted to be a lawyer, he let me know that Mark was on track to be both lawyer and doctor. When I asked Sid to play with Mark he foisted me on his younger daughter, Wendy, a beginner. Sid was known for making horrible line calls. He was a rather cagey player, though, and once after he beat me he issued a condescending comment: You might get there, Joel, one day you might get there.

The implication of course was that Mark was already there. What exactly "there" meant was in the big picture pretty silly. At heart, Mark and I were both cerebral Jews for whom tennis would never be more than a pastime. But concepts such as how tennis fits into the scheme of things are not easily understood by teenagers. At least I didn't grasp it that way. So long as the Binstocks paraded themselves, Barrington Park to me was as much a war zone as Manker Patten, Kalamazoo and Wimbledon were for Connors. Mark, with his two-handed backhand, baseline game and stage father, was a localized version of Jimmy Connors. Given the chance, I wanted to kill him.

Barrington Park was a small, four-court public tennis facility three blocks south of Sunset Boulevard and a mile west of the UCLA campus where Connors still frequently practiced. Few top quality players came to Barrington. But during these tennis boom years, courts all over LA bristled with competition. No longer marginalized, tennis was cool, dynamic, in the thick of mass culture in ways it had never been. In large part, the bombastic Connors triggered this rise, particularly among those of us who played at public parks. Twice a year, Barrington held a tournament. Mark Binstock was seeded first in the "C" division. After two wins, I took on Binstock in the quarterfinals.

Until this match, I'd never grasped how I'd won tennis matches or what it took to emotionally prepare for them. Though aware of my innate ability to disrupt opponents and force them to play poorly, I recoiled from that confrontational aspect of my game. What I wanted to believe was that the better player was the one who hit the most good shots in the right places at the right times. Plausible as this sounded, it was only partially true. As Bill Tilden noted, the primary objective was to make life difficult for your opponent. Tilden didn't mean you cheated. The goal was to understand the essentials of competition and establish a connection not just to your strokes, but with the opponent. Linked to it was a belief I'd never quite fathomed—the notion that I deserved to pursue my ambitions with unrestrained passion. Tennis always warranted Jimmy Connors' desire. Did it warrant mine?

My major problem was the balance between competition and socialization. My one friend, Matt Newman, wasn't a tennis player. Usually we went to the movies in Westwood and I'd spend the night at his house. One summer day, Matt requested he sleep over at my house for the first time. The next day I was scheduled to play the semis of the Griffith Park 12-and-under novice tournament. Matt said if he couldn't come over, he'd never talk to me again. Friendship or combat? For Jimmy Connors, the answer was obvious. It was for me, but the opposite. Matt came. We talked into the night. The next morning, I started slowly and lost, 6-2, 7-6. I was years away from understanding how to balance needs with friends. Maybe the key, as Connors showed, was to refuse to make friends.

So how to take down the hated Binstock? A baseliner, Binstock was more of a steady player like Evert than an aggressor à la Connors. His strokes were nice-looking, clearly the mark of many private lessons. At that point, I hadn't taken any, which gave me another reason to resent him. My game was based more on volleys than groundstrokes. I'd need to rush the methodical Binstock into errors or weak passing shots that I could put away. Netrushing was one tactic I'd employed for a year. But as I headed into the Binstock match I was so filled with bitterness directed at him that I realized netrushing was more than a mere tactic.

For the first time, I smelled the fumes mainlined into Jimmy Connors from birth. I was going to have to get in Binstock's face. As Connors knew deep in his bones for so long, winning this way required that I establish a relationship with the opponent and see who he was—or at least who I wanted him to be for my purposes. He was a snob, someone who rejected me, didn't believe in me, thought less of me, not just as a player, but as a person. He also probably wasn't comfortable hitting too many passing shots. The match with Binstock wasn't a mere athletic contest. It was personal.

Sunday, October 13, 1974. All through the warmup, I felt my anger, which in turn churned its way into my feet. When play began, I was constantly looking for ways to move forward and volley. Every time I looked across the net, I didn't just see an opponent. I saw an enemy. The plan was working. Binstock was harried by my piranha-like movements forward. I won the first set, 6-4.

Binstock broke my serve to open the second. He easily held for 2-love. He was starting to hit harder. My volleys weren't so sharp. By now about half a dozen Barrington regulars were watching. Ken showed up with a friend too. Were I to lose my serve again I'd be in a deep hole, enough to give Binstock confidence to storm through the set and ride the momentum enough to take charge in the third. As Connors repeatedly demonstrated, the line separating control from anarchy was a thin one. Connors butted up against it better than anyone in tennis history. I was barely more than a novice.

Serving at love–40, I fought back to deuce. I earned an ad for the game, but missed an easy volley. Binstock creamed two returns right at me. He was up 3-love. I yelled out, "Fuck!"

I broke back, held, broke again. Binstock's resurrection was halted. My volleys improved. By this time, Binstock's tactics changed. To keep me off the net, he came in—and was quite uncomfortable. With Binstock serving at 4-5, I hit two lob winners and broke him to win the match. We shook hands. He barely looked at me. My body shook. I'd beaten the little twirp who'd dared underestimate me. I'd shoved his dumb-ass baseline game, upscale address and pushy father right up his ass. I'd tasted blood. And I liked it.

Though I lost my next match, that was secondary to my big win. A week later, I began taking private lessons. Hatred fueled improvement. Tennis was one-on-one combat. As Segura told me years later, "Doesn't matter who your daddy is, or how much money you've got, or where you went to school, tennis is pure democracy. It's just you and me, buddy, in the arena. Just you and me."

I continued to despise Connors. It pleased me to see him and Evert call off the marriage, a decision made shortly after they'd looked at condos in LA. Evert went off to Denver. Connors remained in LA, and over the course of a six-hour conversation, the two agreed to postpone their wedding. His love life meant little to me. The bigger factor was his horrific public image. If indeed Connors was Nixon, he was at heart a public person destined to be one of life's losers. I remained a fan of balance and cool over Connors' heated passion. Besides, what was tennis but a hobby? In a pattern that repeated itself all through my life, tennis to me was like The Girl Next Door: I couldn't admit that I really loved her. I had so much more going, didn't I? My background, my limited talents, the incredible depth of Southern California tennis; all roads led me to subordinate tennis. Education came first. Figuring out how to make friends was second. Awkward adolescence was somewhere in the middle.

Even during tennis, my desire to be a lawyer and enter politics took primacy. Each Monday, my mother would drop me off for a 3:30 tennis lesson with Sean Harrington that lasted an hour. Our arrangement was that Sean took me home after his 4:30 lesson. Often he'd suggest I stay on the court and feed balls to his student. It was a good way for me to learn more and work on a few parts of my game. I declined, and instead spent those 60-minute periods in Sean's green Alfa Romeo convertible reading books like Woodward and Bernstein's Watergate caper, *All The President's Men* and William Manchester's Kennedy assassination tale, *Death of a President*. My struggle between thought and action was a closer battle than ever, but thought remained in the lead.

Naturally, I wanted Laver to beat Connors in their Challenge Match. Make no mistake: Laver versus Connors was no mere exhibition. It was a big deal. The early years of tennis' Open Era were heavily splintered, a frontier environment of rival circuits and factions fighting for territory. The four Grand Slams were nowhere near as significant as they became in the late '80s and '90s. Of the 20 Slams played between 1970 and '74, only eight boasted fields with the depth required to make them vital parts of the tennis year. The Australian was a joke. The French Open lacked many top names. The ban of '72 and the boycott of '73 diminished Wimbledon's significance during each of those years. New events filled the vacuum. The U.S. Pro Indoor, played each January in Philadelphia, was much harder to win than the Australian. A WCT play-off in Dallas each May was valued far more by players than the French Open.

Tennis' deregulated calendar made the Laver-Connors Challenge Match exceptionally important. Riordan arranged national TV coverage on CBS and a $100,000 winner-take-all purse (it turned out the loser would walk away with a good chunk of change too). The two had never played. The gap between them was wider than the Grand Canyon. Tennis' man of the '60s, Laver was the quintessential Australian: unflappable, humble, loyal to his mates yet distinctive in his own right. Even as lefthanders the two differed. Laver was a wristy shotmaker, an artist who turned the court into a canvas and wove a tapestry of spins and paces. This was the style I imitated. Connors struck every ball firmly, his two-handed backhand a bazooka-like contrast to Laver's one-hander. Ex-player Gene Scott, covering the match for *World Tennis*, thought Laver's shots "sound like a scratched cassette tape," while Connors' came off "like a pistol with a silencer." Gloria hated Laver's flicky style. It reminded her of Bill Price back in St. Louis. She wanted her boy to blow it to smithereens.

The venue demonstrated how far tennis had come. Caesars Palace in Las Vegas was light years removed from the pristine lawns of Forest Hills. Entertainer Alan King was the hotel's tennis ambassador. He'd poured his own money into hosting a tournament at the hotel. Though he'd been front and center as a spectator at Forest Hills since the '50s, King called it "a horrible place. Everyone at that club looked like Rudy Vallee. So much of that old world tennis culture." King was a spiritual soulmate of the folks who'd thrived on the action at Segura's BHTC. The tennis director at Caesars Palace was Gonzalez. Other Hollywood types like Charlton Heston, Johnny Carson and Clint Eastwood came to Vegas for the big match. To steal one of Frank Sinatra's lines, it promised to be a ring-a-ding time. Less than a decade before this scene was unthinkable.

Like a politician acknowledging a campaign debt, in virtually every interview Connors ever gave he'd praise his mother for teaching him strokes that left his game simple and uncomplicated. Off the court, though, Connors in these years was constantly entangled. Riordan's lawsuits hung like a dark cloud. Connors remained steadfast in his refusal to play Davis Cup. Prior to the Laver match, Connors cancelled his reservations at Caesars and relocated to the Tropicana Hotel because he allegedly wasn't given 10 rooms and 30 tickets. Laver arrived at Caesars carrying his own bags. Then came a debate about when the balls should be opened given the thin desert air of Las Vegas. A coin flip was won by Laver's coach, Roy Emerson, and the balls were opened two days prior to the match. Connors showed up an hour late for a joint press conference the day before the match. Whenever Laver spoke, Connors rustled papers and pranced. Laver chided him for not playing Davis Cup. That weekend, 150 miles away in Palm Springs, the U.S. lost to Mexico.

Instead, Connors hunkered down with his posse. Segura by now was the tennis director at La Costa, a nouveau riche venue near San Diego. There were rumors that La Costa was a front for the Mafia. As Segura said, "Let's just say the boys made me an offer I couldn't refuse." His stature as Connors' coach enhanced Segura's stature as an instructor. Connors came to La Costa for frequent workouts. They were a perfect pair, like Muhammad Ali and Angelo Dundee at Deer Lake. Connors, the heavyweight champ, bounced up and down, a towel wrapped in between his neck after a good sweat. Segura, filled with boundless energy, distinctive in his silver hair and dark skin, shuffled along, ready with a strategic pointer.

To accommodate the national TV audience, the Laver match started at 10:15 in the morning. Laver prepared calmly. He clarified a couple of tactics with Emerson, stretched and sipped a beverage. This was the way tennis had always been.

Connors' suite was a madhouse. A tape recorder blared music. Jimbo bobbed up and down like a fighter. He shook his neck. He jumped rope. He bounced in place. He screamed obscenities. He listened to Segura. "Keel him, keed, keel him," said the coach.

Laver approached the court slowly, Gary Cooper in *High Noon*, ready to save the town all by his lonesome self. Connors bounced up the aisles in a London Fog raincoat. The crowd booed. At the top of his lungs, Connors yelled to one and all, "Fuck you! Fuck you!" *Tennis'* Barry Tarshis took a long look at Connors that morning and wrote that, "Tennis may be a game to most of us, but to Connors it seems to assume a significance of life and death proportions." Was this necessarily bad?

An all-star team of ex-players called lines, including Bill Talbert, Don Budge, Frank Parker, Ted Schroeder, Tom Brown, Gene Mako and Dick Savitt. Likely as it was that they all detested Connors' etiquette, since then I've interviewed virtually all of them and discovered that, as players, they too shared an understanding with Connors that Tarshis and so many others overlooked: yes, tennis was a game, but it was brutal. The only difference, of course, was that these men fought with good manners, at least for the most part. (Years later, I played one of these legendary linesmen. On the few occasions when I won a point with an odd shot, he yelled out, "L.F., L.F., L.F."—short for "lucky fuck.") Unlike Connors, though, they'd never played for $100,000 on national TV. But as I'd learn in all my conversations with top players, classy sportsmanship only cloaked the eyes and hands of a killer. Connors just made that disposition more obvious. Sorry, says the scorpion as he stings the frog, it's just my nature. No matter what the era, there was a lot of scorpion in tennis players.

The literal noise of a Connors match—his words, his squeaky feet, his grunt, the crowd's reaction—obscured a notable aspect of his game. Jimmy Connors had a keen tennis mind. Like Jack Kramer with the serve-volley game, Connors knew he had bigger weapons than virtually all of his opponents. Because of that, it appeared he didn't have need for employing eclectic tactics the way a less-powerful player might. But as Kramer had noted, it's indeed a strategy to employ your guns. The trick was determining where best to aim them. "Jimmy's ploy," wrote Segura in his book, *Pancho Segura's Championship Strategy*, "was to rush Laver by hard, firm returns of serve and deep, hard volleys. Laver's weakness was his excessive topspin which often made the ball bounce short and always made it bounce high. Jimmy hit the ball up or at the top, never giving Rod time for the next shot."

For two sets it worked to perfection. Connors led, 6-4, 6-2. Laver was unfazed. Improving his serve, he won the third, 6-3. He broke Connors for 2-1 in the fourth, but Connors evened the match in the next game. Since Connors started off the set, he could apply constant pressure on Laver's service games. With Laver serving at 4-5, Connors held five match points. Twice Laver erased them with aces. On another, Connors hoisted a topspin lob. No line call. Connors jumped the net. But Ted Schroeder at last made the call: out. Laver knotted the score.

The crowd went nuts. This was the high-stakes, circus-like atmosphere Riordan craved back in Maryland. Comedienne Totie Fields screamed at Connors. Turning towards Fields, Connors made an obscene gesture and said, "shut up, broad."

At 5-all, the momentum was Laver's. I'd been upset to see my lefty hero play so poorly the first two sets. Perhaps, finally, Connors would suffer a public humiliation.

Here again Connors proved he was the master of the right shot at the right time. His serve was rarely an asset. Usually, its left-handed spin kept the receiver off-balance just enough so as not to handicap Connors. At this moment, he aced Laver. The crowd was silenced. Connors held. As he changed sides, Segura offered a tip: return serve down the center. Keeping the ball down the middle would make it difficult for Laver at this tight stage to volley too close to the lines. Connors followed the plan perfectly and broke Laver at love. The King was dead. Long live Jimbo.

Virtually the same discordant sequence of events took place prior to Connors' match with Newcombe at Caesars on April 26. Again there were controversies. The most notable occurred earlier that month. Months earlier, Newcombe entered the WCT Denver tournament. His agreement with Connors was that neither would enter the same event so as not to interfere with the purity of their Challenge Match. But when tournament director Ray Benton offered Connors a wild-card entry—figuring a potential Newcombe-Connors April 20 final on NBC would scoop CBS' broadcast of the Newcombe-Connors Challenge Match—it became a question of who would drop out. The noble Newcombe withdrew, and lost a good chance for keen preparation. Connors' acceptance of Benton's offer was precisely the kind of craven act that made him so despised.

But more than tennis marked the Connors-Newcombe rivalry.

Laver was taciturn, more disposed to letting his racket speak for him. He and Connors had little to do with one another personally. Besides being much more of an extrovert than Laver, Newcombe had a talent Connors couldn't help but notice. Newcombe was a man among men. The Yiddish term tossed around Barrington Park was "mensch," which technically means "a person," but in application means someone like Newcombe: inclusive, hearty, generous, mindful of others. An aggressive netrusher, a ladies' man, a formidable presence in bars and boardrooms, Newcombe was a racket-toting mix of Burt Reynolds and Joe Namath. He commanded the court and the world like a pitcher poised to close out the seventh game of the World Series. Newcombe's trademark mustache captivated me. Was the one-eyed logo on his shirts a pirate or just winking?

Newcombe was my second-favorite player after Laver, who by 1974 was 36 and in the final stages of his career. Newcombe was younger than Laver, older than Connors and still looked to have good tennis ahead of him in 1975. Moreover, he appeared intelligent, not a guy you'd talk to about books, but certainly worldly and inclusive in a way Connors was not. I'd seen this first-hand one August night in the summer of 1974. Ken drove us to the Los Angeles Sports Arena for a World Team Tennis match. I insisted we arrive early so we could watch practice. Sneaking down to court level (a habit I'd continue as a journalist), I saw Newcombe practicing serves. At the other end of the court, I picked up one of the balls he'd just fired. Holding the ball in my hand, I figured I'd take home a souvenir. Suddenly, Newcombe saw me. I was caught. "Take it," said Newcombe. What? "Go ahead, take it," he said. I was stunned. The ball stayed in a drawer for years.

The mark of a first-rate mind, Thomas Jefferson noted, was the ability to hold two opposing ideas in it at once. Does success make the man or does the man make success? Newcombe understood that no matter how much he defined himself by tennis, that wasn't entirely who he was. He beat your head in by day and bought you dinner at night. He could let a 14-year-old inside the game during practice and then go out and compete. Newcombe grasped the lessons that a man can only learn by himself. Certainly they weren't in Gloria Connors' lesson plan.

At one point, negotiations about balls, court surfaces and other topics grew so heated during a meeting in the basement of Caesars Palace that Newcombe told Connors, Segura and Riordan they were "the three biggest shits I've ever had anything to do with in my life. You can all go and get fucked." Newcombe fled the room with plans to quit the whole match. Gonzalez, the referee, ran down the hallway to talk him out of it. Newcombe was aghast. You Pancho, of all people, you would never stand for this bullshit. Gonzalez threw up his hands, but at last succeeded. Newcombe agreed to play.

While Laver-Connors was their first-ever meeting, Newcombe was 2-0 versus Connors. Both matches were in Grand Slams, the first when Connors was still in ascent at Forest Hills in '73. The second was in January '75, in the finals of the Australian Open. From Newcombe's vantage point, his losses to Rosewall at Wimbledon and Forest Hills in '74 opened the door for Connors. Connors said it wasn't his fault Newcombe hadn't reached those Grand Slam finals.

At the Australian, Connors made a rare tactical mistake. In an effort to ingratiate himself with the public, echoing what he'd done versus Bob Kreiss in the 1970 Junior Sectionals, Connors deliberately threw a point after Newcombe received a bad line call. The crowd cheered Connors. But Newcombe recognized patronization when he saw it, and went on to break Connors' serve in that game and earn a 7-5, 3-6, 6-4, 7-6 (7) win. "It's no good being nice," said Connors. He'd shown quite vividly his ineptitude at mixing competition with camaraderie.

When they met in Las Vegas nearly four months later, the lack of tournament play hurt Newcombe. His first serve missed repeatedly, which made it much easier for Connors to dictate the flow of each point. "Serving to Jimmy is like a baseball player pitching to Hank Aaron," said Newcombe. "If you kept throwing the same stuff at him all the time, you're going to get hit out of the ball park." Even had Newcombe been at his sharpest, I believe he would have been severely compromised by Connors on any surface but grass (where the fast surface helped him win more free points on his formidable delivery and play shorter points on Connors' serve). Save for one no-look backhand service return that gave Newcombe the second set, Connors was thoroughly in control. He varied his serves to keep Newcombe off-balance, mixing up serve-volley with groundstrokes. Connors' 6-3, 4-6, 6-2, 6-4 win earned him $250,000.

"The crowd wanted Newcombe," said Connors afterwards, "but it wasn't Newcombe they had. They had Connors, and they will keep on having him, like it or not."

With trademark perspective, Newcombe threw himself a defeat party. More than 40 of his pals crammed into his suite at Caesars. "First to the net, first to the bar," was the unofficial Aussie tennis motto. One of Newcombe's friends suggested he congratulate Connors, man-to-man. An inebriated Newcombe sauntered up to the Connors suite. Gloria creaked open the door and eyed Newcombe suspiciously. Was the Aussie about to make more trouble for her boy? Jimbo had won, what more could they want from him? All I want to do is congratulate Jimmy for a job well done, said Newcombe. The door opened. As the two shook hands, Newcombe said, "You were the better player today. Well done." The room was completely silent. Newcombe was struck by the image of son and mother alone. He found it sad.

Yet few then dared have sympathy for Jimmy Connors. More like the opposite, which made that summer's Wimbledon one of the greatest comeuppances in tennis history. Connors was a buzzsaw, not dropping a set in six matches on his way to the finals. In the semis versus the big-serving Roscoe Tanner—one of many juniors expected to have a better career than Connors—he was brilliant, blasting balls into every possible corner. His final-round opponent was Arthur Ashe. Connors was an 11-2 favorite. The Ashe-Connors matchup conjured up memories of the 1962 heavyweight bout between Floyd Patterson and Sonny Liston. Ashe, like Patterson, was a liberal's darling: sophisticated, beloved and, unfortunately, undergunned. Connors was Liston, the thug from St. Louis with the knockout punch who lacked social polish.

Urbane as Ashe was, he had never been particularly intelligent on the court. His game was based largely on slash-and-burn shotmaking. If the muse was on, he was as good as anyone. Off a smidge, and he was eminently beatable. The night prior to the match, Ashe huddled with a brain trust that included Dell and Ralston. He hatched a plan akin to the rope-a-dope Muhammad Ali employed to beat George Foreman. The cornerstone was to deny Connors pace. Success required suave serving, caressed low balls to Jimbo's weaker forehand, deft lobs and firm volleys.

The bigger subtext was Connors' lawsuits. Since Ashe was president of the ATP, in a manner of speaking, two litigants were about to play the Wimbledon final. As a Dell client, Ashe was also firmly aligned with Davis Cup captain Ralston and the group of Americans Connors snubbed. Ashe made sure the world knew this when he came on court with a jacket that bore the initials "USA" on the back.

But you didn't even need to know the intricacies of tennis politics to see the conflict. Ashe was cool and appropriate. Connors was hot and bratty. The only thing they had in common was that they'd each attended UCLA. A telling difference was that Ashe graduated, while Connors dropped out, which around our house made him nearly as odious as a convicted Watergate operative.

During those years, NBC broadcast Wimbledon on tape-delay. I sat to watch the first set, and was shocked and delighted to see Ashe's plan work to perfection. He won the first set, 6-1. Ashe coaxed Connors into one error after another. After a commercial break, NBC announced that Ashe won the second set, 6-1. The match was only 41 minutes long. It was staggering. It was terrific. Ashe was in what players called "The Zone," an allusion to the TV show, "The Twilight Zone." In other words, it was scary how well Ashe was playing. His forehand volley, often tenuous, held up against Connors' firm pace. For one of the few times in his career, Ashe remembered to lob. He was also aided by the overcast skies, which were normally so sunny this time of day at Wimbledon that it was very difficult for a right-hander to serve at maximum effectiveness. That little twirp Connors was about to have his lunch handed to him.

As she watched on Centre Court, Gloria Connors was by herself. Pancho Segura was 6,000 miles away. In May, he received a message from the Connors camp: Don't bother coming to Wimbledon. Gloria was vexed at all the attention Segura received for her boy's success. Though unquestionably the association with Connors helped him drum up business at La Costa, to jettison Segura on the eve of a Grand Slam was unacceptable paranoia. The Evert relationship fizzled earlier in the year, a breakup allegedly attributed to Gloria's desire to have Jimmy's career take priority over Chrissie's. Riordan, the best father figure Gloria and Bertha could imagine, would be given the heave-ho by year's end for making life too complicated. Besides the various lawsuits, which were becoming millstones, Riordan had yet to pay Connors for his Challenge Match versus Newcombe. And then there was the matter of what Riordan did before the Wimbledon final.

To his credit, Connors has never talked about this publicly, but all through Wimbledon, Riordan took Connors daily to the Chelsea Soccer Club for electrotherapy for a leg injury. He'd suffered shin splints and a groin pull in his first-round match against John Lloyd. The injury got worse. The morning of the final, a doctor recommended Connors not play, lest he suffer a serious injury that required surgery. There was no way on God's earth Connors was about to default a Wimbledon final. He also made another request to Riordan: Don't tell Mom. This omission was a prime piece of evidence in Gloria's subsequent case against Riordan. Did it occur to her that Jimmy deceived her too? Love is blind.

Ashe went up a break in the third. But Connors fought back, and won that set, 7-5. He slapped his thigh and charged himself into gear. Glad as I was to see him lose, part of me was drawn to his overt intensity. I wanted the match to go longer. Yes, Connors was a brat and a bully, but not one who packed up and left when it got rough. He was a contrast to many of my fellow privileged peers who mocked tennis and coasted on a wave of family money and dilettante-like behavior. After I'd beaten Binstock again in the spring of '75, his father told me Mark had other things in his life besides tennis (funny, Sid never said that before our two matches). Though tennis to me then was scarcely what it was for Connors, we shared one thing: We were in it for life.

When Connors took a 3-0 lead in the fourth, a decisive set seemed likely. Ashe rallied. Despite Connors' comeback, Ashe stuck with his plan, and assembled its pieces with the patience of a bricklayer. Prone to choking, Ashe relaxed as he never had. Nineteen seventy-five was the first year players sat down on changeovers at Wimbledon. Chairs have since been placed at opposite sides of the umpire's stand, but in that first year the players sat back to back. Ashe was impervious, a towel over his head. Connors looked ready to combust. Ashe broke Connors twice in the fourth, and at 5-4, served it out easily. Ashe gave a slight fist pump, an unheard of act for him. "I lost," said Connors. "Sometimes it gets to the point that people believe a guy can't lose and they believe every time he steps on the court, he's going to win. You people have to realize I can lose." *You people.*

Bobby McKinley, Jeff Borowiak and Ilie Nastase were among those who'd befuddled Connors with off-pace balls. But this wasn't Tulsa, UCLA or the Riordan circuit. On the sport's premier venue, Ashe authored a blueprint. It wasn't easy to pull off, but it was possible.

Connors' U.S. Open was a fitting bookend. A change that helped him at the start of the event hurt him at the finish. Amid public cries that rallies were too short and complaints from players that the grass was of poor quality, the U.S. Open scrapped grass in favor of a slower clay surface called Har-Tru.

The move triggered a domino effect. Many American tournaments preceding the U.S. Open changed surfaces too. This change benefited Connors more than any American of his generation. Gloria's emphasis on short, compact groundstrokes made him well-equipped for any surface. On the other hand, the shift to clay greatly diminished the possibilities of domestic success for virtually every one of Connors' peers. The likes of Dick Stockton, Brian Gottfried, Erik van Dillen, Sandy Mayer and Bobby McKinley, as well as those a few years

younger like Vitas Gerulaitis, Butch Walts, Brian Teacher and Trey
Waltke, had spent their whole life developing games based much more
on attacking than the attrition-based style called for on clay. All of
them would have thrived much more on grass. The gap between
Connors and his compatriots widened significantly.

For the second straight year, Connors beat Borg on a claycourt,
7-5, 7-5, 7-5 in the semis. The win was particularly satisfying given
Borg's repeat at the French Open (a vindictive Connors, fuming over
his '74 ban, launched his own Paris boycott).

The next day Connors was completely bamboozled by Spanish
claycourt specialist, Manuel Orantes, 6-4, 6-3, 6-3. Orantes played until
10:30 the previous night, beating Guillermo Vilas 6-4 in the fifth after
Vilas led 5-0 in the fourth.

It's likely Connors underestimated Orantes. Connors also played
with more confusion than usual. Segura, banned by Gloria, still adored
Jimbo enough to offer the tactic of hitting to Orantes' forehand.
Nastase, Connors' doubles partner, said he should hit to the backhand.
It wasn't clear which plan Connors followed. Instead, the day was all
Orantes'. The Spaniard jerked Connors around the court with a
variety of dinks, drop shots, passing shots and lobs that all made
Connors look sluggish. Most notable was the way Orantes, similar to
Ashe at Wimbledon, exploited Connors' forehand. The slow clay
revealed even more how hard it was for Connors to handle a short,
paceless ball on that side. His forehand backswing was so straight and
rigid that he lacked the arc necessary to clear the net with safety or
drive with penetration. Since far more of these low balls came from
Orantes' superb slice backhand, Connors probably should have
listened more to Segura than Nastase.

But by this stage of 1975, Connors wasn't listening to anybody. It
wasn't just that he'd lost matches. That was an area where he would
prove deceptively resilient. It's often said that champions cannot accept
defeat, and that no tennis player was more unable to cope with losing
than that spoiled brat, Jimmy Connors. This explains why whenever
Connors lost so many would think he was finished, once and for all.
He'd always deny that he was devastated, but so voracious was his
desire to win that no one believed he was capable of taking a big loss
and moving on. As Connors' career proved, he was always ready to
attempt the climb back up the hill, much more so than Borg or, later,
John McEnroe. So it wasn't the mere act of losing that unraveled
Jimmy Connors in 1975.

It was the way he'd lost, and what he turned to in the wake of those losses, that told the story of Jimmy Connors that year. All his life, he'd been wrapped in the armor of a champion, first by grandmother and mother, then primarily by mother. He'd marched up and up and up, but done so with nary a kind word for the others who were trying quite hard too. Even from the top of the mountain, his reverence or humility was perfunctory. Worse yet, he showed another odious side of his character: disloyalty. The breakup with Evert was likely a case of mutual puppy love dissolving. Riordan? Well, that was less about tennis and more about business, particularly as the Connors family saw how Riordan was less concerned with Jimbo's welfare and more focused on advancing his increasingly shady agenda. (In 1977, Neil Amdur of *The New York Times* broke the story that CBS and Riordan's claim of "Winner-Take-All" matches versus Laver, Newcombe and others was a sham. The revelations triggered an investigation of the network by the Federal Communications Commission and Congressional hearings. That scandal was just one of several traumas that rocked CBS Sports in those years. Scandal hardly mattered to Riordan, who as a solo promoter was accountable to no one.)

But Connors' banishment of Segura, the most devoted of coaches, was inexcusable. When Segura offered advice to Gloria on how Connors needed to add more topspin to his forehand and round out other parts of his game, she told him not to mess with her boy's strokes. Nineteen seventy-five marked the first time Connors' confidence curdled into hubris.

So if humility eluded Connors, others humbled him. Newcombe, Ashe and Orantes did so with panache. Those Connors disregarded on his way up chuckled with pleasure as he fell down (although for a number of quirky reasons he remained number one on the ATP computer rankings, despite being viewed by many as the world's second-best player behind Ashe that year). With his coterie in disarray for so much of 1975, Connors found himself in places he'd probably wished he'd never gone. Singer Paul Anka managed some of Connors' business affairs and landed him an appearance on "The Howard Cosell Show" show, where Connors launched a singing career with a rather inept performance—a perverse reversal of the dilettantism displayed by Dino Martin that Connors had treated with such disdain.

There were other indulgences too. In 1975, said Connors, "I started to think about all the high school dances I missed because of tennis .... Basically I did all the things I missed when I was a kid—missed for 20 years." The fluid mix between work and play that came so easily for Aussies like Newcombe wasn't so smooth for Connors. By late '75, he was 30 pounds overweight. Alone in a hotel room in Acapulco, frustrated by what he'd let himself become, he reached for the phone and dialed the number he knew best. Back with Gloria, he chased one ball after another and lost 18 pounds in two weeks.

Connors' decline pleased me. Jimmy Connors wasn't about to suffocate my beloved tennis. As young as 14, I appointed myself tennis' commissioner-at-large. I'd studied its history, internalized its code of sportsmanship and loved nothing more than holding court on tennis' values and personalities. Connors was Public Enemy Number One. As I watched him fall off his perch, I'd ascended up my own tennis hill. Binstock was finished. After my second win over him, I went on to win the tournament. I now beat Ken consistently, although, to my chagrin, he admitted he wasn't into tennis anymore. As I entered high school, I had dreams of being one of the team's top five singles players, further than Ken, who'd only played doubles.

It's Monday night in the fall of 1975. Sean Harrington has driven me home from another lesson. We're in his Alfa Romeo, outside my apartment building. His knees injured, Sean's quitting tennis instruction.

"You've really improved," he tells me. "You've got a great opportunity right now." It's a nice compliment, but so what? I'm no big-time player, so how much better should I try to be anyway?

"Don't get hung up on people who are pros or who play at UCLA," says Sean. "Just try to be as good as you can be for its own sake. Go out in the morning and practice serves. Find more people to play with. Jog. Jump rope."

"That's a lot of time," I say.

"You're worth it," says Sean. "Think about it."

My contemplation lasts an elevator ride. No way. Who did Sean think I was, Jimmy Connors? It was the poster of "King Arthur" that was taped on my bedroom wall. Arthur Ashe read books (though I'd later learn first-hand that he rarely finished them).

Only years later did I realize that Sean's words weren't strictly about tennis. It wasn't just tennis I was worthy of. It was ambition. It was desire. It was passion. It was something other than the external cool of an Arthur Ashe. How could I let the girl next door in when I couldn't even hear the knock on the door?

Two decades later, I spent a week a year with John Newcombe at a Fantasy Camp held at his ranch in Texas. A natural storyteller, he and his mates regaled us day and night. There were battles won, battles lost, all part of life's journey. True to his ability to celebrate and mock himself, in the lobby of the ranch was a large portrait of Newcombe hitting a backhand—by far his worst shot. It was hard to imagine Connors possessing enough self-esteem to make a joke at his own expense. When I asked Newcombe about Connors, he was full of admiration and puzzlement. "Jimmy was one hell of a player, as rough a competitor as you'd ever see," said Newcombe. "But tell me: Did he have to win so much on hate? Did he have to be so rude?"

As 1975 ended, I wondered the same thing. But hate and anger helped me beat Binstock. Though I wouldn't admit it, in certain ways, Connors was growing on me. On the next-to-last day of 1975, I played a big match at UCLA on the court where Connors often practiced. It was a challenge match for that critical fifth singles spot on the high school tennis team. I was behind, and slapped my thigh several times. I came back, and beat someone I detested so much I wouldn't talk to him for nearly 25 years. During that match I wore a Fred Perry vest, the same garment Connors wore for his 1974 *Sports Illustrated* cover shot. Then again, it hadn't cost much. Six months earlier, after I'd lost in the first round of the 16-and-under sectionals, I'd stolen it from the pro shop of the Los Angeles Tennis Club. A little renegade behavior at the hands of the tennis establishment was OK in my book. I wore Connors on my sleeves, but I wasn't about to buy into him.

5

Break Point

Every Sunday night for a year, Ken and I watched the World War II documentary, "World at War." Week after week, we witnessed Brits weather the Luftwaffe, Yanks trudge through Guadalcanal, Germans slither beneath the Atlantic Ocean and, most important, fellow Jews survive the Holocaust. History in our house was a tool, a moral compass pointing us in its direction daily. My mother, a staunch liberal, wore a popular necklace that said, "War is not healthy for children and other living things."

After we'd watched the last episode of "World at War", I asked my father, "Why can't we all be neutral, like Switzerland?"

Kind as my father was, he was also pragmatic. "That's like saying, 'Why can't we all be nice guys?'"

Couldn't we? Wasn't that how you made friends? Wasn't being nice the best way to succeed?

Ken made friends so much easier than I did. He was magnetic. The day he got his braces off, he showed off his smile like a movie star. Thanks to his friendship with Tony Paris, son of TV director Jerry Paris ("The Dick Van Dyke Show," "Happy Days"), he played poker with actor Ron Howard and tennis player-actor Vince Van Patten. He dated an attractive blonde.

Many times, I felt more like a spectator of Ken's success than a protagonist in my own life. After my parents and I attended his high school graduation in June 1974, Ken went off to a party, while the three of us walked to Baskin-Robbins 31 Flavors in Westwood. As I ate my butterscotch sundae, I reflected to myself that my high school graduation four years later coincided with Ken's far-more significant graduation from UCLA. Projecting further, I saw myself a mere undergraduate while Ken was in law school. Unquestionably, one of the highlights of my win over Mark Binstock was that Ken saw it.

I was a loner, which even my modest tennis success did nothing to change. On the one hand, I wasn't good enough for anyone to tell me I was a worthy talent (well, Sean Harrington, but wasn't that his job?). My junior high was better than virtually any high school in the country. On the other hand, my immersion in tennis distanced me from my one friend, Matt Newman. His anger surfaced when he reminded me how unattractive I was and that I'd have to work extra-hard to get girls to like me. This only enhanced my self-consciousness. Though I finally got my braces off in the summer of '75, I lacked Ken's swagger. I was so eager to be well-liked I had no idea what made me likable. Entering my first semester of high school that fall, I walked around in my warmup suit and thought of the icy elegance that made Arthur Ashe a champion. I figured that to succeed I must strike the right balance of wit and cool.

Sunday, September 12, 1976 was the day Jimmy Connors showed me that fire was better than ice. Success and cool were incompatible.

That Sunday, Connors played Bjorn Borg in the finals of the U.S. Open. As we had so often, Ken and I planned to watch, get inspired and play immediately afterwards. But after I'd started beating Ken, he was far less concerned with tennis. He was much more focused on money. After earning $22,000 over a six-month period selling office supplies over the phone, Ken dropped out of UCLA early in his sophomore year. He and his friend Greg Seltzer started their own office supply business. Ken's exit from school did not please my parents, but surely, they thought, he was young enough to experiment and return to school.

An odd incident occurred the night before the U.S. Open final. Many Saturday evenings, my parents, Ken and I would converge in our living room to watch the 11:00 news. On this Saturday, Ken seemed distraught. He stared into space. He looked haunted. Suddenly, he picked up the rectangular box that was used to select TV channels. He glared at our parents. He didn't push a button. He didn't throw the box. He held the box and stared into the distance. Our father asked him to give back the box. Ken stared more, looked ahead. Then he surrendered the box and walked silently back to his room.

All I did throughout this 10-minute interchange was watch. A self-preserving detachment came over me during emotional crises. When I was 10, our father told me our mother was about to be operated on and have a cancerous breast removed. The image that came to my head

was of a piece of chicken. Our parents loved to tell the tale of a trip to
the pediatrician. Ken was seven and I was three. When the doctor
approached to give us shots, Ken ran around the room. I stood calm as
a British soldier. The pattern repeated the night Ken held the cable
box. My parents talked him down. I said not a word. Nothing further
was said.

I approached this U.S. Open final with a new attitude towards
Connors. Much had changed between the two of us in 1976. A year
previously, Connors' demise was as savory to me as watching Nixon
vanish off that White House lawn. But as Rex Bellamy noted in early
1976 in "Is There A 'New' Jimmy Connors?," the first of two consecutive monthly stories in *World Tennis* about Connors' metamorphosis,
"It's a measure of Jimmy Connors' reputation that some folks are
discussing the finals he's lost as if the guy was ready for a wheelchair."

As 1976 dawned, Connors was 23 years old. He won nine tournaments the previous year and reached three Grand Slam finals. Who
seriously could rival Connors for supremacy? Surely none of his Slam
conquerors. Orantes only shined on clay. Ashe and Newcombe were
past 30. Connors owned Borg.

Guarded and rigid as Connors seemed, he had made changes. Some
worked better than others. In the late summer of '75, he agreed to play
Davis Cup. The captain was my beloved camp director, Tony Trabert.
In October, Connors easily won two matches versus Venezuela in
Tucson. But in Mexico City that December, Connors severely underestimated the emotional pressures of international team play.
Unprepared, out of shape and tactically confounded by altitude, spectators and a shrewd opponent, Connors lost the fifth and decisive
match to Raul Ramirez. The greatest win of Ramirez's career was yet
another reason for Connors to loathe Davis Cup.

More effective was the purge of Riordan. So long as Connors rose
up the ranks, Riordan's ceaseless politicking was a sideshow in Jimbo's
mind. But a few high-stakes losses altered the picture. Driving up in
his car during Wimbledon, Connors saw a headline: "Tennis Star Sues
Kramer" and wondered, "What poor sucker's doing that?" When he
saw it was him, he started to wonder if Riordan was truly looking out
for his interests or treating him like a piece of valued property. In the
spring of '75, Newcombe warned Connors about collecting money
from Riordan for their Challenge Match. By the fall, neither
Newcombe nor Connors had received a cent. By January, Riordan was
out. Stan Canter, the chatty movie producer ("St. Ives," "W.W. and the
Dixie Dance Kings") who befriended Connors at the BHTC, was in.

A chastened Connors launched his 1976 campaign. This was the beginning of those even-numbered years when, like a Congressman, Connors ran for office after a frustrating odd-numbered year. "I hope you all notice my new image," he said in January at the U.S. Pro Indoor in Philadelphia. "I don't have anything to prove anymore. I've won all the big titles and I go on playing tennis because that is just what I like to do." In 1975, he conceded, he forgot his grandmother's advice to "work when you work, play when you play."

Connors won the tournament. More notable than his on-court brilliance was his off-court finesse. "His press conferences were full of extroverted enthusiasm," wrote David Gray in *World Tennis'* "Yes, Virginia, There Is A New Jimmy Connors." "Who could resist such Andy Hardy frankness? He was more relaxed than he had been on such big occasions last year." His convincing 7-6, 6-4, 6-0 victory over Borg in the finals punctuated a comment Connors made earlier in the week: "The King is back."

And gradually, it was dawning on me that I occupied his kingdom. "For better or worse," said a 1975 *Los Angeles Magazine* article, "he is ours." Connors' rackets were strung at Westwood Sporting Goods, the same shop where my friends and I brought our frames. Bill Johns, the store's owner, showed me Connors' T-2000 several times. A keen tennis rival of mine, Steve Smooke, was the ballboy in the background of a Nike poster featuring Connors serving at the Los Angeles Tennis Club. Eddie Berman and his brother, Ron, two high school teammates of mine, were members of the BHTC. Not only did they talk frequently with Connors, they hit with him several times. Stan Canter's son, Jeff, was a high school classmate. Connors pervaded Los Angeles, from tales of his mother paying his parking tickets at UCLA to rumors of trysts and encounters at restaurants, gas stations and nightclubs.

Most of all, Connors often practiced at UCLA. When my friends and I weren't sneaking on the courts to play, we watched the UCLA team and the many pros who came to hit. At first glance, it was remarkable how slight Connors, the hardest hitter in the game, looked in person. Barely 5'-10", not much taller than me, he resembled a moptop elf, a racket-wielding pixie. Before he hit a ball, he jogged several times around UCLA's Sunset Courts. As he stepped on the court and picked up his feet to begin rallying, there was a subdued peace in his eyes that rapidly transformed into the glare of a hawk. Other pros such as Boris Becker were renowned for lightly tapping a few balls at one another for as long as 20 minutes. Connors was at full throttle by the third ball.

Connors' practices were like nothing I'd ever seen. The spring in his legs, the drive in hips, the harnessed and uncoiled body rotation, the ever-squeaking feet, all unified in one resounding, clean drive after another. It was a tennis version of Rule 17 from that classic book about writing, *The Elements of Style*: omit needless words.

Then Connors played points. His appetite for opportunity was massive. Let the opponent hit one slightly tepidly, and Connors pounded on it immediately.

Nothing was more energizing to me than witnessing Connors go from defense to offense. Compromised way back into his forehand corner, he'd dash with fury, striking a hard, deep crosscourt drive, rocking the assailant on his heels and in the process eliciting a short ball. Then he'd approach down the line and promptly end the point. It was the ultimate counterpunch, the fully-realized version of what I tried versus Ken when he'd accuse me of dogging it. As I sought to improve, Connors' schoolyard heat was invariably overtaking Ashe's classroom cool.

Another major reason for Connors' ascent into my life occurred during my first year of high school. University High School was a public facility located two miles west of UCLA. Its district cut a swath through West Los Angeles, reaching far north into ultra-rich Bel-Air on up to Mulholland Drive, and as south as the more middle-class neighborhoods of Mar Vista. Had Connors not attended a private school, he would have gone to "Uni."

The '70s were an odd transition decade in the history of education. Previously, public schools were bedrock institutions. A decade later, with California's school districts gutted by tax-cutting and tumult over integration, affluent families shipped their kids to private schools. But in the '70s, confidence in public schools lingered. In the wake of the social turmoil of the '60s, parents and students demanded "relevance." New approaches emerged, most notably at "Uni" in the form of an alternative school called Innovative Program School (IPS).

IPS addressed the paradox of adolescence: Beset with massive emotional and physical transitions, a teenager is confused, uncertain how to fit in with others and create an identity. Traditionally, schools took students away from their self-absorption with lessons from algebra, literature, science and history. IPS' premise was different. What value were any of these topics if you lacked self-knowledge? IPS' 200 teenagers were exposed to teachings from est, Scientology, Transactional Analysis and a gamut of ideas associated with the nascent Human Potential Movement. Hours were spent publicly revealing emotions, fears and desires on topics like sex, drugs, families, friendships and futures. Each morning, IPS gathered to publicly "share" emotions. With introspection as a base, scholastic activities were tackled sporadically in self-paced coursework.

I enrolled in IPS because of Ken, who enjoyed it for his three years of high school. Each day at dinner, he described an environment where you called teachers by their first names and argued about everything from capitalism versus socialism to the speed limit, the legalization of drugs and America's role in Vietnam. He said little about IPS' penchant for emotional probing.

The leader of IPS was Caldwell Williams, a tall black man who resembled the actor Billy Dee Williams. Caldwell thrived on shoving the assumptions of us cheeky, predominantly Jewish kids right up our privileged butts. He minced nary a word. A coquettish blonde was informed she was "more than a cunt." A surfer was told "you're nothing more than your body and your BMW." In the process, he obliterated my notion of icy elegance. "You all want to be cool, but that's nothing more than your fears of opening up," he said. And he was right. After the initial shock, the comments from Williams and other staff members struck home. Years before America's confessional society emerged full-bloom on shows like "Oprah" or in corporate team-building events, IPS students were set on a road of introspection.

One day, all of IPS made a 10-minute walk down Santa Monica Boulevard to watch the movie, "Harold and Maude." This '70s cult film was the tale of Harold, a death-obsessed, repressed teen who falls in love with Maude, a life-loving, elderly Holocaust survivor played by spunky Ruth Gordon. A seminal scene came when Maude rolled on the ground and performed a somersault. She urged Harold to join her. Harold backed off, fearing he'd make an ass out of himself. Maude countered. "Everyone," she said, "has the right to make an ass out of himself." This was an IPS mantra.

In IPS history and government classes, I started to win friends and influence people, not just by being nice and cool, but by passionately asserting my ambitions. We held debates. Silent for much of my first year, I emerged as vocal, informed and absent of icy elegance. A history teacher, Bill Greene, read to us from a Theodore Roosevelt speech: "It is not the critic who counts. The credit belongs to the man who is actually in the arena, whose face is marred by dust and sweat and blood." Who more than Jimmy Connors personified this idea?

Much of what I learned in IPS gave me the nerve to walk up to Connors at UCLA one sunny Saturday afternoon in January 1976.

Approaching Connors as he finished practicing, I mentioned the Canter family, nervously adding that I'd also lived in St. Louis. "Whereabouts, son?" he asked. Nodding in recognition, Connors asked, "This weather sure beats Missouri, huh? We'll see ya.'"

Two passions ruled my life: politics and tennis. The former marched forward smoothly. I was elected leader of IPS' student government class. Tennis took more effort. Due to an IPS event, I missed the opening meeting of our tennis team and was placed number 48 on the team's ladder. For eight months I clawed my way up the ladder before at last attaining a singles spot.

By the spring of '76, life was opening up. The tennis team named me "Most Improved." On the first day of summer, I was set to earn a Californian's passport to freedom: my driver's license. Even my social life bloomed. Carolyn Bartholomew was an attractive brown-eyed blonde who enjoyed talking with me. Since we were each in 10th grade, we discussed plans for spending three years in IPS. Maybe once I started driving I would call her.

Instead, all summer I wavered. I never called Carolyn. As was the case for virtually every day of high school and in the summer, I dressed for tennis, playing six or seven days a week. But it was still hard for me to understand myself. I purchased the Rawlings rackets endorsed by Newcombe. Playing the semifinals of a local "B" tournament, I won the first set 6-4, broke serve at 2-all in the second and said to myself, "Just like Newcombe, you hold your serve and run out the match." Everything unravelled. I lost six straight games. Down 2-0 in the third, the situation demanded less Newcombe and more Connors—at least what of him I could muster. I counterpunched my way out of trouble and won 6-3 in the third. A decade later I bumped into my opponent. "All you did was fight," he said. So glad was I to reach the final—it meant I was at last an "A" player—that I played a miserable match and lost. My expectations wandered. Call Carolyn? Read more about politics? Play more tennis? Work on my tennis? Are you kidding, I'm just not that good. And besides, I'll admit, I was lazy, unfocused, torn in pieces by disparate desires.

In the summer of '76, here's how I celebrated America's Bicentennial: driving alone up and down Sunset Boulevard, first east to Hollywood, then west back through Beverly Hills all the way to the Pacific Coast Highway. It was a frequent ritual. By night, I read Theodore White's *The Making of the President* series. Since 1976 was a presidential election, I spent hours engulfed in the campaign, and of course was excited about the possibility of sweeping the corrupt and conservative Republicans out of the White House.

The Connors-Borg match started at 1:00 p.m. At 10:00 a.m., I dialed the first three numbers for Carolyn and stopped. Instead, I drove to Barrington Park. Tom Carbonar, a 38-year-old runner trying his hand at tennis, jogged up to me.

"Joel, who do you like, Connors or Borg?"

"Connors, no question."

"But how can you say that? Borg just won Wimbledon."

"Connors hits harder, deeper. He's already beaten him twice this year."

"Yeah, a friend of mine was at that match in Palm Springs. He said Connors was pretty rude to a busboy. What an asshole. How could someone nice like you, Joel, like an asshole like that Connors?"

"And a damn successful asshole," butted in Sid Young. That spring, Sid moved from the flatlands to a house north of Sunset Boulevard with a tennis court and pool. Tom, a confirmed bachelor, lived in a studio apartment. What Tom saw as Connors' inappropriate conceit was, from Sid's vantage point, the oxygen that fueled success. An asshole, Caldwell Williams and Ruth Gordon taught me, wasn't such a bad thing to aspire to. According to Bill Greene and Theodore Roosevelt, an asshole was willing to stick his neck into the arena— like ruthless Bobby Kennedy, like Connors and, maybe, eventually, like me.

Though Sid's income came from a prosaic business painting homes and apartment buildings, he nibbled around the entertainment industry. He constantly dropped names and surfaced at celebrity hang-outs like Matteo's in Westwood, Nate 'N Al's Deli in Beverly Hills and Caesars Palace in Las Vegas. After the Connors-Laver match, he bumped into Connors in the hot tub at Caesars.

"Jimmy's all right," said Sid, and passed on a rumor about an actress who slept with Connors.

Assuming I was nice, Tom thought I was in Borg's corner. But the Swede's game was even drearier to me than Evert's. That Sunday afternoon I realized I was caught up in Connors' quest to win the 1976 U.S. Open. It was the first of a series of Slams where the fate of Connors' career hung as perilously close to the lines as his savage crosscourt backhand. Champion or chump? As Gloria advised him so often, it was kill or be killed. Her philosophy reminded me of all those challenge matches I'd played to earn my singles spot. Life was a challenge match for Connors, one body impaled after another.

Despite being number one on the ATP's computer rankings, as the

Open began, a cloud hung over Connors' head. It was two years since his last Slam title. Earlier that summer, Borg shocked the tennis world by winning Wimbledon. No one thought the Swede's loopy strokes and attrition-based backcourt game could succeed on grass. Borg versus Connors was the sport's preeminent rivalry. Yet it was the placid Borg, not the bombastic Connors, who was considered the player in ascent.

As with most tennis rivalries, Connors-Borg tilted on contrast. Connors invited query. From his mother to his girlfriends to his metal racket to his squeaky shoes and windmill-tilting playing style, Connors compelled attention. Once a match started, his hawk-like eyes bulged, his eyebrows twitched. "There's something definitely wrong with him," Sid Young said the day after the final. You never watched a Jimmy Connors match casually.

Borg repelled engagement. His eyes avoided contact with everything but the tennis ball. Constantly retreating with eyes and body, Borg shuffled across the court, moving quietly, running down every ball, at times so consistent he seemed to numb his opponents to defeat. His understated grace, exemplary sportsmanship and benign nature made him an icon, the "Teen Angel" of Wimbledon—tennis' first rock star.

The Swede's reticence made it difficult even for Connors to find his fundamental motivational tool: hate. Despite his being Connors' foremost adversary, Borg lacked anything Jimbo could grab on and loathe. He was too young to represent the Establishment like Ashe or Newcombe, too withdrawn a baseliner to strike at Connors like big servers Stan Smith or Roscoe Tanner, too foreign to be a fellow American who dared underestimate Jimbo as a youth.

Their matches turned on a simple geographic premise. Connors loved to force the action from a semi-circle inside the baseline, pinning opponents with penetrating drives and selected netrushing. Borg occupied a semi-circle behind the baseline. Endlessly on the patrol, faster than anyone in tennis, Borg was adept when necessary at whipping passing shots. And with increasing frequency, his beefed-up serve was helping him win easy points too.

Even though he was the number one seed at the Open, Connors was hardly favored. The clay, many thought, aided Borg. His claycourt credentials also included two French Open titles.

Connors' desire to win the '76 U.S. Open was so great that Pancho Segura was brought back into the fold just for this one tournament. Joining Segura in the entourage were Doug Henderson and Bob

Harper, two massive African-American former high school players who served as "The James Gang." An antsy coach, a beefy security detail and Connors—his bouncy stride and a towel wrapped around his neck—continued the boxing-like aspects the deceased Bertha and now-jettisoned Riordan initiated.

Segura constantly advised Connors to play more aggressively. Bold as Jimbo was, there were times when he settled for just hitting one groundstroke after another rather than rush the net and close out the point. Against most opponents, groundstokes were often good enough. But not versus Borg. Throughout the '76 Open, Connors and Segura geared up for the Swede. On the practice court, in the locker, in the car, constantly mapping out point construction on a cocktail napkin, Segura demanded that Connors drive forward, pound the daylights out of those tepid short balls and get his butt into the net. On the slow clay, it took both technique and confidence to pull this off, particularly against a player as fast as Borg.

But point construction was only the rational part of Segura's motivational approach. Prior to matches, he recreated the hypnosis of bygone days, not just with Jimbo but with anyone who dared doubt Jimbo's ability to hammer the Swede. Earlier in the tournament, he'd sat with Herbert Warren Wind, the long-standing *New Yorker* tennis writer. Wind expressed his appreciation for Borg. Why do you like Borg, Segura queried. Wind cited his sportsmanship and his topspin drives. "Well, I tell you this buddy," said Segura, conveniently turning a blind eye to Connors' churlish manner, "Mr. Borg hits with topspin—but it's the wrong kind of topspin. That topspin goes short. Jimbo's going to be driving it deep. Then we'll see what Mr. Borg can do. Let Mr. Borg try and hit the lines." Earlier that spring, after winning a tight challenge match, I wrapped a towel around my neck like Connors and thought how much better my tennis would be if I had a Segura in my corner too.

Connors ripped his way to the finals of the '76 Open, winning six matches without the loss of a set. He was exceptionally savage during his semifinal match versus Guillermo Vilas, a topspinning Argentine who played much like Borg. Hammering one ball after another deep into the corners, running Vilas without once letting up, Connors won 6-4, 6-2, 6-1. "If a guy is hitting the ball 200 miles per hour," said Vilas, "you cannot hit it back 400 miles per hour."

In the manner that defined so many of his triumphs, Borg fought his way through several jams. His second-round match had been decided in a final-set tiebreak. Two more went five, including one comeback from two sets to love down. Borg's skill under pressure, what coach Lennert Bergelin called "ice in the stomach," was yet another contrast with Connors. Whereas Connors always felt the need to start pummeling from round one, Borg's mystique grew around his skill at continually raising his game under pressure. In this sense, what Connors and Borg shared as baseliners was the ability to strike big when cornered.

The Connors camp bounced around Forest Hills with jubilance following the win over Vilas. Sitting in the trainer's room afterwards, Connors heard the popular song, "Everybody Plays The Fool." All his life he had thrived on being counted out, and now, one day before the finals, he was keen on once again sticking his finger up the ass of those who dared not believe in him. What else could a counterpuncher do?

Pat Summerall, Tony Trabert and Arthur Ashe called the action on CBS. I was pleased to hear my friend Tony pick Connors. Ashe, perhaps still angry with Connors for all the complications of the previous year's litigation, went with Borg. Ashe's selection—cool repression picking cool repression—accelerated my renouncement of "icy elegance."

The difference between Connors and Borg was audible. There was a firm, ripping thump each time Connors hit the ball, supplemented by his scuffling feet and intermittent grunts. Borg's balls echoed, a distant ping that only sprung to life when he needed to whip a passing shot. Were it a fight, the judges would award Connors points for his willingness to keep throwing aggressive punches. This is where tennis was in some ways harder than boxing: You must knock the guy down to earn the point. Borg, though, constantly hung just close enough to keep the Connors freight train from accelerating too fast.

With Connors serving in the first set at 4-3 and 15-30, he laced a crosscourt backhand, setting up an easy forehand volley. At 30-all, using a play right out of Segura's book, he snuck in for a backhand volley winner. Rushing the net again, he slid a forehand approach down the line, another winner to go up 5-3.

Serving for the first set at 5-4, Connors continually moved forward, striking a backhand up the line winner for 15-love. Two exceptionally forceful forehand approach shots brought Connors to triple set point. Mid-rally, Borg whipped a ball deep into Connors' forehand corner and crept forward. Connors tracked down the forehand. Borg played a half-volley drop shot. Running full-tilt on the clay, forced to let go of the racket with his right hand and play a one-hander, Connors slid forward, pushing a backhand down the line winner past Borg for the set. The U.S. Open record crowd of 16,253 rose to its feet. Connors once again had superbly transitioned from defense to offense.

I was transfixed. No television network was better than CBS at mixing in the sounds of the court, never more visceral than when Connors grunted, scuffled and squeaked.

Ken's attention was intermittent. His friend Mark Gustafson joined us. A large, former high school football player, Mark looked rather bemused at tennis. To him, Connors was a twirp and, of course, an asshole. But I didn't want to argue. I just wanted to watch.

Borg withstood Connors' fevered opening. He took pace off his backhand and sliced it low to Connors' forehand. It drew errors. Borg won the second set, 6-3, and opened the third by breaking Connors at love. Segura looked nervous. Connors broke back.

By the time Borg served at 2-3, there had been eight service breaks in just two and a half sets. Within two years, largely due to the pain inflicted by Connors' returns, Borg developed the best serve in tennis. Today, though, he was mostly spinning it in, just as Connors always did. And Borg's passivity hurt him, with Connors breaking serve and going up 4-2, 40-love after nearly two hours of play. The lights were on. With Connors taking such a commanding lead, I looked forward to shortly inhaling a Connors win and exhaling on the court versus Ken.

Then, disaster.

Connors whacked a forehand wide.

And then Connors did something he once told me professional tennis players should never do: he drove the ball into the net, not once but on four straight points. Since Borg only came to net once, there was no reason for Connors to strike with so little net clearance. He'd choked.

Now Borg took control, winning 11 of 12 points. Connors was serving at 4-4, love-30. I couldn't believe it, that righteous Arthur Ashe was keen to cluck about how wise he was to pick someone as boring as Borg to win the U.S. fucking Open.

Nervously hitting off his back foot, Connors rolled a tenuous forehand that barely stayed in. Then he came to net on a crosscourt backhand approach to Borg's forehand—an odd selection given that Segura (and every other pro) preached the value of approaching down the line and, even worse, Borg's forehand was considerably better than his backhand.

Pushing his foot to the accelerator, Borg whipped a forehand pass down the line, an apparent winner for love-40. Stretched to the limit, Connors reached it and pounded a forehand volley crosscourt that struck both lines—yet another example of Connors winning a big point with a rare shot. Connors, Ashe remarked, had "no idea how crucial that point was."

But the inspiring part about Connors was that he knew exactly how crucial that point was. Overt awareness was his appeal. He was a different cat than cool cucumbers like Ashe, Newcombe, Smith and Laver. Great as those champions were, none of them burst through the wall like Jimbo. *It's a goddamned war out there.* Because it wasn't clear if Connors was referring strictly to tennis, there was a heightened smell and taste during his matches, a climate which expressed that this wasn't just a game, but a personal form of combat. I'd hated Connors for so long because he stood for a part of me I had yet to fully accept. As I watched Connors scrape and claw versus Borg, I was recognizing that those same tiger juices Gloria brought out in Jimbo flowed through my own body. They were necessary.

The set advanced to a tiebreak. The winner would likely gain just enough confidence to take the title.

Leading 2-1, Connors, owner of one of the safest serves in tennis, double-faulted.

Two errors from Connors' forehand put Borg up 4-2.

Despite catching up to 4-4, Connors seemed unable to blend patience and aggression. Borg passed him for 5-4. A stupid Connors attempt at a drop volley plopped into the net.

A distraught Segura shook his head, muttering, "no, no."

Borg, the fastest, coolest man in tennis, playing on a slow, claycourt, had weathered dozens of Connors punches and now held two set points at 6-4.

The next 10 minutes taught me more about how to win than anything in my life.

Continuing his plan of slowly hitting to Connors' forehand, Borg kept floating the ball mildly deep, daring him to overhit. It was maddening. Then, as Segura predicted to Herbert Warren Wind, one fell short enough for Connors to pounce on it. "You've got to want the ball to come to you," Connors told me years later. Connors drove his forehand down the line. Borg whipped a forehand crosscourt. Connors thumped the backhand volley deep, a winner on most surfaces. But Borg ran it down yet again. Forced to take a high volley dangerously close to the net, Connors scorched it for a winner. Set point number two went similarly. Borg lofted another backhand to Connors' forehand. I knew that the play was for Connors to drive it down the line and set up a volley. Instead, he played it even more powerfully, sliding the ball down the line with enough sidespin for a winner to knot the tiebreak at 6-apiece.

Segura jumped out of his seat. I concentrated as I never had during a tennis match, enthralled by the way Connors bore in on those short balls and stuck his nose right into Borg's face. This wasn't simply a matter of Newcombe or Smith blasting a serve from a distance. This was Connors, a little lefthanded twirp like me, engaged in fist-to-fist combat.

Serving now in the deuce court, Connors aced Borg to go up 7-6. For all the body movements that we associate with Connors, he was extremely tranquil during this match. Following the ace, he tensed and thrust his fists up a few inches.

A tepid Connors return gave Borg a chance to come in and force a long backhand pass from Connors.

At 7-7, Connors was long on a crosscourt forehand approach.

Set point number three.

I was paying careful attention to Connors' body language, particularly as he scampered in for those approach shots. Again, another chance to strike a forehand. In dashed Connors. Striking deep and down the line, he drew a weak pass, an easy backhand volley and an even weaker lob from Borg for an overhead putaway.

At 8-8, Connors tried to sneak in and serve-and-volley Borg. But the Swede's return was so flaccid that it dipped slowly. Late on the volley, Connors was only able to push it back into the court, giving Borg the chance to easily hoist a lob. Connors chased it down, but whacked it long.

Set point number four.

Connors' next forehand approach was harder, deeper than any he'd hit the whole tiebreak. It opened up the court for another easy overhead.

9-9. The crowd rose to its feet and applauded.

Connors struck a crosscourt forehand approach shot. Borg hoisted a semi-lob that was too high for an easy volley, too low and deep for an overhead. Connors awkwardly flicked it crosscourt and retreated to the baseline. Borg whipped a backhand crosscourt to Connors' forehand. Connors sidespinned it down the line. With the reset button being pushed now that both players were back on the baseline, the point started to resemble a patterned drill. Borg rolled a forehand crosscourt, fairly deep. Connors drove a backhand crosscourt. Borg hit another forehand crosscourt, shorter than the prior one but certainly not shallow enough for a netrush on clay at this tight stage.

On the 12th shot of this rally, Connors probably wasn't thinking about anything but striking the tennis ball. The ball, notable coach Vic Braden once told me, doesn't know what the score is. That was the eternal message from Two-Mom and Gloria. Whether on muggy days in Belleville, rain-soaked afternoons in North Carolina, on the back-yard court in Belleville to the lawns of Wimbledon, Jimbo was fore-warned: strike or be struck.

Now he struck, taking his weight back and through the ball with his entire body and two decades worth of love and hate. Connors laced the ball crosscourt for an outright winner. He raised his fist to the sky.

The air went out of Borg's balloon. With Connors serving at 10-9, they rallied mildly. Connors knew there was no chance of Borg suddenly striking and coming in. Borg sensed his moment had passed, and tepidly drove a backhand wide.

Connors' effort was amazing. Over the course of the last 10 points, down 6-4, he'd won six of his seven with winners. On each of Borg's four set points, he'd approached the net with his weaker forehand, capping each point with placements. At 6-6, Connors, owner of one of the worst serves in tennis history, hit an ace on a claycourt. And then at 9-9, a backhand winner for the ages.

Since struggle brought Connors a lead, invariably he'd have to scrape and claw his way to the finish line, toothpick by toothpick. By the time Borg served at 2-2, the match was three hours long. Borg went up 40-15. Given how well Connors had played, given how much he'd forced the action, did he have the stamina and will to keep throwing punches well into the fifth set? Borg at this point was in the middle of a five-year run where he never lost a fifth set.

Two solid netrushes brought Connors to deuce, and then he broke Borg. With Connors serving at 3-2, 15-love, Ashe announced he was changing his prediction, sensing the "physical and spiritual resigna-tion" from Borg. Wise as it was by this stage, Ashe's switch irritated me. Why couldn't he live with his prediction?

Borg served at 2-4, 15-40. Inches away from redemption, Connors twitched. But as he would throughout his entire career, Borg hung on the ledge just long enough. Now it was up to Connors to serve the difficult 4-3 game.

There was no backing off. Jumping on Borg's short return, he ripped a crosscourt forehand for a winner. A Borg pass winner on the next point did nothing to discourage Connors, who charged the net on each of the next three points to go up 5-3. Borg held easily.

The first point of this game opened with a 24-stroke rally. Finally, once again, Connors came in off a deep backhand approach. Borg was wide with the backhand. Then Borg netted a benign smash. Connors missed two backhands, including one where Borg dared rush the net. At 30-all, Connors' ripping crosscourt forehand set up an easy volley. At championship point, Connors drove a crosscourt backhand from midcourt. Borg whipped a forehand crosscourt pass for a winner.

Deuce, and Connors nailed a backhand up the line for a winner and his second match point.

A good deep forehand from Borg forced a long Connors forehand.

My palms were sweating. Another penetrating Connors backhand approach, and a long Borg lob.

Match point number three. Connors again took a short forehand, driving it safe and moderately deep to Borg's backhand.

Would the Swede lob? Rip it up the line? Roll it crosscourt?

The backhand went into the net.

Connors raised his arms up in the air. It was the first of many redemptive triumphs. If he couldn't hate Borg as a person, he surely hates him as an idea, as surely and powerfully as he'd loathed all those others who'd dared count him out for so long. *Everybody plays the fool.*

Coming after the losses in '75, this triumph was exceptionally sweet, a pointed reminder that Connors was no mercurial dilettante, but a champion for the ages. Curiously, in the campaigning spirit he'd shown all year, the cantankerous Connors expressed concern for how he was regarded. "I didn't say one word," said Connors after the match. "I didn't do one thing. I just hit tennis balls this time. I don't know if you like me better this way or the way I used to be."

I loved the way Connors emphatically revealed his ambitions. The man in the arena, I'd learned from Theodore Roosevelt and Bill Greene, "knows the great enthusiasms, the great devotions; who spends himself in a worthy cause, who at the best knows in the end the triumphs of high achievement." The twitch, the jump, the run, the arms outstretched at match point; it all showed just how sorely Connors craved victory. And what was so bad about that? Tennis, the way he played it, it wasn't just a parlor game. It was a battle, no different than the cavalcade of NFL games CBS reported on throughout the Borg-Connors match. "The New York crowd is a tough one to play in front of," said Connors. "They come to see blood. I didn't want to give them any of mine." Only later in his career would Connors realize it was better to be a donor.

I was primed to play. Ken remained remote. Three years ago, inspired by Newcombe's serve-volley Forest Hills win, we'd charged out with hunger, playing two sets with breakneck intensity. On this day, I drove to Barrington, but we were of two different minds.

It was a strange set. I was pumped, eager to charge forward like Connors. Ken was sleepwalking. The points were intriguing. Ken's forehand and athleticism remained good weapons. But this day, with me fully-grown at 16, our four-year-age gap wasn't so vast. I spun in my lefty serve, pecked away at Ken's backhand and, like Connors, kept coming in for volleys. I won the set, 6-4, but Ken's indifference made it all pale in the wake of Connors' great win. I was primed for more. Ken wanted to go home. I gave him the keys to the car, looked for other tennis, found none and went home.

No one was in the condo. This was common, but usually my parents left a note and a $5 bill for dinner money. Tonight, nothing.

Only past midnight did my parents and Ken surface. They had bailed Ken out of jail. After Ken left me at Barrington, he visited a woman he knew. We've never quite known what happened, but in the course of that evening she filed assault charges. The cable box incident made more sense. There was something going on with Ken. We had no idea what. I felt nothing.

Two days later, the '76-'77 school year began. Whether inspired by Connors, presidential politics or my own success in debate classes, I decided to run for president, not just of IPS but all of University High School. I announced this publicly at IPS one morning during our confessional "sharing" period, and felt myself transformed. No longer was I just a nice guy fitting into the background. No longer was I Bobby Kennedy the helpful younger brother. I was a candidate, like Connors, a contender entering the bloody arena. I thirsted for the challenge—and, most of all, loved the recognition. Four years earlier, I posted a McGovern sticker in my locker, but removed it after my Nixon-loving partner threatened to beat me up. In the fall of '76, I was determined to make a stand for myself. I craved power and public validation. I had no idea that this desire was likely connected to the private agony engulfing my family.

On a Saturday afternoon in late September, IPS gathered at Rancho Park in Cheviot Hills for a picnic. The warmth of a Southern California autumn day is enchanting in its sensuality and long shadows. As the days grow shorter, desert heat gives way to at least the pretense of winter and the scent of odd possibilities and alluring intimacies. Alison Mogull, a brown-haired, slim-waisted, sharp-tongued 15-year-old wearing a pair of blue jeans and a white tank top, approached me. "So you want to be president?" she asked. Looking at me clad in my tennis clothes, she added, "Nice legs." Hooking her arm around my waist, she asked me what I'd do if I were elected.

Alison knew all about presidents. Her father, Artie, was president of United Artists Records. He drove a Mercedes 450 SLC with a license plate that read, "THE MOG." The Mogull house, high up over Benedict Canyon, was filled with gold records, many of which Artie had earned from his association with Bob Dylan. Alison wanted to introduce me to Artie, current president meeting future president. Like Connors, I'd made my ambitions clear, and the rewards, I was seeing, could include fame, friends, sex and glory.

Two weeks later, Alison sat in my lap in a large lounge chair during a break between classes. I was told there were two visitors waiting for me outside the school's gate.

It was my father and Ken. Ken wore a pair of navy White Stag tennis shorts identical to the ones I had on when I first met Alison. He looked giddy. Our father told me they were on their way to check Ken into The Westwood, a nearby mental hospital. Ken's status, now identified as a "condition," was vintage '70s: a "nervous breakdown." It was only the start.

As I walked back from the gate, I sensed myself detaching. Alison flirted with another boy. I watched myself from another camera, precisely the opposite of the tactile immersion of the Connors-Borg match. I felt a slight urge to tell Alison what had just happened. It passed. I was the soldier. It didn't matter that I was attending a school where teenagers were given license to openly reveal emotions. God damn it, I was the candidate, running for president. Ken had descended. I would transcend. Like Connors, I would make a charge for the number one ranking. Like Bobby Kennedy, I would carry my wounded brother's torch into the bright California sunshine.

A fellow student approached me to talk about tennis. Having watched the Open final, he was staggered by the way Connors "came through" amid so much pressure. "To be able to hit that kind of shot, without losing your nerves, that's amazing," he said. No question, Connors' nerves held up. Ken's hadn't. All I wanted to think about was that tiebreaker, the way Connors refused to surrender and kept moving forward.

6

Seasons of Sorrow

ermit a confession. "Emma Bovary," wrote the novelist Flaubert of his most well known character, "is me." So goes my desired link to Connors. Birth order, love of the counterpunch, the T-2000, a puny body, the left hand. In a writer-subject Stockholm Syndrome, I've imposed my life arc into Connors'. It's selfish, unequal, intrusive. Having inhaled Connors for decades, all I see are events and patterns, the threads of our lives circling one another. We occupy two disparate circles connected by tennis, life's highs and, as we discovered between 1976 and '78, its lows. Events proved how sorrow squeezes its way into corners, only to emerge in odd places.

Years later, when I sat on a therapist's chair and retold what happened to Ken and my family over those two years, the picture that constantly surfaced was of a sweaty Connors grimly pacing the court in the late stages of a match, his left hand clasped around the frame, his shoulders hunched over to return serve—Jimbo the warrior, on the trail again, his body and heart taking him and all who followed to places the most rational minds ignored.

But that's hindsight. From the vantage point of 2004, it's a lie to claim that as a teenager I was aware of what preyed upon me in the wake of Ken's first breakdown and what came next. I was disconnected from pain. It was a survival instinct. My body let me play tennis. My head let me run for president.

By October, Ken returned home from a 10-day stint in The Westwood. Our father convinced him it was best to sell his part of the office supplies business to Greg, calm down and contemplate a return to college. As a Hanukah present that year, I bought Ken a picture frame bearing an inspirational message: "Don't Worry." Ken gave me two long-sleeved plaid shirts that he felt "would be a little different and cooler than the tennis clothes you wear all the time." The bigger message in our home was simple. Since we assumed that what happened to Ken was merely a one-time incident, better not to stigmatize him by talking about it with anyone.

Silence fit me like a glove. My parents excluded me from Ken's tumult. There was be no family therapy, no need for me to get involved in any of the messy complications of his recovery. I was left alone, which freed me to draw heavily on LA's common currency, celebrity. Alison Mogull called me "Mr. President." My first campaign team meeting was at the Mogulls' house up in the hills north of the Beverly Hills Hotel, in a room where Artie Mogull's gold records lined the walls. Alison showed me his bedroom, pointing to the mirrors on the ceiling. A bitter Carolyn Bartholomew confronted me a week later. "Why didn't you call me?" she asked. "You're more into that Mogull crap." She was right. Long before Ken's illness, I felt like a second-tier player. No more. Though I never advanced any further with Alison than schoolyard flirtations, it wasn't her love I sought. It was her proximity to power and fame that intoxicated me.

Two weeks after Ken's return from The Westwood, we drove to Jerry Paris' house in Pacific Palisades. He had a few extra tickets to that Sunday's football game between the Rams and the Seattle Seahawks. Ken told Jerry I was a tennis player.

"Can you be another Connors?" he asked me.

"Well, no, but at school I'm running for president, and—"

"Connors, what a guy. Do you know Connors?"

"No, but—"

"You don't know Connors? Gotta know Connors."

Yet, on another level, in a way Jerry Paris or anyone else in LA would surely dismiss, I knew Connors. As Gloria put it, yes sir, you're damn right I knew Connors. It was a private relationship. When I played, Connors' visceral spirit infused my senses. My eyes saw him when a short ball came to my forehand and I'd pounce on it and charge forward to the net. I heard Connors when I scrambled on the baseline, threw up a lob and found myself back in a point that seemed lost. I smelled Connors when I took charge of a match late in a third set, or, for that matter, early in the first, when one scrappy volley could hypnotize the other guy for an entire match. And I tasted Connors when psyching up for yet another challenge match versus a teammate who dared try and wrestle my coveted singles spot away from me. "You dislike the guy for the match," said Connors at Forest Hills in '76.

"Once you get out there, friendship ceases. It's like this—I'm on my side of the net, you're on the other side, don't come over here or we'll do battle. We're playing for blood out there."

Only my sense of touch failed me—and, in retrospect, the absence of touch left me fundamentally senseless. Connors was an electric fence, too lively for me to admit I fed off his sparks to anyone but myself. Touch, wasn't that meant for more delicate matters? Wasn't that what I thought I wanted from Alison? No, touch eluded me, even when it chased me. Touch was off the agenda when it came to the more personal matter of Ken's breakdown. Lack of touch kept me distant from what was buried deep inside me, the fear that I later unearthed like the Dead Sea Scrolls: I had made Ken sick, and since I'd followed in his steps so often, my breakdown was imminent. A hearty touch, a good hug of reassurance, was what my whole family might have benefited from that fall of 1976. Instead, I attempted to touch people from the remove of a stage. In my high school yearbook, there is a photo of me awkwardly shaking hands with another student as we hold a mock document, a parody of a political photo opportunity. Of course I'm wearing tennis clothes.

In 1977, Connors and I each encountered tragedy and the debris of emotional fallout that most painfully and obliquely strikes those who lack the tools, capacity or desire for introspection. Even when messengers arrive to provide solace, there can be no learning if the student isn't ready. Instead, what results is anguish and solitude. There was no way I could reconcile my tennis warrior with my smiling candidate. Connors was unbalanced in his own odd way too. As he had on the court for so long, all he could do was hit for the lines and tilt towards the edge.

Estranged from his father since childhood, Connors was adept at forming casual relationships with older men. From Bill Riordan to Pancho Segura, to Stan Canter and assorted cronies from tennis, Hollywood and business, Connors enjoyed the company of men who were no threat to him on or off a tennis court. One such figure was Frank Hammond, an avuncular linesman more than 20 years Connors' senior. As the two played backgammon one December day, Connors asked Hammond what he'd like for Christmas. Hammond's request was simple: Call your father. Connors went ballistic. "Big Jim" simply wasn't part of his life. Though Gloria had returned to Belleville soon after Jimmy's pro career took off, the marriage remained one in name only. "There was a civil war in that house," a Connors friend told me. "She took Jimmy, he took Johnny and that was that." Rumor had it

Jimbo didn't take his father's congratulatory phone call after he'd won Wimbledon. Never was he seen at one of the boy's pro matches.

By late 1976, Connors' father was suffering from cancer. On January 30, 1977, Connors lost a five-set final in Philadelphia to Dick Stockton. There was a melancholy mood at the tournament. Word had come that Big Jim was on his deathbed. Connors quickly left Philadelphia, and arrived home to grasp his father's hand moments before he died.

The death of his father cast a shadow over Jimmy Connors in 1977. If for some the passing of a parent opened a door into the soul, in Connors' case, much of what he did that year was to slam that door shut with malice—on people, on venues, on history. Its echoes muddled his legacy forever.

Ilie Nastase was the first to bear Connors' brunt. Though Connors had returned to the top of the world rankings in 1976, Nastase beat him four out of five times that year. Connors admitted it was hard to get motivated versus a friend, and throughout '77 began to distance himself from the man he'd regarded as an older brother. Given Ken's penchant for Nastase and my own effort to get out from under his thumb, it was an emotional challenge I understood too. On March 4, 1977, shortly before Nastase and Connors were due to play an exhibition in Puerto Rico with a purse of $650,000, an earthquake rocked Nastase's hometown, Bucharest. Nastase wasn't aware of the disaster. As his managers sought to clarify the extent of the damage and determine if Nastase's family was imperiled, they also agreed not to tell the moody Romanian what had happened lest he fly off the handle. Even newspapers were hidden from his view.

A few hours before the match, as Connors and Nastase headed to the court to warm up, Connors said, "Hey, buddy, you'd better call Bucharest. You might not have a house anymore." Nastase figured Connors was only joking. Connors won easily. Only later did Nastase realize Connors' remark was below-the-belt gamesmanship.

Several weeks later, Connors and Nastase were in St. Louis. It was the first pro tournament Connors played in his hometown in his career, which made him edgier than usual. An impish Nastase, good-hearted enough even after the Puerto Rico incident, snuck into a training room and gave Connors a friendly hug from behind. Connors flew him against a locker and said, "From now on there's no fooling around between us, buddy."

The Connors-Nastase schism came to a head that May when the two met in a nationally-televised challenge match at Caesars Palace in Las Vegas. Connors had never lost on this court. He and Nastase always ribbed each other during their matches. On this occasion the jokes were meaner than usual. After Nastase made a few wristy winners, Connors referred to "that fucking backhand" on a changeover. An angry Nastase yelled back, "You think it was lucky?" Connors leaped out of his chair, confronted Nastase face to face and let fly with a series of obscenities.

Nastase countered. "Why don't you get your bloody mother down here on the court?" he said. "You know you can't win anything without her."

Connors was floored. Silent for the rest of the match, he turned from lion to pussycat. Nastase won handily.

It was an odd period of bluster and vulnerability in Connors' life. Upon hearing of Elvis Presley's death that summer of '77, Connors said, "What a shame, there are only a few of us kings left." Like Presley, Connors was a backwoods boy from the boondocks, the darling of his mother's eye who'd rocked the world and warmed to the middlebrow charm of Las Vegas. As a Connors confidante told me, "Connors didn't like the Beatles. They were a group, a team, and they were British. In some ways, Connors thought he was competing with the Beatles. Elvis was American. Jimmy loved that Elvis did it on his own."

But there were also signs in '77 that Connors didn't always want to soldier alone. The romance with Evert was rekindled. Since the breakup of '74, each pursued several public romances, including Evert with Burt Reynolds and President Ford's son Jack, Connors with actress Susan George and 1973 Miss World Marjorie Wallace. The Evert-Connors reunion set off marriage rumors. By the next year, though, each started relationships that led to marriage.

Connors also explored the intriguing notion of a mentor-player relationship with, of all people, John Newcombe. That spring, Connors and his mother met with a psychologist. The doctor believed Connors' lack of a male role model was costly on and off the court. Newcombe was approached as a potential coach, which in those days meant more of an intermittent advisor than a constant courtside presence. He and Connors agreed to talk. They never did. Had it happened, tennis history might have been quite different. The savvy Newcombe, exceptionally keen at parsing the strands that separate victory from defeat, would have brought Connors insights into his opponents dramatically different from Gloria's mix of technical and paranoid.

It was unfortunate for Connors that he and Newcombe didn't connect, particularly since Connors' ambition was grand as ever. The resurgence of '76 proved he was no flash in the pan. Everyone in tennis knew Connors was dedicated to tennis for the long haul, and believed in himself with exceptional confidence. Finally he'd left the Riordan circuit for WCT. Mike Davies, a WCT official, once explained to Connors the rules of a complicated round-robin event. "If you win every match," said Davies, "you win $180,000. And if you lose one match—" Davies never finished the sentence. Said Connors, "I'm not interested in what you get for losing a match."

Neither was I. Elections I could afford to lose. I finished last in the school's presidential election. Defeat meant nothing. It was a delightful campaign, capped off the day before the vote. On a brilliantly sunny day, I rode around the school in the back seat of a convertible. It was the pictures of Bobby Kennedy in the 1968 California primary that inspired me more than anything. I made myself a celebrity. Schoolmates commended me on my courage for having entered the arena. One of them compared me to John Kennedy.

But there was no way I would be so carefree about the outcome of a high school tennis match. As the last singles player on our team, I warded off one invasion after another. After playing more than a dozen without a single loss, our coach, Tom Anderson, asked me to play Jai Li. Jai was tall and powerful. Anderson considered him, "a real athlete rather than a tennis player." I hated to hear Anderson talk like this, and constantly routed the many so-called athletes he'd sent my way. The afternoon he made me play Kelvin, a center on the basketball team and seven inches taller than me. I hit one low ball after another, twisting him into knots. Anderson insisted that an athlete like Li could beat me. Infuriating. Why should a sport apologize for itself? By dint of playing tennis, wasn't I automatically a good athlete? Hadn't Connors proven once and for all that tennis players—no matter how big or small— weren't sissies?

Jai Li beat me. A week later, we were set to play again for the precious singles spot. Lose it, and I'd have to play doubles.

This would have been a perfect occasion to draw on the power of the IPS community. It was common in IPS for students to publicly share their feelings and seek support. From driver's training to dental exams, from the SAT to the ménage à trois, all was fair game.

There was no way I dared mention Ken's travails. That spring he had another breakdown and landed in The Westwood again. I stuffed my family life so deeply it wasn't on my mind. But if family was too heavy, tennis was too light. In an alternative school in the '70s, competition was frowned on. Two IPS teachers, Bill Greene and Don Chronister, frequently played tennis during lunch hour. Their matches were marked by long, attrition-based rallies. Each stood at the baseline and floated back one ball after another in a poor man's imitation of Bjorn Borg playing himself. I suggested to Don that he'd probably win more points if he charged the net and attacked Bill's flimsy backhand. "We're not about competition," he countered. "We're playing cooperative tennis. Winning at all costs—that's what hurt us in Vietnam and got Richard Nixon into trouble. That's not us."

The odd thing was that though I was regarded as one of the more vocal people in high school, I never spoke of my family or my tennis. I sought votes for president but didn't dare address matters of my heart. Like Connors, I was a loner.

Versus Li, I won the first set, 6-3, forcing him into repeated errors with good volleys. He took the second, 6-2. My forehand fell apart, and his prior mistakes now found the lines.

One set for all the marbles. How it took place is rather fuzzy, but points accumulated one by one. Li lost his focus. I came to net, surprised him with a few lobs, and closed it out, 6-3. As I walked to the bench, I turned to Coach Anderson and said, "No more challenge matches. Please, no more challenge matches." Naturally, I didn't tell the news of this triumph to anyone in IPS. Nor did I want to bother my family with it. Ken's recovery was the priority, wasn't it?

Another setback came that April. At 5 a.m., our apartment's lobby buzzer rang. Two of Ken's friends begged our mother to come downstairs and drive with them to a hotel room near Beverly Hills where Ken was "freaking out" due to a mix of drugs and mania. With our father out of town, my mother drove east on Wilshire Boulevard to coax Ken home. He was naked, under the covers of the bed. Suddenly, he darted out of the room and dashed into the streets of Los Angeles.

When I woke up, and saw no one home, I figured my mother and Ken had gone their separate ways a bit earlier than usual. Just as I left for school, I saw my mother and my uncle Frank with a batch of clothes in their hands. Within an hour, an off-duty policeman found Ken on the streets of Santa Monica, a good five miles from the hotel. Say hello, The Westwood.

A few words on my uncle, Frank Drucker. The good news was that he was a psychiatrist, and able to help my parents gain some understanding and logistical assistance for mending Ken's psyche. The bad news was that Frank's temperament was light years removed from the brand of humanist, touchy-feely therapist that might have made Ken's struggles more palatable. In contrast to our father, a salesman who usually looked at the sunny side, Frank was a brooder. A month after the episode triggered by the assault charge, with Ken tucked away in

The Westwood, Frank spoke bluntly. "I don't want to sound like a Dutch uncle," he told us over dinner, "but what happened can eventually lead to a diagnosis like schizophrenia and institutionalization."

It was a horrific image. How could one incident send Ken to such depths? And yet through 1977, the episodes and altercations added up—including violent interactions between Ken and my parents. Surely, at any moment, what my parents called Ken's "condition" could be rectified with a mix of medication, relaxation and, hopefully, yes, a return to college. There was a long history in West Los Angeles of privileged kids who briefly inhaled too much of the region's hedonism before setting themselves on a path to law, medicine or business.

Here I must confess to a lack of participation. Between the excitement of my presidential campaign and the nonstop tennis season, I was exempt from duty. So removed was I from what was happening to Ken, so willing were my parents to distance me from it, that I became a free-floating nation state. Driving my own car, earning money teaching tennis and filing for my uncle, I was self-reliant. I played tennis with newfound confidence. Save for the first Li match, that year I never lost to an opponent I was expected to beat. Up against players who'd routed me before, I tested them more severely. So long as I made my way forward into the net—Connors' physical approach shots had shown me a whole new level of movement—I believed I at least was a contender versus any player of my level. In the semifinals of the high school playoffs, held at the Los Angeles Tennis Club, I won a tight singles match, 7-6, 7-6 that proved pivotal in our team's march to the finals.

There was a girl in IPS I'll call Tonya Johnson with brown hair and large doe-like eyes similar to Bambi. Tonya asked me frequently if she could watch me play tennis. I demurred. Was it that the cheerful candidate wanted to separate himself from the driven netrusher? Where precisely was my arena anyway? Finally, Tonya convinced me to play paddle tennis with her one Saturday morning on the Venice boardwalk.

After a few minutes of friendly rallying, Tonya insisted we play a few points. The similarity to tennis made the game easy for me, particularly since the small court emphasized the ardent enterprise and quick reflexes that made me an instinctual volleyer.

Several points into our match, Tonya walked to the net. "There's something else in you when you play that's different," she said. "You hold on to so much, and then, when you play, it's as if you're letting it all out, as if you're holding on to something you don't want anyone to know. You're so courageous, you probably don't even know it." The depth of her insight drew me to her but also, on a level I dared not recognize then, scared the daylights out of me. This girl knew me, was attuned to me in a way no one in my life was. She'd zoomed to the heart of my soul. Maybe that was why I was so reluctant to have people watch me play tennis. The notion of becoming president was ephemeral, fame an illusion. My tennis matches were real, occasions when I was vulnerable. It was the tennis court that was my true arena. But I was too scared of what all that meant to let someone in on it.

Tonya lived in an apartment near the Venice Beach. As was the case for so many kids in our generation, the apartment was frequently vacant. Other 16-year-olds, such as my best friend, Jeff Poe, would have been attuned enough to kiss Tonya. Not me. I thanked her for the paddle tennis and left. My fears weren't conscious, but I was unquestionably acting on them. This girl knew me not just as someone running for office, but as someone running from something. Tonya requested I call her that summer. I never did. Ken suffered another breakdown. By the end of June, he was home again.

There were days when Ken was healthy, seemingly on his way to normalcy. Then there were bizarre interludes—at least we thought they were interludes—when he was listless, unmotivated or even surly. On Saturday, July 2, Ken, his friend Mark and I gathered to watch the Wimbledon final between Connors and Borg.

Mark continued to despise Connors. Turning to Ken, he asked, "What do you think of Connors, psycho?" After Ken laughed at Mark's joke, he wondered why Nastase wasn't in the finals. Borg was the defending champ, but Connors was number one in the world. Connors' mission was to derail the Swede and prove he was once and for all the king of tennis. To me, it was a challenge match on a global scale.

Connors' 1977 Wimbledon campaign couldn't have started any worse. Practicing with Newcombe shortly before the tournament, an errant ball bounced off Connors' frame and hand. He felt a sharp pain, but continued the session. At the doctor's office afterwards, the diagnosis was not good. Connors' right thumb was broken. Of course, said the doctor, you won't be playing tennis for several weeks. The hell I won't, said Connors. A splint was dug into his thumb so deeply that it drew blood.

As with the leg pains of '75, Connors has never spoken publicly about the effects of the injury. Though his bouts of on-court vulgarity and off-court solitude contrasted with the tranquil and collegial Australians, Connors' refusal to discuss his physical traumas was right out of the Aussie sportsmanship manual. As Roy Emerson said, "If you're hurt, don't play. If you play, you're not hurt." I drew a connection between the Aussies and one of IPS' main ideas: People invoked "reasons" for their failures rather than take responsibility. It made me angry every time I won a match and heard an opponent whine with an excuse.

Classy as Connors' privacy about his injury made him, his next very public act was reprehensible. Nineteen seventy-seven marked the Wimbledon Centenary. To honor this anniversary, every living Wimbledon singles champion was invited to participate in a parade on the tournament's opening day. The man I'd spent four summers with, 1955 winner Tony Trabert, left Southern California on a Sunday, flew all night to London, marched in the parade Monday afternoon and flew home the next day. Connors had been in England for weeks. As dozens of tennis greats basked in the applause, as fans and players alike honored the glory of Wimbledon and the collective community of tennis, Connors practiced with Nastase on a Wimbledon backcourt. "There was something acutely symbolic in Connors' snub of the proceedings," wrote Peter Bodo in *Tennis*, "for it cast him as the mythic king in exile, a man who would return to the domain of Centre Court only in conquest." As he had his entire life, Connors thrived on putting as much tension and distance between himself and others as possible. When he took Centre Court for his first match, he was heavily booed.

So dominant were Connors and Borg at this point that their meeting in the finals was taken nearly as gospel, even as each played sluggishly in the early rounds. The semis were a bit more dramatic. Vitas Gerulaitis extended Borg to 8-6 in the fifth set in a superb display of all-court tennis. More notably, Connors met the future, an 18-year-old, talented, temperamental, lefthander of Irish descent, John McEnroe. That first Connors-McEnroe match was a generational flashpoint, like the Bette Davis character in *All About Eve* encountering her successor, Anne Baxter. Out to show McEnroe who was boss from the outset, Connors refused to speak to him in the locker before the match. The match was tougher than Connors desired. He won the first two sets, but McEnroe snuck out the third with adroit variations in spin and pace. Connors at last took charge in the fourth. "This kid is difficult to play," said Connors. "He tees off on everything and makes shots from impossible places." Just six months ago, Connors' place on tennis' throne seemed assured. It was clear McEnroe was a star. Borg had improved. With younger players in the ascent, Connors for the first time in his career felt the wind at his back.

Connors started the final in fifth gear. He struck 21 winners to take the first set, 6-3. From the Players' Box, Gloria Connors pounded her fist into her hand. The tiger juices were flowing. But as ex-player Gordon Forbes wrote, "He's playing too perfectly altogether—like a complicated machine that has been programmed to hit hundreds of risky winners and then been overwound. Watching him one senses over-kill. Feels instinctively that his best shots would be worth more than only one point."

This was precisely the critique many of Connors' elders made of his game. There was a belief that he tried to hit the ball too hard too often. Added to this was a perception that his shots cleared the net so low that he had little margin for error. I explored this topic with noted teaching pro Vic Braden. Disputing the assumptions that Connors' game was too high risk for his own good, Braden's scientific research proved that Connors' drives actually cleared the net by several feet. That was the only way he could generate consistent depth. The deceptive factor was his consistency. Not since Budge had a groundstroker struck so many line drives.

Still, Forbes' point was magnified by Borg's languid playing style. Since the Swede was as fast as anyone who'd ever held a racket, he relied more on innate gifts than trained skills. While Connors covered the court with the tiny steps of a crab Gloria had pounded into him since he could walk, Borg loped like a gazelle. It was a new approach in movement. Borg repeatedly tracked down Connors' best drives and floated them back with exceptional clearance over the net. The enhancements Borg had made to his monochromatic baseline game were particularly potent on Wimbledon's grass. His serve was a well-placed bullet, able to produce cheap points for him in a way Connors' delivery never could. Big serves helped Borg bail his way out of four break point opportunities at 1-1 in the second set. Borg also learned how to hit a low-bouncing chip backhand crosscourt to Connors' forehand—the major weakness Ashe and Orantes uncovered in '75.

Errors cascaded off of Connors' T-2000. Borg won the next two sets, 6-2, 6-1. I was dismayed. Ken and Mark stood up and left. "This thing is over," said Mark. "Your boy Connors is through."

I sat alone and fretted through one point after another. Connors wasn't about to back off and try to outsteady someone as airtight as Borg. Just as Alex Mayer warned his son Sandy back in the juniors, this boy Connors took more chances when behind. Connors' sense of enterprise made rooting for him a nerve-wracking process. He played the game the way it was meant to be played: strike confidently to the lines, force the action, move forward. No one tilted to the edge of the lines better than Jimmy Connors. No one was a steadier defender than

Borg. Who would blink? The Swede's deep topspin drives and short slices made it hard for Connors to land a knockout punch. At 4-4, Connors saved two break points. From 5-all, he won eight of nine points, breaking Borg at love to even the match.

In what seemed a 10-second period, Borg won the first four games of the fifth and held break points for a 5-0 lead. His mother, Margarita, began crying.

Connors found another gear. Hold, break, hold, break again— evening the match with a massive forehand volley that nearly clipped Borg's ear. Unbelievable. Connors, the man who played on emotion and momentum better than anyone in tennis history, was about to ride the wave to an incredible comeback and another Wimbledon title. There he was, slapping his thigh, his head rolling back and forth. Borg was strictly a one-timer. What did Mark and Ken know? This seemed even more obvious once Connors won the first point of the 4-all game.

And then Connors committed the rarest of possible errors. He double-faulted. At 15-30 he hit a backhand 10 feet long. Borg then broke him when Connors missed a forehand. "I got excited and rushed," said Connors. "I played the ninth game like a dummy."

Borg served out the match at love.

What? How could that be? I couldn't believe it. Ken was gone. Connors had lost. I had no one to play with, no victory. Redemption must wait. As Connors said, "the year is very young, my friend, Forest Hills is yet to come."

Connors created goodwill for himself at the 1976 U.S. Open. He remained cocky, but was far more gracious, his churlishness blunted by the fidelity of his desire to regain his title. Returning as defending champion in '77 was another matter. The summer was frustrating. As he attempted to recuperate his thumb, Connors also suffered back pains and bad losses. For the first time in his pro career, he failed to win a title during the summer. One of his more abrupt exits came at the Longwood Cricket Club. Like Wimbledon, Longwood was yet another venerable venue where Connors was once a champion. As with the Wimbledon parade, Connors in 1977 opted for the snub. After his mysterious default in the quarters he skipped out so fast he slammed a car door in journalist Bud Collins' face. "I think Jimmy was crushed by the death of his father," said Riordan that summer. "It really shook him, and affected him very deeply. I think he may still be confused about it."

As the U.S. Open began, many favored Borg or the ascending Argentine, Guillermo Vilas. A cranky Connors, asked about his injuries after an early-round match, responded testily, "You're inside my back, why don't *you* tell me how it feels?" The off-court chasm between Connors and his peers, narrowed significantly in '76 (he'd even played doubles with Ashe in one tournament), widened. Said Bob Lutz, one of the more friendly players on the tour, "None of us know what Connors does, and none of us really care."

If Connors seemed incapable of winning with his words, he never doubted his ability to let his racket make his case. In the quarters he gained partial revenge for his '75 final loss when he pummeled Orantes 6-4, 6-2, 6-3 in a crisp display of all-court fury. Afterwards, pumped up by the victory, Connors walked back to the clubhouse, as tightly wound as a drum. Gloria asked if he was still annoyed by a female spectator who yelled at Connors during the match. "Yeah," said Connors. "She said 'fuck you' to me. I told her I'd fuck her, see me after the match." One of Connors' bodyguards said someone in the crowd had said, "fuck you too." At which point Connors said, "Bring him around." As the body-guards laughed, the devoutly Catholic Gloria stared silently. Said Connors mid-Open: "It's my title, they'll have to take it."

Connors' petulance was a tragic yet appropriate part of the U.S. Open's last year at Forest Hills. Having outgrown the West Side Tennis Club, the tournament announced plans to move to new quarters in 1978. That final go-round at Forest Hills was a carnival of commerce and commotion. The new breed of boisterous fans attracted to tennis, the inception of night play in 1975, the hustle and bustle created by more corporate sponsors, and even the roiling tempers that pervaded New York City that summer of 1977 (marked by a nasty blackout and the "Son of Sam" murders) all made the U.S. Open as much public spectacle as sporting event. A spectator was randomly shot while watching a match. Another day fans were so upset at a mistake in scheduling they staged an act of civil disobedience, refusing to abandon their day session seats. Tournament officials relented.

To the old guard which cherished the pre-Open Era Forest Hills, the commotion caused by the tennis boom was personified most of all by Connors. This most American of players, this massively-selfish indi-vidual, stated publicly what the likes of Bill Tilden, Ellsworth Vines, Don Budge, Jack Kramer and Pancho Gonzalez always thought, but lacked the forum or, depending how you looked at it, arrogance, to air their views publicly.

"If you're going to play tennis, then I say play it the best you can," said Connors. "That's just the way I am. If it wasn't tennis, I'd be number one at whatever I was doing. That's something born in me." With a playing style that harkened back to the '30s, Connors overlaid a '70s swagger. It wasn't understated like those older Caucasian champs, but it was damn compelling. It was also, perhaps, necessary. Now that tennis had gone Open, it was in the marketplace, subject to the deregulation and vulgarities of commerce rather than the self-regulated amateur environment.

No one more than Connors delivered the game into American living rooms. Players like Arthur Ashe and Billie Jean King had used tennis as a means towards a broader series of political goals. In the process, they showcased what made tennis such an attractive sport. Connors, of course, was strictly a one-man army. He so wanted to make himself a big deal, and possessed such an exceptional set of fundamentals with which to accomplish his goals, that in the process he lifted himself and the sport off its feet. Unquestionably, his behavior and antics got people inside the circus tent. Once they were inside, though, he transcended the sport not as a social icon like Ashe or King, but largely through the brilliance of his tennis. From his choreographed, electric footwork to his sizzling returns and tenacious retrievals, Connors' all-out baseline attack was grand theater. By the end of the decade, Connors played 15 of the 16 highest-rated TV matches in tennis history. "I don't think anybody will ever play the game like I do," said Connors. "I push myself to the point of no return."

Invariably, Connors left his mark on Forest Hills' swan song in a way even he vowed never to repeat. In the semis, he played Corrado Barazzutti, a steady baseliner known as someone who played within himself. In Barazzutti's case, that meant he virtually never hit the ball particularly hard. Nicknamed "The Soldier," Barazzutti was similar to Borg in that he was proficient at running, fetching and forcing his opponent to hit yet one more ball. Also like Borg, his subdued persona offered Connors no overt emotional resistance. Connors was forced to provide the pace, direction and emotional intensity on every point. Adept as Connors was at dictating, it was a contrast to his upbringing. Gloria and Segura built a game designed to repel attacks from netrushers. By now, thanks to the presence of clay at Forest Hills and the ascent of players like Borg and Vilas, tennis was much more of a baseline game than it was at the start of the '70s.

Always quick out of the blocks, Connors jumped off to a 3-1 lead. Barazzutti stiffened, and at 3-3 the two played an epic game. Connors erased two break points. At deuce, he netted a low forehand. Clearly, Barazzutti was going to make a go at this match. On the next point, Connors struck an inside-out backhand to Barazzutti's backhand corner that landed very close to the line. After the linesman called it good,

Barazzutti stared at the clay in hopes of having the umpire inspect the mark left by Connors' shot. This was a common practice on clay courts.

Connors then validated all the beliefs of those Forest Hills patricians who detested him. Running across the court, he scampered to the area where his ball had landed, scuffed out the mark with his feet and impishly jogged back to his own side of the net. The crowd of 12,587 booed. Said Barazzutti afterwards, "If they let him get away with that, what else?"

"Mister Connors, Mister Connors, Mister Connors," said umpire Jack Stahr. "Your attention, please." Connors looked elsewhere. Finally, he shrugged impishly and turned to Stahr. "Mister Connors, you really had no right to do that although you meant it in fun. But the ball was good and it's deuce." As the crowd booed, Connors yelled, "I'm the last [American] you've got left, so you'd better pull for me."

On the next point, when Connors missed yet another forehand, the crowd gave a massive cheer. Said Pat Summerall on CBS, "He's got the crowd against him, but he likes that." Another group of fans countered the boos with applause for Connors. After Connors saved six break points to win the game, another loud cheer echoed through the stadium. Though Barazzutti was far from finished, Connors eventually earned a 7-5, 6-3, 7-5 win. For the fourth straight year, he was in the U.S. Open finals. His opponent was Vilas, vastly improved since Connors routed him in the '76 semis. Borg defaulted in the fourth round with a shoulder injury.

I watched alone. Ken no longer cared about tennis. It reminded me of earlier days when we played games like Monopoly, Careers, NFL Strategy and, finally, tennis. In all these competitions, Ken initially dominated me. I worked hard to be his equal. And then, just as I reached the stage where I was ready to beat him, he lost interest.

That summer of '77 Vilas acquired some of the aura of physical invincibility Bjorn Borg possessed his entire career. Coming into the U.S. Open final, the Argentine was on a 38-match winning streak. A moonie-like devotion to his coach, the crafty Ion Tiriac (formerly Nastase's mentor) and an increased fitness regimen made Vilas exceptionally formidable on clay. The morning of the final, he ran for more than two hours.

Windy conditions made it hard for either player to strike with as much confidence as usual. The lefthanded Vilas' plan was simple: hit every ball possible to Connors' forehand. Whether slicing his backhand down the line to keep it low, or whipping his forehand crosscourt, Vilas was intent on breaking down Connors' weaker side.

Connors jumped all over Vilas to win the first set, 6-2. Vilas grabbed the second, 6-3. The crowd yelled for both players. This was the magic of Connors. No matter how much he angered people with his behavior, the precision of his tennis overrode his immaturity. Connors' charisma had little to do with cracking jokes or pumping fists. Connors scarcely did either during the Forest Hills years. As he liked to put it, the U.S. Open was all about business.

As many forehands as Connors was forced to hit, he proved quite effective on that side. He drove one ball after another deep into corners. Vilas covered yard after yard. Vilas served at 1-4, 30-40 in the third. This time he was the aggressor. He struck a big serve and rushed to net to close out the point. At deuce, Connors netted a forehand approach shot and advised himself to "take your fucking time." Vilas held.

With Connors serving at 4-2, 40-15—virtually the exact lead he'd held in the '76 final—he missed two backhands and let Vilas get back on serve. In our living room, I felt a sense of dread. A tennis player knows there are only so many openings, and after a year of feeling Connors deeply in my bones, I worried about his ability to create more.

He did. With Vilas serving at 3-4, Connors reached 15-40. A big serve erased one break point, but at 30-40, Connors netted a backhand, and soon, after more than two hours, it was dead even.

Yet in another sense, it wasn't tied at all. Connors had thrown most of the punches, but let Vilas off the ropes. The cumulative impact this has on the player who's squandered the lead creates subdued anger. And the opposite for the escape artist, who on the heels of survival feels a rush of confidence. At 4-5, 15-40, Connors held two set points. Vilas, not known as a spectacular server, aced Connors. On the next point, Vilas ripped a backhand passing shot that forced Connors to net the volley. Vilas held for 5-all. Said Tony Trabert on CBS, "Man, you could cut this tension with a knife."

After the erasure incident versus Barazzutti, Connors said he'd never done something like that on a court. Now he did something I'd never seen him do on a court either. Jimmy Connors panicked. A horribly executed drop shot, a ridiculous serve-volley effort and soon Vilas served for the set.

Vilas played a terrible game. It was merely a hiccup. As the tiebreak began, I recalled what Connors had done to beat Borg the previous year. But everything was askew versus Vilas. The conditions and Vilas' variety were much harder to attack than Borg. Two netted forehands gave Vilas a quick lead. Despite catching up to 3-3, Connors netted another forehand, missed a backhand volley. It was slipping away.

Leading 5-4, Vilas ripped a deep topspin forehand. Connors thought it was out. It was called good. Taking a long look at the baseline and the linesman, clearly on the verge of a tirade, Connors bit his tongue. On the next point, Connors crept to the net. His volley wasn't good enough, and as Vilas ripped a winning passing shot the crowd erupted in the loudest cheer of the day. Chris Evert, watching from outside the referee's office, went back inside. Said Trabert, "they used to call this a sissy sport."

His anger bottled up, unsure whether he cared if Forest Hills liked him or how to fight an opponent who'd extricated himself and now appeared unbeatable, Connors was more lonely and vulnerable than ever. As Trabert noted shortly before the tiebreak, "Connors has to wonder where he's playing this match, because it seems more people are for Vilas than Connors." Despite Connors' declaration that he liked the crowd to hate him, I suspected that in 1977 a civil war waged inside him. It was one thing to make your way up the ladder on hate. People didn't like Connors, and he didn't like them, but that didn't matter if you wanted to get to the top. So his arrogance carried him through '74 and early '75. The comeuppances of '75 were the price of hubris. Connors felt that way too. But 1976 marked the first time Connors saw that people applauded a champion. His glorious tennis and tenacity made significant members of the public warm to him. Even after the first boos at Wimbledon following the parade episode, the British crowd hardly vilified him. They respected Connors for the champion he was in 1974 and the feisty competitor they knew he'd always be. Gloria was deaf to this kind of recognition. All she saw were the doubters. Jimbo, though, had glimpsed the beginnings of appreciation and perhaps envisioned another way.

Connors' senses melted in the fourth set. As Connors rushed, Vilas dialed in. Evert shook her head in dismay. Connors served at 0-5, love-40. He fought back to deuce, earned a game point. I wondered if he could come back, toothpick by toothpick, as versus Borg. Then came a double-fault. A forehand volley into the net.

On Vilas' fourth match point, Connors approached with a forehand down the line and put away an easy forehand volley. Vilas stared at the linesman and beseeched him to call Connors' approach shot wide. After a long pause, the linesman complied and stuck out his right hand.

At 7:21 p.m., umpire John Coman declared the match over. Vilas jumped up in the air, as the crowd descended on the court, fans carrying him on their shoulders as if it was the finals of a soccer game. So many spectators were on court it was impossible for the two to shake hands. Stunned, Connors walked towards his courtside chair. As a spectator tried to grab him, Connors reached forward, his arms in the air, his fists primed to coil. Pulled away by his bodyguards, Connors snarled, "Who's next?"

Connors once said, "I love winning titles with U.S. in front of them." This was not Jimmy Connors' America. It resembled an assassination scene in a Costa-Gavras movie, set amid a coup d'etat in a banana republic. A cross Gloria Connors came on the court. Connors turned to his bodyguard, Doug Henderson, and said, "Let's get out of here." Connors scampered to his locker, fetched his bag and left the West Side Tennis Club. No Wimbledon parade. No Longwood. Tonight he'd snubbed a third classic tennis venue. On his way out of Forest Hills, Connors spat on a tree. It was 7:29 p.m. Another of his handlers sat behind the wheel of a rental car. Though in the course of his career Connors perfected the Elvis-like getaway in the limousine, this evening his number one aide de camp, Lornie Kuhle, whisked him into a far more plebeian vehicle: a blue Ford Pinto. He held a small white tissue in his left hand. That evening he visited Evert, who I'd once jokingly called Connors' Pat Nixon in waiting. Maybe Don Chronister was right: competition was toxic. Wrote Peter Bodo in *Tennis*, "A man who in his own troubled way wanted to be nothing more than a hero had fallen." Years later, Connors said, "that match is still going on."

The next day I reviewed what happened with my mother. We joked and compared Connors to Nixon as someone who might one day say we won't have to kick around anymore. She wondered about his ugly lust for competition and thought he was mentally unbalanced. Borg and Vilas, dominated by Connors a year ago, had overtaken him at the high-stakes occasions he lived for. "How long," my mother asked, "can someone keep that up without losing his mind?" I flashed on what went on with Ken over the last year. I said nothing. The conversation we were having was only about tennis, wasn't it?

Yet perhaps the unraveling versus Vilas was revelatory for Connors. To steal from Winston Churchill, that last match at Forest Hills was not the beginning of the end. It was the end of the beginning.

Transition issues were on my mind that fall and winter. It was my last year of high school. Until 1976, my plan was to follow Ken and attend UCLA. Only decades later did I realize the new desire triggered by his breakdown. I wanted to go to school away from home. Given my love of politics, there was a natural, affordable choice 400 miles to the north. The University of California at Berkeley instantly captivated me when I visited it twice that fall. I sat in on two political science classes, discussed Karl Marx at a party in the hills and, most of all, was drawn to the school's history of political engagement dating back to the Free Speech Movement in the '60s. I applied and waited.

With college on the horizon, certain there was an imminent end to my competitive tennis career, I considered quitting the high school team. I'd so convinced myself to back off my ambition on the tennis court that it was difficult for me to compete with the intensity of the previous four years. Many a Friday night I'd attend a party the day before a tournament. Invoking tennis, I'd leave early. But the next morning I'd never quite give tennis its due either.

At 17, I figured I'd made the most of my limited potential. Mike Anderson, my best friend on our team, was equally unexcited about tennis. Not only did we fail to believe we could improve, we were tired of our high school coach's insistence that every time anyone on our team played each other it counted as a challenge match. A system designed to create urgency made our entire squad avoid each other.

Mike and I were burned out. It was more fun to spoof Connors than to emulate him. Just like Connors, we tugged on the sleeves of our tennis shirts and dragged our toes when walking between points. As Mike watched me go down a set and 5-2 at a tournament in Ventura, he yelled out, "the car is waiting." After the final point, I responded, "Lornie, we're out of here." Minutes later we were on Highway 101 listening to the "White Album" and engaged in one of our favorite highway activities, staring at the drivers next to us and wondering which celebrities they resembled. "Who's that guy with the big nose, Ringo?" Mike asked. That fall I began a part-time job as a clerk at The Wherehouse, a record store in Westwood. Though Alison Mogull was no longer in IPS, the memories of her father's gold records remained.

Ken continued to waver. He and Mark loved to joke about Ken's odd moments as "psycho." Ken laughed when I compared him to John Lennon. Like the ex-Beatle, Ken didn't do much of anything anymore. January 5, 1978 was the date he planned to reregister at UCLA. My parents hoped a return to school would be the right fit. Yet if it was one thing to jest about what had happened to Ken with him, I maintained a tight lid on it. Though a few of my friends who worked for Ken in his office supplies business were slightly aware of his episodes, they heard nothing about it from me.

One Friday morning, Tonya walked up to me and said, "What are we doing tonight? I'll be over at 7." As we met in the lobby, we bumped into Ken. "Your brother, what does he do?" asked Tonya. "Uh, he's in sales, but he's going back to UCLA," I blurted out, quickly changing the subject. Over quesadillas at the Sundance Café in Westwood, Tonya told me how much fun we'd have if we could go to plays, movies, museums. She said once again how she wanted to watch me play tennis.

There is a parable about what it takes to get a message. A flood hits a town. With the water reaching dangerous levels, the citizens evacuate. The preacher is told to get in a truck headed to safety. He refuses. God will save me, says the preacher as he heads into a tower. As the water rises higher, a boat comes. No way, says the preacher from inside the tower. God will save me. With the flood 20 feet high, a helicopter arrives for the clergyman. Sorry, he says, God will save me. The next day he is drowned under a violent wave. Arriving at the pearly gates, he asks God, "Why didn't you save me?" To which God says, "I sent you a truck. I sent you a boat. I sent you a helicopter. What more did you want?"

God sent me Tonya. Why did I resist her? She was friendly. She was pretty. She was curious about my passions, that is, my true passions. That was the problem. By then I was so used to a lack of genuine attention—my parents were engulfed in Ken's crises—that I lacked any clue of what to do when sincere interest came my way. Like Connors, I succeeded as a loner, counterpunching the hard way as tennis player and candidate. A candidate, after all, is someone *vying*, campaigning if you will, for acknowledegment. The presidential campaign was a way to wrap myself in the armor of celebrity. When others wanted an intimate glimpse, I scoffed with skepticism. I wasn't worth it. I was scared the secret of Ken would be discovered. And if the person I'd looked up to more than anyone was unstable, what did that say about me?

Yet few of those worries were on my mind consciously then. The only emotion I permitted myself was loneliness. Caldwell Williams once molded a room of 20 students into separate sculptures, twisting us into shapes based on his perception of each of us. He took my right hand and placed it on a girl who was flexing her bicep. He took my left hand and placed it on a boy posed like Rodin's Thinker. There I was, smack between action and thought.

Weeks passed and I didn't call Tonya. On New Year's Eve, I drove to a party by myself in Encino. While my best friends, Jeff Williams and Jeff Poe, enjoyed the mix of flirtation and music, parties exacerbated my loneliness. During school days, I felt productive, engaged in IPS' nonstop conversation and activity. Relaxation was harder. That evening, Tonya surfaced again. She walked up to me, grabbed me by both hands and looked into my eyes. "I want to spend more time together," she said. "I like you. I think we can get to know each other better. You have all this tumult in you, and yet you persevere. I admire your courage. I know the pain you're facing." Just how prescient she was would be proven profoundly within a week. As the water rose, I headed further up the tower.

Thursday, January 5, I arrived home at 5:30 p.m. to an empty apartment and the odd sound of Ken's stereo. The screen door to our patio, always closed, was open. No note from our mother. Our father was in Chicago on a business trip. I wasn't worried.

From my mother I inherited an incredible memory. We're each able to summon up the names of schoolteachers, movie premieres, phone numbers and enough random tidbits to impress the staff of Trivial Pursuit. Neither of us recalls what time she came home that evening. We will never forget what happened earlier.

Ken had leaped off our third-floor patio. All morning and into the afternoon—the day of his anticipated college registration—he wandered silently around the apartment. And then, standing on the ledge of the balcony, he jumped and landed on the concrete adjacent to our building's swimming pool. Paramedics whisked Ken to UCLA Medical Center. Both wrists were broken. His back was brutalized, soon encased in an igloo-like body cast. "What are we going to do?" asked my mother that night. All I felt was my cocoon of detachment. In my life were friends, and if I wanted, the possibility of greater intimacy with Tonya. Why not call her? I didn't even give those options a chance.

Three days later, Connors played Borg in the finals of the season-ending Masters tournament in Madison Square Garden. It was a rainy Sunday afternoon in Los Angeles, and I was more alone than ever. When my parents weren't visiting Ken at the UCLA Hospital, they grappled with dozens of problems. Over the first 15 months since Ken's first breakdown, each episode required a singular series of tactical steps. Hospital stays started and ended. A business sold. A car purchased. Legal tiffs settled. This latest disaster was far more complicated. Clearly, Ken's problems were chronic. Where would he go after his hospital stay concluded? What was the state of his psyche? What caused him to jump? With his body in three casts, how would he care for himself? And, crude as it sounded, how much did all this cost? We were affluent, but far from immune to these concerns. I figured, per usual, it was best to shut up and not make a nuisance of myself.

It was an odd tournament for Connors. The Thursday night of Ken's leap, Connors lost to Vilas 7-5 in the third, yet emerged from it curiously ennobled. With more than 18,000 fans packed into Madison

Square Garden, Connors and Vilas staged a three-hour epic. This was one case where Connors wanted to know how he'd be rewarded should he lose. The tournament's round-robin format meant a player could lose and eventually win the tournament. After the Vilas loss, Connors uttered four of his favorite words: "Don't count me out."

More importantly, this match marked a turning point in public sentiment to Connors. The New York crowd began to see Connors as a kindred soul. Away from the patrician lawns of Forest Hills, inside the intimate hulk of Madison Square Garden, Connors' affinity to New York City became more apparent. Like New York, Connors was a road-weary, seasoned warrior who'd scaled the heights, tasted the depths and kept on fighting. Like New York, he wasn't pretty, but he too dared to be nothing less than The Big Apple of his world. "If you ask me who's number one," Connors said during the Masters, "it's Guillermo Vilas. If you ask me who the best player is, it's me." Wrote Peter Bodo that spring, "Fans walk away from a Connors match feeling that they have carried away of piece of him, after becoming engaged with him in an almost personal way."

Two of my high school teammates, Ed and Ron Berman, practiced with Connors several times at the BHTC the week before the Masters. The distance between LA and Madison Square Garden seemed short that Sunday. The Connors-Borg final was a perfect distraction for me.

Connors, per usual, drove balls deep and sent Borg on the run. Connors revealed a few tactical wrinkles. In the middle of several rallies, he looped a topspin forehand to Borg's backhand in hopes of drawing a short ball. Connors also came to the net more than usual. In the first four games, Connors broke strings in two rackets. The indoor court, coupled with CBS' unsurpassed courtside microphones, made the sounds exceptionally vivid. It was a contrast to NBC's coverage of Wimbledon that seemed remote, more the texture of a regal coronation than a brass-knuckled sports event. Up 3-2, Connors served a second-serve ace to Borg's stronger forehand and closed out the game with two superb volleys, going on to win the set 6-4. At 30-30 in the first game of second set, primed to break Borg and crack the match open, Connors just missed a crosscourt forehand. He glared at the linesman, but said nothing more. Borg picked up the pace with his serve and forehand. Soon Borg led 4-0. Connors wasn't about to let the set go. The intimacy of an indoor tennis match, the rainy day, what happened to Ken, the tactile feel of the CBS broadcast, Tony Trabert's commentary—as Connors and Ken hung in the balance, there was something more at stake to me than a tennis match. If at the '76 U.S.

Open I was a Connors admirer about to become a loyalist, by January '78 I was fully invested. Even if I wasn't so enthused about my tennis anymore, I needed Connors to win that match. When Borg won the second set 6-1, and broke Connors early in the third, I worried that the two disappointing finals of '77 were about to be joined by a third. Who knew how Connors would react if he lost this time?

Borg served at 2-1, 40-15. Connors drilled a crosscourt backhand return that forced an error. On the next point, Connors half-volleyed a backhand off the baseline that drew another mistake from Borg. Twice Connors reached break point but was unable to convert. At deuce, Connors drove a forehand down the line approach. Borg whipped a forehand pass up the line. Connors lunged and surprised Borg with the angle of his volley. The Swede poked a backhand down the line, but Connors dashed to his right and knocked off a winner to earn another break point—at which point Connors hit a letcord forehand. Connors raised his arms up in the air. The crowd of 17,150 went nuts.

For the balance of the match, the two staged the classic ice versus fire points that made their rivalry so electric. Borg won on footspeed and defense, as if he were playing primarily not to lose. Connors earned points with a potpourri of scorching backhands, sidespin forehands, lunge volleys, scampering lobs and clever serves. Were it indeed a boxing match, the judges would have awarded Connors more points for landing more punches. As the third set wore on, Trabert and Summerall noted how sluggish Borg seemed. Borg's disinterest angered me. Point to point, match to match, in victory or defeat, the Swede, at least on the surface, was cool as a cucumber. It hardly seemed that he wanted to put himself on the line. Borg fans loved the Swede's cool. I hated to hear that. It was an insult to the lessons I'd learned about passion and success, drive and emotion from IPS and Connors. "I'm an asshole, you all know that," he said that year. Borg seemed to float through the arena. Connors was up to his elbows in the arena. He wanted to pound the ball into every possible corner. "I was taught that lines were there to be hit," said Connors. He wanted to prove he deserved the crown, and was willing to risk the pain of defeat to earn it.

With Borg serving at 3-4, Connors twice reached break point, but erred on two forehand volleys. At 4-4, the match was nearly two and a half hours long. Connors played a perfect serve game, reaching 40-love with a delightful creep into the net, a sharp forehand volley and a resounding overhead. A game away from the match, Connors forced Borg into a backhand error and closed it out with a resonant forehand volley. The King, yet again, was back.

Just when I was thinking of chucking the whole tennis thing, Connors rescued me. Like Ken, irrational emotions had frequently gotten the best of Connors in 1977. Like Ken, that year he was moody, remote, paranoid. Like Ken, he'd engaged in inappropriate behavior. In resurrecting himself to beat Borg, Connors showed me how to tilt to the edge without falling off. "I don't look back," Connors said in early 1978. "I can take the heat. I might be humbled when I lose as much as when I win. Life is like tennis, or business, or anything else—you have to get hit in the mouth a few times before you learn. I got hit in the mouth by things a lot bigger than tennis, but I'm still here." To see Connors defeated on a large stage and rise yet again was far more intoxicating than anything on Artie Mogull's wall. Maybe quitting the team wasn't such a good idea after all. My parents agreed. A week later I quit my job at the record store.

After Ken was operated on at UCLA, he returned to The Westwood. A body cast kept his back in place. Each of his wrists was in a cast. He complained about the pain. Not once did he admit what he had done to cause it. "I can't take it," he told me. As I saw my older brother look so dejected, I thought of the Kennedys, to the night three years earlier when Ken and I had watched "The Missiles of October," a TV movie about the Cuban Missile Crisis. Afterwards, Ken gave me his paperback of *13 Days*, Bobby Kennedy's account of that event. As Ken whined, I countered as Attorney General Kennedy might have. "You're not a wuss, are you?" I asked. "Don't be a wuss right now. Tough it out."

Ken's stay in The Westwood was short. The daily rate was over $100 a day, far more than my parents could afford for anything other than brief stays. He returned home, complete with casts and a live-in nurse. In a small, three-bedroom apartment, Ken and his pain were omnipresent. "I can't take it," he said several times a day. Our father, guilty that he'd been away during two of Ken's episodes, watched his blood pressure rise. Our mother attempted to provide normalcy with meals and domestic duties. One afternoon I heard Ken yell at my parents, "I didn't ask to be born." Another day he sat in our living room and said over his tears, "You try to make things work, and they don't. They don't, they don't, they don't." Various diagnoses of Ken's "condition" surfaced, but it seemed most clear he was schizophrenic.

I was a witness, a survivor about to launch himself into another realm. All around me, pain was in abundance. For so long, I competed versus Ken. The match was suspended. When a sibling becomes ill, writes Victoria Secunda in *When Madness Comes Home*, "normal sibling rivalry and individuation, resentments and idealizations, are moot, and the well sibling is stranded in a limbo of confusion. It is as if all the rules suddenly changed in the middle of the contest. One cannot enter a healthy competition when one's afflicted brother or sister can barely enter the gate. It wouldn't be fair. The relationship as it was—familiar and predictable rhythms of reciprocity—in many ways withers, and with it a part of the well sibling's identity."

I regained my identity in the most basic way for a resident of Los Angeles. I took to the road. With Ken incapacitated, my parents loaned me his car, a long-hooded white 1976 Ford Elite with power windows, red vinyl interior and an 8-track player. The winter of 1978 was the wettest Los Angeles winter since we'd moved to California. I waded through the water and listened to Ken's tapes, most notably his collection of Beatles songs. Alone in his car, I reflected silently, constantly playing the song, "Let It Be." One stanza in particular puzzled me. On the album, the song, "Let It Be" included the words, "there will be an answer/let it be, let it be." But in the movie I saw the week before Ken's jump, Paul McCartney sang, "there will be no sorrow/let it be, let it be." All that winter I wondered which phrase best fit.

News of Ken's jump was kept quiet. I mentioned it briefly to Jeff Poe. His brother, also Ken's age, had recently suffered a mental breakdown. Rather than commiserate on our respective siblings, Jeff and I distracted one another with drives down Sunset Boulevard and gossip. I remained obsessed with power. Who in IPS had clout? Who commanded attention?

With my other best buddy, Jeff Williams, we focused on the future. Jeff was IPS leader Caldwell Williams' son, and like me was a firm believer in the school's focus on commitment and responsibility. We spent hours talking about our dreams. Both Jeffs loved it when I told them the biggest story from my senior prom. It was held at The Ambassador Hotel, the same spot where Bobby Kennedy gave his last speech. I ditched my date (not surprisingly, I didn't ask Tonya, opting instead for a girl who was merely a friend) and searched in vain for the spot where he was shot.

Yet no matter how I tried to avoid it, the ill effects of sorrow shadowed me. One February night I went with a group to see Pat Collins, the "Hip Hypnotist" who performed on Sunset Boulevard in West Hollywood. Alan Deitch had received his acceptance letter from Berkeley that afternoon. I was still waiting. Alan and I were both eager to get hypnotized. He submitted to Collins' spell instantly, rapidly clucking like a chicken, singing and engaging in all the fun of the show.

When I sat in front of her, nothing took. "You, my friend," said Collins, "are too distracted to be here now. So just enjoy the show."

A month later I sat in the lobby of the Church of Scientology in Westwood. Since Scientology's ideas were part of IPS, many students enrolled in its courses. At the behest of a friend, I took Scientology's free personality test. As the sounds of the Atlanta Rhythm Section echoed through the room—"I am voodoo into you"—I filled out dozens of multiple-choice questions. The Scientologist who evaluated my quiz said to me, "You can't go forward in life until you identify that wall between you and others." What was he talking about? Even after I'd obliquely made reference to Ken during IPS' public sharing period—"My brother is having some problems"—I remained adept at letting my mind talk me in and out of anything.

My body wasn't so cooperative. My tennis results plummeted. A year earlier, with Ken's episodes mostly taking place off the stage of my home, I was a rock of mental toughness. With proof of his illness in front of me daily, as I watched my parents worry, I grew concerned about their health and my future. One night, I had a dream. Tonya hugged me, then walked away as she told me there was no money for me to go to college. "You'll have to figure it out," she said. I'd rejected her, and who knew if my family had the emotional and financial resources for my next big step?

I was distracted and negligent. Eager to spend as little time as possible in our apartment, I'd dash out after dinner and spent week-ends drifting between tennis and solitary drives. I felt pains in my chest. One afternoon I went to Santa Monica for my annual checkup. Forgetting to eat all day, I fainted in the waiting room. Tests revealed I had almost suffered an ulcer.

If not exactly a haven, tennis at least became an escape valve. I still held a singles spot, but started to lose the tight matches that had been my forté. My singles reached its nadir versus Crenshaw High, a team so weak that we'd often drop our top five players from the line-up and still win easily. Our coach figured it would boost my confidence for me to play number one and earn a victory. It didn't happen. My opponent was hardly skilled. His backhand was horrible, but he had a reasonable forehand and good courtspeed. A year ago, this was the kind of player I was so deft at picking apart that he invariably screamed out, "How can I lose to this guy?" This time I asked that question. I missed easy volleys and overheads. I netted passing shots where the opening was wide as a truck. Down I went, 7-5 in the third. Where was Mike with the car to take me away?

One evening, after losing yet another close match that I didn't tell anyone about, I was in my bedroom, working on an exercise for the next day's French class. Ken and his nurse were in the living room. My parents were on a brief vacation, no doubt a form of relief. Ken yelled at his nurse to get him some lemonade. We didn't have any more. Ken was frustrated. I heard their conversation, but didn't bother to emerge from my room. It bugged me. I picked up my racket and swung it in the air. I took the racket and hit the globe I'd received that snowy night a decade ago in Connecticut. Dare I forget the pleasure Ken and I had that first evening as we'd illuminated the continents? I wanted to forget everything going on in my house. My racket took a divot out of the globe. I hit it a few more times, each piece crumbling the world more and more. I slipped into the kitchen and fetched a garbage bag. After pouring all the pieces into it, I scampered down the hallway and tossed the bag down the incinerator.

Our coach dropped me to doubles to play with Ron Berman. I felt dejected. I shared none of this anger with anyone. Certainly it was too trivial for my family, too indulgent for my peers.

Doubles was far less pressure-filled than singles. Collaboration creates shared responsibility. There's also less court to cover. My guile meshed well with Ron's power. Against Palisades High, the rival school that defeated us in the previous year's finals, we held a match point, which I blew with a missed backhand volley. Though we lost, buried within that defeat was the idea that Ron and I might put our grumbling about not playing singles aside and become an effective team. As Connors said during this period, "It's like I lose the battle sometimes, but I know I'm going to win the war."

By April, my spirits picked up. The acceptance letter came from Berkeley. The death of my mother's mother the previous fall left me with a small inheritance. For $3,000, I purchased a used VW Scirocco. I took this yellow car to heart. Over a five-month period, I drove it 8,000 miles. The Scirocco liberated me. I wasn't an occupant of Ken's car. Instead of Ken's 8-tracks, I listened to my cassettes. I was my own man.

One Friday afternoon that April, Mike Anderson and I drove east to the Los Angeles Tennis Club. We didn't want to play. We just wanted to stare at our favorite venue. Three minutes later, we headed west on Melrose Avenue, turned north on La Brea Boulevard and west into West Hollywood on Sunset Boulevard. Our destination: Tower Records. This was an epicenter of fame, in the shadows of the massive billboards featuring rock stars and upcoming movies. As I whisked the Scirocco into the parking lot, we saw a Porsche with Kansas license plates wedged at an angle. What asshole dared take two spaces? Fuck him. I jammed the Scirocco into the half-space to the Porsche's right. As we got out, Mike noticed a man in a Prince Valiant haircut slumped in the Porsche's passenger seat.

Mike made our favorite joke. "Who's that, Jimmy Connors?"

I peered closely.

It was Connors.

There we were, two 17-year-olds. We were nice, friendly Jewish boys, one a lefthander like Jimbo, the other so into Connors he hit with two hands on both sides. Our idol was a 25-year-old college dropout and momma's boy who admitted he was an asshole.

I looked at Connors and walked closer. "Hey, Jimmy," I said.

"Hey, boys, what's shaking? How's everything?"

We didn't know what to say. Then I began my first interview with Connors.

"Jimmy, are you going to be number one again or what?"

"Well, we'll have to see about that, son, won't we?"

"What do you make of Vilas?"

Connors eyes narrowed in the familiar slit-like look he hunkered into before he returned serve on a big point. *Son, they're all big points.*

"You gonna tell me a guy's the best in the world when he loses to Mark Cox?" Cox was a journeyman.

Probably best to change the subject. I noticed a small bracelet on Connors' wrist, the plastic kind attached to patients' wrists in hospitals.

"Where have you been, Jimmy?"

"Little bit of mono, boys, little bit of mono. Take it easy."

Only two decades later did I realize what made Connors particularly vulnerable to me that afternoon. For 20 years, Mike and I have reviewed that conversation—the quintessential LA venue, the Porsche, the Scirocco, the mono (who was he kissing?). Only recently did I realize that Ken too wore a tiny plastic bracelet days after his leap.

Too excited to shop, I backed out of the parking lot. As we winded our way west on Sunset Boulevard through Beverly Hills and Westwood, on through to Mike's house in Santa Monica, we talked nonstop about how Connors would surely beat Borg the next time they met at Wimbledon. Between Mike, Ron Berman and myself, we devoted far more energy to talk of Connors, Borg and the Beatles than our own tennis.

All that lack of interest in our own was what made the finish of that tennis season the biggest surprise of my tepid playing career. The morning of June 15, for the only time in three years of IPS, I made a public announcement about my tennis. "Today's my last match, at the LA Tennis Club," I said. Our team was a heavy underdog versus Palisades, and figured we'd come in second once again.

As Ron and I walked out to the LATC's Court 13 for our doubles match, one of our opponents made a request. I'd known Mark Rifenbark since we played on the same team in Santa Monica Teen Tennis. A ranked junior, he carried himself with a cocky swagger. "Let's make this fast, Joel," he said as we unzipped our racket covers. "I've got tickets to Bob Seger."

Something about that vexed me. Nothing like the anger I'd felt towards Binstock, but anger nonetheless. You want to make this fast, I thought. Well then, fuck you. After Ron and I squeaked out a tight first set, 7-5, we dropped the second, 6-3. In the third, we played our best set of the season. Ron pasted returns. I aced Rifenbark on a key break point, and opened the final game with a rolling backhand topspin service return winner. Ron's sharp volley on match point gave us the final set, 6-1. At least we'd won our match.

Then we learned that Mike had won his singles and that we were ahead in the other matches. Within an hour, our team had pulled off a major upset. We were the champions, the best high school team in Los Angeles, perhaps for that moment one of the top squads in the country. And I was the captain. It was a great way to conclude my competitive playing career.

Wimbledon started 10 days later. To the surprise of no one, Borg and Connors reached the finals. Borg was out to become the first man since Fred Perry in 1936 to win three straight Wimbledons.

I'd watched six years of Grand Slam finals in our living room, virtually every one of them with Ken. I wanted no part of that this year. That Saturday, I went to watch NBC's tape-delayed broadcast at my teammate Steve Smooke's house.

Steve's father, Barry, knew the result. We begged him not to reveal it. "You'll see everything you need to see in the first two games," he said.

Soon enough, Barry's prophecy revealed itself. Connors stormed out of the gates to go up 2-love. Borg was cool as ever.

Then everything changed. Borg didn't miss a ball. Serves found corners, volleys died short, drives nicked lines. Barry's prophecy was a joke. In 109 minutes, Borg routed Connors, 6-2, 6-2, 6-3. Asked afterwards by *Tennis'* Peter Bodo how he wanted to be remembered, Borg said, "That I am a nice guy. No. I think I want to be remembered as a winner. Yes, put that!" Reflecting on Connors, Borg later noted that, "He has one weakness. He can never say his opponent played well.

That's why it feels good to beat him and why other players would rather beat him than any other player."

Connors was curt. "My serve took a day off," said a man whose delivery never set the world on fire. With Borg having started the Slam season with a win at the French Open—for the fourth straight year, Connors had refused to play in Paris—and now with Wimbledon in the bag, the Swede was halfway towards a calendar-year sweep of the Slams. When an Australian asked Connors if he'd head Down Under should Borg win in New York, Connors gave one of his more memorable responses: "I'll follow that sonofabitch to the ends of the earth .... Every tournament he enters, I'll be waiting. Every time he turns around, he'll see my shadow across his."

Connors stood at the crossroads that summer. As he had for all but one week since 1974, he remained number one on the ATP computer rankings. No player more than Connors spoke frequently of his desire to be king of tennis. "Being number two is like being number 200," he said. Yet a sense of incompletion nagged him. Much as Connors prided himself on seizing the big occasion, he'd lost six of his last seven Grand Slam finals. Though consistency kept him atop the computer, in two of those years—'75 and '77—his failure to win a Slam left him trailing others in the year-end rankings. Like a company that forecast high earnings, Connors created an expectation of success, and because he only got as far as the finals in these Slams, the defeats left his reputation on the precipice.

Never more than in 1978 did journalistic heavyweights weigh in so inquisitively on the dark clouds that loomed over Connors. The tidiness of his later résumé belies the hung jury that deliberated his case. Peter Bodo's May story in *Tennis*, "Have You Noticed? Jimmy Connors Has Changed" argued that by dint of durability and persistence, Connors had "beaten many of his critics into submission." Others weren't so laudatory. *World Tennis'* Mike Lupica wondered "Has The Champagne Gone Flat For Jimmy Connors?" The piece quoted Riordan: "Physically I still think he's the best player in the world. It's just a question now of whether he's ever going to be able to tie up all the emotional and mental loose ends and become the champion again that he really ought to be." Throughout the summer, Barry Lorge researched "Star-Spangled Hero or Ugly American?" another *World Tennis* story that criticized Connors' vulgarity and contrasted Connors' vitriol with Borg's classy ability to handle wins and losses with equanimity. "Small in stature," wrote Lorge, "he must rely on an inner turbulence to power his game. He plays well in an atmosphere of villainy, thriving on it."

But no probe proved more incisive and enduring than Frank Deford's *Sports Illustrated* profile, "Raised By Women To Conquer Men." Published just before that year's U.S. Open, the story explored the origins of Connors' game, with exceptional insight into the roles Gloria and Two-Mom had played—and, rather poignantly, the absence of a father figure and the resulting psychological havoc. "It is not Bjorn Borg who is the target," wrote Deford. "It is his own man that the boy is chasing. Jimbo will be 26 next week, and the boy and his mother can only go so far. There must be the man to accept the harsh truths, so that once again he can win finals, win other people." Deford, an even-handed, sensitive writer, went to great lengths to show how much of what Gloria and Jimmy Connors did was based on love. Yet even the compassionate Deford couldn't help but see the stew that emerged from this clannish cauldron. As he concluded: "It is strange that as powerful as the love is that consumes the Connorses, Jimbo has always depended on hate in order to win. And all along that must have been the hard way. There is no telling how far a man could go who could learn to take love on the rise."

This was far more introspection than Connors wanted. In Connors' defense, while Deford's story took him to task for doing little more in practice than bashing a few balls with significantly-weaker players, through that summer of '78 Connors made notable technical and tactical improvements. Throughout his entire pro career, a Connors on the comeback trail always focused more on throwing his service toss further in front of him and coming to the net more. A better toss helped him generate more power, placement and better court positioning. Against many, one baseline drive after another worked—but not against the remarkably steady Borg. As Segura told the teenaged Connors, he'd throw even more fear into his opponents if he took advantage of the openings created by his penetrating groundstrokes. Segura's advice worked at the Open in '74 and '76. The Ecuadorian was brought back into the Connors camp as a special consultant for the '78 U.S. Open. Gloria stayed home.

So angered was Connors by Deford's story that he refused to talk to the press during the '78 U.S. Open. So what if fans were starting to warm to Connors? So what if the tournament had ditched snooty Forest Hills for nearby Flushing Meadows, a new public facility more in line with Jimbo's down-home attitude? So what if the tricky clay was replaced by a more Connors-friendly hardcourt? If there were an available bunker, Connors crawled into it. *People put me down 'cause that's the side of town I was born in.*

CONNORS AND ME: With Connors, playing together in a Pro-Am at Pebble Beach, 1996. The next day I turned 36. After Jimbo asked what I wanted for my birthday, I requested a wild card into his next event. He politely declined, but bought me a hot dog.

RIGHT: Family foursome at the height of the tennis boom. Los Angeles, Thanksgiving Day, 1972. From left to right, Mom, me, Ken and Dad.

BELOW: Ken (right) and me, summer 1980. I'm about to start teaching at the Tony Trabert Tennis Camp.

ABOVE: With Tony Trabert, July 1973. One week later our respective T-2000s helped me win my first tournament and Connors take the U.S. Pro in Boston—his first major title as a pro.

LEFT: Dad and me, in San Francisco on vacation in the summer of 1975. Note the Fred Perry vest à la Connors.

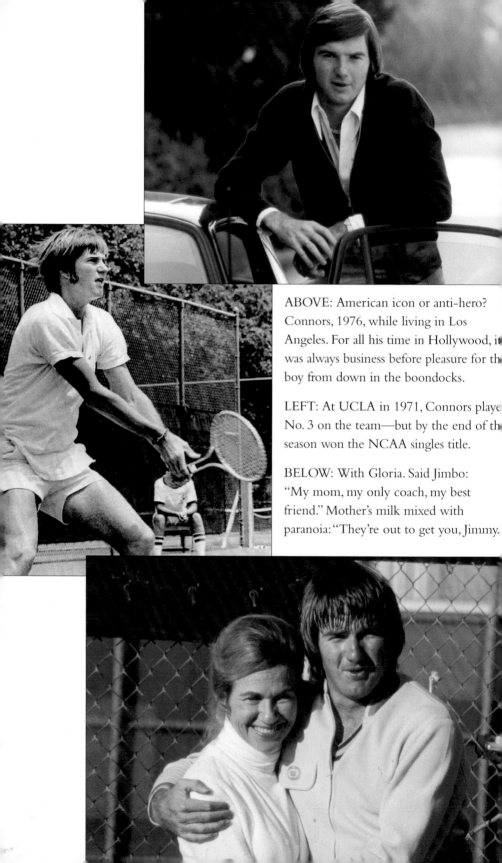

ABOVE: American icon or anti-hero? Connors, 1976, while living in Los Angeles. For all his time in Hollywood, it was always business before pleasure for the boy from down in the boondocks.

LEFT: At UCLA in 1971, Connors played No. 3 on the team—but by the end of the season won the NCAA singles title.

BELOW: With Gloria. Said Jimbo: "My mom, my only coach, my best friend." Mother's milk mixed with paranoia: "They're out to get you, Jimmy."

LEFT: Connors' first manager, Bill Riordan, was to tennis promotion what Colonel Tom Parker was to Elvis Presley: a rogue with a super-nova in tow.

BELOW: Pancho Segura, one of the most generous and insightful men in tennis history, buffed and polished Connors from a diamond in the rough into a sparkling gem. Years later, Connors barely acknowledged his help.

LEFT: Shaking it up at the venerable Longwood Cricket & Croquet Club in Boston.

LONGWOOD US Pro Tennis Championships

ABOVE: April 1974. Peas in
pod, Chris Evert and Connor
leaped to the top that year. B
then, I hated them both. The
changed my mind.

LEFT: At the Wimbledon Ba
1974, at the first dance after
pulling off the "Love Double
both won the singles at 33-1
odds. Calling off their planne
wedding later that year, Ever
Connors remained close in a
unique to athletes and erstwl
lovers.

REDEMPTION: Wimbledon 1982, and Connors wins his first Slam in nearly four years—and at last claims his second Wimbledon. During our first interview later that month, he tells me, "They can't call me a one-timer anymore."

WITH ILIE NASTASE: An older brother figure of sorts who for a time was Connors' closest friend, doubles partner and rival. Said Nastase to me: "It is difficult to talk about Connors."

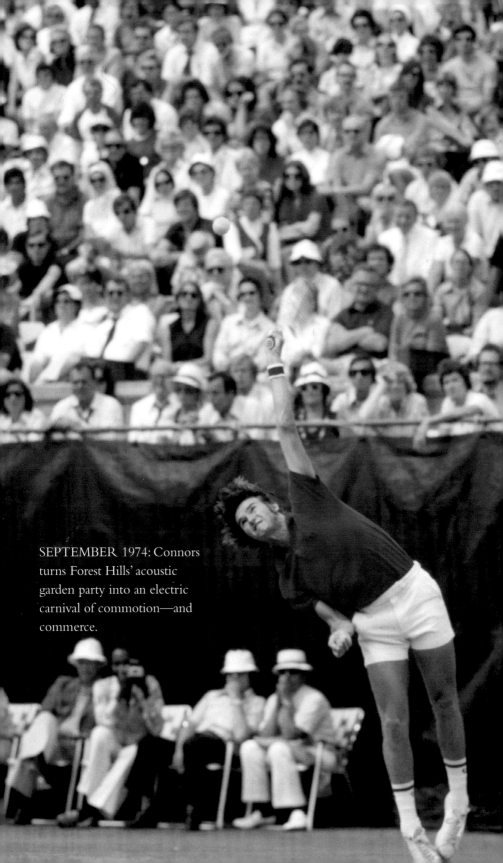

SEPTEMBER 1974: Connors turns Forest Hills' acoustic garden party into an electric carnival of commotion—and commerce.

After playing tepid tennis to reach the round of 16, for the second year in a row Connors faced a threat from a dangerous Italian. Barazzutti in the '77 semis occupied one end of the spectrum, a man with nary a pulse who attempted to bore Connors to death. This day's opponent, Adriano Panatta, was at the opposite end. The only man to ever beat Borg at the French Open, when Panatta was on he was one of tennis' premier shotmakers, able to paint every corner of the court with winners from all sides.

Mike and I glimpsed this match from a tantalizing distance. We drove that summer from LA to New York to watch the first few days of the Open. Before Connors' first-round match, I lay on my stomach and stared under the fence of a court where he practiced. Three days later, we snuck into box seats to see Connors' third-round match versus Pat Dupre. After more than three weeks on the road, we drove past the U.S. Open site one last time. The big scoreboard showed Connors-Panatta. Naturally we had no idea how much this match transformed the shape of Connors' entire career.

Panatta took advantage of Connors' sluggish play to win the first set, 6-4. But when Connors won the second, 6-4, and the third, 6-1, he appeared on his way to a routine win. Panatta didn't merely win the fourth set. He won nine of the next eleven games. He trounced Connors, 6-1, and even after Connors rallied from 3-1 down in the fifth to level the set, Panatta broke and held for 5-3.

What happened next was probably the most important single passage of games in Connors' career. As Peter Bodo noted in *Inside Tennis*, a book on the 1978 tennis year, "Connors had yielded this title to Vilas last year. He had been subdued by Borg at Wimbledon for two consecutive years. McEnroe was pressing. For Jimmy Connors, this was Armageddon." For Connors to lose to Panatta at his beloved U.S. Open was unacceptable. A Connors defeat would likely open the door for Borg to win the Open and widen the gap between them. It's doubtful, though, that when Connors picked up the balls to serve at 3-5 he dared let himself think of long-term implications. All he knew was that he was in the arena—and a new one at that. "I loved that chance to inaugurate a new facility," he told me years later. "I wanted to make my mark there. And I thrived on it when people said I couldn't do it anymore."

He held easily. Panatta served at 5-4. At 30-all, two crisp down-the-line returns off Connors backhand and forehand gave him the break. His emotions held in check throughout the entire tournament, Connors proceeded to exult as he never had. Always an ardent thigh-slapper, he punched the sky, thrust his hips and shook his head like a boxer. Between points, he walked his Cagney-like strut. It was an amped-up version of the shtick honed back in Beverly Hills. But there was nothing disingenuous about it. As *The New Yorker*'s Herbert Warren Wind wrote, "Most times in the past, many of us have felt that Connors' purpose in parading these antics was to show up his opponent and glorify himself. Not this day. Unmistakably, he was simply exhibiting for himself alone the joy he felt at playing such sensational stuff when nothing less would have done."

As he had from the outset of his pro career, Connors broke through the sport's patrician wall. For so long, tennis was held in the tight hands of wealthy people who may have competed at work, but deluded themselves into thinking tennis was purely a leisurely pursuit. Connors differed. To satisfy his needs, to generate the emotion a runt from Belleville needed, Connors had pried tennis open. Though Wind, a guardian of the game's old world values who also wrote about golf, emphasized that there was "nothing belittling or mugging" in Connors' behavior versus Panatta, he also called him "an odd duck" who "plays his best tennis when he is dramatizing himself all over the premises in his own eccentric fashion." But what Wind overlooked was that Connors' fashion was in sync with the sensibility of contemporary sports: self-dramatization. Joe Namath guaranteed a Super Bowl victory. Muhammad Ali dispensed with Sonny Liston as much with his mouth as his fists. Connors brought tennis as close to the masses as this rarified sport could ever come. Wind's odd duck was the public's prized swan.

The fans, Connors said nearly 25 years to the day after the Panatta match, "that pay their money to come watch tennis, they're begging, begging, to get into it and to be a part of it and to be sucked into what's going down there on the court. You don't ask them to be quiet at a basketball game or football game or baseball game or a hockey game. So my career was spent on trying to make a tennis crowd into those fans, the team kind of fans." Given Connors' refusal to join forces with colleagues as a member of the ATP or the Davis Cup team, it was ironic that he'd at last found a source of renewal through a connection with others. Of course, he shared himself from a stage where there was room for but one star.

This was a far cry from the ugliness and solitude Connors felt at Forest Hills. Connors' character was still revealed in bizarre forms of action, whether he was darting in and out of his limo, stiff-arming reporters or mooning a practice partner. New York fans, he told *Rolling Stone* two years later, "either love me or hate me, but it's good because at least I know they're involved." That 1978 U.S. Open began Connors' campaign to open the gates of the fortress Gloria kept him in for so much of his first 25 years. It started in January with the loss to Vilas. It accelerated by leaps and bounds versus Panatta.

Connors held to go up 6-5, and soon reached triple match point on Panatta's serve. Panatta fought back to deuce, saved another match point with an ace, then earned an add to take it into a tie-break, but just missed a forehand.

At deuce, Panatta hit a fine serve, attacked the net and forced Connors to pass him with a forehand. The Italian keenly anticipated its direction down the line, and struck a crosscourt forehand volley angled sharp enough to take the ball into the doubles alley. Connors sprinted. Stretched so far on his backhand side, he let go of his racket with his right hand and hit a one-handed drive—which whistled around the netpost (a legal shot) and landed just inside the sideline. Connors jumped up and down as if on a pogo stick. "The shot of my life," he called it.

Up against match point number five, Panatta double-faulted. As the two shook hands, they exchanged a long, soulful look at one another. "We have a saying in Italy," said Panatta, "he would not die. That is Jimmy." Crawling out of his bunker, Connors relented on his media ban and agreed to talk to the press for five minutes so long as questions were confined to the match.

In four brilliant games, capped off by one of the greatest shots in tennis history, Connors christened Flushing Meadows. He rode the wave of momentum to straight-set wins over Brian Gottfried in the quarters and McEnroe in the semis. The two victories represented twin poles of Connors' career. Gottfried was a peer, as much a friend on the pro tour as Connors allowed himself to have. The two shared a respect that preceded adolescence. Since Connors felt familiar and unthreatened by Gottfried's game, the match hinged strictly on who played better tennis. Connors won 6-2, 7-6, 6-1.

McEnroe posed another problem. After they'd played a three-setter in Indianapolis the previous month, Connors called him the future of American tennis. How fast time flew. That year at the U.S. Open, as Mike and I watched McEnroe play, I thought how much I hated this lefty punk. There I was, 18, linked to the older generation led by Connors.

Versus McEnroe in the semis at Flushing Meadows, Connors won the first two sets handily. McEnroe took a 5-1 lead in the third. Connors fought back. After he broke McEnroe at 5-3 to get back on serve, he took a swig of water, walked past McEnroe's chair and spat the water down at his opponent's feet. This nastiness wasn't too far removed from what he'd done to Barazzutti, but in this case, Connors' covert, courtside churlishness was precisely the kind of tactic he knew an elder statesman could get away with. Who was McEnroe but a teen punk? Connors went on to close out the match, 6-2, 6-2, 7-5. Borg was equally dominant versus Gerulaitis. For the fourth time in the last two years, he and Connors would meet in a Grand Slam final.

What happened that Sunday off-court overshadowed what happened on-court. Borg had suffered a blister in his thumb that was so bad he was advised to default. The Swede refused and instead took a cortisone shot.

Connors was primed. Revenge, payback, victory, history—the whole crock of emotions stirred in him, all contained in his legs which churned like pistons in practice and throughout the match. Though Connors' handlers attempted to conceal information about Borg's injury from him, he was well aware of it. It's tricky to compete versus someone who is hurt. Eager not to let the injured opponent earn any free points, the temptation is to ease up and play cautiously. This can lead to badly tentative play, the exact brand of defensive tennis that hurt Connors versus Borg at Wimbledon. The hardcourt surface favored aggression. Its true bounce also virtually eliminated the soft, short shots that forced Connors into numerous forehand errors on grass and clay.

The combination of Borg's injury, the 6 p.m. start time and the cacophony of planes flying from nearby LaGuardia Airport made the U.S. Open seem light years removed from the gentility of Forest Hills. Borg, never as comfortable in America as Europe, was even more unsettled. A couple of times, the racket flew out of his hand. Connors jumped on every possible short ball, striking drive after drive into corners. After he won the second set to go up two sets to love, Connors let out a blood-curdling, motivational scream. Not once did Borg reach break point. On match point, Connors struck a service winner to win 6-4, 6-2, 6-2. He was redeemed—and in the process, became likely the only man in tennis history to win the U.S. Open on three different surfaces.

Though Borg was classy enough to never cite his injury as an excuse, the blister reduced the impact of Connors' win. I watched the match with Steve Smooke at his tennis club. Afterwards, Steve said, "Borg would have won if he hadn't been injured." But he didn't, I countered—nervously. As Herbert Warren Wind noted, "It was impossible not to feel sympathetic towards both finalists." Connors played so well he might have beaten a healthy Borg. At Wimbledon '77, Connors played well enough, come close enough to make his injury a non-issue—and felt the agony of defeat. Borg hardly seemed to enter the arena. That '78 Open final will always remain shrouded.

What wasn't so cryptic was Connors' post-match speech. A year earlier, as Connors stormed out of New York, the Illinois native was the anti-Lincoln: kindness to none, malice to all. On this evening, as USTA president Slew Hester handed Connors his winner's trophy, the crowd's response was muted. There was a mix of mild applause, and a few boos. As a plane flew overhead, Connors waited to speak.

"It seems that every time I come to New York," said Connors, "I play my best tennis." Light applause. "Whether you like me or not, I like you."

Thirty years earlier his grandfather, Mayor Connors, handed the keys to East St. Louis to President Truman. Now here was Jimbo on the stump. Only two years previously he'd called the New York crowd "difficult" and confessed how reluctant he was to drip his precious blood. After a two-year exile from a Slam win, Connors discovered something Gloria and Two-Mom never taught him: You could win and be liked. Better yet, being liked could help you win. Competing was more fun when the people were in your corner. Never again would a New York crowd root against Connors.

A week after the U.S. Open final, I arrived at Berkeley to start college. The night before my drive north, I watched Muhammad Ali regain his heavyweight title. Calling the action for ABC, Howard Cosell quoted Bob Dylan's song, "Forever Young"—"May your hands always be busy/may your feet always be swift." Naturally, I thought of Connors. Connors and tennis ruled my adolescence. He reached his first Grand Slam final when I was 13, back when I was barely five feet tall and hated him. Ken was a senior in high school that year. His whole life lay in front of him. I was ready to trail behind. So much had changed. What did the future hold for Ken and me?

"It's all history now," Connors said after the '78 Wimbledon final. "I don't care about history. I'm not going to brood." I was in a new arena, 400 miles away from our living room, and held my destiny in my hands. On my dorm room wall I hung up a cover from *Sports Illustrated*'s post-U.S. Open issue. It was a close-up of Connors. His Prince Valiant hair flew through the air as he ripped a two-hander. The headline: "Connors Comes Through." Could I?

7

Lessons

As happened frequently with Jimmy Connors and me, the tale of how I came to see that my purpose in life was to become his biographer began in a period marked more by exile than glory—at least on his part.

At the end of 1978, Connors occupied a peculiar spot. For the fifth straight time, he finished the year ranked number one on the ATP's computer. In two of those years, 1974 and '76, he'd clearly been the best in the world. In '75 and '77, his inability to win a Grand Slam led most experts to place others atop the rankings (Ashe in '75, Vilas in '77).

Nineteen seventy-eight was trickier. Connors concluded strongly at the U.S. Open, but Borg's win at Wimbledon was more emphatic. The Swede also earned another Slam in Paris. In future decades, Borg's two Slams would have ended any discussion. But because many top men played World Team Tennis or were more focused on Wimbledon, the French Open field was not particularly deep until 1979, when WTT disbanded and even Connors returned to Paris for the first time since 1973.

Tennis Magazine believed Connors deserved the top ranking for 1978 partially because his wins in Washington, D.C., and Indianapolis were roughly equivalent to Borg's French title. Most others saw it differently, particularly since Borg's blister at the U.S. Open downgraded Connors' victory. True to his Garbo-like persona, Borg spoke nary a word about topics like rankings or his place in history. Connors, like the title character in *Citizen Kane*, was and always would be one thing—an American, forthright, optimistic, bold. "I want to finish up the 1970s being recognized as the player of the decade," he said. By the end of 1979, there would be no doubt of where Connors stood in the tennis hierarchy.

The year began with news from the Connors camp that did not involve tennis. Gloria Connors announced that Jimmy had secretly married Patti McGuire in Tokyo the previous fall. McGuire, Playmate of the Year in 1977, was the cover girl for the issue of *Playboy* featuring the infamous Jimmy Carter interview that appeared prior to the '76 presidential election. Originally from Webster Groves, a suburb of, of all places, St. Louis, McGuire met Connors at a hangout created by Connors' fellow Illinois native: Hugh Hefner's Playboy Mansion in Los Angeles. Yet for all the sexuality that lurked around such Jimbo hotspots as Hefner's and Caesars Palace, Connors was considered a prude. Rarely was he seen around the locker without a towel tied to his waist. He blushed like a choirboy when Patti sent an erotic birthday greeting to him at the U.S. Open. And when *US Magazine* ran pictures of her in a bunny outfit as an accompaniment to a lauda-tory profile of Connors, his first instinct, he told me, was "to beat the shit" out of the publisher.

Since it was soon revealed that McGuire was pregnant, many believed Gloria made up the autumn marriage story to avoid the taint of a shotgun marriage. It was acceptable for her offspring to use every form of profanity in front of thousands in person and millions on TV (one of Connors' most notable tirades saw him calling an umpire "an abortion" while a cross dangled from his neck). But the notion of a love child was intolerable. The Connors camp huddled. Soon, Connors left LA for Florida. Gloria was never seen again at a Grand Slam tour-nament. On August 1, Patti gave birth to a boy, Brett. Connors called his son "a cool little guy" who gave him "new incentive."

The unanswerable question about the impact of Patti and Brett on Connors: anchor or distraction? Prior to the '70s, athletes were written about as if they barely had private lives, so the topic went unanalyzed. But a number of factors—the growth of television, the collapse of walls between public figures and journalistic inquiry, an increased audience of media consumers—pried open the doors. The only pattern I've found is that journalists in happy relationships grant credence to the anchor notion, while those unattached or anguished take the opposite view.

There were two people far more significant than Patti or Brett who posed challenges for Jimmy Connors in 1979: Bjorn Borg and John McEnroe. That year marked the first time Connors faced a two-front battle. It was one thing when an Ashe, Newcombe, Orantes or Vilas played the match of his life to beat Jimbo at a Slam. Those were one-off occurrences, and in their own way, tributes to Connors' excellence. So it was when Borg beat Connors at Wimbledon in '78. "Borg took lawn tennis to new heights," wrote veteran British journalist Lance Tingay, noting the high quality of Connors' tennis. Even the Swede agreed it was the best match he'd ever played.

In 1979, the Swede's aura of invincibility grew even greater. If Connors' defiantly solo, swagger manner made him tennis' Elvis, the stoic Borg was the Beatles, dubbed the "Teen Angel" when he became the first tennis player to attract swooning teeny-boppers at Wimbledon.

For much of the '70s, Connors was the only man with enough fire-power to melt Borg. And then, in the last year of the decade, as if to prove in his own quiet way which man indeed was the best player of the '70s, Borg stepped on the accelerator. His serve, already one of the best in the game, grew faster and more accurate. His baseline drives went deeper and harder. In prior years, Borg tried to beat Connors with a game different than his own, attempting the mix of finesse and attack employed by most Connors conquerors. In 1979, he whipped Connors any way he wanted. Borg easily won all six of their matches that year, his dominance most emphatically demonstrated with a 76-minute, 6-2, 6-3, 6-2 bludgeoning in the Wimbledon semifinals. Said Borg, "I was scared of Jimmy before because he had beaten me so many times. I didn't know how to play him, but it's a different story now." The aura that had enveloped everyone else smothered Connors.

Despite the repeated losses, Connors remained upbeat. Much as Connors hated losing to anybody, there was never a sense when he lost to Borg that the loss eroded his concept of himself. Connors had beaten Borg before when the big money was on the line, and with just a few more solid strokes, felt confident he could beat him again. Versus merely one solitary Swede, Jimbo was still the number one contender and America's great hope. Throughout 1979, no matter what happened versus Borg, Connors and the world knew he held the U.S. Open title.

Connors' pot boiled quite differently once McEnroe arrived near the top. He'd charged boldly in late '78, winning the first four singles titles of his career, capping the year with a win at the Masters in January '79 that included his first victory over Connors. Down 7-5, 3-0, Connors retired due to a blood blister. It appeared that he preferred to default rather than give McEnroe the satisfaction of a complete victory. Two other McEnroe achievements that fall of '78 were exceptionally notable. In Stockholm, McEnroe played Borg for the first time and beat him 6-3, 6-4. It was Borg's first loss to a younger player. And for all Connors' talk of how he loved America, it was McEnroe who in December led the U.S. Davis Cup team to its first title in six years. McEnroe's eagerness to represent his country sharply differentiated him from Connors. He earned kudos from tennis greats such as Davis Cup captain Tony Trabert, as well as Don Budge, Jack Kramer and Rod Laver. McEnroe's stalwart Davis Cup record also went a long way towards nullifying concerns about the hostility he frequently displayed with officials, sponsors, media and fans.

Connors felt a much more visceral antipathy toward McEnroe than Borg. He and McEnroe were lefthanded, emotionally volatile Irish-Americans who lusted for victory. Like Connors, McEnroe was a bloodthirsty competitor, a consummate opportunist who hit the ball on the rise and created a climate of oppression for his opponents. There was a kindness to Borg that separated him from his warrior self. He came off the court relieved to have completed the requisite task. No such gap existed in the psyches of Connors and the young McEnroe (the older McEnroe proved different than Connors or Borg). Each wanted to demonstrate dominance in every way possible.

But notable differences between Connors and McEnroe made it very difficult for the older lefthander. First, McEnroe had a weapon Connors sadly lacked: an outstanding lefty serve. Though McEnroe's sideways-to-the-court motion was rather unorthodox (and the bane of teaching pros who spent hours undoing students who'd try to emulate McEnroe), his skill at turning his hips, shoulders and arms into the ball was exemplary. He was unrivalled at pinpointing corners with the precision of a racket-wielding Sandy Koufax. Though as a junior McEnroe played a rather subtle allcourt game, once his serve blossomed in the pros his netrushing attack became ferocious.

Connors had built his game to repel serve-volley invasions, particularly versus such classic, clean hitters as Stan Smith, Brian Gottfried and others of that era. But McEnroe struck the ball differently. Insensitive as McEnroe was towards people, the delicacy of his hands was like no one in tennis history. Taught by a former Mexican Davis Cupper, Tony Palafox, McEnroe's game synthesized the best of both worlds: the poetic finesse of a Latino with the killer instinct of an American. This extraordinary package made McEnroe adroit at befuddling Connors in two ways. First, he anticipated Jimbo's passing shots with remarkable quickness and agility. Second, McEnroe was extraordinary at mixing paces and spins from all corners of the court. Said Arthur Ashe, "Borg and Connors are like sledgehammers. But this guy's more of a stiletto. A nick here, a piece there, and pretty soon you're bleeding to death."

Connors was a body puncher à la Joe Frazier. McEnroe resembled Muhammad Ali: float like a butterfly, sting like a bee. The serve stung most of all. And whenever Connors served, McEnroe's variety continually kept Connors off-balance and neutralized him long enough for McEnroe to either attack directly on his service return, make his way to net mid-rally or force Connors into errors. When necessary, McEnroe stayed back on his second serve and was one of the few players able to win points from the baseline versus Connors.

Connors lost this way to Nastase early in his career. He was similarly massaged by Ashe, Orantes and, to a lesser degree, Newcombe, in his Slam losses of '75. But Ashe and Newcombe were past 30. Nastase lacked staying power. Orantes was only effective on clay. McEnroe turned 20 in February '79. That May, at the prestigious WCT Dallas event, he became the first player since Ashe at Wimbledon '75 to beat Connors and Borg in the same tournament. After Connors was routed, 6-1, 6-4, 6-4 in the semis, he was in no mood to talk. "Ladies and gentleman," said WCT PR director Rod Humphries, "Jimmy Connors has left the building, left the city, and has probably left the country." Though Connors beat McEnroe many times well into the '80s, to do so he needed to be clicking both as counterpuncher and aggressor.

Oddly enough, the previous week Evert, the defending U.S. Open champ, lost for the first time to Tracy Austin, a younger American who played much like Evert and was regarded as her successor. And just as Evert could to some degree stomach a loss to an improved European rival in Martina Navratilova (who'd beaten her at Wimbledon in '78 and would do so again in '79), surrendering the crown of America's best galled her too. The keen parallel in Evert and Connors' paths as competitors helped them draw closer to one another in a way unprecedented in sports history. How many athletes have been engaged to one another and fought similar battles? Several years later, on the eve of the U.S. Open, Connors watched Evert practice. "Hit the ball," Connors encouraged the former love of his life. "Hit it like you did before the war." Which one?

The coincidental link between Connors–McEnroe and Evert–Austin became exceptionally vivid at that year's U.S. Open. There were rumblings prior to Connors' semifinal versus McEnroe of a Connors back injury. He said nothing. McEnroe's racket said everything. His 6-3, 6-3, 7-5 rout of Connors showed exceptional prowess and maturity. McEnroe read Connors' service returns and passing shots like a book. From the baseline, he numbed Connors with so many different paces and placements that he started to make Connors retreat. John

Newcombe, calling the action with Tony Trabert on CBS, assessed the tactical and generational implications. Given McEnroe's penchant during this match for hitting fairly benign service returns and off-pace groundstrokes, Newcombe was surprised how reluctant Connors was to occasionally serve and volley or sneak his way into net from the baseline. The emotional toll was even worse. "It was only a few years ago," said Newcombe, "Connors was the guy beating up on Rosewall. Now, he's got a young guy putting him in all sorts of trouble." But whereas Rosewall was a 39-year-old a few ticks short of midnight, Connors in 1979 turned a mere 27.

Newcombe also noticed something in Connors-McEnroe that Connors soon enough used to his advantage. McEnroe's mouth was often louder than his racket. Certainly Connors displayed his share of vulgarity and hostility towards opponents, officials and spectators. But Connors rarely lost his temper when he was in control of a match the way McEnroe did. Connors also attempted his share of jokes that, however base ("Jock slipped on that one, folks") were his attempts to build a connection to the crowd.

But here in this semi, with McEnroe beating the daylights out of Connors, McEnroe berated linesmen. Years later, McEnroe admitted that he often thought at these times of defusing his on-court tension with a joke. But that was one area where he lacked finesse, so instead he either said nothing, yelled or scowled. It was not particularly attractive to see someone with a significant lead lose his temper. While McEnroe stewed, Connors became the people's choice, not just for the sake of endurance the way he had the previous year, but for the sanctimony of the game itself. Versus McEnroe, Jimmy Connors became not just the more liked player, but the better behaved one. When McEnroe jawed with the chair umpire, Connors turned in mock disbelief to the crowd. Connors is wondering, joked Newcombe, "How can you carry on like that?" As Connors later noted, "They came up with someone worse than me."

The generational changing of the guard was made official the next day when McEnroe beat Vitas Gerulaitis in straight sets to win the tournament. Earlier that afternoon, Austin ended Evert's four-year run of Open championships with a dominating 6-4, 6-3 victory. That fall, Evert spoke for herself and her ex-fiancé. As she drove along a Florida turnpike with *World Tennis'* Steve Flink, Evert said, "I watched Jimmy play McEnroe at the U.S. Open, and he had the same look in his eyes as I think I have when I play Tracy. McEnroe and Tracy are so young and confident. They really look forward to playing us, and they go out there thinking they're going to win. You can feel it, and it can be very intimidating."

Though at the end of 1979 Connors was ranked number two on the ATP computer, this was largely a spot earned by dint of his consistency and a few subpar results from McEnroe. Connors reached the semis of all three Grand Slams and won eight tournaments. But his losses to Borg at Wimbledon and McEnroe at the U.S. Open made it clear he was the world's third-best player.

Unquestionably, Connors ranked head and shoulders above others. He threatened Borg and beat McEnroe (twice in best-of-five set matches in early 1980), but as the decade began, the men's tennis marquee showcased Borg and McEnroe. Connors was the third wheel, a critical, important part of the conversation, but increasingly the odd man out.

The incredible Borg-McEnroe final at Wimbledon in 1980 further diminished Connors' significance. Only after McEnroe overcame seven match points did Borg win his fifth straight Wimbledon, 8-6 in the final set. Borg-McEnroe's sublime fourth set tiebreak, won by McEnroe 18-16, obliterated memories of the '76 U.S. Open tiebreak between Connors and Borg. Connors lost to McEnroe in the semis 6-3, 3-6, 6-3, 6-4 after squandering a 4-2 fourth-set lead. He also further advanced his statesman campaign. After McEnroe badgered an official, Connors said, "Shut up. Grow up. You're a baby. I've got a son your age." The irony of Connors as a spokesperson for maturity was not lost on anyone.

The Thompson half of his family had made Connors a champion. Now it was time to engage the Mayor Connors side and kiss his share of babies. Yet what came off as acceptable cornpone in New York wasn't as successful on British soil. Wimbledon's fans eventually accepted Connors as champion and competitor, but the link between Britain's Church of England, upper-crust reserve and Connors' Catholic, boisterous upward mobility was more a platonic affinity than the romance he built with New York. "Spill your guts at Wimbledon, and they make you clean them up," said Connors.

There was also the matter of how Connors' massive ego meshed with each event. Win the Open, and, as in America, you are the man, a bold, ruthless conqueror, accountable to nothing but the idea of individual success. Such is the code of democracy and the marketplace. Win at Wimbledon, and you remain humbled by the event's grandeur. This is what made classy sportsmen such as Laver, Newcombe and Borg so revered by the British: their acceptance of Wimbledon as a cathedral, where you bow and take your place beneath a greater presence. McEnroe, embarrassed that he excelled at a minor sport rather than the major team sports he loved as a kid, valued the way Wimbledon blunted individualism. Connors, of course, bowed for no one. His cause at Wimbledon also wasn't aided by the fact that 1980 marked his sixth straight failure to earn a second title there. By then it was clear the heir apparent to King Bjorn was McEnroe. Connors was a ruler from an earlier era—and one with a rather short term at that.

Yet there was an edgier side to McEnroe when he played Connors. Versus Borg, he behaved impeccably (or at least tried to). Certainly, McEnroe respected both of his rivals as champions. But while he revered Borg, there was something in his own background that made him, as he frequently put it, "clash" with Connors.

The son of a Manhattan attorney, raised in an upper-middle class home, McEnroe was educated at an exclusive prep school and spent a year at Stanford. While Connors came from a middle-class town where kids likely did not attend Manhattan prep schools or elite private colleges and often ended up in blue-collar jobs, McEnroe's New York City peers went on to be well-behaved, educated, white-collar professionals. Underneath his bluster, McEnroe, if not particularly cultivated in manners and the arts at that age, possessed the capacity for intellect, introspection and something that eluded the ever-combative Connors: appreciation of the talents of others.

Borg's angelic qualities inspired McEnroe. Besides knowing that he could ill afford to fritter his energy versus the formidable Swede, McEnroe was also enamored by Borg's tranquil command of everything from baseline rallies to groupies and even opponents. In only the third match between the two, an upset McEnroe screamed at himself and officials. At 5-all in the third set, Borg motioned for him to come to the net. McEnroe anticipated an admonition. Instead, Borg politely told him that everything was going to be OK and that they should enjoy the great tennis they were playing. To the young McEnroe, convinced until he became a great tennis player that he was an unattractive bundle of nerves, what was more appealing than a kind Swede who attracted chicks by the dozen and competed with such poise? Add to this the delightful stylistic contrast between McEnroe the attacker and Borg the defender, and the table was set for matches that were at once competitive and aesthetically pleasing. Borg-McEnroe represented a tennis utopia. Nowhere was this better demonstrated than at Wimbledon, where the lushness of the grass and the brief points harkened back to the pre-Open days.

If Borg-McEnroe promised the dream, Connors-McEnroe delivered reality: a knockdown, kick-in-the-pants brawl, contested most vividly on the utilitarian hard courts of America's metallic public tennis center, Flushing Meadows. Wimbledon was tennis' ultimate club, so exclusive it literally took decades for applicants to get in. Flushing Meadows was the ultimate public park. Save for the two weeks of the U.S. Open, all it took to play there was a few dollars for court time.

A consummate feel player, McEnroe absorbed the sensual differences between Borg and Connors. Where Borg floated, Connors grunted. Connors wasn't cool. He was hot, red-hot, his ambitions based in a desire to escape the streets of Belleville and East St. Louis. The urbane McEnroe, though hardly a patrician, found the intensity of Connors' ambition at once distant and, in some ways, uncomfortably familiar in its rawness and generational proximity. McEnroe's father, the son of a security guard, had put himself through law school at night. For all of McEnroe's New York sophistication, he knew—and dreaded—the narrowness it took to be a champion. Connors' focus scared him. Versus Borg, McEnroe felt transcendent, his racket in the clouds. Versus Connors, he was more bound to the ground than he dared desire. McEnroe-Borg hinged strictly on the impersonal matter of execution: one man's offense versus another's defense. With Connors, it was personal, bound up in the mutual animus of two dogs fighting for the same bone. If Borg was the Beatles, then McEnroe was the Rolling Stones, another cool British band. And if both cited Elvis-Connors as an inspiration (there is no doubt that Connors' initial dominance over Borg and McEnroe aided their improvement), neither Borg nor McEnroe had Connors' voracious, unsophisticated fidelity to tennis. For even though Borg was a champion, he also emanated a certain indifference to tennis that McEnroe, a dabbler in music and art, a man who fancied himself more than a tennis player, found attractive.

After the Paul Anka musical foray of '75, Connors stripped himself of cross-cultural delusions. He was a tennis lifer. It was just so different for McEnroe to compete against Connors than Borg. A loss to Borg merely meant he'd been outhit by a reluctant killer. But Connors was a hungry assassin, at the first signs of hope ready to drag McEnroe into a cesspool of doubt, rage and raw, sloppy ballstriking. With Borg, McEnroe brought out the paintbrush. With Connors, he strapped on his boots. A sharp Connors could outrally McEnroe from the baseline, hit solid returns from close in, back McEnroe off the net with good lobs, make his way to net and expose McEnroe's lack of conditioning—and, what I believed, was his twirpy desire to be cool.

The coolness of Borg-McEnroe infuriated me. It annoyed me to see people talk about tennis and think that victory was merely a matter of flicking the right passing shot like Borg or tapping a drop volley like McEnroe. Cool was what IPS taught me to despise. It was chickenshit. I knew better, because Connors showed me that success required commitment and visible intensity. But it was hard for Connors to make a player like McEnroe grind it out at Wimbledon. The U.S. Open, Mike Anderson and I believed, was a different matter. There, we thought Connors could derail McEnroe's muse and play real, mano a mano hardcourt tennis—to get down in the boondocks where the game was truly fought.

Few believed in Connors by 1980. "Mention the name Jimmy Connors to tennis mavens," wrote Michael Segell in *Rolling Stone* on the eve of that year's U.S. Open, "and, in most cases, you'll hear a sweeping denunciation of his talents: He's washed up." Of course it was testimony to Connors' cultural impact that he was deemed a worthy topic for this magazine. "Since his marriage and the birth of his son," wrote Segell, "the word is that Connors has a new attitude—more mature, less abrasive. He also hasn't won many tournaments during this time." The truth was that the seven titles Connors won since Brett's arrival trailed only Borg's 11 and McEnroe's nine. What mattered was the perception that Connors was in decline. At a party that summer I saw a high school friend. He wore a Fila warmup jacket similar to Borg's. "Connors is through," he said. "I don't pay attention to him anymore. From now on it's all Borg and McEnroe." This person played a little tennis, but compared to him, I was a touring pro.

"What the fuck do you know?" I asked. Even I was surprised by the intensity of my response. But I shouldn't have been. It was an even-numbered year, and Connors had won the Open in '74, '76 and '78. The day before Connors played McEnroe in the semis, Evert avenged herself, thrashing Austin 4-6, 6-1, 6-1. Just before the Connors-McEnroe match, Evert beat Hana Mandlikova in the finals. The Queen was back to the throne. In a hallway just outside the stadium court, Connors congratulated Evert's mother. No doubt the King recognized the symmetry.

And so when Connors took a 3-1 lead in the fourth set versus McEnroe, having already gone up two sets to one, I had two thoughts. The first was to call Mister Fucking Fila and ask if he still believed Connors was finished. The second was to call Mike Anderson, watch Jimmy close it out and discuss how he'd beat Borg the next day. After all, he'd lost but one set to the Swede in three U.S. Open matches.

Connors-McEnroe started off as a rerun. Just as in '79, McEnroe won the first set, and as he stayed ahead in the second, I felt a sense of dread. I was in our living room, alone. At this point, McEnroe seemed to have drained the day of possibilities. His play blunted Connors and minimized the crowd's enthusiasm. Said Pat Summerall on CBS, "I've got a feeling they're about to get into it." He was right.

Connors served at 4-5, 30-30. McEnroe took his backhand return exceptionally early, bumping it down the line to reach set point. Connors hit a wide serve to McEnroe's forehand. The return sailed long. For the first time, the crowd erupted. Connors held, and stepped up to return serve. Unlike Borg, who stood so far behind the baseline to receive serve that McEnroe controlled most of the court's geography, Connors stepped on the baseline—and moved inside it to return McEnroe's second serve. Connors wanted to crowd McEnroe and let him know he was primed to pound every ball possible. With his trademark squeaky shoes and little steps, Connors moved in and struck fierce returns and passing shots. At break point, Connors dashed across the court and hit a one-handed backhand down the line to go up 6-5, then held at love to square the match.

McEnroe grew distraught. He thought the chair umpire, Don Wiley, hadn't noticed a let cord serve on the last point of the second set. "Tell me," McEnroe demanded, "when you're going to get one right, Mr. Incompetent." Trabert noted how quiet Connors was. The crowd was in Mayor Connors' corner. He wasn't about to lose a single vote.

Among those watching were Jimbo loyalists Nastase and Segura. No matter how rudely Jimbo treated them, no matter if they were in or out of his circle, they continued to watch him battle. Segura sat literally on the court in a special corner box the USTA built to seat tennis legends. As Connors and McEnroe paced into corners, the likes of Segura, Jack Kramer, Don Budge, Bobby Riggs, Vic Seixas, Althea Gibson and Fred Perry gazed and conjectured. None felt Jimbo's ups and downs more viscerally than Segura. Much as he respected McEnroe's serve and volley, Segura believed McEnroe's groundstrokes were, as he put it, "flimsy." With sound forward movement, Jimbo must exploit this weakness.

As the third set wore on, Connors did just that. As long as Connors returned McEnroe's serve, he was in charge of the points. Trabert noted how body language told all. McEnroe pouted, Connors walked with confidence. Connors won the third set, 6-0, broke McEnroe early in the fourth, and was up 0-2, love-30 on McEnroe's serve. He'd won eleven straight games. Two good serves leveled the game. At 30-all, Connors' return forced McEnroe to float his volley. Per Segura, Connors moved forward, primed to volley McEnroe's volley into the open court—and missed. McEnroe got out of the game. Connors remained sharp. Serving at 2-1, 30-30, he surprised McEnroe by serving and volleying on his second serve. Another fine serve put Connors just three games away from his first Grand Slam final in two years. Said Trabert of McEnroe's listless play, "That's not going to get it done." I was jubilant, but held off on calling Mike and risk losing my focus.

McEnroe held. Connors served at 3-2. Service games at this point become like late innings in a baseball game. The server-pitcher wants to sit on his lead like a mother hen, carefully giving just enough air to apply pressure. Closing out a match is rarely clean.

If the clash between McEnroe's serve and spins and Connors' return and pace were the two obvious points of conflict, the less-analyzed factor was that each of them was lefthanded. As a lefthander myself, I knew the awkwardness this created regardless of playing level. Since lefthanders are only 10 percent of the population, they're used to playing righthanders. As righties try to adjust, lefthanders build instinctive patterns. But when a lefthander encounters one of his own, the circuits go awry. Rod Laver felt uncomfortable versus lefty Tony Roche. Emulating Laver, McEnroe played a more classic lefthanded game than Connors. A textbook lefty strategy is to swing the serve wide in the ad court to the righty's backhand. But versus Connors, it went to the forehand, a side with much more reach and power than a righty backhand. McEnroe also liked hitting angles to get his opponent off balance, but Connors' compact strokes, agility and powerful counterpunches made them far less successful. How could McEnroe float like a butterfly when he felt crowded and shoved?

Connors ran his share of pet plays, too. Though his forehand wasn't as strong as his backhand, he proficiently pounded it deep and hard all day long, particularly crosscourt to a righty's weaker backhand. This often yielded an approach-shot opportunity—or better yet, a high floater Connors was able to volley for a winner. Versus McEnroe, alas, a crosscourt forehand went to McEnroe's forehand. The younger lefthander was so deceptively quick (his experience as a soccer player was apparent when he glided across the baseline) he retrieved and confounded Connors with a variety of high, low, short and deep replies—often crosscourt, but occasionally slapped down the line. Connors' twisty serve, with just enough spin to find a righty's backhand, posed little problem for McEnroe, who was extremely adept at moving forward with his short strokes to attack the net off a return on either side. Finally, Connors loved to lace his backhand crosscourt. The penetration of Connors' drive made it hard for the opponent to drive through the ball enough to pin Connors back. Instead, the topspin that was applied to every righty forehand caused the ball to land short and give Connors yet another chance to rip it deeper or approach down the line—back to the righty's backhand. This was a textbook play for Connors when he'd beaten Borg. Here again, McEnroe posed a problem. Connors' crosscourt backhand went to McEnroe's backhand. McEnroe was better than anyone in tennis history at blunting pace. In his instance, he sliced his backhand into nooks and crannies with just the right mix of depth and off-pace so that Connors felt unsettled and ill-prepared to drive the ball and move forward. McEnroe's backhand slice also went deep and down the middle, nullifying any angles or, worse yet for Connors, down the line and to the shot Connors missed more than any, his low forehand.

To net out the lefty-lefty comparison, McEnroe had a much better serve, volleys and was more adept at mixing spins and paces. Connors' game was more patterned and predictable, and because of that, he was more hindered by playing another southpaw.

For Connors to beat McEnroe, he needed to stay on the attack that to this point had earned him 12 of 14 games. And here, so close to the finish line, he lost his way. A backhand approach, normally struck instantly down the line to the righty's backhand, was hit crosscourt and wide for love-15. Connors' failure to put away a benign forehand volley made it easy for McEnroe to hit a passing-shot winner. At 15-30, Connors wisely served and volleyed off his second serve—and missed an easy backhand volley. But then Connors recovered. A forehand volley winner, a good serve and a rip-roaring crosscourt backhand pass gave Connors an ad. But it disturbed me that Connors needed a big winner when earlier in the point he passed up a prime chance to come to net. Was he backing off the attack?

A point away from a 4-2 lead, Connors served to McEnroe's forehand. McEnroe hit one of the rarest shots you'll ever see in pro tennis—an off-pace, underspun, crosscourt forehand return. It's a shot you see all over the world on Sunday mornings, a mini-chop, barely hacked over the net. Once again, the lefty to lefty geometry vexed Connors, as he overhit a crosscourt forehand wide. Versus a righty, driving deep to the backhand, Connors wouldn't have felt quite the need to hit the ball as close to the line. Credit also goes to McEnroe's great speed.

McEnroe appeared to be baiting Connors. Go ahead, he dared, tag the ball and come in—but it better be on a great approach shot, or else I'll dink another one just annoying enough that you won't be able to put away the volley. And unlike McEnroe, Connors was not as comfortable hitting more than one volley to win a point. Connors preferred a big approach shot and a crunching volley. McEnroe wasn't going to let him get off easy. Like Corrado Barazutti, McEnroe played within himself. The difference was that unlike the monochromatic Italian, McEnroe's range of colors was wide as the rainbow.

The next two points, 19 and 17-stroke rallies, ended the same way. Connors approached, and McEnroe struck his passing shots just hard enough to force him into volley errors. 3-3 in the fourth.

I called Mike Anderson. We spoke so often we never identified ourselves. "I don't like this," I said. Not until Connors and McEnroe shook hands did our conversation end.

Connors served at 3-4. Everything about McEnroe now was firmer—deeper, shorter, sharper, crisper on offense, airtight on defense. Facing his sixth break point of the game, Connors made a forehand drop volley that McEnroe ran down, but drove into the net. As the crowd roared, Connors grinned, but as Trabert noted, "He's smiling, but it's a nervous smile." With a point for 4-all, Connors overhit groundstrokes on three straight points to hand McEnroe the game. McEnroe held at love.

And when Connors lost his serve to open the fifth—he'd now dropped six straight games—Mike and I were numb. After more than three hours, after he'd taken such command, now versus the best serve in tennis under the lights, what more could Connors do? I asked Mike, "Why isn't Jimmy getting in more?" Mike, who hit clean, hard strokes à la Connors, countered. "McEnroe's doing what you do, Joel," he said, "he's not giving him the right ball to hit. It's awkward." But if Mike usually beat me, why couldn't Connors take it to McEnroe?

The answer, of course, was that I was no John McEnroe on or off the court. There was room for only one hotheaded lefthander in my life. Besides, like Ken, Connors was older than I was. He'd carried me through adolescence and, as I turned 20 in 1980, was attempting to do so into adulthood. Connors came from a place I knew nothing about—the nonintellectual boondocks of Belleville—to the very city where I'd grown up. McEnroe was a peer in age and upper-middle class background. But as Mike reminded me, McEnroe wore the self-contented sneer of the juniors who'd beaten us. No question, he and Connors were both stuck-up little tennis players. But we only recognized McEnroe with our eyes. By the time he emerged, we viewed tennis through the lenses of young men rather than as the adolescents who'd felt Connors far more viscerally.

With McEnroe up 1-0, 30-30, Connors struck yet another backhand down the line return that set up an easy lob placement. Break point for 1-all. Another down the line return opened it up for a penetrating backhand approach and backhand volley winner. McEnroe was so distraught that he threw his racket to the ground—at such an odd angle that it soared from his baseline over the net past Connors' baseline. The crowd booed loudly. The Mayor owned the town.

Connors stood near the net. He sauntered back towards the baseline where the racket lay, picked it up and pretended as if he was going to throw it back over the net. McEnroe was walking to his bench, which happened to be on Connors' side of the court. Connors gently tossed him the frame. McEnroe explained to Wiley and the tournament referee, Mike Blanchard, that what he'd done was an accident. The whole sequence revealed everything about Connors-McEnroe: great serve, great return, break point winner, temper tantrum from the younger, milked by the elder, the younger's case for his defense and, finally, the skill of both at managing the flow and tempo of a match. More than anyone in their era, Connors and McEnroe were geniuses at strategic pauses, Connors often with a towel or a long ball bounce when serving, while McEnroe often juggled balls or fiddled with his strings and shoelaces. Add to this the aptitude each had for hectoring umpires, and it's no wonder their matches always took a long time.

"We've gone this far," said Trabert soon after McEnroe's racket flew, "we might as well have a tiebreaker in the fifth. That would make it perfect."

McEnroe broke to go up 3-2. Connors had break points at 15-40, but both his backhand returns hit the tape. After he missed the second, Connors rubbed his crotch with a ball. "Not good, not good," Mike said to me—not the vulgarity but that its presence revealed Connors beginning to crack. McEnroe held, and three games later, he served for the match at 5-4.

The crowd screamed. CBS showed a split screen. Connors bounced up and down like a boxer. McEnroe rocked, ready to serve. A firm Connors return, a McEnroe drop volley. Connors ran forward and poked up a backhand high to McEnroe's forehand—a very easy volley that McEnroe netted. Two good serves brought McEnroe to 30-15. A series of planes flew overhead, and both players held off. The sound of the ball coming off a racket is critical for tennis players. Airplanes make it impossible to hear. Connors hit two sharp backhands that forced McEnroe to miss a volley. McEnroe threw up his hands in disgust. Mike and I held our phones in silence.

At 30-30, McEnroe struck a crosscourt forehand volley that wasn't quite angled or deep enough. Still, for most players it would be difficult to pull off a forceful passing shot with the best volleyer in the world stationed at the net. This is where Gloria's years of demanding a committed stroke paid off. Connors rocketed a crosscourt forehand that clipped the net and skipped over McEnroe's racket. Connors thrust his pelvis—and then netted a forehand return. At deuce, McEnroe cracked a serve into Connors' backhand. This was a wise play, as it's not easy for a returner to find an angle sharp enough to avoid an incoming volleyer. But Connors' early, compact swing made that possible, and his backhand again squealed up the line—and another pelvic thrust. McEnroe served again to Connors' backhand, right down the middle of the court—yet another smart serve lest McEnroe open the court for a forehand angle. And once again, Connors struck another winner, inside-out to level the match.

The crowd was on its feet. This was Connors at his best, drawing on the energy of the occasion—the crowd, the commotion of the airplanes, the hardcourt—to wrestle the intruder and kick him out of the house. The U.S. Open was Jimbo's house, wasn't it? He'd won it in each of the last three even-numbered years. Here was the fourth. He held easily and sprinted to his chair.

All signs pointed to a Connors break, but despite several fine returns, McEnroe held at love.

Heading into the tiebreak, Mike and I were nervous and doubtful. Connors versus Borg in '76, Vilas versus Connors in '77, McEnroe versus Borg in '80—tiebreakers usually favored the more aggressive player. Mike and I recalled that the one time we played each other in a tournament, I won the first set in a tiebreak by dint of coming in frequently. McEnroe's serve and volley were perfect assets for tiebreak tennis. Just how many sharp returns did Connors have left? At 1-2, Connors served into McEnroe's backhand and drew precisely what he wanted: a high forehand volley. He drove it into the net. Mike and I winced. Segura's shoulders dropped. "Jimbo, Jimbo, not that one," he said. "No, no, no, no." That one volley turned the entire four-hour match.

On the next point, Connors overhit a backhand. McEnroe served, leading 4-1, then going up 6-1. After Connors won both points on his own serve, a sizzling delivery down the center of the ad court from McEnroe ended it. Mike and I were on the phone for more than an hour. Connors was gone, McEnroe the winner 6-4, 5-7, 0-6 (!), 6-3, 7-6. The next day, McEnroe and Borg played a five-setter nearly as elegant as the Wimbledon final that McEnroe won 6-4 in the fifth. McEnroe and Borg were way up the mountain. Connors was left behind.

And I wanted blood. I called Josh Marks, a former high school team-mate. Since Josh was also in IPS, our matches were often quite cordial. Not this one. On the Sunday morning after the Connors-McEnroe match, he and I met at UCLA. I focused more than I had on a match in two years as I scampered into corners, darted in after approach shots and crushed overheads to win 6-2, 6-2. At least in some measure I purged myself of Jimbo's loss. A week later I returned to Berkeley. It was a strange feeling. Even as my ambitions occupied places and subjects far away from tennis and Jimmy Connors, he continued to infiltrate them.

"How could you call it that way?"
"That's how I saw it."
"I thought it was good."
"I didn't see it that way."
"No way. I don't believe you. Get someone else to look at it. I want to hear it from someone else."

This is not Jimmy Connors yelling at a linesman. It's me, engaged in a furious discussion with an instructor. My poetry paper was in my hands. A C+ for my comparison of Robert Frost and Wallace Stevens? How could that be? Worse yet, there was nary a comment. What was wrong with my ideas? What was right? There were more than 100 students in American Literature 130D, and I was deter-mined to get recognition and rewards. This conversation repeated itself for four years. Even when I got an A, I wanted to know why, and how much more it would take to make my essay worthy of *The New York Review of Books*.

My tennis racket was shelved. From ages 13 to 18, I played virtually every day, including more than 400 competitive matches. In four years of college I rarely played more than once a week. Save for the occa-sional match such as versus Josh, I competed with minimal intensity. But if my racket was in the closet, Jimmy Connors was with me. "Normal development," writes Diane T. Marsh in *Siblings: Forgotten Family Members*, "may also be affected in other ways. For instance, siblings may strive to become 'perfect' . . . . They may also experience 'survivor's guilt' for having been spared a similar fate, which may intensify the need to demonstrate their 'invulnerability' and competence." What the Beverly Hills Tennis Club meant to Connors, Berkeley was to me. *I couldn't see it as being just a little tennis. It had to be great tennis, top-of-the-pile tennis.*

"Look at the person next to you," said an administrator during Berkeley's freshman orientation. "One of you won't be here next year." It would not be me. My scholarly model came more from the court than the classroom. After all, tennis and Connors, not school, electrified my adolescence. College was yet another challenge match. If it took extra tenacity to get the best possible education at a large, impersonal institution, I'd run down every hall, write personal letters to professors to gain admission into their classes, study syllabi weeks ahead of each quarter, determine which courses I'd take years in advance. Over pizza in my freshman dorm, I heard my floormates discuss their plans to spend junior year in other countries. I had another idea. I'd write my undergraduate thesis as a junior, one year ahead of schedule, so I could enroll in a special honors program.

Driving down Highway 5 to LA with my roommate Phil's girlfriend, Suzanne, I listened to her describe a graduate student she knew. "If you can believe this," she said, "he wants to think about one idea for a while." I was dazzled. Though it would be years before I understood why the idea I found was so vital to me, the notion of digging into one topic appealed to me.

Mine emerged. The initial thought was that since I wanted to enter politics, I'd be a political science major. Ken had pursued the same plan at UCLA. But then, through odd twists in scheduling, I took a history class my first quarter, and was fortunate to come in close contact with a professor rather than the teaching assistants who taught most of Berkeley's courses.

In Sheldon Rothblatt's Modern Europe course, I read *Young Man Luther,* a book written by Erik Erikson about the man who'd launched the Reformation. Psychologist and historian, Erikson coined the term "identity crisis"—that period in a young man's life when he makes the transition from adolescence into adulthood. Erikson tapped into ideas that lurked within me, notions of destiny, success, desire and the future. At stake, I wrote in my paper, was Luther's very survival. He'd done what he could to survive and discover his identity.

Rothblatt summoned me to his office. He thought I had the potential to become a first-rate student. He particularly admired the way I passionately thrust my beliefs into the paper, as if there was something much more at stake for me than the mere explanation of ideas. The study of history, Rothblatt explained, was a fascinating way to understand so much of how people adapted to change and what made humanity tick. A month later, I wrote a paper on Franz Kafka and his tortured view of history. I didn't know it then, but I'd stumbled on to a topic that soon consumed me: the individual in society. Law was remote (Borg?). History was personal. I changed my major from political science to history. I wanted to become a writer.

From Luther and Kafka to F. Scott Fitzgerald and Norman Mailer, Voltaire and Freud, Marx and Machiavelli, Thomas Mann and William Faulkner, I found myself continually drawn to notions of individual freedom, power and transcendence. Individualism eventually led me back to tennis and a professional obsession with Jimmy Connors. But tennis meant nothing to me then.

Many years later, an ex-roommate explained how he generated good grades whenever he recited certain ideas back to a professor, as if each were engaged in a charade. I was aghast. From the get-go, I played for keeps. Ideas were weapons, to be accumulated and deployed. Insights were mine and mine alone. Like a tennis player, most of all like Connors, I went solo. Study groups were popular, but I declined to prepare for finals with others after my freshman year. I hated to discuss my paper topics with others. When others drew on such secondary sources as Cliff's Notes to provide interpretations for literature papers, I called them cheaters.

But as I later discovered, the subtext of this obsession with individualism was triggered by a bigger topic I didn't want to acknowledge existed. As one of my heroes of that period, George Orwell, wrote, "The autonomous individual is going to be stamped out of existence." Wasn't that what I feared would happen to me as Ken fell apart? Wasn't that pretty close to the dream with Tonya? Hadn't I watched horrific events overturn my society? It made so much sense that I was drawn to the study of great intellects and heroes. Tennis was one way to find strength in my role as loner and outsider. But that was just a game for a boy. Now, as I became a man, I sought greater meaning through the study of the transcendent. Ken's descent accelerated my unconscious sense that identities could be lost. To survive, I needed to learn what greatness was all about so that I could emerge not as a loser, but a winner.

Intellect became a form of action, an arena where, like a tennis player, I could become a singular star. Unlike in tennis, my physical limits were meaningless. I was a ravenous student, my books and notepads marked up with comments, exclamation points, underlined quotes. The day I heard a professor explain the term "sensibility"—the notion of a singular artist's vision and how it is projected onto the page—gave me as much increased power as the T-2000 had for Connors. In a history and literature seminar, I took a copy of Edith Wharton's novel, *The House of Mirth*, and threw it against a wall. "This woman," I said, "is an anti-Semitic, snooty bitch." I hated Wharton's insular tales of manners among the rich. I loved novels of ambition like *The Great Gatsby*. "With most students," a professor told me, "it's a challenge to get them emotionally engaged in their papers. You scare me. You're pathologically subjective." *Lines are there to be hit.*

It was 10:15 p.m. on a Wednesday night during finals week of my sophomore year. I paced my living room in my Fred Perry warmup suit and scribbled concepts for the next day's double-header—an 8 a.m. three-hour sociology final, followed that evening by an equally long history exam. The phone rang. It was a friend from LA. I kept it short. "We're going to kick some major ass tomorrow," I told him. The tennis player in me loved the fact that the goal was to "ace" an exam. The next morning, I put on my final piece of clothing: two yellow wristbands. Twelve hours later, the second test completed, I threw off the wristbands and raised my arms in the air à la Connors after his U.S. Open wins.

There is a concept in Jewish families known as "nachas," whereby the children's success provides the parents with a chance to revel in a constant, self-congratulatory feedback loop. *My son, the doctor.* Back to our childhood, Ken and I were programmed to produce ample quantities. But Ken's breakdown crashed the program. And here I must confess: If my desire to produce ample quantities of nachas was conscious, the reasons were not. Not for another 10 years would I sit with other siblings of the mentally ill and share tales of the desire to compensate for loss.

Ken's illness reached a significant crossroads in 1979. As I went north for my first year of college, Ken completed his physical recovery from the leap of '78. There were no episodes for most of this period, but also no signs of motivation. That summer when I came home, Ken's lethargy continued. My parents were relieved there were no violent episodes.

One August morning that summer of 1979, Ken suddenly directed his violence towards me for the first time. I was wearing one of the flannel shirts he gave me three years earlier. Suddenly he demanded I return it to him, since he claimed it was his in the first place. Then he threw several punches at me. Fuck it, I said, you can have them both. Enough. I felt a chill go through me and left the house. By the fall, there were more episodes. After three years under siege, my parents finally decided it was untenable to have Ken under the same roof. He was sent to a board-and-care facility just outside of Beverly Hills. When my parents told me this on the phone that fall, I felt a wave of relief for them and, again, my familiar sense of detachment. Besides, I needed to finish my paper on John Locke's concept of freedom. I was two weeks away from lasting longer in college than Ken. The next quarter, my grades improved significantly.

In September 1979, my parents and I flew east to celebrate the 50th wedding anniversary of my father's aunt. It was implicitly understood that Ken was best left in LA. At the airport on the way home, I chatted with my uncle Frank. He expressed concern about the impact of Ken's illness on us over the last three years, particularly on my own develop-ment since, as he put it, I was "pretty much an only child these days." When I passed that on to my parents, they were livid that he should so discount Ken. He was ill, but not dead, right?

But Frank was more accurate than I dared admit. If asked, most of my college friends believed I was an only child. Never did I mention my brother unless asked, and then I, usually chatty to a fault, said hardly anything. I was particularly mute when my roommate Phil's brother visited us the day after he learned he scored a 760 out of 800 on the law school admissions test. I was exceptionally uncomfortable when another roommate and I visited a friend in a hospital. I reinvented myself into an independent person. After all, Caldwell Williams had taught me that I was the cause, not the effect, of the entire universe.

My dreams of greatness came together when, as planned, I wrote my history thesis in my junior year. At my thesis advisor's suggestion, I researched the life and times of Norman Mailer. Little did I realize that Mailer addressed so many of my passions. "I have been running for president in the privacy of my mind," he wrote in *Advertisements for Myself*. He too was obsessed with the Kennedys. A random mention of Mailer by movie critic Pauline Kael inspired the title, a concept that to me touched everything from the Halloween costume I'd worn at age five to my presidential campaign: The Man Who Would Be King. As one critic noted, "In all Mailer's novels, it is the individual, and indi-vidual integrity, that must be fought for and preserved."

Mailer's ideas about America and the challenges of ambition capti-vated me. "We set ourselves around the knoll and get ready to play King of the Hill," he wrote. "Soon one of us is brave enough to take the center and insist it belongs to us. Then there is no rest until the new King is killed." His edginess, based as it was in a comfortable urban Jewish lifestyle, pointed to that border of sanity and paranoia I'd watched Ken teeter over. "The only life-giving answer," wrote Mailer, "is to accept the terms of death, to live with death as immediate danger, to divorce oneself from society, to exist without roots, to set out on that uncharted journey into the rebellious imperatives of the self."

When Joan Didion, a Berkeley-educated, LA-based writer I started to read at that same time, referred to The Doors as "Norman Mailers of the Top Forty, missionaries of apocalyptic sex," the connection thrilled me. The Doors were one of Ken's favorite groups when we first moved to LA. They were also the most popular band at his board-and-care facility. The summer of 1979, Ken suggested I buy *LA Woman*. I listened to the title track constantly on my car stereo.

At age 12, I'd read John McPhee's explanation that a tennis game grows out of a personality. Why couldn't a personality grow out of a tennis game? However down the food chain I was as a junior tennis player, I never lacked for tenacity. As I wrote The Big Paper, Norman Mailer, Joan Didion, Jim Morrison (often called "Jimbo") and a host of Jewish intellectuals and American icons danced around in my head. To write about Mailer was more than a challenge match. It was a Grand Slam.

It was 1 a.m. on Friday, February 13, 1981. As I sat at my desk, I wore the bottoms of my Fred Perry warmup suit and a green adidas sweatshirt. Papers, notecards and books were strewn on the desk and at my feet. A bag of cherry jellybeans lay near my lamp. The first draft of the thesis was due that day. Thirty to 50 pages was the acceptable length, but my paper was barely two-thirds complete and by that evening I'd written 70 pages. Through the night I composed and typed an additional 30 pages. At 8:00 a.m., I started proofreading (rather poorly). I felt delirious as I trotted around the Berkeley campus with a shopping bag filled with hundreds of bound pages.

Two days later, my advisor called to tell me he liked the draft and offered a few suggestions. A month later, I typed it again, this version 110 pages long. The honors committee chairman told me he looked forward to reading it. I was 20 years old and convinced I was primed to set America on fire. My thoughts were my form of action. Unlike tennis, where I backed off from my ambition, in the world of ideas I jumped in headfirst. When another professor offered to give me more advice on how to become a better writer, I recalled Sean Harrington's advice about improving my tennis and how I demurred. But in this case, I accepted every bit of input.

"Look at me, going everywhere," says the title character in Saul Bellow's breakthrough novel, *The Adventures of Augie March*. That's how I felt when I came home to regale my parents about my Big Paper. They were appreciative, but as we made plans to visit Ken, my father issued what he no doubt saw as a kindly piece of advice. It was probably best, he suggested, that I refrain from talking about my paper so as not to upset Ken. I obeyed. Who I was to think my glories were so important when someone else in my family was suffering? Naturally, this made me eager to return to Berkeley, where I wanted to believe I had friends who understood me.

But at Berkeley I was isolated too, trapped between my deeply-buried, private emotions about Ken and my fear that my desires would come off as too crass. "Ambition," I read earlier that year in a book that bore that title, "is most often confounded with aggression; and aggression, make no mistake, is scarcely thought an admirable quality." I was so proud of my great paper and my place in the honors program. But whenever I heard a peer talk about how she didn't think it was worth getting so hot and bothered about a research paper, or another friend say that grades didn't really matter, or another one denigrate Norman Mailer, I felt lonely, misunderstood and invalidated—too much of a jock-of-action around aesthetes, too thoughtful among jocks. Like John McEnroe, I came from a privileged background where cool disinterest carried more weight than hot passion. But I had no intention of taking a distant, ironic or disaffected route. Connors' ups and downs, Ken's downs and my ups pointed me elsewhere.

The pursuit of success occupied so much of my time that while I had many an acquaintance, I rarely made close friends. Living in a house with three men and two women as a junior, I decided to spend the last two quarters of my senior year alone as a border in the basement of a house in the Berkeley hills (and spent hours on the telephone). I was far too wrapped up in my next set of courses, which books I must read, the next big paper I needed to outline *immediately*. Years later, I worked in television with a former top-10 tennis player. Having turned pro in his teens, he never attended college, and romanticized the life of an undergraduate. "You think it's all bull sessions and pizza?" I asked him. "Well, try grinding it out for four hours in the library! Try finishing a blue book exam when your wrist is killing you because you've been writing nonstop for three fucking hours!"

For a year, I was close with an equally ambitious graduate student who shared my love of American history and literature. She and I spoke daily, and one summer while in separate places wrote letters to each other describing the various books we were reading. She was Ken's age almost to the day. Just before I left Berkeley one summer, I considered telling her about him. But I didn't.

The funny thing was that even if I rarely played tennis, my friends recognized how much the sport defined me. When a roommate and I drove to Napa for a small pro tournament, he noted how comfortable I looked as we watched and talked about the sport. I enjoyed tennis, but so what? I wanted to write about America and explore politics, society and culture. Tennis wasn't part of that world. But it was as if my friend was trying to help me see what I was blind to: for all my desires, it was the girl with the racket I loved most.

Only in the summer could I let tennis return to my life. My five-year campaign to work for Tony Trabert had worked. The summer after my sophomore year in college, I was a counselor at his tennis camp. At first, I thought I'd only work there one summer. My plan for the next year was to earn a select spot in Berkeley's Cal-in-the-Capitol program and intern in Washington, D.C. But I so enjoyed the counselor job that I decided to do it again. The internship would wait until I'd graduated in June 1982.

And naturally, it was during these summers when I thought of Jimmy Connors. Summer, after all, started with Wimbledon and ended with the U.S. Open. In July '81, as we ate breakfast, Trabert made an announcement. It was always thrilling to hear the same voice of my childhood summers talk on CBS. Quite often, Trabert made the same pointers about the pros on the airwaves he told his campers. On this morning, he updated us on the Wimbledon semifinal between Connors and Borg. "Jimmy Connors," he said as I looked up from my Fruit Loops, "has taken a two sets to love lead." I thought it was the greatest thing I'd heard him say since he handed me my trophy for winning my group eight years earlier. With that kind of edge, surely Connors was headed to the finals. I went out to teach that morning with an added bounce in my step.

Two hours later, as the entire camp took its daily break for a piece of fruit, I looked up from my apple to hear Trabert say, "Jimmy Connors"—and here I expected him to say *will play the Wimbledon final*—"and Bjorn Borg have just started the fifth set." The odds still favored Connors. Never mind that Borg had lost but one fifth set in the last five years.

At lunch came the final announcement. "Bjorn Borg," said Trabert—and I knew the rest. Were Trabert a radio, I'd have clicked it off. Connors lost that final set, 6-4. He rocketed off to a 6-0, 6-4 lead. In the fifth he held break points for 3-1 but failed to convert. Throughout his first three service games in that final set, Connors fought off eight break points until, at 3-3, 30-40, he erred on a routine forehand. "After all those breakpoints, I was getting nervous," said Borg. "If I don't get that last one, Jimmy maybe leads 4-3 and then the pressure is really on me."

I staggered out from lunch depressed. It was always such a roller-coaster to root for Connors. Unable to even watch this match, lacking an opponent to take out my anger, I returned to my teaching court and fed one ball after another in a daze. The U.S. Open was even worse. Connors lost to Borg in the semis in straight sets. The symmetry was striking. From 1979 to '81, Connors lost six semis at Wimbledon and the U.S. Open, three each to Borg and McEnroe. Added to that were losses in Paris to Victor Pecci, Vitas Gerulaitis and Jose-Luis Clerc. When McEnroe toppled Borg in both the Wimbledon and U.S. Open finals, it seemed certain he and the Swede would vie for these trophies for the better part of the '80s.

Late in the year, there was a small victory that to Connors was major. It came in London, at an indoor tournament where he played McEnroe in the finals. I was home on a short break, and watched this match in the living room with my parents and a high school friend, Pablo. McEnroe took a two sets to love lead. "Connors," said Pablo, the son of an art gallery owner, "such a punk, so crude. Now McEnroe, there's creativity." My father countered. "Don't say that around Joel," he warned. I was restrained, but wanted to throttle Pablo. Didn't he understand that tennis wasn't a beauty contest? Did he have no appreciation for Connors' precision? Or was he just piling on the carcass of a former champion in decline?

Connors fought back. McEnroe lost his temper. Connors made his share of rude comments too, but by this point in their careers, McEnroe was what psychologists call "the identified patient." Nowhere was McEnroe more studied than in England. A few choice tantrums in his '77 Wimbledon debut earned him the nickname "SuperBrat." An early exit in '79 was not particularly graceful. There was the verbal fracas with Connors in '80. In '81, McEnroe was a mess of manners from day one, issuing one of his most famous statements— "you're the pits of the world"—in his first-round match. So cantankerous was McEnroe on his way to the title in '81 that the All-England Club refused to grant him the honorary membership customarily given to singles winners.

McEnroe's tirades at Wimbledon spawned a national industry of armchair psychologists, apologists and prosecutors. One reason for this was that by the time McEnroe surfaced, tennis (thanks in large part to Connors and Borg) was a much larger part of the global sporting culture. In barely a decade, the perception of tennis players had morphed from amateur pretty boys to professional athletes to, at least in the case of McEnroe, celebrities worthy of Andy Warhol silkscreens.

Another explanation for why the British scrutinized McEnroe more than Connors was that while Connors was regarded as a young, arrogant punk and a momma's boy, his rudeness in England was largely confined to isolated episodes, such as the parade snub of '77. Connors' sportsmanship truly had improved, he was losing more and, with wife and child in tow, he appeared to be settling down. No doubt bigger tantrums were on the horizon for McEnroe. McEnroe also played with a refinement, delicacy and net attack that was a much better fit for the short points of contemporary grasscourt tennis than Connors' base-line-based style. Connors actually played more similarly to the last British men's singles champion, Fred Perry, who like Connors was a cocky outsider (son of a Labour Party MP). But Perry's wins were way back in the mid-'30s.

Finally, there was the matter of social class. In McEnroe, the British recognized a kindred soul: a disconsolate prep school lad attempting to reconcile breeding with combat. No such conflict occupied Connors' boondocks-based, Ugly American sensibility. McEnroe's deeper inner struggle was between temper and talent. This too fit well with Britain's social structure. Talent, like social class, was merely something you were born with. Extremely lax about practicing, McEnroe often projected an artistic fatalism, the sense that his game was more based on inspiration than perspiration (even if he was a voracious competitor).

In contrast, Connors, as intense a practice player as the game has ever seen, built his success toothpick by toothpick, a self-made man. Connors felt no affinity for McEnroe's privileged artistic anguish. McEnroe resembled Holden Caulfield, the tortured yet precious narrator of *Catcher in the Rye* who fretted over his briefcase and possessed a sheltered boy's delusions of a perfect world. Connors was Gatsby, the Midwesterner who stood alone and in rising to the top, experienced first-hand enough of humanity's corrosive qualities to know there was no such thing as perfection.

By '81, decline also made Connors that British favorite, the likable loser with a hint of the rogue in him. Connors, the politician's grandson, the boy from the Midwest who came to Beverly Hills, shrewdly reached out for support. At last he'd seen how his counter-punching style—fighting off incoming missiles, scampering into corners—was a source of endearment rather than resentment. "I like the crowds on my side and that makes me get up and try even harder," he said in '81. McEnroe, an artist, saw the court as his own personal canvas. He seemed to be saying, you people have no idea what I'm doing out there, so just leave me alone and let me paint a masterpiece.

On a fast indoor carpet that day in London, Connors came from two sets to love down to beat McEnroe, 3-6, 2-6, 6-3, 6-4, 6-2. The victory snapped an eight-month title drought, probably the longest since Connors had picked up a racket. Afterwards, he turned to his security guard, Doug Henderson, and said, "Man, I began to wonder if I'd ever win a five-setter." In his victory speech, Connors spoke of how hard the last few years were for him and that he hoped to get back to the top in 1982. After London, he and Henderson went to Israel. Visiting the Church of Nativity, built over the manger where Christ was born, Connors bought a candle and prayed, perhaps not just for his family, but also, Henderson imagined, for "just one more big one."

Not many anticipated Connors winning Grand Slams. By the end of the year, though Connors was number three on the ATP computer, others, such as *World Tennis'* highly-regarded editors, ranked Connors fifth. "Perhaps it is true," said the ATP's 1982 Media Guide, "that time waits for no one, even Jimmy Connors."

I didn't want to believe this. Connors conducted his career with such urgency, had risen so high, lost so bitterly, fought so diligently, it was hard to see him actually relishing life anywhere but the pinnacle. As always, he emphatically declared his intentions. "I'm working to be number one in the world this year," Connors said in 1981. "I don't want to hang around if I can't be the best in the world. As far as I'm concerned number one is the only number, and for me not to think I can be number one is ridiculous."

And yet, even in decline, or maybe even *more* in decline, I began to see Connors in richer terms than in his years at number one. As the joke goes, why does the South have so many good writers? Because they lost. Two articles I read that year demonstrated two ways to understand Connors. Mike Lupica's "The Best and the Baddest" in the February '81 issue of *World Tennis*, tipped its hat to Connors' signifi-cance as a warrior: "The bad guy is still a bad guy, but he is a challenger now, and tennis fans have come around to his side." But the story's emphasis on results led to a conclusion I found unacceptable (however apparent it seemed to so many). Connors, wrote Lupica, "probably won't be number one again…. His best days, his very best days, are behind him."

Tennis' Peter Bodo took a different view, regarding Connors' results of the last three years less as proof of inevitable decline and perhaps, just possibly, transitory occurrences in the journey of a man who certainly loved to win, but also knew most of all how to fight again and again. Connors, wrote Bodo, "has survived triumph, and endured disaster. Neither Borg's merciless groundstrokes nor John McEnroe's shotmaking genius have dulled Connors' passion for excellence or his willingness to put his entire being into what, to so many people, is merely a game. No less now than ever before, the sum total of Connors is more than his game and more than his person. He is an attitude." Because he failed to bury Connors, I favored Bodo's view.

Yet there was an aspect to all the commentary that disturbed me. I hated to see Connors reduced and shoved off to the sidelines as if he was an old Senator who once campaigned hard for the White House but should now simply be venerated. Connors as statesman? Once unlikely, now plausible. Connors as contender? Once plausible, now unlikely. Even in Connors' eyes the titles he once considered his right to win took on fatal implications. Or maybe they always had. "Before I quit, before I die," Connors told Bodo, "I'm going to win Wimbledon or the Open again. It might kill me, too, but you know, I'm gonna do it."

With Connors' public history nearing the eulogy stage, I chose to view him personally. The journey began elliptically. In a writing class I took in the spring of '82, I crafted an essay about the split between Ken's woes and my life. Ken's board-and-care facility was just eight blocks south on Robertson Boulevard from Tony Trabert's office. Yet in the essay I was unable to put on paper a word of Ken's schizophrenia, or any information about his episodes. "You're beating around the bush," said my instructor. "But this tennis thing seems very important to you. Why don't you write about some aspect of tennis that really interests you?"

That same month, in a history honors seminar, I was reading Hegel's lectures on the philosophy of history. He wrote extensively about individuals in history and the way greatness grows out of desire. According to Hegel, "A man who accomplishes something excellent puts his whole energy into the task …. That a man can thus devote his whole energy to a particular cause suggests a kind of instinct of an almost animal quality." I also reread *The Great Gatsby*, that grand tale of an American man of action, told by another American man of thought, the narrator Nick Carraway (who, like me, gets carried away by his subject).

Nothing more than tennis helped me turn thought into action. Who better to demonstrate that than that animal-like competitor, Jimmy Connors? Like Norman Mailer, Connors may not have been the best of his time, but he was arguably the most important. And to quote from *Gatsby*, "If personality is an unbroken series of successful gestures, then there is something gorgeous about him, as if he were related to one of those intricate machines that register earthquakes ten thousand miles away." The impact of Connors' tennis on me was seismographic.

My essay was called, "The Great Connors." Connors, I wrote, "was not so much a hero as a reference point. And even that status may make him a hero." In 1982, Connors and I were set to mark notable birthdays, him turning 30, me 22—the same age he turned in 1974 when he became number one in the world. On life's rollercoaster, through wins and losses, he (me?) continued to fight. "Though I would love to see Connors win a major title once again," I wrote, "our relationship has long since crystallized. A Connors triumph would stoke rather than rekindle the fire he has ignited in me for so long." The child in me knew what I wanted—Connors back on top. But the young adult saw a sober reality. The essay was dated May 17, 1982.

Two weeks later, Connors lost in the quarterfinals of the French Open, winning just six games in three sets to a journeyman named Jose Higueras. Tony Trabert was at the match and told me that, "Jimmy looked like he'd never change anything in his game."

Connors left Paris for England to prepare for Wimbledon. I was two weeks away from graduation, and on a Friday afternoon that June, completed the last book I'd ever read in college, Garry Wills' *Nixon Agonistes: The Crisis of the Self-Made Man*. Wills' understanding of each American's connection to this unsavory politician made me think of Connors: "We must not, even, despise Nixon, but forgive him—absolve ourselves." Buried in all of us ambitious Americans were strands of the paranoia that fueled Nixon and Connors. But Connors mattered less to me than Nixon. Of all the capitals Ken and I quizzed each other on as children, none held my attention more than America's. Soon I'd be there.

8

Love & Love

"When will you fall in love? When you least expect it and where it's most likely." —Caldwell Williams

In the spring of 1982 I studied the Cleopatra's Nose theory of history. The theory explored the role of chance in shaping historic events. It was based on the premise that if Cleopatra's nose was smaller, Mark Antony might not have been attracted to her, and instead focused more on the Roman Empire's military strength. Little did I know as I debated the credibility of Cleopatra's Nose that chance was about to shape history for Jimmy Connors and myself.

Roll Call, a weekly newspaper that covered Capitol Hill, accepted me as an intern for the summer after graduation. To learn more about journalism, that spring I attended a "Magazine Fair" in San Francisco. I met Mary Jane Ryan, the editor of *Inside Tennis*, a regional tennis publication based in Oakland. Ryan asked if I wanted to cover the California State Open, a small pro tournament held in Berkeley. Since it was local and she offered me a whopping $75, I agreed. Though I'd never reported on a sports event and my one tennis story was the Connors essay, after studying a few issues of the magazine, I thought I could imitate prior stories.

It went smoothly. I intuitively knew what questions to ask, what mattered during key matches and which peripheral notables were worthy of mention. Granted, it was only a 500-word story.

Two weeks later, one month before my flight to Washington, Ryan asked if I wanted to interview for the editor's job. Despite receiving résumés from many qualified journalists, none knew as much as me about tennis. I pondered the scenario. *Roll Call* paid nothing. *Inside*

Tennis paid $850 a month. At *Roll Call* I'd be yet another fish in a big pond. At *Inside Tennis*, my role was far more significant. Aware of my lack of experience, Ryan said she'd make sure the publisher, Bill Simons, paid her to train me during a month-long transition period.

Simons was an ex-hippie with a lifelong love of tennis. He was extremely ill at ease with himself, but his mind was agile. From Australians and Americans to various philosophies about instruction, travel and feature stories, I spilled out one idea after another. Having paid much more attention to coursework than tennis for four years, I was surprised to see how opinionated I was. Mary Jane Ryan warned me that Simons was not always the easiest person to work for.

I accepted the offer and started full-time two days after graduation. Though in my head I justified it on financial and vocational grounds, in my heart I was following love. When I told a high school friend about the job, he said, "Of course you're supposed to be editor of a tennis magazine."

There was good news in the tennis world. Mike Anderson called to tell me about Connors' June 13 win over McEnroe at Queen's Club, a Wimbledon tune-up tournament. The more notable tidbit Mike passed on was that Connors served extremely well. Even more than in his redemptive Opens of '76 and '78, Mike noted that Connors' toss and motion was more aggressive. As Wimbledon neared, there was a belief that Connors might well break his Grand Slam drought.

There were two reasons for this. The first was Borg's exile. At the '81 U.S. Open, McEnroe beat him in four sets. Two lob winners from McEnroe turned it around, to the point where Borg was so upset he left the court immediately after the match ended, skipping out on the awards ceremony. In early '82, a burnt-out Borg decided to sit out the first three months of the year. Due to a number of complicated political factors related to tournament commitments, Borg's partial sabbatical spread to the entire year. He vowed to return in 1983.

Factor two was McEnroe's discomfort at the top. "Those years '79 and '80, chasing Borg and Connors were the best for me," he said. "Then I got there, and it felt strange to be at the top of the mountain all by myself." The increased demands on his time that accompanied the number one ranking pained McEnroe. A lingering ankle injury and the adjustment to a new racket didn't help him. Borg's departure jolted him too. With the Swede gone, how could McEnroe wield his paintbrush? Instead, he was left back in the combat zone with Connors, and worse yet, the rising Ivan Lendl, who a month prior to Wimbledon beat McEnroe for the fourth straight time.

Wimbledon began on June 21, my 22nd birthday, two days after graduation. I started at *Inside Tennis* the next day. Unfortunately, Simons refused to pay Ryan $1,000 to train me. Instead, he created a two-pronged editor job, wherein I shared the position with Kathleen Fenton, an experienced journalist with no tennis knowledge. Fenton had started three weeks before me. When it came to assessing Simons, Fenton was less diplomatic than Ryan. She called him a tyrant, a micro-manager known to yell, bully and make last-minute changes that created chaos. Despite that, I remained confident. If the job didn't work out, I planned to teach tennis and apply to graduate schools in journalism.

My first week on the job, Simons fired Fenton. His replacement was one of his colleagues, who spent more time rewriting stories and none teaching me how to edit a publication. I didn't have a clue about how to be an editor, a job that has much more to do with technical matters like layout and planning than knowledge of John McEnroe's playing style. Reporting was also new to me. I didn't understand how a journalist must cultivate sources to develop stories. Nor did I agree with Simons' firm request that certain advertisers be quoted. Two days after he and I went to Lake Tahoe to play a Pro-Am event, he asked when I'd complete my story. What story? The most notable encounter came when Simons and I met Mark Heffernan, a world-class skier who told me he knew Connors. Simons called Connors "one of the greats from the '70s, probably fading now." Heffernan and I disagreed. We thought there was more great tennis ahead for Connors. It was one of the first signs of the many ways Simons and I collided. Intellectual quarrels were no doubt the grist of any magazine. But at *Inside Tennis*, Simons did not respond well to dissent.

He explained how I needed to write a laudatory feature on the resort that hosted us. I complied, and wrote an innocuous story that read more like a travel brochure than the insightful pieces I dreamed of writing. Then again, I was a young, headstrong Berkeley graduate who believed he knew tennis front and back. I had yet to learn that journalism was more complicated than merely issuing your own ideas. Simons lacked patience for my education on his watch. To some degree, this was understandable. To another, it was regrettable.

Yet those problems were secondary. Immersed in tennis, I was where I was meant to be. So was Connors. The chance principles of Cleopatra's Nose brought me to the job. Now the same theory would bring me to Connors. My first two weeks at *Inside Tennis* coincided with his best Grand Slam effort since the week before I started college.

Not once in my four years at Berkeley did Connors reach a Grand Slam final. Now, in his first Slam after my graduation, he was in the Wimbledon finals.

It was one of the wettest Wimbledons in history, rain interrupting play for 10 of the tournament's 13 days. A backcourt-based player like Connors benefited more from dry weather that made the bounce off the courts truer. Conditions that were moist, or as they say at Wimbledon, "greasy," aided volleyers like McEnroe. A player who hit the ball in the air as frequently and proficiently as McEnroe eliminated the issue of dealing with odd bounces. Volleying also greatly reduced the opponent's response time.

Still, Connors' disciplined, compact strokes made him more adept at Wimbledon than any other baseliner of his time save for Borg. In 1982, the combination of his improved serve and commitment to aggression meant he was coming to net more than usual. The night before the final, Segura saw Connors. Their days of hours together were gone, but Segura, eternally generous, offered Jimbo one quick tip: As soon as you hit the return of serve, move forward. This sequence was always one of Connors' strengths, but on grass it was even more critical. A tepid volley or half-volley from McEnroe that bounced up high on a hardcourt was quite effective on slick grass; on the soft lawn, the ball merely died. As usual versus McEnroe, Connors needed to charge hard on offense and defense.

Early in the morning of Sunday, July 4, I sat to watch the final.

After losing the first set, Connors won the second. Up a break in the third, he was executing just the right mix of sound serves, forceful groundstrokes and net attacks. McEnroe, ill at ease all day, continued to whine about calls and mope between points.

I called Mike Anderson, sitting in his living room 400 miles to the south. "Gotta like it," I said. Most pleasing was Connors' forward movement to the net, which on grass made it very hard for McEnroe to play effective passing shots. Serving at 4-3, Connors charged the net on each of the first three points to go up 40-love and take the game at 15. At 5-4, Connors served for a two sets to one lead. After a long backhand put him in a love-30 hole, Connors again charged forward and earned two points to square the game.

Then, again, alas, as in '77, the unthinkable. A double-fault for 30-40. And then another.

Recall that Connors was never known as the kind of server who went for too much. Here, with an improved delivery, it let him down when he needed it most. As the set advanced to 6-6, I sank in my seat.

The '80 U.S. Open semi proved how perfect McEnroe's game was for tiebreakers.

McEnroe hardly needed brilliance. Connors played one of the worst tiebreakers of his career, starting off with a tepid volley and sprayed approach shot. A McEnroe let cord volley winner and a fine serve put Connors down 1-4. Maybe if Connors won his next two service points he could press McEnroe.

Double-fault number 10. 5-1, McEnroe. McEnroe ran it out, 7-2. I picked up the phone. "Not good," I said to Mike. He was staggered too. Despite leading 2-0 in each set, despite winning more than 70 percent of points when at the net, despite breaking McEnroe's serve four times, despite a 5-3 lead in the third, after two hours and 18 minutes, Connors trailed two sets to one. For Connors to win Wimbledon he'd require an unprecedented double achievement. Besides never winning a Slam after losing the first set, Connors had never won one in a fifth set. As Connors told me the next spring, "That was unusual. One way or another, I'm usually out of there pretty fast."

The fourth began on Connors' serve. McEnroe reached break point. The roulette-wheel fashion of grasscourt tennis, combined with the proficiency of McEnroe's serve, made this virtually a match point. Connors served and volleyed and struck a let cord winner. McEnroe glared, asking chair umpire Bob Jenkins if he'd heard a let on Connors' serve. Five deuces later, Connors held.

McEnroe's serve improved. At 1-2, McEnroe's ninth ace flew by Connors for 2-2. Upset with the accuracy of the electronic linecalling device, Connors jawed with the service linesman, albeit far quieter than in previous years. Jenkins gave Connors a code violation warning for abusing an official. "Thank you very much," said Connors. The crowd laughed. Connors said nothing the rest of the match.

The quality of play, patchy and disjointed in the third set, improved. McEnroe's tirades continued. "Baldy! Bald eagle!" he yelled at a linesman. The match passed the three-hour mark. McEnroe, said Bud Collins on NBC, "wants the haven of a tiebreaker." Besides the last set of this match and the '80 Open semi, McEnroe toppled Borg in the '81 Wimbledon final with two superb tiebreaks. And of course there was his grand effort in the 18-16 classic back in '80. There was such a delightful margin for error in McEnroe's game, particularly on grass, where he slithered balls and made his way into the net with the improvisational manner of a jazz musician. With his more structured swings, Connors was less fluid. Added to this was the difference in their serves. As the two started another tiebreak, the telling difference was

McEnroe's 15 aces and Connors' 12 double-faults (he usually served no more than one or two a match).

At 2-2 on his serve, Connors struck a backhand passing shot wide. McEnroe was four points away from a successful title defense, and about to serve into the ad court—the side of the court lefty serves love most because the skill and threat of a wide slice gives them such a range of possibilities.

McEnroe wisely served into Connors' backhand. With the ball coming into his body this way, it was very difficult for Connors to do much more than drive the ball back into McEnroe's strike zone. Connors return accomplished a bit more. It went wide and low to McEnroe's forehand, short enough that McEnroe was forced to half-volley it rather than hit the ball in the air. This gave Connors just enough time to apply Segura's lesson. As McEnroe tapped the half-volley down the line, Connors ran diagonally across the court full-steam and ripped his backhand down the line. Against many opponents, Connors' backhand might likely have been a winner or yielded an error. Not McEnroe, who stood his ground and promptly flicked a forehand volley back down the line. Connors' forward movement brought him so close he intercepted McEnroe's volley. His racket wielded awkwardly like a lacrosse stick, Connors connected with a two-handed backhand volley winner to get back on serve at 3-3. As he walked to change sides, McEnroe tossed his racket across the width of the court, then aced Connors to go up 4-3.

Connors struck one of his best serves of the day, McEnroe unable to return it. At 4-4, Connors came to net and struck a short, crisp backhand volley winner.

At 4-5, McEnroe missed his first serve. He served wide to Connors' forehand. Connors ripped a crosscourt forehand so hard that McEnroe netted the volley. Two set points for Connors. McEnroe spanked a forehand volley winner.

Connors toed the line at 6-5. Go for the serve or merely get it in? Risk a big one and miss and McEnroe might charge the net on the second serve return. Underplay it and get in a nervous rally.

This time Connors' toss and serve was on the money. His best serve of the day went down the middle, scooting through the grass so sharply McEnroe barely stabbed at his backhand return. Connors yelled and thrust his body in jubilation.

After nearly three-and-a-half hours, the match was dead even. And yet, from McEnroe's vantage point, just as happened to Connors versus Vilas in the third set of the '77 U.S. Open final, the emotional impact overwhelmed the rational reality. With Connors' confidence in ascent, McEnroe started to press, unsuccessfully trying to hit his serves harder, deeper and sharper. Serving at 1-1, 15-30, McEnroe netted a half volley. At 30-40, McEnroe's second serve went to Connors' backhand. The bounce was true, the ball a bit shorter than usual. Connors teed off like he was in a batting cage—a down the line winner for the break. "That return just might be enough," said Bud Collins.

Now it was a question of reaching the finish line. Complaining about line calls, tossing his racket, McEnroe appeared as if he was looking for a good reason to lose. The camera intermittently showed his father, who looked dyspeptic. It was uncertain if he was more anguished by the results or his son's behavior. In those days, McEnroe's father reminded me of Sid Binstock, a narrow parent with little regard for others than his prized possession. It was perverse, but true: McEnroe's tantrums transformed Connors into a gracious sportsman. Coming to net four times, Connors took a 4-2 lead. He was now 51 of 68 at the net. McEnroe held.

The match reached the four-hour mark. To serve the 4-3 game is akin to a pitcher working the 7th and 8th inning. It's not quite the close, but it's precisely what's required to reach the finish. And as Connors learned the hard way in the third set, to blow a lead at this late stage can shift momentum so drastically that the whole match can slip away.

With Connors serving at love-15, McEnroe stood on his baseline and elected not to play a Connors forehand. It was called good. "That's just not fair," McEnroe said to Jenkins. But it was McEnroe who made the mistake. It was always best to hit the ball and play the point rather than assume a shot so close was out. McEnroe's failure to even hit the ball showed how mentally brittle he was. But McEnroe won the next point with an overhead. At 15-30, Connors was a pitcher with runners on second and third.

Refusing to back off, Connors made his 70th charge to the net. His forehand approach nicked the baseline. McEnroe hit one of the most creative shots in his arsenal, a hybrid mix of a high passing shot and low lob. Too short to be struck as an overhead, too high to establish a comfortable volley position, the shot was eminently easy to miss. It wasn't much different from the floater Connors hammered into the net in their '80 U.S. Open fifth set tiebreak. It required adept foot-work. Connors attempted his own awkward putaway, a variation of his sky hook overhead. He drove it crosscourt, but not particularly deep or angled. Any place else but the late stages of a Wimbledon final, and McEnroe would have easily swept a forehand passing shot down the line. So stunned was he by the gift right in front of him that he hit it long.

At 30–30, Connors missed his first serve. His second barely tickled the net for a let cord. His serve spun into McEnroe's backhand. Wisely, McEnroe bunted it down the line to Connors' weaker forehand. This was normally a no-lose placement for McEnroe on grass versus Connors. If the chip went deep, Connors had to come up with the goods from a tough spot of the court. If it went short, well, that was Connors' famed weak shot. This one came just past the service line, but here again, the effort Connors had put in for weeks on charging forward after his serve paid off. Though he didn't serve and volley, Connors was well inside the baseline to field McEnroe's return. He dashed in for the forehand and ripped it past McEnroe for a down-the-line winner. Connors pumped his fists and screamed a warrior's cry.

On the next point, McEnroe's backhand return went inadvertently short, an unintentional drop shot. Showing his keen grasscourt opportunism, McEnroe ran forward. His return was about to bounce very low. Even if Connors arrived at the net in time, getting the ball past McEnroe was no easy task. Out of the corner of his eye, Connors saw how the point shaped up. He sprinted forward. It was necessary to hit this backhand with one hand. Connors sliced the ball down the line, a rare off-pace push, but all he could do. It went past McEnroe and raised chalk. 5–3. Connors ambled like James Cagney. He wagged his index finger. One more. He bounced up and down to return serve like a boxer.

I called Mike. "We're not going anywhere," I said. McEnroe held easily. Mike and I stayed on the phone through NBC's long commercial break at 5–4. Borg and McEnroe, said Bud Collins "bypassed Connors. Those whole years got longer and longer and longer."

There was the business of closing it out. Borg stood at this same point versus McEnroe in '80 in the fourth set, reached double match point and was forced into a fifth. "He's capable of hitting four or five winners," said Connors. "I just wanted to stay dangerous. I didn't want to do anything spectacular."

But he did. On the first point, Connors served and volleyed to McEnroe's forehand. Anticipating the direction of the return, Connors leaned into a backhand volley and struck it emphatically crosscourt for a winner. On the next point, he surprised McEnroe with a second serve netrush and another firm backhand volley. From the baseline at 30–love, Connors rocketed a crosscourt forehand that raised chalk and drew a McEnroe error.

The fans started their traditional closing scream. Match point at Wimbledon is a public release. The spectators, wise to tennis, treat Centre Court less like a noisy sports event as we know it in America and more like grand theater. When players arrive on Centre Court, they are applauded like Shakespearean actors. Throughout the match, each is clapped for appropriately. On match point, the noise grows shrill. So many times over the last eight years, I had heard those cries at Connors' moment of extinction. This day was different.

"Come on, Jimmy, you can do it!" yelled a fan.

Double-fault number 13.

At 40-15, another big serve skidded through the baseline. McEnroe barely touched it.

"Can you believe that?" I asked Mike. "Unbelievable! Unbelievable!" We barely said much more. Four hours and 14 minutes, the longest final in Wimbledon history. Connors motioned to Patti and hugged her.

Back in 1974, Connors said, "Maybe one day I'll be the sentimental favorite at Wimbledon." Wrote Bud Collins, "I should live so long."

After the awards ceremony, Collins waited inside a hallway for NBC's post-match interview. As Connors entered, Collins asked, "How long, James Scott Connors? How long?" Not since Bill Tilden in 1930 had a player won Wimbledon after such a long gap between titles. Connors spoke about the match and how hard it was to win such an epic. He appeared to be choked up and sniffling, but told Collins it was merely a slight cold. I doubted it. Said Connors, "I hope my mom's watching."

With Connors headed to San Francisco for a tournament in September, *Inside Tennis* considered him as a cover subject. My idea was to amend "The Great Connors" to include the great Wimbledon victory. Simons rejected my proposal and lectured me on what he called "mythomania." Given that he'd recently written a story about his efforts in a Pro-Am and that the latest issue included a writer's personal reflections on Evonne Goolagong, I was perturbed. But Simons was right. Connors warranted a conventional profile, but only, stipulated Simons, if I landed a one-on-one interview. He offered no suggestions on how to make that happen.

Later, I grew familiar with publicists, agents and managers. But in the summer of 1982, I knew nothing about how to arrange interviews with celebrities.

But I did know tennis, and in my own twisted way, knew Jimmy

Connors. That spring I mailed "The Great Connors" to Dave Engelberg. A former counselor of mine at Tony Trabert Tennis Camp, Dave was a tennis instructor who was also a member of the Beverly Hills Tennis Club. His father was Connors' dentist.

Connors was set to play an exhibition versus Sandy Mayer and Borg in a LA suburb the weekend of July 24-25. Simons and I thought that might be a good place for me to pursue the interview. Dave liked "The Great Connors" so much that he left a copy of it for Connors at the BHTC the day before the exhibition, thinking that since Connors was in LA, there was a strong chance he'd drop by the club.

My plan was to introduce myself to Connors on the Sunday of the exhibition after he played Borg. On the Saturday, I was with Dave. Just past 6:00 p.m., he suggested we drop by the BHTC. Connors, Dave said, often dropped by in the early evening.

Fifteen minutes after we arrived, Connors walked through the door. "Dave," he said, "Thanks for that story, it was great."

"Well, meet the guy who wrote it."

"How are you, son? If there's ever a favor I can do for you, let me know."

"How about an interview?"

"It's a deal."

The next day, Dave, Mike and I drove to watch Connors-Borg. More was at stake than at most exhibitions. Borg planned to return the next year. Connors wanted to prove he was a valid Wimbledon champ. The best of five sets format and the national broadcast on ESPN, both rare for exhibitions, enhanced the match's importance. "I don't want to lose to that guy anywhere or anytime we play," said Connors.

This was the first time I watched Connors play as a member of the press. Mike and I snuck close to the court. When the fourth set went into a tiebreaker, with the sun setting over Southern California, with Connors and Borg toe to toe, Mike turned to me and said, "Can you believe we're here, right now, and you're about to talk more with Jimmy? Weren't we just with him at Tower Records?" Wasn't I just in school? Now I was about to interview the Wimbledon champion.

As Connors took charge in the fifth, I contemplated how to reach him. The press conference would be a mob scene. With Connors ahead 5-2, I left Mike and sprinted near the players' benches. When Connors won, I ran on to the court. Four security guards flanked Connors, but I drew closer to him before they arrived. I was inside the perimeter. Connors greeted me, and gave me the number where to call him the next day. On the way back, Dave, Mike and I were euphoric.

"There you were," said Mike, "you were right in there." On the freeway we saw Connors with his UCLA doubles partner, Jeff Austin. We honked, they honked back and then Dave shared an idea that had never crossed my mind. "It all makes sense, Joel," he said. "You know history, you know tennis, now you know Jimmy. You're going to write his biography." Right there, on Interstate 10 headed west, late on a Sunday afternoon, Dave pinned the tail on the donkey. No matter how hard it was to deal with Simons, no matter that at 22 I lacked skills or experience, my purpose was clear. Me on Connors, a perfect fit.

Our interview took place in the dining room of the BHTC. Three tables over sat Mark Heffernan, now a tennis teacher in LA. As he watched me interview Connors, we nodded to each other.

"You wrote that in May, huh?" Connors asked about my "Great Connors" essay. Once the interview began, he was forthright (or full of himself?) in the way expected from a recent Wimbledon champion. "The wins are all great," he said, "but it's the losses that teach you the most. That's when you learn who your friends are—and who you are. And that's when it's time to learn." Pleased as Connors was with the Wimbledon title, he said, "My job isn't quite finished yet. I would like to win the Open one more time." When I asked him what his most disappointing losses were, Connors joked, "I've got a lot of them. How much time do you have?" He also noted that the likes of Ashe, Orantes and Vilas were "one-timers"—players who played one great match against Connors but were unable to repeat it. "I didn't want to be in that one-timer group," said Connors about his second Wimbledon.

Over the coming weeks, I interviewed many inside and outside the Connors circle, from Pancho Segura and Stan Canter to Tony Trabert and Jack Kramer. Invariably, Simons and I fought about the angle. He believed Connors was a near has-been, a player ranked out of the top five by the end of 1981 whose career was completely resurrected by his Wimbledon victory. Though I agreed it was a comeback, I felt Connors had nibbled quite closely over the last three years and finally broken through. Simons thought Connors was a changed man, mellowed by marriage and parenthood, humbled by defeat. I thought Connors was every bit the same upwardly mobile, feisty fuck he was since childhood. What changed most of all, I argued, was the public's perception of Connors. "I think just a little bit of age has come between me and the so-called critics," Connors told me. "I still do the same things I've always done. The only thing is that I do it now at 30, and it's a little different from when you're 18, 19, 20, coming up like that." A little more maturity from both Simons and myself and we'd have found common ground. Neither of us was right or wrong. Who truly knew the answers to any of these questions anyway? Instead I dug in my heels. Soon enough, I paid the price.

Most of all, I wanted to focus on Connors' tennis rather than his image. To me, again disagreeing with my boss, the emotional life of Connors between the lines transcended matters of image. As I foolishly asked Simons once when he demanded I attend a press conference, "If you know about painting, must you interview the artist?" I was too cocky for my own good.

Simons also wasn't pleased when without asking his approval I dashed off a letter to *Sports Illustrated* on *Inside Tennis* letterhead. The magazine's account of the Wimbledon final decried the quality of play. Acting as a one-man Connors Defamation League, I disagreed, comparing Connors-McEnroe matches to the raw, hard-fought football games between the Oakland Raiders and Pittsburgh Steelers in the '70s. Connors loved it when I showed him this letter. Simons was justifiably angry I didn't let him review my letter first. Or, I wondered, was he upset it appeared under my name and not his?

In August, I was fired. Simons believed it simply wasn't working out. Three months prior, I was barely a journalist. This I knew. What made anyone think I was an editor? My severance: an additional $150 to complete the Connors profile. I felt more relief than anger. Now I could relax, teach tennis and go to graduate school. Better yet, no longer dependent on Bill Simons for a job, I pursued the angle most personally of interest to me: Connors' continual desire to prove himself. At 30, he'd made a career out of overcoming those who doubted him. At 22, fired from my first job two months after graduation, I found that message deeply inspirational. Simons had written me off, but I vowed to make my mark.

There was also a delightful twist in my life. I was in love. Caldwell Williams' prophecy came true that summer. I will go to my grave convinced it had to do with the happy ions I pumped out because I was enmeshed in tennis. It helped that I'd drawn yet closer to my true passion in Connors during his Renaissance Summer. Joan Edwards, *Inside Tennis'* art director, was attractive, friendly, intelligent and humorous. Like many art directors (or editors for that matter), her expertise was in process rather than content. That didn't stop me from talking to her nonstop about tennis. As my roommate noted a year earlier, around tennis I was in my element.

By the end of August, we saw each other every night. I took Joan to an electronics store so she could buy an $89 black and white TV. At

11:30 each night, we sat on a futon in her Oakland apartment, ate Häagen-Dazs chocolate chip ice cream and watched the CBS Late Night U.S. Open highlight show, with guest commentary by Tony Trabert and John Newcombe and ample match footage, of course, of Jimmy Connors.

As at Wimbledon, Connors rode a strong wave of support based not just on sentiment but performance. McEnroe's year-long funk continued in New York, his three-year title run ended in the semis by Lendl. Much as he was admired as a tennis genius, McEnroe never quite connected with the public at the U.S. Open as a tennis player like Connors. It baffled him. "I'm from New York, I'm one of them," he said. But if he was geographically, he wasn't in spirit. An odd paradox governed the climate of the U.S. Open. Even as the event grew, its seat-holders remained primarily from the same upper middle class strata where McEnroe came from. But those very same privileged spectators now attended tennis tournaments with the expectation they were not at a garden party, but at a rough and tumble sports event. New York tennis fans wanted something raucous. If the British empathized with McEnroe's prep school lad anguish and delicate game, New York fans treated McEnroe in two ways. If they shared his upper class background, they sure didn't want to be reminded of it at a tennis tournament. And if, like many of the new fans who came to tennis, they had not attended prep schools, they despised McEnroe's insularity. He was a twirp. Besides, he'd won too much, and often quite easily.

During the U.S. Open, it was Connors' boondocks-based, ripened swagger that captured the hearts of cabdrivers, ushers, hot dog vendors and those loud fans who made their annual trek to watch a tennis tournament. Eventually, McEnroe too became popular, but far more as some mix of grand ambassador, chief justice and likable rogue. In New York, Connors was the Mayor, the man who walked the streets with the fireman, the man who stirred emotions and sought votes. He conducted himself in Louis Armstrong Stadium like Huey Long cracking the whip over the Louisiana state legislature, a mix of coercion, charisma, humor, bluster and demagoguery. On the middle Saturday of the U.S. Open, Connors walked onto Louis Armstrong Stadium to play Jimmy Arias.

"Go Jimmy!" yelled a group of fans.

"I'll try," Arias yelled back.

"You're not the Jimmy we're rooting for!" They yelled back.

Connors chuckled.

Lendl was yet another new rival. In only his second year on tour in

1980, he beat Borg and finished ranked number six in the world.

Connors loathed Lendl. In his early years on the tour, Lendl was shy and arrogant. The Czech's sharp yet caustic manner put many on the defensive. Though quite different from Connors, he too had a hard time becoming one of the boys (it was much easier for a team sports lover like McEnroe). Another major reason for Connors' antipathy came in January 1981 at the Masters. The two met in the final stages of the round-robin. An odd outcome awaited. The winner played Borg in the semis, while the loser drew a lesser player, Gene Mayer. After extending Connors to a tight first set and losing, 7-6, the pragmatic Lendl barely tried in the second. Connors won it, 6-1. Afterwards he ripped into Lendl, calling him a "chicken." It was an insult not just to the fans, but to Connors personally. Was Jimbo worth so little that his opponent failed to even try? When Lendl skipped Wimbledon in '82, Connors told me, "I give him an 'F' on his report card for that."

But there was an unstated factor for Connors' wrath. As when he spat at McEnroe's feet, he wanted to mark territory. He knew how good Lendl was, but also recognized Lendl's Achilles heel was mental toughness. Lendl had a reputation as someone who dished it out but couldn't take it. Intimidation by any means was worth it, particularly now that Connors was a venerated elder. By the summer of 1982, Connors was 8-0 versus Lendl. Just before the Open, Lendl beat him 6-1, 6-1 in the semifinals at Cincinnati. Yet while some saw that as a changing of the guard, others wondered if Connors let that much go to give Lendl false confidence.

Lendl's one win over Connors was not the only reason he felt hopeful coming into that year's U.S. Open final. Besides never losing to McEnroe in '82, Lendl came into the Open with 11 tournament titles (albeit, like Connors in his youth, he earned many on a weaker circuit). Eight years younger than Connors, Lendl owned the game's best forehand and a superb serve. Experts like John Newcombe saw many Slams in his future, and picked him to beat Connors.

The day before, Connors won a very physical match versus Vilas. Connors was aided by the true bounces of the hardcourt and an opponent who wasn't quite as fast he was in the '77 final. Lendl ended the day by hammering McEnroe. Asked afterwards on CBS how he felt about playing Connors, Lendl asked, "Oh, did he win?" At his hotel, Connors heard this, and instantly felt angry. Face it: If Gandhi were on the circuit, Connors would find a reason to despise him. But there was condescension in Lendl's answer. Surely he knew the result of Connors' semi. As Connors told me, "I know all about him. You really shouldn't say things unless you can back them up. He has no credentials." The next afternoon, Lendl walked into the locker and saw Connors' bodyguard, Doug Henderson, engrossed in a gin rummy game with Johnny Connors. Lendl boasted he could beat Henderson at gin.

"You may be able to," said Henderson, "but I'll bet you $5,000 that Jimmy kicks your ass today." As Lendl recovered from the verbal body blow, Johnny piled on. "I'll bet you another $5,000 that he turns you into Lendl soup."

Five minutes later, Lendl tried to joke back with the 6-foot-3, 220-pound Henderson. "Be quiet before I beat you up," he said.

Suddenly, from another corner, Connors piped in. "I'd like to get a piece of that action." Lendl sulked to another corner of the locker.

The role of the brain in tennis is misunderstood by spectators and poorly explained by players. Two opposing ideas joust. One declares it's not good to think too much. The other says it's important to use your head intelligently. Beneath this lie our assumptions about the physical and the mental. In a sport, it is one thing to shrug off a loss simply by saying the victor was merely physically stronger than you. Physical gifts, after all, are traditionally considered as innate as the color of one's eyes. But to say you were beaten mentally is different. Our society places a premium on intelligence, and to admit you were stupid is far more damning.

The literal sound of Connors' game was so audible it overwhelmed its cognitive aspects. He liked it that way. It was fine for him for fans, coaches and opponents to think he merely played one way. He often said, "I was taught to play one way, by mother, and if I'm not playing that way, I'm not playing my kind of tennis."

But the notion that he only played one way was also part of Connors' con job. Certainly, like everyone who's ever picked up a racket, Connors had a few ways he liked to win a point. He wasn't likely to serve and volley with the frequency of a McEnroe. Nor was he about to stand 10 feet behind the baseline like Borg and float balls high over the net.

Yet within his series of strokes there were a number of distinct ways to construct and end points. In the '82 Open semi versus Vilas, for example, Connors saw that Vilas' slice backhand was a trickier shot to handle than his higher-bouncing topspin forehand. Accordingly, as the match wore on, Connors aimed more balls to the forehand, driving to the backhand mostly when he could take offense with approach shots.

Everyone in tennis knew that Lendl's forehand was superb. The

typical strategy was to stay away from that side and break down his
backhand. When Connors and I spoke about the '82 Open final months
later, he said he made no game plan. I wasn't sure if I believed this. Then
again, Connors' skill as a competitor relied less on planning and more
on his predator-like aptitude for assessing how his strengths matched up
against the opponent's on that particular day, and, in many cases, to alter
it subtly as the match wore on. The bedrock of his foundation was so
strong he felt the confidence to add layers to his strategy, knowing that
he could always fall back on his base of deep, hard groundstrokes. Said
one lifelong Connors rival, "You would be on the court with him deep
into the fourth set and suddenly he'd do something he hadn't done all
match. He was so dialed in to what he could and couldn't do that you
didn't feel you got him off his game. He knew what he wanted to do
even when he wasn't yet doing it. He had the guns."

His biggest gun was his crosscourt backhand. Like a dentist wielding
a drill, Connors liked to probe with this shot and see what he uncovered. Quickly, he spotted a soft spot on Lendl's side. So accustomed was
Lendl to running around his backhand that he hit his forehand better
when he moved to his left and drove the ball inside-out than he did
when forced to move to his right. Lendl was particularly vulnerable to
balls short, sharp and low to his forehand—a spot Connors could find
all day by lacing crosscourt backhands.

After five games, a nervous Lendl had made 10 unforced errors on
his forehand side. More notably, Connors' drives were so penetrating
they were forcing Lendl to hit the ball shorter. With Lendl serving at
2-3, 30-30, he blasted a serve down the center to Connors' forehand.
Connors flew into the ball and rocketed it deep to Lendl's forehand.
The short reply gave Connors a chance to approach to Lendl's backhand and put away a tepid lob. On the next point, Connors concluded
a 20-ball rally with a series of balls to Lendl's forehand that opened up
the court for Connors to drive a backhand down the line winner. As
Connors thrust his pelvis, he glared back at Lendl. "I have no doubts,"
said John Newcombe on CBS, "that Connors is going to his forehand.
I think we're going to find out how good Lendl's forehand is today."
Did Connors make this plan beforehand? Proud of himself more as
man of action than thought, Connors will never say. But I think deep
down there was a part of Connors that hankered to charge right at
Lendl's strongest shot.

To a finesse player like McEnroe, it was an untenable plan. Lendl
merely hit through him. But at that point in tennis history no one on
the tour hit harder than Jimmy Connors. So why not bring his

strength right up against Lendl's? As Connors drilled away at Lendl's cavity, each player's entire game went in opposite directions. Connors' serve, weaker than Lendl's, was often spun wisely to Lendl's forehand in the deuce court, hence opening up the court for Connors to take charge of the points. Yet, as Connors ground his way through one point after another, going after Lendl's forehand was but one tactic in a grand design. It wasn't a design Connors necessarily planned in advance, but as the match evolved, he built it as he always had: toothpick by toothpick. For Connors in this match did far more than hit balls to Lendl's forehand. Connors' own forehand was rock-solid as it pounded its way deep to Lendl's backhand or slithered down the line to his decaying forehand. Frustrated to see his major strength betray him, Lendl pressed on his serve, only to watch Connors scrape and drive one return after another. Lendl grew tentative on his backhand, uncertain if he should drive powerfully and move Connors or chip it low to his forehand in hopes of drawing an error. Most of all, the battle was won at foot level. Connors' feet churned like pistons, his confidence rising in each rally. Lendl plodded.

This wasn't simply Connors in the zone. It was the grind. Through rallies that lasted eight, 10, 15 balls—far more physical on the Open's hardcourts than Wimbledon's grass—Connors built points with just the right mix of baseline depth and forward attack. He won the first set 6-3 and opened the second with eight straight points, capped off by a forehand down the line approach shot winner to go up 2-0. I called Mike. "Taking away someone's strength," said Mike. "That's actually how it's taught, but only Jimmy can do it."

The CBS team, most of all Newcombe, remained surprised. As the Aussie applauded Connors for his "150 percent" effort, he wondered if such effort would hurt Connors as the match wore on. Trabert, who taught me to hit the ball with a straight backswing somewhat similar to Connors', felt Lendl's loopy swings made it tough for him to establish any tempo versus Connors' onslaught.

Lendl served at 2-4 in the second set. A series of crosscourt backhands from Connors opened up the court for him to drive a forehand down the line behind Lendl, earn another break and take the second set. Ahead 6-3, 6-2 after one hour and 20 minutes, Connors glared directly at Newcombe in the CBS booth in the southeast corner of the court. Newcombe mentioned this on TV. Months later, I asked Connors if indeed he looked up at Newcombe. "I don't look up to Newcombe anywhere, on or off the court," he said. Then there followed one of those long pauses that I knew meant Connors meant more than a mere quip. "People were talking about Lendl and how he was going to win the U.S. Open," he said. "Well, we were going to see about that, weren't we?"

Lendl served at 1-3, love-30. It almost seemed too easy, I thought, as I sat on my couch. Just past 3:00 p.m. in California, I wondered if there was someone I could call for a match. Lendl came back, and then at 3-2 Connors played one of the strangest serve games of his career. At love-15 he struck a backhand long. On the next two points he served consecutive aces for one of the few times in his life. At 30-30 he double-faulted, and then surrendered his serve with a backhand into the net. Lendl held to go up 4-3. Newcombe noted how Lendl fought from two sets to love down to beat Vitas Gerulaitis earlier that year in the Masters final. He also pointed out how Connors continued to stretch his legs. Connors cramped after the Vilas match. How important was the eight-year age difference between Connors and Lendl?

After Connors held for 4-all, he reached break point on Lendl's serve. But Lendl had picked up his quality of play significantly, and began to run Connors into corners. Lendl held. At 4-5, 30-love, Connors missed easy backhands on three consecutive points. "No doubt about it," said Newcombe, "something is happening with Connors." My palms started to sweat. I thought of what happened in '80 versus McEnroe and '81 versus Borg. After Connors fought off a set point with a backhand approach winner, he missed several forehands, and then, on set point number two, Connors netted another backhand. "We've got a new ballgame," said Trabert. My first instinct was to throw the phone against the wall. "Not good," I said to Mike and quickly hung up.

A tennis player cannot run out the clock, or shut down the other team's offense. He must continually earn points. So it was that Connors started the fourth set with offense. He'd come to net more than 40 times in the first three sets, but as the fourth began he attacked with yet more urgency. In the first game, he broke Lendl's serve with a skidding forehand down the line winner. He took a 2-0 lead with a backhand volley placement, his 51st point at the net.

But Lendl held to love and broke Connors with a backhand down the line pass to level the set. As much as Lendl's strokes had improved, his body language was hardly positive. Connors, meanwhile, looked to have aged 10 years in 30 minutes. His beard looked darker. His hair glistened, a result of sweat and pouring water over his head on changeovers. When the match started just past 4 p.m. it was more than 100 degrees on the court. Past 6:00 p.m., it was cooler, but Connors seemed depleted.

With Lendl serving at 2-2, 30-30, the match was nearly three hours long. Newcombe noted how brutalizing rallies were. Connors floated a backhand service return deep to Lendl's backhand. Lendl undercut his response, short to Connors' forehand. Connors scampered in cross-court. With far more confidence than he'd shown the first two sets, Lendl ripped a backhand pass crosscourt. Connors lunged and the ball dropped over for a winner.

On break point, Connors' return floated to Lendl's forehand. Lendl hit this one crosscourt too. Connors approached down the line with his backhand. A lob might have been a good play from Lendl, but both players were too amped up for finesse at this stage. Lendl's pass flew right to Connors' backhand volley. Connors stabbed it behind Lendl down the line to earn the break. Another phone call. "Maybe we're in the clear," I said to Mike.

Connors held for 4-2 with a crosscourt forehand volley place-ment—netrush number 60. Each of his four games was won with winners. He seemed weary, but just might make it. From fluids and footwork to volleys, he looked for energy wherever he could find it.

Now Lendl gave him some more. At 2-4, 15-15, the two both ended up at net. Connors attempted a feeble lob volley. Lendl hit his smash perilously close to Connors. It was a legal play, but it was also known throughout the sport that Lendl liked to intimidate opponents by hitting them with tennis balls. Connors admonished him. What did you say? I asked Connors. Again a long pause. "I don't recall," he said, an obvious lie. As Connors moved to return serve, the most primitive lip-reader saw him mouth the word, "Motherfucker." Said Trabert, "That might just be enough adrenaline pump for Jimmy to carry him right on through." On the next point Connors approached off Lendl's serve—a rare play for Connors, but one that Segura had taught and urged him to execute constantly—and struck his trademark skyhook for a winner. Then he wagged his index finger at Lendl. Though Lendl held serve, Connors indeed was energized. Trabert wondered why Connors continued to exert energy on every point. The serve-volley players were more prudent with their output once up by a service break. But Connors had spent his whole career turning that model upside-down. His manner was to apply pressure on every point, to let the opponent know there was no way out of the noose.

The 4-3 game opened with a 14-ball rally, Connors again pounding deep into Lendl's forehand to set up a sliding backhand down-the-line approach. Lendl drove the passing shot into the net. The next point was similar, a 10-ball exchange, Connors driving a forehand approach shot so deep Lendl was only able to lob long. Next, a gift: Lendl struck a service return wide. At 40-love, Lendl's tepid forehand and weak backhand placed the ball short to Connors' backhand. It was a drill he knew from Belleville. As his feet squeaked with the trademark short steps, Connors laced the backhand crosscourt for a winner. He raised his arm up in the air and extended his index finger. One more. I called Mike.

On the first point of Lendl's service game, the Czech whipped a crosscourt forehand approach and angled a backhand volley. Full tilt, Connors ran and struck a forehand down-the-line winner. He thrust his hips at the crowd. As much as Connors said he adored New York, was this gesture more a manner of making love or something more perverse? Regardless, the Connors who looked so tired 20 minutes before had found another gear. Lendl held.

Connors stood by his chair the entire changeover. Pat Summerall on CBS failed to report this. As the 5-4 game began, he said, "Lendl, out quickly and out first." Could Connors close it out? On the first point he served and volleyed, but struck the backhand volley long. The match was now three hours and six minutes long. At love-15, Lendl smacked two forehands. He was at last seeing he could open up the court if he drove his forehand down the line rather than hit it crosscourt to Connors' backhand. With Connors stretched into his forehand corner, Lendl rocketed his next forehand crosscourt, inches inside the baseline. A tenacious Connors scampered and virtually half-volleyed his reply. Lendl, not comfortable in the net area, failed to move in close enough and was wide with the volley. At 15-all, Connors sliced his serve deep to Lendl's backhand. Seeing Lendl's racket face open up—a sign that the return would float high—Connors scampered in and nailed a forehand volley down-the-line winner. He raised two fingers and screamed out, "Two! Two! Two! Two!" On the next point he served, drove his backhand deep into Lendl's backhand and dashed forward. "All I wanted to do was rush him," said Connors. Lendl's pass went 10 feet wide.

"This crowd will tear this place apart if Connors wins this one," said Trabert. Connors now stood one point away from his best season since 1974. Back then, a boy, a punk, someone I detested. Now he was 30, still a punk to me, someone I adored. Who changed more? Again he scampered in, his backhand barely going past the service line. Lendl lined the pass into the net.

Mike and I screamed. For years after we would re-enact this final point, me serving a lefty spinner to his forehand, Mike hitting short to my backhand. The crowd roared.

Connors, far more exhausted than at Wimbledon, staggered to his chair. His body soaked, his face grizzled, his body wrapped in towel and warmup suit, he looked more like a boxer after 15 rounds. So worried was Connors of cramps that he stood up through his entire press conference. "When I won before, everybody thought I would," said Connors. "When I won now everybody thought I wouldn't. And that's pretty satisfying."

Two weeks later, Connors came to San Francisco to play the Transamerica Open. My profile was *Inside Tennis'* cover story that month. Copies of it were all over the event's venue, the Cow Palace. I took a seat right behind the court for Connors' first-round match.

As he walked to my side of the court to serve his opening game, Connors and I made eye contact. He gave me a brisk nod. I was staggered. Afterwards, he said how much he liked my story.

"Are you coming tomorrow?" he asked.

"I don't know. My publisher wants this press credential back." I added that Dave Engelberg was coming too.

"We'll fix that. Get your butt here tomorrow." He told me to meet him.

The next night, Connors was right on time. He took Dave and I into the event's office, turned to tournament director Barry MacKay and said, "Take care of these guys." We were handed VIP passes. For the balance of the tournament, Dave and I were courtside for Connors' matches, usually sitting with one of the key members in the Jimbo Posse, a photographer named John Heller. After each match, Heller, Dave and I huddled with Connors. With Connors back on top, it was one big lovefest between him and the public. Even after he lost the final to McEnroe 6-1, 6-3, he (and McEnroe) knew the defeat did nothing to damage his splendid 1982.

As Dave, John and I waited for Connors to emerge from the locker after the finals, a long line of fans stood nearby hoping to get Jimmy's autograph. Many of them held copies of *Inside Tennis*. Dave asked a few if they liked the story on Connors. After several said yes, Dave pointed to me and said, "Here's the guy who wrote it." Hankering for Connors, they settled for me. I made my way up and down the line, signing my name dozens of times. When Connors at last came out and saw what was happening, he laughed.

The night before, Dave, John, Connors and I dined in San Francisco. It was a swift, informal meal, but by this point I'd launched—at least, like Mailer's presidential aspirations, in the privacy of my mind—my campaign to earn Connors' trust and eventually become his authorized biographer. We chatted about tennis, football, baseball, the weather. When I explained to Connors about being fired from the magazine, he said, "That might turn out to be a good thing for you. You'll have to figure it out in your own time, in your own way." It was the same message Tonya told me years ago in a dream.

The question was, how? After the finals, Connors hustled out of the Cow Palace with Heller in his classic, Elvis-like manner of limo and private plane. Like the circus, the tennis was gone. I was left behind.

As I completed grad school applications, I taught tennis. Why didn't I move to New York and find a job at *World Tennis* or *Tennis*? First, I wanted no part of cold East Coast winters and muggy summers. I was starting to play more tennis than I had in four years. As I'd written about the sport, and spent time with Connors, I realized how much I loved to play, particularly outdoors in California.

Second, but no doubt more important, I was in love. There was a way I was able to understand and accept myself with Joan that I had never felt with anyone in my life. I felt safe with her. She wanted to know me in ways no one ever had. She also had an illness, lupus, which helped me explore my unstated fear: Did I make people get sick? Very early in our relationship, Joan became the first person I ever told about Ken. She told me how much she appreciated me trusting her enough to confide in her.

Then I did something I'd never done. Soon after we started living together in the spring of 1983, we were eating brunch at The Zuni Café, a San Francisco restaurant. The weather on this Sunday morning was brilliant, the sky blue, the view of the San Francisco Bay perfectly clear. I had a tennis match scheduled that afternoon. The poignant Pachelbel's Canon echoed through the café's speakers. "Do you remember this music?" Joan asked. "It was used in *Ordinary People*." *Ordinary People* was a movie about an upper middle class family torn apart by the accidental death of the older brother and the younger brother's feelings of guilt which triggered a suicide attempt. As I heard the music, I began crying about Ken for the first time since it all started nearly seven years before. "It wasn't my fault," I said. "It wasn't my fault." Life with Joan in California meant far more to me than any East Coast job or graduate school. And I wasn't about to make her relocate.

So instead the plan called for me to apply to Berkeley's graduate school in journalism. The only trouble came when my application was rejected, the Connors piece in *Inside Tennis* cited as evidence of my shortcomings. Joan reminded me that no one needed a degree to become a writer.

Fortunately, Connors was once again in my life to prove her point. In April '83, he was in LA for a tournament at the Los Angeles Tennis Club. I successfully pitched a Connors profile to a new national magazine called *Racquet Quarterly*. Following the plan that worked so well, I left a copy of the magazine and a note for Connors at the BHTC. Connors was so relaxed that as he walked on to the court at the LATC for his first-round match, he spotted me in the crowd and yelled out, "Hey, I called you." As he unzipped his racket cover, we scheduled our interview.

For 21 years I've owned a cassette. I misplaced it for a decade. For another three years it sat in my trunk beneath an old T-2000. It's that week's interview with Connors. It opens with my recording of the telephone message he left for me at my parents' house. The primary focus of the story: Connors' comments on his '82 Wimbledon and U.S. Open finals, many of which form this chapter's accounts.

The tape oozes my assumption of friendship. Cheekily, I told Connors he could have won each final in straight sets. He paused for a long time, then said that, "Hindsight is 20-20, but the way each worked was perfect. That Wimbledon was so long, and at the Open, if I'd just won it in three sets, they'd have said Lendl had a bad day." I asserted how much he didn't like low balls to his forehand. "I don't mind that shot," said Connors. I asked why he didn't play Davis Cup. "I'm a non-participant," he said, "for reasons of my own." As I mentioned Newcombe's concerns about his fitness for a fifth set, Connors said, "But it didn't go five sets, did it?" When I told Connors about interviewing Patti on the phone, he asked, "You interviewed my wife?" I had no idea they were in the middle of a separation that wasn't resolved until the summer of '83.

Looking back, I see my approach was at once callow and informed, fawning yet inquisitive. I genuinely wanted to understand Connors, not just as a transitory celebrity but as an enduring athlete. Most young journalists started at the bottom and worked their way up to the stars. I was barely beginning, and juggling the complicated relationship between writer and subject.

And yet, a connection formed between us. Most of all, I was younger than the world-weary journalists who'd covered Connors his whole career. There were few journalists Connors felt comfortable calling "son." But he also recognized how much I knew, that I tallied up his netrushes in each match and that my curiosity was genuinely aimed at what he called "the tennis" rather than "all that other crap." Connors also appreciated that we had mutual friends. As I interviewed him that afternoon, his aide de camp, Lornie Kuhle, played on a court in front of us versus my old doubles partner (and Connors' one-week hitting partner five years earlier), Ron Berman.

"You know that guy?" asked Connors.

"Know him? That guy once threw a racket at me in the middle of a challenge match."

Pinching his nostrils, looking me over, Connors retorted, "I can see that."

It was blarney, a conversation between two tennis players utterly forgettable save for the fact that one of them was at that point the best player on the planet. If it was meaningless to Connors, yet one more chat adjacent to a court with yet one more civilian, to me it was all-important. I didn't know how I was going to find my way into the world of writing, but at least there was Connors. And if at 22 I could already publish thousands of words on the world's number one tennis player—not the has-been Bill Simons said he was—who dared stop me from anything?

Shortly after interviewing Connors at the BHTC, I arrived at the LATC to watch his second-round match. A player named Eliot Teltscher had just lost a match. "I play pretty much the same way, and that's what I'm going to do, win or lose," he said. It was one thing for a multiple Slam winner like Connors, McEnroe or Borg to say this, but for a top 20 player like Teltscher to say this was, depending on how you looked at, either too realistic or too depressing. A fellow journalist loved it. "Eliot's like me," he said. "He's a journeyman who knows his limitations." Still basking in the glow of my interview with Connors, I wanted to throttle the journalist. You sir, I wanted to say, are nothing more than a hack. Where was ambition?

Much as I dreamed big for my career, I was always brought down to earth when we visited Ken. At 26, his violent episodes were over, thanks in large part to a series of medications. He lived at a board-and-care facility, or "halfway house." Often he went days without bathing. Other times he barely spoke. My father admitted to me he had diffi-culty sleeping after talking with Ken at night. Dutiful son that I was, I said nary a word about Jimmy Connors to Ken. In my Los Angeles, there was the sun, and there was the moon.

By May I stopped teaching tennis and searched in earnest for a job. I'm yet another of those liberal arts graduates who will share how hard it was to find a job in communications and that the economy that year was particularly difficult (isn't it always?). Contacting newspapers, magazines, public relations firms, advertising agencies, I sent dozens of cover letters, made hundreds of phone calls, built networks of contacts. One afternoon I walked into the offices of a publication and sold an idea on the spot. For three weeks I made $5 an hour writing for a suburban weekly newspaper. Constantly throughout this period I thought of Connors grinding out one point after another. When an editor's job at a monthly sports publication resulted again in my termination (besides the production skills, I loathed revising the words of others), I naturally thought of Connors back on defense, forced to scramble back to offense. Having saved some money from teaching tennis, I had until the end of September to either find a full-time media job or apply for a less-desirable position as an administrative assistant.

Connors' lovefest at number one continued through the first half of 1983. Oddly enough, he finished 1982 ranked number two on the ATP computer, yet another of those technical anomalies that benefited him in other years. But through the end of '82 and into '83, no one doubted his status not just as the sport's premier player, but something even bigger.

The aspiring biographer in me was reminded of Norman Mailer. Like Connors, Mailer saw life as a war. Like Connors, Mailer was regarded as pushy, obnoxious and full of himself. The two each debuted strongly, Connors with his breakthrough '74 campaign, Mailer with his 1948 popular and literary success, the World War II novel, *The Naked and the Dead*. Each wanted nothing less than to be number one, yet because each often came close but short, were regarded as unsuccessful, to the point where each was in danger of becoming more known for their losses. Like Connors, an allegedly mellowed Mailer enjoyed late career success. His Pulitzer Prize winning book, *Armies of the Night*, written 20 years after his debut, cast into relief the relentless tenacity of his vision and high quality of work. As one critic wrote in *The New Republic*, "He has willed himself into pertinence and power . . . Mailer has intervened in the age so that he has come to count, more securely as time goes on."

"For Connors," wrote Peter Bodo in the January '83 *Tennis*, "1982 was a year of crystallization. On the morning after his U.S. Open victory, he awoke as a man with a history, as a man who the public finally perceived in a broader, richer context than before. He is a hero now, rewarded for all those semis and finals in which he came up, despite his strongest efforts, a service break short or a second serve long."

Connors' stock was further enhanced in January '83 when Borg shocked the tennis world and announced his retirement in the middle of the Masters tournament. Until then, everyone thought '82 was a mere sabbatical. That very month, a *World Tennis* article asked, "Can the Iceman Cometh Back?" Connors spoke with a confidence he hadn't had since the late '70s: "He's going to have one main obstacle in his way and that's me … it's going to make for one hell of a rivalry again."

Borg's exit altered perceptions of him and Connors. For so long, Connors was considered the man unable to accept losing—a skill the classy Swede seemed to master. Now the picture looked quite different. Connors went nearly four years without reaching a Slam final and returned to fight another day. Borg, dispatched in the '81 Wimbledon and Open finals by McEnroe, was the one unwilling to attempt a climb back up the mountain. Contrasted with Borg's exile, Connors' tenacity shined even brighter. I wanted to find my friend in the Fila warmup suit and ask him how he felt about Borg's dominance and Connors' decline now.

Connors rode into Wimbledon with a wave of confidence, defending his title at Queen's with a 6-0, 6-3 win over Lendl and a 6-3, 6-3 victory over McEnroe. Yet when I looked at Connors' Wimbledon draw, I saw a name that worried me. Kevin Curren owned one of the biggest serves in the game. Sure enough, versus Connors in the round of 16, he served 70 winners, including 33 aces, to eliminate Connors in four sets. McEnroe won the tournament handily. Most notable was his straight-set rout of Lendl in the semis. It was his third straight win over Lendl, proving how much McEnroe had shaken off his '82 staleness.

As the '83 U.S. Open neared, McEnroe and Lendl were the two favorites. Besides having never successfully defended his Grand Slam title, Connors would turn 31 in New York. "Should he manage to win the Open this year," wrote Steve Flink in September's *World Tennis*, "it would be the greatest accomplishment of his career."

That month a friend 12 years my elder taught me how to put on a tie. He also gave me counsel. It was time, he said, to let go of tennis. I was 23, likely not to play as well as I aged, and that maturity required thinking about more than Jimmy Connors. But as I sent out one résumé after another, as I interviewed for jobs left and right, could I abandon Connors? Of course my friend was right. I just needed some more time, a few more hours in rapture of Connors. He might not win the U.S. Open that year, but he was still someone I needed to take seriously.

But when McEnroe lost to Bill Scanlon in the round of 16,

Connors' draw opened up. Instead of the treacherous McEnroe, he faced Scanlon in the semis, beating him easily to set up a second straight final versus Lendl.

"Now don't get me wrong, to win Wimbledon, to win a Slam after four years, that was a great thrill," Connors told me that April at the Beverly Hills Tennis Club. "But the Open, well, that was business. Business as usual."

Given all the tumult generated by Connors in New York over the previous decade, it was an odd metaphor. It was hard to compare Connors at the U.S. Open with the predictability of a quarterly earnings announcement. The '83 Open final was no exception. More than any of the 15 Slam finals Connors played in his career, it was one where mitigating factors told the story.

A bone spur on the tiny toe of Connors' right foot made it hard for him to move. He also had diarrhea. Per the rules, he would be permitted one bathroom break, though if necessary, he could sprint to a nearby lavatory on any changeover and likely get back on the court within the 90-second time limit. Earlier in the tournament he had received a death threat. Security guards, disguised as photographers and others with courtside access, swarmed around Connors. As the match started shortly past 4:00 p.m., it was 107 degrees on the court, with 95 percent humidity and winds of 18 miles per hour. And of course there was the matter of Lendl, still Slam-less at 23, but unquestionably a better player since last year's final. At 31, was Connors improved?

As typically happens with back-to-back finals, there was an air of déjà vu. With Connors serving at 2-2, 30-15, he and Lendl engaged in a 20-ball rally. Eleven of Connors' drives were aimed at Lendl's forehand, and when Lendl struck one long, Newcombe noted the psychological battle and Connors' effort to go "strength to strength." Trabert pointed out how the wind was less of a problem for Connors than Lendl due to the Czech's longer, loopy swings.

Lendl served at 3-4, 30-40. His first serve went deep to Connors' backhand. Leaning into it, Connors struck deep to Lendl's backhand. Shocked by the penetration of Connors' return, Lendl's reply was short. Connors approached. Lendl's backhand flew 20 feet past the baseline. Connors pumped his fists and held at love to close out the set, 6-3, in 31 minutes.

"Here we go again," I said to Joan. We watched the small black and white TV. I sat less than a foot from the screen.

When Connors broke, held and reached 15-40 on Lendl's serve, I wanted to start dancing. But not only did Lendl fight back in that game, he won four straight games and soon served at 4-2. The toe injury clearly made it hard for Connors to push off and drive the ball with his customary force. Lendl was more precise with his forehand than in '82. But Connors broke to get back on serve. Then, Connors' eyes watering, he approached chair umpire Rich Kaufman and said, "It's time." Quickly he went to the bathroom. Upon returning, Connors' serve was broken again, and Lendl now served for the set at 5-4. Saving two set points, Connors again took Lendl's serve. After having only lost his serve five times in his first six matches, Lendl had been broken just as much by Connors in less than two sets. Said Newcombe about Lendl's struggles, "It's one thing to get up to the line, it's another thing to cross it." It made me think of how hard it was to find a job.

Connors now served at 5-6. Down set point, he hit one of his rarest serves—right down the center for an ace. A superb volley and a retrieval that led to a backhand winner took the set to a tiebreak.

With Lendl up 3-2, Connors played four horrific points. He netted an easy forehand pass, drove a forehand volley long, was wide with a forehand and then drove another forehand long. It was now one set apiece. The psychological edge Connors had from both the '82 final and the start of the match appeared gone. Physically, Lendl looked sharp and Connors seemed to have every reason to grow weary.

When Lendl took a 3-1 lead in the third, it was hard to see how Connors could win. From the baseline, Lendl played with far more security and intelligence than in '82. He drove forehands to Connors' forehand instead of backhand. He served with greater pace and variety. He withstood Connors' charges too. Connors thus far had only won half of the points when he came to net, significantly lower than the desired 65-75 percent.

So here is the question: How does a player become a champion? Obviously, he must build the best set of skills possible through practice and competition. And he must execute them constantly. Yet, having interviewed the likes of Connors, Newcombe, Trabert, Segura and Billie Jean King, I've come to understand that skill plays but one small role. Champions from every era in tennis history have told me that there were always several players with skills as good as anyone else's. As tennis grew, there were even more. In 1983, there were probably 80 players able to test Connors.

What makes the difference? It is a matter both rational and spiritual. The brain tells the player why he's better, just as when Segura used to run through the inventory of strokes with Connors before the match. But it's the heart that nurtures faith and confidence, as Segura and Gloria did for so long with Connors. Or, for that matter, as Connors did with himself. It's the heart that becomes particularly important when a player is not hitting the ball as well as he has in the past. In '82, Connors stripped Lendl of his confidence and the Czech was unable to regain it. Lendl had stopped believing in himself that day, and by the time he recovered, it was too late. This was Connors' strength. His confidence never ebbed, even through years of losses for the highest stakes. No matter what compromised him—injury, conditions, the opponent—Connors accepted the terms of the struggle and sought to impose himself on them as best he could.

In fact, Connors knew compromise came with the territory. He would scrape and claw and fight his way through it. If he lost, there was always another day. Tennis was not the art of excellence. It was the craft of enthusiasm, in a player's willingness to pound ball after ball and know that so long as he stayed alert, good things could happen. For all my friend's recommendations that I abandon tennis and grow up, it was Connors' mix of youthful optimism and hard-boiled maturity that guided me. He'd propelled me through adolescence and college, and now he beckoned me into the arena as an adult.

But it was still more fun to win than lose. As Lendl served at 5-4 to take a two sets to one lead, it was hard to see Connors winning this in five. A year ago, fully fit, he barely got through it in four. With a point for 5-all, Connors' forehand approach went long. Lendl reached set point. His first serve nearly aced Connors, but was called long. Then Lendl committed a cardinal sin for playing big points. No matter what, goes the wisdom, make the opponent play. Force him to at least hit the ball. Lendl's second serve spun into the net. At deuce, Connors crept forward and struck a forehand volley winner. On the next point, a superb crosscourt backhand volley. The crowd went nuts. So did I.

At 5-all, Connors closed out his service game with that rarity for him, an ace. Newcombe noted how Lendl's "psychological inner battle" continued. Moments earlier, he had Connors on the ropes, and somehow failed. At 5-6, Connors resolved to force Lendl to play. Lendl erred badly, wide with a backhand for love-15. The court open, Connors just missed a backhand. At 15-15, Lendl netted a forehand, then a backhand. Now it was double set point for Connors. Connors' backhand approach was long, but on the next point, Lendl netted a forehand. It was far from elegant, even for Connors, but there he was, one set away. Newcombe was justifiably amazed at Lendl's meltdown. "You *win* U.S. Open titles," he said. "People don't give them to you."

When Connors slid a forehand down-the-line winner to break Lendl for 2-0 in the fourth, he stood at the precise point he was in '82—same lead in sets and games in what I hoped was the final set. Though he continued to throw himself virtually horizontally to return Lendl's services—retrievals that repeatedly rushed Lendl into errors—I wondered how Connors would consolidate the break. Certainly he wanted to get to net more, but again, his toe injury made it difficult to thrust into the court.

At 2-0, Connors did something he likely never did at any point in his career. He served three aces. 3-0. "Where is this coming from?" asked Pat Summerall.

"From his heart," said Trabert. I turned to Joan and hugged her.

It fascinates me how the muscle we associate with love is also linked to combat. "We're going to kill each other in the process," Connors said before the match. "It's going to be fun."

But Lendl wasn't enjoying himself at all. Connors broke him for 4-0, held easily for 5-0, and now stood a game away from the first successful Slam defense of his career.

At 15-30, Connors wiggled two fingers. He "smells blood," said Trabert. At 30-30, Lendl was long with a backhand. But then he aced Connors, and did so again after Connors earned a second match point. At deuce, Connors whipped a running crosscourt forehand winner. "Unbelievable," said Newcombe about Connors' fight. Another ace. Soon Lendl earned an ad. Not about to let go of a 6-0 victory, Connors lunged and struck a backhand return winner. Again a Lendl ad. Connors scorched a backhand passing shot. Lendl with another game point. The Czech hit a drop shot, but Connors ran it down and rolled a perfect forehand lob over Lendl's head.

On Connors' third match point, Lendl missed his first serve. Connors took the forehand return and drove it crosscourt. Lendl didn't even move. The second Connors saw the linesman call it good, he raised his left hand. All five of his fingers were in the air. He had won ten straight games.

"I love New York when I win and I love it when I lose," he said to the crowd just before he accepted his trophy. The Vilas defeat was ancient history. Borg was retired. Lendl lacked the goods. McEnroe was formidable, but failed in New York the last two years. There was nothing incomplete or withered about Jimmy Connors' résumé now. Of course since childhood, backed and revered by mother and grandmother, he'd never felt he lacked anything. Perpetual self-belief had brought him everything. As Bud Collins noted at the '82 Wimbledon, Connors was "the once and future king."

Just 15 months earlier at my college graduation, Connors was a man who hadn't won a Grand Slam singles title in four years. The future belonged to Borg, McEnroe and Lendl. Over the period from June '82 to September '83, that trio earned one Slam. Connors snapped up three. Much as Connors seemed in the middle of a grand second act, his resilience—particularly when compared to Borg's departure, McEnroe's discomfort and Lendl's performance—showed new-found character. Once considered a man for whom a second act was unlikely, Connors now looked like he'd lived a lifelong encore. In '76, '78, '82 and '83, he proved how dangerous it was to count him out. With eight Slams and 100 titles, it was all gravy from here on in.

As Connors prepared for his victory laps, it was time for me to get to work. "He just finds a way," Trabert said during that Open final. Of course he was talking about Connors, but I also felt the message was aimed at me. Four days after that year's Open final, more than 100 cover letters and phone calls later, I was offered a full-time job at a public relations firm. The next day, Connors withdrew from the San Francisco tournament due to his foot injury. At the Cow Palace the next week I overheard Donald Dell—now Connors' agent—offer career advice. "To get back to tennis, I had to get away from it," he said. "I had to learn how to do a job, had to get some skills and experience. Then I came back. Seven years away from it. Seven years." *In your own time, in your own way.*

9

Business As Usual

It was Sunday, September 1, 1985. I was in New York for the U.S. Open. Not since 1978 had I seen Connors play in New York. It was more than two years since I'd last seen him in person. After paying a scalper $25 for a ticket, I wandered outside Louis Armstrong Stadium, hoping to catch a glimpse of Connors as he headed from the locker to the court for his third-round match. Suddenly I heard lots of yelling.

"Jimmy! Jimmy! Jimmy!"

"Go kick ass, Jimbo!"

"Jimmy!"

"Kill 'em, Connors!"

This was a very different atmosphere than the evening in LA when we spoke like two friends at a park. Flanked by a quartet of security guards, Connors shuffled slowly through a thick crowd. Fans grabbed his hands and touched his navy blue vest. I couldn't help but think of Bobby Kennedy on the campaign trail in California. But while Kennedy gripped and grinned, Connors stared ahead in silence. "It sure is hot today," a Connors practice partner once said to him. "Son, this is business, no time for talk," said Connors.

I followed the trail and snuck into a vacant box seat behind the court. I looked into each corner. At the south end of the court was the spot where Connors stood when he served out the '82 final. Up in the northeast was the ad court from which he struck the winning return in '83. To my left was the small box where Segura, Budge, Perry and Kramer often sat. Up to my right, tucked into the southeast corner, were Tony Trabert, John Newcombe and Pat Summerall in the CBS booth. Louis Armstrong Stadium began to fill. In another box along the east side of the court I saw Nastase.

Even in a routine straight-set victory over Thierry Tulasne there were plenty of entertaining points. Connors played with such continual effort that he brought out the greatest ambitions from his opponents. They'd each push one another to the edge. Most of the time, it was the other guy who fell off.

Soon after match point, I sprinted outside the stadium. Earlier that afternoon I'd chatted up Nick, a security guard just outside the entrance to the players' lounge area that was off-limits to ticket-holders. In his thick Brooklyn accent, Nick explained why he liked Connors so much more than other players. "Jimmy cares, you can see it on his face, in the way he plays, how he tries so hard," he said. When I showed up after the match to spot Connors, Nick greeted me like a familiar friend.

I wondered if Connors would recognize me. Since our last encounter in LA there were dozens of tournaments, thousands of fans, countless journalists. When I'd first written about Connors in the spring of '82 he was perceived more as a grand fighter than an impact player. Three years later, the Slam victories in '82 and '83 had rounded him out. Connors' rough edges were smoothed into endorsements with the likes of McDonald's and Paine Webber. It was an image rehabilitation worthy of Richard Nixon. "Always the consummate competitor and performer," read a 1984 profile, "Connors now looks more like the all-American hero." In his New York element, who would I be to Connors but some kid he'd met years ago back on the Coast?

"Hey, Jimmy," I yelled to him.

"Where have *you* been?" he asked.

The next day I smuggled a bottle of champagne into the USTA National Tennis Center, a present for Connors on his 33rd birthday. My plan was to find him as he came off a practice court. Better yet, he was inside the stadium, working on his day off as an announcer for CBS. Two hours before showtime, Connors and Trabert were on the court together running through logistics for the broadcast with a producer. Pumped up by the sight of my hero and mentor together, I snuck past the security guards and made my way onto the court with paper bag in hand.

"You know this troublemaker?" Trabert asked Connors.

"Yes," said Connors, thanking me for the gift. "So where have you been?" I gave a quick answer and dashed off to a seat.

I'd done precisely what Donald Dell advised. I was an account executive with Edelman, one of the world's largest public relations agencies.

The phrase "public relations agency" evokes images of Hollywood entertainers, flim-flam entrepreneurs and dreary press releases. But these areas comprise only a speck of what public relations practitioners do.

The public relations agency business was a way for me to acquire a range of skills and experiences I hoped to bring back to tennis. "This job," said my boss, "isn't for dilettantes who just want to think great thoughts and write. It's a job that's all about tenacity, little steps and making things happen. You've got to pay attention and create opportunities." In other words, I thought, it's a lot like being Jimmy Connors.

For every client project, there were dozens of micro-details. The image in my head was of Connors as he constantly shuffled his feet. Like a young actor who plays all sorts of roles, I cut my teeth on dozens of stories and projects in subject areas where I lacked innate passion. Love, which is often blind and potentially indulgent, gave way to craftsmanship. Whether I arranged an event for the San Francisco Zoo, or booked a series of interviews for the inventor of that quintessential '80s product, the wine cooler, or wrote a case study for an engineering trade publication on an industrial fabric company's pond liner project in Pennsylvania, I took one tiny step after another. Love meant nothing, but persistence meant everything when I wrote a newsletter for an airline, or determined the news value of a gas station and a slab of cheese in the same morning. All day long, whether on the phone or in a meeting, with a letter or a video, I became adept at telling the stories of others. As in football, school and tennis, I built a reputation as a tenacious practitioner, one who, just like Connors, would chase a project to the ends of the earth.

But I wanted more from Connors than a figurative form of motivation. My apprenticeship would take some time. Besides, Connors continued adding chapters.

"Two more years," a Connors' friend told me in late 1983. "Jimmy wants to play 'til the end of '85 and then do other things." I wasn't sure if that was true, but felt confident those "other things" might include an autobiography. The signs pointed towards a kind ride into the sunset. What I didn't count on was how bumpy that ride would be. I should have known better.

The 1984 Wimbledon final promised much. Connors, the '82 champ, was out to regain the title from defender McEnroe. In June '83, after beating McEnroe in the Queen's final on the eve of Wimbledon, Connors still led their rivalry 11-9. Over the next 12 months, McEnroe won five straight times with the loss of but one set. Connors' semifinal win at Wimbledon over Lendl was yet another show of classic resilience, Connors rebounding from a break down in the third to take the fourth, 6-1.

McEnroe joined the club of men who played the finest match of his career versus Connors in what happened to be a Grand Slam final. In 80 minutes, he committed just two unforced errors and destroyed Connors, 6-1, 6-1, 6-2. There was little animus from Connors in defeat. This was a different man in a different time. As Kim Cunningham noted in the July issue of *World Tennis*, "Connors still makes questionable gestures, mimics querulous opponents, stalls, grunts and mixes up the momentum of a match with comedy that can turn to combat at the drop of an expletive. But his timing has improved because now when he laughs, the world laughs with him." Besides, what was Wimbledon but a prelude to the Open?

The Connors-McEnroe U.S. Open semifinal concluded one of the greatest days in tennis history. "Super Saturday," September 8, 1984, began with Lendl's fifth-set tie-breaker win over Pat Cash and continued with Navratilova's three-set victory versus Evert in the women's final.

Connors was on a 19-match Open winning streak, compiling a sparkling 41-3 record and three titles since the move from Forest Hills. McEnroe was 39-3 and also a three-time winner. No man besides these two had ever won the title at Flushing Meadows.

It was nearly 7:30 when Connors and McEnroe started. Of the eight times they met at Grand Slams, this one was unquestionably the best mix of playing quality and drama. Like two top-rate lawyers in a courtroom, McEnroe and Connors each argued their cases eloquently, McEnroe out to prosecute with his serve and volleys, Connors countering for the defense with his returns and groundstrokes.

On the opening point, Connors drilled a backhand return down the line for a winner. Over the course of the match, he hit this shot frequently and successfully. "How 'bout the crosscourt?" McEnroe yelled after yet another flew by him. Barely an hour into it, the quality was so high, the score so tight, that Tony Trabert said, "It wouldn't be right if this didn't go five sets." At one set all, McEnroe served at 1-3, love-30. Visions danced in my head of Connors going on to win a third straight Open. But McEnroe held, broke and held again. With Connors serving at 3-4, deuce, the two had a 31-ball exchange that ended with Connors netting a forehand. "You could teach a whole tennis lesson out of that rally," said Newcombe. McEnroe broke to serve for the set at 5-3—and then Connors broke back and held for 5-all.

But at 5-6, 30-15, just as a tiebreak seemed inevitable, Connors tried to out-cute McEnroe with an angled backhand volley (again that lefty-lefty mix derailed Jimbo's instincts), and though Connors saved one set point with a lunging backhand volley, two points later he lost a 23-ball rally with a high volley that was barely wide. McEnroe now led 6-4, 4-6, 7-5. Under the lights, in what proved to be the best year of his career, McEnroe appeared invincible. His serve crackled into corners. He feasted on Connors' delivery, repeatedly coming in on Jimbo's first serves. His volleys nicked corners. His groundstrokes were appropriately low, deep or angled.

Yet when the fourth set began, Connors was fresher. He broke McEnroe immediately. McEnroe misfired on volleys and groundstrokes. Connors served at 5-2. Though he went on to win the set, it was in the fourth that he lost the match. McEnroe broke Connors at 5-2, held again and forced Connors to play a tough game to serve it out. That tiny sequence of three games was enough for McEnroe to get his teeth back into the match. Had Connors closed it out 6-2, he might have generated enough momentum to seize the night in the fifth. But McEnroe—particularly in 1984—was as formidable a competitor as Connors. His great serve made him even more adept at raising the level of his game than Connors. After three hours and six minutes, McEnroe opened the fifth in a much higher gear than Connors. He held at love, broke Connors at 15, held again at love for a 3-0 lead and soon had another break point for 4-0.

Here again the momentum shifted. Connors held, and when McEnroe served at 4-2, Connors reached break point—but was inches long with a forehand. McEnroe closed out the game with an ace, then held again at love to close out the match, 6-4, 4-6, 7-5, 4-6, 6-3 after three hours and 46 minutes. "I thought it was a great match," said McEnroe. "I had a feeling he was the only guy that would be able to stop me so I had to take matters into my own hands. I served 70 percent of my first serves in and the guy broke me seven times. That's got to tell you something."

Hard as it was to believe, this was an acceptable loss for Connors. Minutes after shaking hands with McEnroe, five-year-old Brett Connors made his way to the court. Jimbo, no longer the fiery warrior, hugged his son and waved his hands through his hair. Long past midnight, Connors, his brother Johnny, Doug Henderson, McEnroe and McEnroe's coach, Tony Palafox, were just about the only people left in the locker. "That match was really the final," said Palafox. There was no doubt in Connors' mind he would have found a way to beat Lendl. The next afternoon, over lunch at the Hard Rock Café, Connors and Henderson talked about a few points from the match. "There's always next year," said Connors. Three years prior, Connors hoped to win one more Grand Slam. He'd since tripled that goal. At this stage in Connors' career, it was, though he'd never admit it, honorable to lose so closely to a player as brilliant as McEnroe was in 1984 (82-3 for the year).

But dare one expect pure grace from Jimmy Connors? When Dell began to manage Connors in 1983, he convinced Connors that the one jewel missing on his crown was participation on a winning Davis Cup squad. Connors played one prior tie for the Ashe-led American team in the summer of '81. But when asked to join the team for later rounds, he declined, invoking a ski trip when invited to play in the finals. On the eve of the finals that year, Ashe appeared on a television call-in show. One call came from none other than Connors, who asked Ashe how things were going. "It would be a lot easier if you were with us," said Ashe.

In 1984 Connors agreed to play Davis Cup for the entire year. Unfortunately, Davis Cup exacerbated tensions between Connors and McEnroe. Connors lacked any affinity for the team event. McEnroe was a stalwart, in seven straight years never turning down a request to represent his nation. McEnroe's preeminence made it hard for Connors to accept being the team's second-best superstar. Much as Ashe tried to play the diplomat role, he was repeatedly stymied by Connors' discomfort with collaboration. There were numerous misunderstandings between Ashe and Connors. Since the Cup began, all matches were three-out-of-five sets, so naturally Ashe was shocked when Connors asked if they were only two-out-of-three. There were also quibbles over practice times, hotel accommodations and sportsmanship. "To Mac and me," wrote Ashe in his posthumous autobiography, *Days of Grace*, "that silver cup was the Holy Grail. To Jimmy, it seemed that it might have been made of Styrofoam." An even bigger factor was that Connors was 32, still a major factor but not likely in ascent. McEnroe was 25, at the height of his powers.

It reached rock-bottom at the finals in December. A different draw, and the U.S. team might well have hosted a hapless nation on native soil with Connors and McEnroe happily leading America to victory. Instead, the venue was Sweden. The surface was an indoor claycourt, with an opposition that starred Mats Wilander, a rough player who'd frequently beaten Connors and McEnroe and was exceptionally formidable on clay.

Both of America's stars were on edge. The previous month, in Stockholm, McEnroe threw a temper tantrum highlighted by him thrashing courtside water cups with his racket. Suspended for 21 days, he came back to Sweden stale and cranky. With Patti Connors pregnant, due in December, Connors felt anxious and worn out from a long year. He'd also lost his only two matches to Wilander, most notably blowing a 4-0 third-set lead in Cincinnati the past August. When Ashe and Jimmy Arias were 15 minutes late for a practice session, an irate Connors scrawled an obscenity on the clay court.

In the opening match, Connors was unable to dent Wilander. The 12-year age difference between the two was notable, as was Wilander's sharp focus versus a tepid Connors. Frustrated by everything from Wilander's consistency to the odd bounces of the court, Connors barked out profanities, grabbed the umpire's chair, and came within a point penalty of being defaulted before losing 6-1, 6-3, 6-3. After Connors was fined $2,000, referee Alan Mills gave serious thought to barring Connors from future Davis Cup matches. But the intervention of Dell, coupled with a profound apology from Connors, smoothed things over. McEnroe was upset in the next singles match, and when he and Peter Fleming lost the doubles to give Sweden the Cup, Connors' Davis Cup career was over for good. "What was I thinking?" Ashe asked me the one time I interviewed him at length. "All his life, Connors was trained not to trust anyone and to look out for no one but himself. He was never going to understand the dynamics of team play."

The next year did not start off well. In January '85, up 5-2 in the third to Lendl in the semis of the Masters, Connors lost the match 7-5, 6-7, 7-5. Connors then suffered a series of losses earlier than usual in Philadelphia, Memphis and La Quinta—tournaments where he had earned 14 titles. Spotting Connors' decline with the alertness of a dentist detecting the first signs of a cavity, *World Tennis'* Steve Flink dared ask "Is Connors All Washed Up?" in the magazine's May issue. "The feeling grows that Jimmy Connors has moved irrevocably past his prime," wrote Flink. "One wonders whether this proud and complicated man is any longer a serious threat to win a major championship." I didn't want to believe this, but, at 32, without a title nearly halfway through the season, with losses now coming to lesser players, the signals were not encouraging.

In large part, Connors' struggle to reconcile desire and decline—

or competition and commerce—was symbolized that year by his racket. By the early '80s, the T-2000 was as dated as an 8-track player. Wilson stopped making the frame years earlier. Connors issued a public plea for T-2000s. At the '83 U.S. Open he carried the same frame he'd used in '74.

Eager to capitalize on his late career resurgence, Wilson wanted to make Connors the successor to Jack Kramer: not just a man with a racket, but a grand corporate ambassador. A deal was signed for millions, but the terms demanded Connors change rackets so he could at last endorse a frame players might purchase.

Wilson's representative on the pro tour, Max Brownlee, worked with Connors and Wilson's product development team to build a suitable frame. The Wilson Pro Staff was unveiled in the summer of '84, complete with a massive print and broadcast advertising campaign starring Connors in a tan blazer. "It's perfect!" said Connors in the ads. He began to use the racket just before the Open. It added more power to his serve, and, on other shots, a player with the disciplined technique of Connors would probably strike the ball well with a garbage can lid. That fall, Connors won two tournaments with the Pro Staff, including a 6-0 third-set win versus Lendl in Tokyo that proved to be Connors' last victory over him. It was also the only tournament title Connors would win for nearly four years.

But the relationship with Wilson was one case where time was not on Jimmy Connors' side. A 32-year-old tennis player, competitive 11 months a year, has significantly more mileage on him than other athletes. As the bad losses accumulated in early '85, Connors looked for reasons. What changed that caused him to suffer? According to a source close to Wilson and Connors, at one point Connors told Brownlee the money meant nothing to him. Connors said he had all the fucking money he wanted. What he wanted most of all was a racket that would help him win. So, Max, find it! At La Quinta in March, Connors lost 6-3, 6-0 to a rank-and-file player named Greg Holmes. As Connors walked off the court, he dumped the frames in Brownlee's lap. At Connors' press conference, a representative from rival manufacturer Prince asked Connors if his racket was responsible for his loss. Pointing to Brownlee, Connors said, "Ask that guy." Connors went back to the T-2000. (An adolescent Southern Californian named Pete Sampras started to play with the new Pro Staff and used it his entire career.)

Connors' lifelong peers were now retired. Several wondered what continued to motivate him to play when it seemed unlikely he could ever be number one again. Even McEnroe, seven years younger, groused about the demands and pressures of being at the top. "I've never been wild about being number one," he said in 1985. The next year, at 27, McEnroe took a six-month sabbatical. He reached but three more Grand Slam semifinals the rest of his career before he quit at age 33 (Connors between 27 and 33 advanced that far 15 times and won three Slams).

There was never going to be an exile for Jimmy Connors. What kept him going? Money was one motivator, but as the Wilson incident proved, Connors wanted more than dollars. More likely he loved recognition and applause. Beneath the fighter in Connors was a people-pleaser. The little boy who'd started off performing for the two women in his life now made thousands cheer with each word, gesture, step and shot. Victories at this point were less a matter of making his résumé substantial and more a chance to perform yet another day. Who wanted to give that up? And then there was the matter of competition. In a team sport, a player's decline hurts the squad. But in an individual endeavor, why not soldier on? Connors was still one of the top five or six players in the sport at this point. "But why should he fade into nothing?" a friend asked me. That's when I realized why people want their athletes to leave sooner than later. When an athlete declines, we face our own mortality. If Jimmy Connors erodes, what does that say about the rest of us? Eager as I was to write Connors' biography, I wanted him to play as long as he wished. In his own way, Connors' steadfast refusal to stop was yet another way for him to counterpunch the pace of conventional wisdom. "Why should I retire?" asked Connors. "What else can I do where I can make a living like this? But beyond that, I still like to play the game. I like to compete. I *live* to compete. What's more, I like to prove people wrong when they say I can't do it anymore."

There was still the possibility he might live up to his word. When Lendl and McEnroe both lost early at Wimbledon in '85, Connors' arrival in the semis gave me hope. The winner of Connors' match versus Kevin Curren would play Sweden's Anders Jarryd or the German teenager, Boris Becker. Surely neither the yeoman Jarryd nor the youthful Becker was ready to topple Connors in a Slam final. Despite Curren's win over Connors two years earlier, who believed he had the goods to do it again?

On July 5, 1985, Joan and I planned to watch Connors and then have a couple of friends over for dinner. On the first point of the match, Connors lofted a forehand lob over Curren's head for a winner. "There, that's it," I said, "Jimmy's going to open things up with a lot of good lobs. I like this."

I was mistaken. Curren won handily, 6-2, 6-2, 6-1.

That night I was one of the worst hosts you'll ever see. All I thought of was how anemic Connors looked. And this wasn't versus a champion like Borg or McEnroe.

"You know what you have to do," said Joan.

"What?"

"It could be Jimbo's last Open. You have to go to New York."

Eager to endear myself to Connors, I made an initial contact with *Tennis Week* and proposed an article about Connors' relationship to the U.S. Open. "Business As Usual For Jimbo" was a Valentine, pointing out how the growth of tennis and Connors at the U.S. Open were intertwined. His New York run, I argued, was anything but business-like. I joined the chorus who'd compared Connors to Frank Sinatra. Who else was better-equipped to sing "My Way" than Jimbo? The editor liked the story, but thought my praise should be countered with another piece.

I proposed a solution designed to enhance my campaign to become Connors' appointed biographer. Richard Evans, *Tennis Week*'s long-standing senior writer, was a classy, elegant British journalist deeply simpatico with the older generation of Ashe, Newcombe and the embryonic ATP (a place where he once held a job). He detested Connors, not just for his sportsmanship—curiously, Evans adored McEnroe—but also, I suspect, for Connors' base mix of individualism and ambition. McEnroe's upper-middle class prep school anguish was acceptable, but Connors' white-hot desire, blue-collar sensibility and crude humor were anathema to Evans. I suggested Evans write the counterpoint piece. His story, "Let Your Racket Do The Talking, Mister Connors" took Connors to task for everything from Davis Cup to his weakness on the low forehand. As a journalist 20 years older than me, Evans in the '70s no doubt absorbed far more of Connors' toxicity than I had as a young fan. Yet much as I agreed with certain aspects of his case against Connors, I felt he wasn't seeing the whole picture. Then again, how could a British writer understand someone as American as Connors? I'll admit I was more advocate than disinterested journalist. By bringing Evans into the dialogue, I wanted to create a Challenge Match. No one truly could win, but if Connors read both pieces, I'd surely triumph.

Connors was featured on the cover of *Tennis Week*'s U.S. Open preview issue with the headline, "Jimmy Connors—The People's Choice." I gave Connors a copy along with the bottle of champagne.

The next day, when I saw him after his win over Stefan Edberg, he complimented me on the story. Later that afternoon, with Connors making the introduction, I spoke to Donald Dell. He liked my story too, and later that day I asked him if Connors was considering writing a book. Three hours later, Dell told me a book wasn't in the cards now, but that we should keep in touch. Looking back, I realize the matter of a book was barely on Connors' radar screen then. He and Dell were in cahoots not for history, thought or any of the topics that captivated me. They were partners in commerce. Dell could generate more revenue for Connors with three nights of exhibitions than a book deal. Now that was action. But even the smallest signs of encouragement were all I needed. In more ways than I wanted to admit, I was deluding myself.

Though Connors reached the semifinals of the U.S. Open for the 12th straight time in 1985, he was beaten handily by Lendl, 6-2, 6-3, 7-5. Hours before that match, Connors turned his ankle practicing with Dick Stockton. Yet even a healthy Connors was hard-pressed to beat Lendl by that point. The next day, Lendl blitzed McEnroe to emerge as the world's best player. By the end of the year, the likes of Lendl, McEnroe and Wilander were clearly better than Connors. Becker and Edberg were rising rapidly. Connors remained one of the top six players in the world, but for the first year in his career failed to win a single tournament.

Lendl vexed Connors. After the Tokyo win of '84, Connors led their rivalry 13-5. Just as McEnroe turned the tables on Connors in '83-'84, Lendl did so in '84-'85, beating Connors seven straight times. Fanatical devotion to fitness, coupled with wise guidance from his coach, legendary Australian lefty Tony Roche, helped Lendl overcome his innate weaknesses as a competitor.

Back when Connors still believed his best days were ahead of him, he relished the chance to compete against Borg and McEnroe. Much as he detested losing to either, he knew he was up against two tennis geniuses. Good as Lendl was, there was nothing inspiring to him, no aura like Borg or artistry like McEnroe. If Connors was Elvis, Borg the Beatles and McEnroe the Rolling Stones, Lendl was little more than Led Zeppelin—a fine band, yes, but nothing like the supreme music of bygone days. That Lendl's rise coincided with the crest and fall of the tennis boom validated Connors' belief that the sport was better when he ruled the world. Granted, there were other reasons for this decline in participation, ranging from the difficulty of the game to economic shifts such as the entry of women into the workplace, but that was a level of abstract sociology and thought disdained not just by Connors, but virtually any top-tier athlete. *Sports Illustrated's* cover headline after the '86 U.S. Open summed up a more cogent view towards Lendl that Connors no doubt savored: "The Champion That Nobody Cares About."

Criticizing Lendl for failing to "jump right in" and compete with the top players in the early '80s, Connors ripped him for "biding his time" with a schedule of weaker tournaments and limited entry into more competitive events. Connors seemed to have forgotten that he was similarly selective when he bypassed WCT in favor of the Riordan circuit. Speaking of Lendl to John Feinstein in 1989, Connors said, "to a large degree, he became number one by default. Look, Borg quit, I got old and McEnroe went a little brain dead for a while. Somebody had to be number one. Lendl was a patient man and it worked out for him."

Were anyone to have disparaged Connors' ascent this way—such as how he was able to win Wimbledon and the U.S. Open in '74 without facing Newcombe, Nastase or Smith—they likely would have received an obscene tirade and a subpoena. Lendl spoke with his racket. He beat Connors the last 17 times they played. Granted, these wins all came when Connors was past 32. Credit Connors once again for helping someone improve. Debit him for stingy compliments— and, versus Lendl on February 21, 1986, a terrible act once thought even beyond Connors' capabilities.

That day, I received a phone call at work. "You're not going to believe what Jimbo just did," said Joan. In front of a national TV audience on ESPN, he and Lendl met in the semifinals of the Lipton Championships in Florida. It was their first match since the '85 Open. At 33, Connors started the match on fire, taking the first set 6-1. Lendl ripped through the next two, 6-1, 6-2. But Connors squared matters with a 6-2 fourth-set victory. It was a sticky, uncomfortable Florida day. Connors' body was soaked. Throughout the early games of the decisive set—the stage when Connors once was able to over-take Lendl—it was Lendl who hung tough, Lendl who produced the right shot, and Connors who misfired. Lendl served at 3-2, 30-love and struck a volley. Assuming it was long, Connors let it go, only to see it called good.

Connors flew into one of the biggest rages of his career. He screamed at umpire Jeremy Shales. He shook his arms and fists. He ranted some more. He sat on his chair. The invariable penalty stages occurred—a warning, a point penalty, a game, then the match to

Lendl, 5-2 retired in the fifth set. For all of Connors' determination, on this day he had snapped and thrown in the towel. His penalty was a suspension of 70 days and a fine of $20,000. Months later in San Francisco, he told me that event was "the royal screwing." But who'd been screwed, player or public?

When I told what happened to a colleague, she asked, "What, is Jimmy Connors having his second childhood?"

"No," I said. "He's ending his first."

So was I. At 25, I began eight years of psychotherapy. Healthy as it was for me to be in a relationship, my ability to understand and express emotions was limited. My childhood, coupled with Ken's illness, helped me learn to be independent, accountable only to myself. Now, as I tried to sort through love and maturity, the tricky matter of intimacy and interpersonal negotiations was difficult. For so long, feelings were bottled up inside me that with Joan they leapt out in all sorts of odd ways. I broke my share of the instruments of time and communication: alarm clocks and telephones. Did I want to marry Joan? Did I deserve love? Did I warrant tennis? I was primed to play, but was no longer able to stay as calm as I was in my teens. I yelled when I missed easy shots, fired balls into corners, even threw my racket. In all sorts of safe venues—from the comforts of Joan to the tennis court—I sought to make up for lost emotions.

Yet what was I truly angry about? I excavated what went on with Ken and my parents. I tried to understand how his illness affected my relationships with everyone from friends to colleagues to clients. I realized how worried I was about being overlooked, how my life quest was to generate recognition for my achievements. I saw how my role in my family left me feeling lonely. Soon I learned that I was not alone. I found a support group of siblings and children of the mentally ill. For the first time in my life, I shared and listened to the tales of others with similar experiences. Twice a month for two hours, we discussed not the horrible episodes of our loved ones, but our own narratives. There was T, so mature as a child she knew she lacked the emotional desire to be a mother. There was D, worried she might become schizophrenic one day (the chances of this happening rise by tenfold if one sibling is so afflicted). There was N, resolved never to be pushed around by any boss or lover. There was S, master of the preemptive breakup lest she be abandoned. Forget Jimmy Connors. These were life's true grinders. And I was one of them. Every time I attended this group I felt as if a knife cut across my body and stitched it back together. Sheltered, privileged, blessed with a Berkeley education and a white-collar job, I was at last giving myself permission to say I'd been in the arena, a survivor of my family's emotional plane crash.

My own self-exploration made it both easier and harder to accept Connors' decline. On one hand, I rationally saw how his career must indeed end, such as when he lost in the first round of Wimbledon in 1986. But during this time, as I discovered emotions I previously didn't know existed, I felt raw, attuned to the slightest tics that might trigger anger or tears. Songs, movies, even the sight of two boys in a park—all was fair game. "Because of the power of the sibling partnership," writes Victoria Secunda in *When Madness Comes Home*, "brothers and sisters of the mentally ill inherit certain enduring legacies, chief among them feelings of entrapment and enduring grief."

On Sunday, August 31, 1986, I watched the U.S. Open. "That is not a typo," said Pat Summerall of a graphic that appeared on the screen. The score showed Connors trailing 5-0 in the first set of his third-round match versus Todd Witsken. Todd Witsken? Well, surely Jimmy would turn it around in the next set, particularly after he'd won two games in the first to at least get into the match. But Witsken masterfully hit one ball after another to Connors' forehand. Connors was unable to close out points. Witsken won the second set, 6-4, and despite a game effort in the third, Connors lost it, 7-5. It was his last match with the T-2000. For the first time since 1973—half my life ago at that point—Connors was eliminated before the final weekend.

This defeat was more than I wanted to handle. What so upset me by then about a Connors loss? Everything was gravy by now, wasn't it? Was his defeat the passage of my carefree youth? Wait a second— you mean my youth of repression and anxiety? Given what had happened to Ken, given the decadence and cynicism of Los Angeles in the '70s, it was a lie to call my love for Connors a passion based in innocent, pastoral bygone days. No, it wasn't the past I was crying for that afternoon.

It was the future, and my desire for transcendence. Two weeks later, dining in San Francisco, Connors asked, "How old are you, son?" When I said 26, he noted that, "You've got a lot ahead of you." Since Connors was only eight years my elder, I countered, "So do you." But he begged off, "No, not me anymore. I'm headed off into the sunset. But you, you've got a lot of years left."

Success was up to me. I followed a familiar post-Connors ritual. An hour after the Witsken loss, I was on the court with Craig Gold. Of course I wanted to kill him, but this match in my mind was less about tennis and more about ambition. Comfortable in his job as a lawyer, Craig struck me as complacent. We shared an interest in the business of sports, but I doubted if he had the guts to pursue it. Craig cautioned me about the perils of trying to "break in" to another world. Versus Binstock in '74, I wanted to kill Connors. Versus Josh in '80, I wanted to avenge Connors. Versus Craig in '86, Connors was buried. I was out to win for my own sake. I beat Craig 6-3, 6-1. Though any Connors loss bothered me, never again did one bring me to tears.

I knew I wanted something other than a life in a public relations firm. Of course, there was the idea of a Connors biography, but that was a distant constellation. Surely there were other planets within my grasp. Making time around my job, I freelanced tennis pieces for several publications, most notably a regional sports magazine called *City Sports*. I also thought I might find work not as a journalist, but in some realm of communications and marketing with a sports management firm such as the one Dell ran. Each year, I spent nights and weekends at the San Francisco tournament, nominally working on a story, but most of all I networked. Since I looked so young in those days that I was often asked if I was a ballboy, in 1986 I decided to wear a jacket, blazer and tie every day I was at the tournament. With Connors in San Francisco for the first time since 1982, I also took four days of vacation time.

Connors first-round match was his first since the Witsken loss. Three hours before it was set to start, a tournament official told me he hadn't seen Jimmy all day. The official speculated that Connors pulled out of the tournament at the last minute. I was crushed. I walked through the dimly lit Cow Palace hallways and waited.

Five minutes later, with racket in hand, gray warm-ups and a light green sweatshirt, Connors walked my way, shook my hand and kindly grabbed the lapels on my gray blazer. "Very nice," he said. "Now come out here while I do some work." It was one of my favorite moments at a tournament: the period in between day and night sessions. As the facility's staff cleaned the seats, music piped in while players practiced. Connors began a light pre-match hit. When he finished, I wished him luck. He told me to find him after the match.

But Connors found me. He won a routine 6-1, 7-6 match versus Dan Goldie, a player just out of Stanford. "Goldie," Connors joked near my seats between points, "That's the name of my dog." After his press conference, Connors told a security guard to let me accompany him to the locker. Near Connors' bag was a tin of cookies, a gift from a tournament volunteer. "Have one, have two," he said as he waved the tin near my face. He asked what I was up to. He recognized one of my current client's products. He asked, "You'll be here tomorrow, won't you?" Where else on earth would I want to be? I was so excited I hardly slept.

Donald Dell arrived for Connors' next match. Dell and I sat together just behind the court. I tried to pry my way into a conversation, but the match turned out to be too tight for much chatter, a rough three-setter versus Peter Fleming. At 34, Connors took no wins for granted. As he at last grabbed the go-ahead break versus Fleming at 3-4 in the third, Dell barked out, "Close the door. Get that first serve in." Connors turned back and gave us both a jestful look that seemed to say, Wow, great idea, get the first serve in. The next afternoon, Connors beat a Swedish Borg clone, Peter Lundgren, 6-3, 6-4. After each match, he made sure to ask if I was planning to watch the next one. We chatted about the kind of topics most popular in lockers: sports, weather, food.

One question I've commonly asked tennis players: In a one-week tournament, which day of the week is it acceptable to still be in contention? For the rank and file, the common answer is Friday—the quarterfinals, a fine week of quality tennis. Well into Connors' 30s, the lifelong answer was Sunday, nothing less than victory. But I think by 1986, even a man with Connors' ambitions scaled back his expectations. His childhood ended that day versus Lendl in February. Now he was an adult. Saturday, the start of national TV coverage, was acceptable to him. Less than a half hour after the Lundgren match, still sweating, Connors grabbed a payphone and called John Heller in Los Angeles. "Heller, Heller, Heller," he said, "Come on up." It was time to send in reinforcements. Though San Francisco was drastically less significant than London or New York, Connors wanted all the support he could muster.

"I'm sitting down to your left," Heller said to Connors just before his semi versus Anders Jarryd. Though Jarryd won the first set in a tiebreak, he appeared to be slightly limping. "Watch this," said Heller, "Jimmy is going to make Anders run so much he'll be gasping for breath in half an hour." Heller was dead-on. Many times, with openings to take the net, Connors elected to stay back and keep Jarryd on the string. By the third, down 2-0, a hobbled Jarryd retired. Connors was in the finals, only the fourth such showing of the year from a man who used to reach them by the dozen.

Heller and I met with Connors in the locker room. He was glad to be in the finals. Eschewing a shower, he asked for a ride from my indoor press parking space to a friend's car at the other end of the parking lot. As Connors, Heller and I walked out, a security guard, seeing me in my blue blazer, asked if I was Connors' agent. I laughed, but of course was pleased. As we threw Connors' bag into the backseat of my small Toyota, fans milled around us. Connors signed autographs. Heller and I watched. I wanted to bottle that moment and learn about the thousands of other times Connors emerged from arenas and tennis clubs around the world. I dropped Connors and Heller off at a corner of the parking lot where he met an old UCLA friend named Kim. Just when I was about to tell Connors I'd see him before the finals, he told me to meet him and Heller at the top of the Mark Hopkins Hotel at 6:30. I walked back into the Cow Palace in a daze. The Connors biography seemed several light years closer. It normally takes 30 minutes to drive from the Cow Palace to the Mark Hopkins. Not wanting to get caught in any San Francisco traffic jam, I left at 5:00 and spent an hour walking around Nob Hill.

One thing I have learned from dining with celebrities is that conversation is only moderately reciprocal. That evening, Heller, Kim and I gathered in Connors' presence. But then again, he was the sun. What were we but mere planets? We three scarcely cared about each other.

Connors was curiously vulnerable. He loved his family, regretted how his life took him away from them so often. But then he admitted how he still loved the fight and the roar of the crowd. "You watch," he told us. "I may invent some new fist pumps for next year." If in some ways the words echoed his press conferences, in other ways he was far more personal, even, quite rare for an athlete, inquisitive. He asked me what I wanted to do with my life. I told him about my desire to work more in tennis. "Don't let anyone in this sport take advantage of you," he cautioned. "Because they can, they will. They'll see how much you love the tennis, and they'll penalize you for that. Don't let them. There are only three or four people in the world who write about this sport as well as you do. Don't forget that." Then he spoke to us all about the factor he valued most: loyalty. "People always want to be my friend when I've won," he said. "But it's the people who come by when I lose that matter to me. That's why I'm glad you all came to see me." No question, 1986—the suspension, the first round loss at Wimbledon, his early exit in New York—pained Connors deeply. As with my essay in the spring of '82, I was grateful my timing coincided more with his downs than ups.

What happened the next night between Connors and me was more notable for what happened off the court than on it. Connors played McEnroe. It was a well-played match, McEnroe winning 7-6, 6-3. In the first set tiebreak, Connors fought off a set point with a dashing crosscourt forehand that led to both players landing on the ground. But McEnroe's serve and speed were too much.

After it was over, Heller suggested we sit near Connors during the awards ceremony. Connors was in a good mood. "The final, that's not bad, is it?" he asked. "Not bad for a 34-year-old man nobody thinks can play anymore." (He was still ranked number seven on the ATP computer.) In his victory speech, McEnroe thanked Connors for supporting him during his sabbatical. "Why would he want to thank me?" joked Connors from courtside. "Everyone knows we hate each other. That guy, Mac, he's something." But any genuine anger he felt for McEnroe was gone. Both were unified in friendship by their mutual contempt for Lendl.

As Connors, Heller and I walked back to the locker, I felt the familiar melancholy of a tournament's last moments. The circus was about to leave town. This week was one of the best shows yet. But I was still left behind. Naturally, there was a limo waiting to whisk Connors and Heller off to some exclusive airstrip for the private flight back to Santa Barbara. Moments before we said good-bye, Connors pressed a piece of paper into my hand. It was his home number. "Call me," he said. "Just call me. You come to Santa Barbara, you'll come to the ranch and we'll watch the sunset. But call."

Though I never saw the sunset from Connors' ranch, we spoke many times. I've often wondered why he felt the need to give me his private phone number. Was there something he craved? Or was he simply being a friend? I'll never know. Years later, a Connors colleague told me, "Jimmy's always known you were the press, and treated you just how the press should be treated." Around that same time, Connors told me, "You know I don't give a shit what people write about me." I suspect the opposite. Connors was particularly vulnerable in 1986. He no longer seemed an important factor in tennis. But he knew I carried a candle for him no matter what. A music reporter who traveled for a week with a band once realized, *you can't be in these peoples' lives.* Yet in the wake of that week in San Francisco, I thought perhaps Connors and I found common ground in our desire for recognition and connection. I wasn't sure which mattered most. I hoped my loyalty would be rewarded.

His expectations dramatically lowered by his results in 1986, Connors competed with renewed zest for the balance of the decade. "Jimmy just doesn't care anymore," a friend of his told me late that year. Oh, I thought, he cared all right. But in some ways, he'd come full circle. As a boy, Connors likely gave no thought to long-term tennis goals. Once a pro, he couldn't help but think of a sustained, epic career, the over-the-top success he first imagined when he moved west to Los Angeles at 16. Twice that age, his legacy firmly established and not likely to post any more significant results, Connors lived match to match. "I'll play as long as I feel like playing," he said in 1986. "If I show up and I'm playing a tournament, don't ask me if I'm not going to play much longer, 'cause I'm there."

There was just enough edge to those comments to sustain Connors' ambitions. No longer was he tennis' hardest hitter. Nor was he able to strike the ball as early as in his best years. But he remained one of the game's formidable competitors. In a play right out of the BHTC, he was like the old guy who tells the kids to go easy on him—and then suckers them into acquiescence. The crowd firmly in his corner everywhere he played, feeling zero pressure to win, Connors was determined to squeeze every bit of juice from his career.

His passion for competition was particularly refreshing in the late '80s. Lendl was driven, but remote, cold as an MBA compared to the more entrepreneurial Connors. Lendl's blunt and overt belief that only Slam results mattered created a negative expectation from spectators all over the world. How would concert-goers have felt if Sinatra had said he only cared about Madison Square Garden? McEnroe whined repeatedly about the dedication required by competition, a screech soon to be echoed by Wilander, Becker and Agassi. Said Connors, "Money took away all that single-mindedness to be the best—the tunnel vision to eat, to sleep, to breathe, to drink, to do whatever it took, tennis, tennis, tennis all the time. Guys at the tournaments now are more involved in trying to play the softball game and going out and doing this and that than in trying to play top tennis."

Connors remained the most refreshing player in tennis. He committed himself no matter what the city. But an athlete is not merely an entertainer. He must win. In 1987, Connors showed yet another level of resilience. At Wimbledon, he recovered from a 1-6, 1-6, 1-4 deficit to beat Mikael Pernfors 1-6, 1-6, 7-5, 6-4, 6-2 in the round of 16 (complete with the promised new fist pumps). "When it was the beginning of the fifth, you just knew he was going to win it," said Evert. "He'd die out there if he had to. I've never seen anyone pull out a match like that." One win later, and Connors was back in familiar territory: his 11th Wimbledon semi. Though he lost to eventual champ Pat Cash, he was quite happy when we spoke two weeks later. "That was a lot of fun," he said. "It played pretty well on TV, didn't it?" Later that summer, he reached the semis at the U.S. Open, losing again to the tournament's winner, Lendl. During his round of 16 match versus Henri Leconte, Connors' foot began to bother him. When a tournament official asked if he could continue, he said, "I'll play on a pegleg if I have to." Bill Simons, the publisher of *Inside Tennis* who'd fired me five years previously, offered me $150 to call Connors for an interview. I refused. My sights were set on much bigger fish. It was more than a decade before I ever called Connors for a single quote.

In '86 and '87, Connors remained the top-ranked American, fourth on the ATP computer at the end of '87. Losses hardly fazed him. He took delight in ending his nearly four-year title drought by snapping up two titles in both '88 and '89, including a dazzling straight-set victory over McEnroe in the finals of a tournament in Toulouse, France. In the quarterfinals of the '88 U.S. Open he met Agassi, a player half his age who'd once hit with Connors at Caesars Palace when he was four years old. Agassi's sizzling groundstrokes and flashy image made him Connors' heir apparent. Agassi won, 6-2, 7-6, 6-1, but when he said he was surprised that Connors put up that much resistance, Connors fired back, "He made a mistake." A week later, Connors beat Agassi at an exhibition in Detroit. If his long-term vision was minimal, on a given night, the lion still roared.

"I don't really care what people say," Connors said in the late '80s. "I never really have. I've always done my own thing, I've always enjoyed it and I think that's driven a lot of people along the way, which has been kind of fun. On the other hand, seeing is believing and staying in tip-top form all the time is difficult for me. I've done it for 14-15 years and I've reached the point now where I become a little stale and flat. So the best thing about it is I realize that and understand that. Now I have to sit down and figure out what is the best way to pull myself out of that. If I can do that, then it will be fun again more time to make a lot of people eat their words."

It was a comment he might have made in '76, '78, '82, '83 or '87. During the Pernfors match, writers began to compose obituaries for Connors. In a London newsroom, a headline with Pernfors as victor was written and nearly set in type. Instead, on the bus home from work, I saw this in the San Francisco *Examiner*: "Connors Rallies From the Brink." He was the Harry Truman of tennis players.

In 1989, after not playing a single match between Wimbledon and the U.S. Open, Connors again surprised the tennis world. In New York, seeded 13th, at age 37 he upset the third-seeded Edberg to reach the quarters. For the second straight year, he faced Agassi. After nearly fainting in the second set, Connors stormed back to take a two sets to one lead. Agassi accelerated, and went up 5-1 in the fifth.

By now I was at another public relations firm, one far larger than Edelman called Burson-Marsteller. I thought constantly of Connors, pined to get into tennis, but Connors was right: management firms, sponsors, tournaments and tour organizers were tight-fisted and exploitive. It was classic supply and demand economics. For every position, there were dozens of applicants. I met several times with a representative from IMG, the world's largest sports marketing firm. No longer was I barely out of school. The IMG man liked my skills and ideas. But as he said, "We've got Stanford MBAs who want to work for us for free." I countered with a line I'd read in a business book: "You pay peanuts, you get monkeys." Burson-Marsteller had a sports marketing division, but the only assignment available for me in San Francisco was the promotion of a man who raced big rig trucks in cities like Nashville and Louisville. I still knew tennis was where I wanted to be, but was frustrated when it came to clarifying how to get there.

I watched the Agassi-Connors match in Washington, D.C. Burson-Marsteller had sent me to a seminar for aspiring supervisors. I hated the process of supervising others. Sports, I told a boss, was good training for business, but perhaps I played the wrong sport. Collaboration was not always easy for me.

I stared at Connors and Agassi on a TV inside a hotel fitness center. "Well, that's it for Connors," said a man on an exercise bike.

"Well, let's see," I said.

Connors fought. He was back in the boondocks. "Give this guy a chance to choke!" he screamed into the courtside microphone. He held, broke, held again. Agassi served at 5-4. Connors bounced up and down. He sharply angled a backhand return, sidespinned a backhand approach down the line and put away a forehand volley for love-15. But on the next point he netted a forehand. Then Connors' return betrayed him when Agassi struck a fine serve down the center. At 30-15, Connors stormed forward, but was wide with a backhand volley by mere inches. Two match points for Agassi. Again, Connors came in, and this time Agassi was just wide with a backhand pass. As always, from the backyard with Gloria to Flushing Meadows, Connors and his opponent were headed to the edge. At 40-30, a long rally, but the dynamic wasn't favorable. As Connors pounded his forehand cross-court, it went to Agassi's backhand. But this wasn't a one-hander from a Connors peer, or even a floater like Borg's. Agassi struck with both depth and pace. And then he keenly undercut one down the line, a drop shot that Connors chased down but pushed long. It was the first time Agassi had ever won a fifth set. Once again, Connors was the roadblock for another tennis player's rite of passage.

Loser and still champion, Connors was exhausted but delighted. He'd once again proven his point: Don't count me out. When you think of Connors, cherish the fight. Cherish the struggle for survival, a keen factor for siblings and children of the mentally ill. Understand the need to scrape and claw, and you'll never see tennis or anything else as particularly pristine. *It's a goddamned war out there.*

Those ideas were at the center of "Play It Again, Jimmy," my 1990 *World Tennis* piece. Once the story appeared—particularly after talking with Connors about it—I knew my one true weapon in the sport was as a writer. "You have your own way of seeing this game," Connors said to me. "Don't let that go." There was no way I dared let my personal vision be subsumed by any management firm, tournament or sponsor.

"Tell me," Connors asked in one of our conversations, "how's *your* tennis?" It was no joke. Since he'd asked, I felt no need to apologize for my playing level or the insignificance of the previous weekend's club tournament where I'd won the singles and the doubles by playing nine sets on the last day. "You're in the arena," said Connors. Blarney or sincere? It hardly mattered. Time after time, writing about Connors helped me navigate through one arena after another.

10

Requiem For
A Lefthander

The night at the U.S. Open when Connors requested I write a proposal to become his ghostwriter, I asked him what autobiographies he liked. Connors confessed it was 20 years since he'd finished a book. His candor was persuasive. If Connors trusted me enough to reveal such long-term disengagement with the world of thought, surely we could make a great team. I was a biography junkie. Little did—or should—Connors care about the hours I'd spent on Kennedys, King, Malcolm X, Sandy Koufax, Bob Gibson, Norman Mailer and so many others. "I never looked up to anybody or had any idols," he told me. No historical context, no ATP, no Davis Cup team or any other power would shackle Connors.

But he was about to let me in, and if he did, perhaps I'd uncover depths and secrets about tennis I—and those millions I felt so misunderstood my favorite sport—never knew existed. If the world recognized and understood tennis, it would recognize and understand me. Said Connors as we ate lunch one day, "Out there by yourself, hot and tired, you just—well, me and Borg were in the locker before the '78 Open, and . . ." at which point an ex-pro barged in and slapped Connors on the back and started talking. I wanted Connors away from the cronies, toe-to-toe with me in our own verbal rally.

If Connors wasn't a prolific reader, he knew a good story. "There's a movie you have to watch," he said. It was not the tale of a famous athlete, entertainer, military leader or politician. It lacked the classic up-from-nowhere themes I knew jocks like Connors loved. The movie was *Best Seller*. It starred Brian Dennehy as a policeman (a descendent of Al Thompson, Jimbo's grandfather?) turned author. Dennehy's character is approached by a former hit man, who wants him to pen his story as a way to right old scores. "I want people to know what I had to do—and why," he says. Along the way, Dennehy finds out that he and his subject share a past. He also discovers that the term "former hit man" is an oxymoron.

I found it striking that Connors gained inspiration from the tale of an assassin. Was that how he regarded his life, as a tale of one kill after another? Who were the enemies in the shadows? Who taught him to pull the trigger? How many were left in the dust? How was he able to balance hate with love without annihilating himself? Connors' narrative alter ego was no pretty boy. It was the pockmarked, whiney-voiced James Woods. The poster for *Best Seller* showed Woods in dark glasses and the subhead, "If words could kill." Thought for Connors was a form of action. "Nobody gets it right," he said to me. "I want to get it right. Do you have what it takes to help me get it right?"

Three weeks after our day at the Open, Connors arrived in the Bay Area for an exhibition. Joan and I, married a year earlier, went to watch. She met him for the first time. "Keep him out of trouble," advised Mayor Connors with a wink and a pat on her arm. That weekend the tournament director's wife told me she dined with Connors and heard him mention the possibility of collaborating with me.

If his wrist compromised him physically, verbally Connors remained a lion, and, naturally, not so smooth about his entry into winter. Emerging from the shower after an easy first-round win, he quickly faced a scant three reporters (including me) and talked about how he wanted tennis to "rock and roll again. That's what this sport needs, someone who actually cares." Then he invited me into the locker, where for another hour he regaled and ranted with myself, tournament director Erik van Dillen and a local teaching pro named Chris Bradley who knew Connors from his junior days.

"This Sampras guy looks pretty good," said Bradley. After Connors left that year's Open with his injury, Sampras beat Lendl, McEnroe and Agassi to become the youngest U.S. Open men's champ in history.

Connors glared. "What do you mean?"

"Well, he's got all the shots," said Bradley.

"What do you mean, all the shots?" asked Connors.

"Well, he just won the Open," said Bradley.

"The Open," said Connors. "The Open. One fucking 19-year-old kid wins one U.S. Open. Has he defended it? Has he come back and played it again and again? The Open. Let's see what this kid's got not just for this year."

There was a time when Connors' lack of grace towards Sampras would have irked me. To some degree, he was as disdainful of Sampras as others were towards Connors in 1974. Granted, Sampras in 1990 had only won a single U.S. Open. But there was a bigger battle at stake for Connors. I felt as he ripped into Sampras that he was contemplating history, longevity, significance. Or was it that Sampras was just another pretender to the throne? Either approach—long-term thought, short-term action—appealed to me. A tennis friend of mine named Mark who I beat frequently acknowledged the quality of my tennis game only rarely. Instead, he spoke constantly of the potential of another player, Bill. "If Bill played more," said Mark, "He'd be the best one here." For months I listened to Mark sing Bill's songs. Finally, one day, I blew up. "If my ass," I said. "Bill's not here, so it doesn't matter." What matters, I wanted to add, was that Mark couldn't beat me, so why was he so busy telling us how good Bill might be? Yes, I understood Connors' contempt for Sampras. He didn't hate Sampras any more than I hated Bill. What he hated was the lack of recognition for his lifelong dedication.

Unfortunately, Connors' wrist continued to bother him. He was forced to default the final versus McEnroe. Rather than leave that evening, though, Connors stayed, and in the locker afterwards, I was with him as he bantered with McEnroe. "Connors, man, how could you get injured?" asked McEnroe. "I flew all the way out here to play you, and thought it would be like old times—a little yelling, throw the racket, some good points." Connors laughed. After McEnroe left, Connors asked if I was working on the proposal. I told him I was grinding it out. "Don't stop," he said.

For all I know, Connors' request to me was an idle thought. For all I know, he might have made the same suggestion to two, six, 10 writers. It didn't matter. A random suggestion to Connors was in my mind salvation. The proposal was the tunnel I was digging in hopes of escaping public relations. Arriving at my office at 7:30 in the morning, squeezing in time at lunch and throughout the day, I wrote a 60-page document. I wanted Connors to see how I understood where all the bodies were buried, that I grasped the flow of his life and had the right mix of curiosity and reverence. "By now," I wrote, "virtually everyone in tennis has told a Connors story. Everyone except Connors."

In a section titled "seven words that make me the right co-author," I hoped Connors would most appreciate two: independence and desire. For the latter I used a trite but effective motivational pitch. What is the difference between involvement and commitment? Take ham and eggs. The chicken is involved. The pig is committed. A month after Connors left Stanford, I overnighted "Jimbo! Taking It On The

Rise" to his house. He told me he was glad to receive it.

For weeks that turned into months, my mind occupied two territories. There was the present. Clients required updates, counsel, story angles, research, articles and speeches. But then there was the future. Often, whenever my phone rang, I imagined it was Connors, telling me the proposal was great and that a publisher was set to give me $200,000 to start on his autobiography. The notion of writing Connors' story upped my expectations. It was like feeding a sample of steak to a man used to eating hamburger. My boss, having read my *World Tennis* story on Connors, wondered why it sounded so differently from what I wrote for clients. I told her it was a matter of angles, omitting to say how little I cared about our various clients' products and services. When I was younger, during my apprenticeship years, the mere process of succeeding on behalf of myself and my clients was sufficiently motivational. But now, with bigger possibilities ahead, having turned 30 that year, I grew increasingly bored. I wanted Connors to save my life. But he was busy saving his own.

Connors spent that winter recovering from wrist surgery, his arm in a full cast for 11 weeks. At first, he was barely able to hit for 10 minutes. By early 1991, he was training more vigorously. His ranking, 14 at the end of 1989, plummeted to 936 at the end of 1990 (years later, the ATP created an "injury-protected" ranking). The tennis world moves so rapidly—Becker once called tennis years "dog years"—that in early '91, Connors was hardly considered a factor. But certainly he recalled how in the '89 Open his last two wins were over Andres Gomez and Stefan Edberg. Gomez won the '90 French Open. Edberg won the '90 Wimbledon and finished the year ranked number one.

Hours before his first match back, I called Connors' house and was told by Patti to contact him at the Ritz Carlton in Chicago. Per usual, he was upbeat, the customary mix of focus and blarney. "How's everything out in California?" he asked. "I'm just hoping to try and hit some good balls out there tonight and see what happens." Prior to the call, I decided not to mention the proposal. A book was the domain of thought. Connors was now hours away from reentering the world of action. How was I to know action was about to carry him into the clouds all year?

"I liked some of the things I did out there," he said after losing in Chicago 6-3, 6-0 to journeyman Jaime Yzaga. A month later, after taking a set from Edberg in Japan, Connors exulted, "I'm back in business!" One set?

But then, at the French Open, a one-week effort triggered a summer-long lovefest. Most thought Connors' main focus in Paris would be his work for NBC, where he was a commentator in '90 and was set to do so again in '91, his producers figuring he wasn't likely to advance so far as to create a conflict. In the second round, Connors won a five-setter versus Roland Agenor. His next match was versus Michael Chang, the '89 French champ who was born the year Connors turned pro.

I was in an all-day meeting at a software company near Santa Cruz, two hours away from San Francisco. On breaks, I called Joan for updates. It pained me to be locked in a conference room discussing strategies for a trade show when my protagonist was in action. I knew no one at the meeting cared about tennis or Jimmy Connors. My mind drifted between the meeting and Paris.

It was the most memorable match Connors ever played at Roland Garros. Yes, he had reached four semis, but that was when he was expected to advance far into the draw. Versus Chang, he was grateful merely to be on the court. For more than four hours, Connors scampered all over the dirt. Chang's game, based on footspeed and defense, was in some ways reminiscent of Borg's. The 38-year-old Connors again showed his deceptive mastery of tactics. Connors repeatedly struck the ball deep and down the middle of the court, nullifying Chang's keen ability to hit on the run. The younger player's topspin drives often landed short enough for Connors to attack the net. It was a fascinating all-court match. Connors took the first set, 6-4. Chang won the next two, 7-5, 6-2, winning six straight games to close out the third. Connors' back was wracked with pain. Twice in the third set he called for help from the trainer. "Don't leave," Connors said to a couple that was leaving their box seats. "It's not over yet." As the fourth wore on, it appeared Connors had merely given a good effort. Spotting Ion Tiriac, Becker's manager and former coach for Vilas and Nastase, Connors cried out, "Getting old is a bitch."

But at 4-all, Connors snatched Chang's serve, and then closed out the set. The crowd rose to its feet. On the first point of the fifth, Connors struck a backhand down-the-line service return for a winner—and then defaulted. "I can't move my back anymore," he told umpire Bruno Rebeuh. "I'm trying my ass off out there." Following a massage and an IV, Connors faced the press, arguably happier in defeat than for many of his victories. "I've been run ragged, my back is stiff, and I feel like shit," he said. "But, boy, was it fun. To get a stadium rocking like that is a kick you can't believe."

As I drove back with my colleague, talking about future meetings with editors and technology experts, I wondered what Connors' ascent into public consciousness meant for my proposal. I hoped for the best, and looked forward to my next encounter with him. There was no way this year, though, that I could attend the U.S. Open. There was one client's product introduction, another one for whom I was conducting a big research project, another requesting a speech for its CEO. Planning, research and ghostwriting were all skills worth honing. But now I wanted to aim them strictly at Connors.

The world's love affair with Connors continued at Wimbledon. It was one of the wettest Wimbledons in history, backing up play so much that the All England Club took the unprecedented step of scheduling matches for the tournament's middle Sunday. Tickets were made available to the general public, creating far more commotion than usual at this understated venue. Who better to play on this "People's Sunday" than Connors? As fans cascaded him with cheers, Connors smiled through the entire warmup of his third-round match versus Derrick Rostagno. Though he lost in straight sets, he left the court with his head high. At both the French and Wimbledon, fans were every bit as excited to watch Connors enter NBC's broadcast booth as they were to witness the finals.

My chance to see Connors came three weeks after Wimbledon. Back in October, the same night I sent him my proposal, as Connors sat at home recovering from his wrist surgery, World Team Tennis announced that it had signed Connors for the 1991 season. At a time when few in the pro game cared about Connors, Billie Jean King's league extended him a lifeline. Connors' short runs at the French and Wimbledon boosted his valuation. Witnessing his increased profile also taught me a lesson I'd conveniently overlook for many years.

The World Team Tennis match was at the Forum, home then of the Los Angeles Lakers. Connors was friendly as ever. With far more people milling around him than in the fall of 1990, I made doubly sure not to discuss the autobiography. Soon, the others drifted away. Two hours prior to the match, just Connors, myself and the Forum's director of tennis events, Jeannie Buss, sat in a row of empty seats. The daughter of the Lakers' owner, Jerry Buss, Jeannie was somewhat of a Los Angeles legend since the '70s, a girl my age who'd been given responsibility for the Forum's small mix of tennis events by her father the way other kids were handed automobiles. As the three of us made small talk, Buss and I each transparently fixated on Connors, she turned to him and said, "Jimmy, one day I've got to get you to play an exhibition at the Forum."

"That would be terrific," said Connors.

"It would be like that time you played Borg here," I said.

"I never played Borg in the Forum," said Connors.

"Yes you did," I said, "Back in '82."

"Never played Borg at the Forum," Connors repeated.

"No, you never did," said Buss.

I made the point again, and wished I'd had enough nerve to bet every cent I owned that on November 15, 1982, I snuck in to the event through a side door at the Forum Club. I sat on the side of the court, and on the way out saw one of my childhood crushes, "Catwoman" Julie Newmar. But I backed off. I was certain my time with Connors would come. Soon enough I'd find out what went on with him and Borg in that locker in 1978. Soon enough he'd take me down into the boondocks. The conversation with Buss veered elsewhere. Connors remained friendly and went to the locker. Now unattached to the celebrity, Buss regarded me as little more than a distraction.

"That conversation was off-the-record," she said to me. "You're not going to use it, are you?"

I told her I doubted it.

Prior to Connors' exploits in Paris and London, Jeannie Buss wasn't likely pondering him as the star of an exhibition. But as Connors put it earlier that year in the most unwittingly mercantile of ways following his loss to Edberg, he was back in business. No longer was he an injured man pondering mortality. He was a property. Much as Connors knew how insincere and transitory Buss' brand of flattery was, the sound of money was a familiar, welcoming tune. It wasn't that he needed a single dollar. But the acknowledgment of the marketplace had lined the pockets of Connors and so many in the tennis industry. The previous fall, when Connors referred to his mononucleosis of '77, I corrected him and said it occurred in '78. But now, history gave way to myth. And when others can make money off you, they'll abet your myth. Of course Buss let Connors think he'd never played Borg in the Forum. If he'd said the world was flat she'd have agreed with that too. All the better for everyone to cash in on the Jimbo myth.

I, of course, wanted what Connors demanded that night on the taxi from Flushing Meadows to Manhattan: a chance to set the record straight (and, yes, earn fame and money). But for all Connors' noble promises to me that we'd stay in touch, we were each working with our respective myths, all the better to brace us against the harsher realities that awaited in our futures: his invariable decline and exit from tennis, my confrontation with a whole other side of Los Angeles.

The next day, my parents and I visited Ken. He was now in a facility called Meadowbrook. With its various game rooms, TV, playground, group meals and activities, Meadowbrook resembled an urban youth center. The only difference was that no residents were permitted to leave it without Meadowbrook's directors unlocking its gates. Ken was more alert than many others there, but even with his scheduled mix of medications, there was no way he could hold even the most basic of jobs or be completely responsible for himself. Our father had at last accepted that Ken was not likely to regain full health and function in society. The best to hope for was that he would inflict no harm to others or himself. Even then, there were moments of cognition. "It wasn't long ago," Ken said to me, "that you were younger than me." Ever the counterpuncher, I noted, "I still am." But we both knew that a fact was not the same as a truth. At Meadowbrook, there was no Jeannie Buss armed with lucrative delusions for Ken, me or my parents. While Connors floated into myth, I walked in history. Ken's mental fuzziness only accelerated my desire to capture every moment of anyone's life—mine, Connors, my family's—as accurately as possible.

So it was that Connors, the man with the story I barely knew with the depth I craved, called me "son" and made me vastly younger than the eight years that separated us. Ken, the man with the story I knew quite well, a tale that scared and scarred me to the bone, said I was older. Years later, a scientist told me that siblings shared 50 percent of the same genes. I was relieved the ones I had in common with Ken were different than those that afflicted him.

Or maybe that wasn't true. As I'd learned from Connors, to succeed you had to hit for the lines. But as Ken's illness and my connection to him showed me, the line separating healthy from sick was not so easy to discern. Every time I went to LA, each visit and meal with Ken, each step up the tennis ladder, I bumped against those lines, either in pursuit of a winner or an emotional electrocution.

Were I from a family that drank, my father, mother and I might well have had a stiff one after each visit with Ken. But we were a Jewish family of eaters, not drinkers. Once after seeing Ken, my father and I stopped for a donut, what my father called "a little bite of suicide." Anger, grief, guilt and relief were the byproducts of survival. Yet I was the lucky survivor. I was the one with the window office in downtown San Francisco, the pretty and attentive wife and the budding friendship with the champion tennis player. Life was backward or forward, just like those backyard one-on-one football games Ken and I once played.

Tenacity made me earn Ken's respect so long ago that it was an embedded part of my soul, the skill I knew brought me everything from an education to a career. His illness taught me to take nothing for granted. "Beat me today," rang the Connors soundbite I loved most, "and I'll play you tomorrow. And I've followed guys to the ends of the earth just to play them again."

> *At the still point of the turning world. Neither flesh nor fleshless;*
> *Neither from nor towards; at the still point, there the dance is.*
> —St. Louis-raised poet T.S. Eliot, "Burnt Norton"

Composers who wish to create a requiem are often able to do so on desirable terms. Athletes are not so lucky. While an artist's mind improves with age, an athlete's body invariably declines. Robert Frost was a better poet at 40 than 30. Not so for the likes of Willie Mays or Michael Jordan. An athlete's hope is that his final moments are dignified and possibly even memorable. Then again, as I pointed out repeatedly during Connors' twilight years, is it so bad to witness a well-rewarded athlete's decline? As we shudder about the declining hitter, the slowing runner or the tennis player who can't hit as hard, aren't we merely fearful of witnessing our own passing? My own joke is that I intend to go out drooling. But as Connors proved at the 1991 U.S. Open—and as I like to think I'd proved by willing myself into his story—there might well be truth in an adage Gloria Connors probably loved: the harder you work, the luckier you get.

A year to the day after Connors and I walked the grounds of the U.S. Open, he took the court for his first-round match versus McEnroe. Only this time it was Patrick McEnroe, John's younger brother. As I knew quite well, Patrick McEnroe demonstrated the disparities between siblings. Well-behaved to a fault, Patrick's game was devoid of the artistry that oozed from his brother. He was a craftsman, precisely the kind of baseline-based all-court player in the mold of Connors—but lacking his genius too. Still, by 1991, McEnroe was good enough to reach the semis of the Australian Open and become a solid, effective pro. For two sets, he proficiently moved Connors around the court to lead, 6-4, 7-6. Back in Belleville, Gloria Connors turned away from the television and started scrubbing her kitchen floor. As the third got underway, McEnroe began to pull away. Mrs. Connors turned her attention to cleaning her bathrooms. Connors served at 0-3, love-40. Fans began to drift out of Louis Armstrong Stadium. The venue Connors hoped to rock was turning into a tomb.

Then Connors got the only thing he ever needed to charge forward: one point. Soon enough, a game, and even though McEnroe remained far ahead, Connors, liberated completely from any need to etch his résumé, at once dangerous and existential, continued to fight strictly for the sake of the fight. Gloria peeked at a few points. Connors won the third set, 6-4. The stadium was less than half full. CBS' Mary Carillo said, "Patrick's just keeping the ball in play. He's going to let this match die." As the match neared midnight, more people left. Connors won the fourth, 6-2. The announcer on USA Network described how Connors had "clawed" his way back. Said Joan in our living room, "Just like you." Connors waved his fluorescent yellow racket in the air ("I'd give you one," he told me a year earlier, "but I've only got a few right now.") The Mayor wanted the people's support. Of course he got it.

By the fifth set, there were less than 6,000 people in the stadium. Connors went up 4-2. It's over, I thought, yet another comeback—Connors seventh—from two sets to love down. But then McEnroe caught up to 4-4. Connors broke and, despite being down love-40, at last closed out the match after four hours and 18 minutes, at 1:35 a.m. "I'm not going to roll over and let things just go," said Connors. "I just have to stick in there. That's what they pay to see. That's what I'm *supposed* to do."

He'd done nothing more than something utterly routine for a player of his caliber: win a first-round match. All his life, Connors treated every match he played as if it was a final. Now, at 38, they all were. The world took note. Later that afternoon, Becker walked over to Connors' practice court and shook his hand. Defending women's champion Gabriela Sabatini stared at him with the rapture of someone who's just spotted a messiah.

It was as if Connors had won the entire tournament. In some ways, he had, stepping into the aching vacuum that pervaded tennis during this time. The Super Saturday of 1984 was an apex, a Woodstock celebrating the promise of the early Open Era. But the rest of the '80s was more an Altamont. As the tennis boom ebbed, the sport failed to fulfill its promise. Constantly there was talk of increased prize money and attendance, but at the core, tennis in the late '80s and early '90s, particularly in the United States, was rife with tales of dissatisfied sponsors and internecine squabbles between various powers and increasingly remote players. The latter was particularly troublesome. Those that delivered results, like Europeans Ivan Lendl, Stefan Edberg and Steffi Graf, were thought to lack the charisma of Americans such as Ashe,

King or Connors. Those with appeal, such as Agassi, McEnroe and Becker, lacked consistent results and dedication. Most of all, there was an aching gap in the area of desire. "How badly do these guys want it?" Connors asked me once. Others may have played tennis better than Jimmy Connors, but was there anyone who pursued success with more visceral fury? The '91 Open was a two-week Valentine between Connors and everyone from public to rivals. "I wish I had the love of the game he's got," said John McEnroe.

As I inspected Connors' future opponents, I remembered a conversation I'd had at the '90 U.S. Open with Connors' long-standing St. Louis near-contemporary, Trey Waltke. Though Connors' wrist injury was a major reason he withdrew from the tournament, it was notable that he didn't announce his withdrawal until after the draw was made. His opponent: Kevin Curren, twice his conqueror at Wimbledon— and also someone who'd come from two sets to love down to beat Connors in '89. Waltke noted that Connors often benefited from good draws at the U.S. Open. In '74, Newcombe and Smith were eliminated. In '76, the troublesome Nastase. In '78, Vilas. In '83, McEnroe. And now, two seeds in Connors' section, Agassi and Becker, were beaten, respectively, by Aaron Krickstein and Paul Haarhuis. "The more twisted irony," wrote Curry Kirkpatrick in *Sports Illustrated*, "is that at 39, Connors seems only to be arriving, while Andre Agassi, 21, or at least the Image of Andre Agassi (with this guy, one can never be sure), may well be leaving."

Connors' next two opponents, Michiel Schapers and Karol Novacek, were made to order, clean-hitting, dim-witted ballstrikers unable to cope with Connors' skills or the bigger matter of taking on the Mayor on his turf. The Jimbo Express burst past the sports pages. ABC's Ted Koppel devoted a "Nightline" to Connors' invigorating heroics. Madison Avenue, never far from Connors' mind despite his statements to the contrary, joined in with new endorsements for Nuprin and Pepsi. Asked John Lloyd, Evert's ex-husband, now a member of Connors' posse, "But is Jimmy's price rising by the hour or what? By the time he's finished, corporate America will be up for ransom."

From players and sponsors, to fans and press, everyone wanted a piece of Connors. What was it they wanted to touch? "What Jimmy has is what we all would kill for," said Nastase. "Just one more time." Certainly that was part of it. But it wasn't just the matter of a comeback. It was Connors' willingness to squeeze every drop out of his tennis life. Borg's premature retirement initially seemed an aberration. But a decade later, that possibility seemed to lurk around the corner for so many tennis stars. Players like McEnroe, Becker and Agassi were constantly lamenting the complications of life as a professional tennis player. The whines of a tiresome millionaire are hard to stomach. These whiners were leaving cards on the table.

Meanwhile, here was Connors, strictly playing point to point, as unconcerned with his future as a man on death row, making sure he savored every minute. Defending champ Sampras confessed he was somewhat relieved to have lost his title upon elimination in the quarterfinals, referred to its burden as a "bag of bricks." Informed of this, Connors jumped on it like a short ball. No doubt he'd been waiting a year—at least since that night in the locker at Stanford—to send a message to a potential heir. "What?" asked Connors. "Don't tell me that! That's the biggest crock of dump! Being the U.S. Open champion is what I've lived for. If these guys are relieved at *losing*, something is wrong with the game—and wrong with them." Give the Mayor an inch of a mandate, and he was ready to take a mile.

Connors' run reached its crescendo on Labor Day, which also happened to be his 39th birthday. His opponent was Krickstein, a frequent Connors' sparring partner, close enough to Jimbo to have watched the Super Bowl at his house one year (hey, I thought I was going to get that invitation). In five matches versus Krickstein, Connors had lost but one set, most recently beating him at Wimbledon earlier that summer, 6-2, 6-3, 6-0. Save for his powerful topspin forehand, it was hard for Krickstein to damage Connors. Their matches featured many long rallies, Connors invariably forcing an error or coming to net. In large part, for Connors, Krickstein was a less stressful Borg replica, a steady enough player but lacking the Swede's incredible footspeed, nimble backhand and robust serve.

The gap between Connors and Krickstein showcased the tragic evolution of tennis players in the Open Era. In 1968, at 16, Connors won the National 16s title. Realizing how far he was from being as diversified a player as possible—and also aware that only the very best in the world earned big money—Connors relocated to Los Angeles and honed his game for nearly four years until he turned pro. In 1983, also at 16, Krickstein won the National 18s title. Yet though his game was still woefully incomplete, by then there was a massive marketplace ready to capitalize on Krickstein's potential. You didn't need to win big to make lots of money. Anointed with endorsement contracts, proficient enough to earn sufficient money, Krickstein turned pro at 16. Though he was number seven in the world a year later, skill-wise he was a paper tiger. Alas, there was no way he could refine and broaden his game under the demanding pressures of the pro tour and the expectations of those corporations that were counting on him to deliver. Even if his strengths improved incrementally, his weaknesses atrophied. Krickstein's lack of dimension would cost him dearly versus Connors.

Even in spite of his limitations, Krickstein had his own distinguished U.S. Open history: 8-1 in career five-setters at the Open (Connors was only 4-4), reaching the semis in '89. He was also 15 years younger than Connors, a key factor given that Connors came into this match having played more tennis than he had at a single tournament in two years.

But when Connors stood to serve at 5-1, 40-15 in the second set after losing the first 6-3, he seemed in control.

Then all went awry. A double-fault, a forehand into the net and Krickstein broke. Soon it was 6-all, and apparent to all that for Connors the tiebreak was paramount. One comeback from two sets to love down was incredible enough. A second, particularly on a warm afternoon versus a steady opponent, was nearly-impossible. Stepping in as a guest commentator for CBS, John McEnroe said, "This is blood and guts time for Jimmy."

Krickstein held a set point at 5-6. Connors hit a rare shot: a serve powerful enough to force a long return. At 6-all, Connors laced a backhand down the line, sprinted into net and played a perfect forehand drop volley. He waved his racket in the air. Though he'd invariably cite the crowd's screams as the catalyst to his success, watching this match repeatedly, I'm more struck by the discipline of Connors' footwork, the precise metering out of those little steps. With a set point in hand, Connors again charged forward, but Krickstein came through with a forehand crosscourt pass for a winner.

At 7-all, Connors approached again. Krickstein lobbed. Connors struck a crosscourt overhead deep into the northeast corner of the court, extremely close to the line. The linesman signaled the ball good. An angry Krickstein complained, at which point umpire David Littlefield, all the way over on the west side of the court, exerted his right to overrule the call and awarded the point to Krickstein. Connors approached Littlefield.

"He called the ball good!" said Connors, a cross dangling off his neck (the "TIG" necklace was gone). "You didn't see the goddarned ball."

"It was clearly wide," said Littlefield.

"Clearly bullcrap! Bullcrap! You wouldn't have known anything unless Krickstein asked you! Get out of the chair! Get your ass out of the chair! You're a bum. You're a bum! I'm out here playing my butt off at 39 years old and you're doing that? Very clear my butt!"

Said John McEnroe on CBS, "that was a very unfortunate decision. At 7-all, that far away, to overrule like that … if anything, that ball was no more than an eighth of an inch out, and there's no way he could have seen it."

At 7-8, down set point again—ostensibly match point—Connors had found an enemy. It wasn't Krickstein, who he actually liked. It certainly wasn't the crowd, as was the case back at Forest Hills. It was the chair umpire. Again Connors came in, and after he struck a volley winner, he pointed at Littlefield. The crowd screamed its approval. At 8-8, Connors rocketed a crosscourt forehand hard and low enough to creep in and put away another volley. Said Mary Carillo, "David Littlefield gave him the best birthday present he could have." At 8-9, Connors applied a lesson Segura wished Connors had employed more frequently throughout his career: charge the net on a return of serve. Driving his backhand return deep to Krickstein's backhand, Connors stormed in, lunged for Krickstein's down-the-line pass with a cross-court backhand volley, and then perfectly read Krickstein's next fore-hand—a crosscourt drive that Connors punched into the open court. Forty-five minutes after his first set point, Connors was even.

After the 84-minute second set, Connors tossed the third, letting Krickstein win it 6-1 in 25 minutes. After three sets, a CBS graphic showed Connors with 50 winners and 24 for Krickstein. During the same years when Krickstein was posing for clothing contracts, Connors was learning how to close out points.

Sensing Krickstein's limitations, Connors yelled aloud to "get in there!" Up 4-2, Connors felt Littlefield failed to overrule a bad call. Knowing the crowd's noise would give him support and, perhaps more importantly, recovery time between points, Connors took the law into his hands. "That ball wasn't going fast enough for you not to see that one," Connors said to Littlefield. "Kiss me before you do anything. Just kiss me." Littlefield, prudent enough to know that admonishing Connors would likely trigger more demagoguery, stayed silent. As the political philosopher Machiavelli wrote in *The Prince*, "for the vulgar is always taken by appearances and the issue of the event; and the world consists only of the vulgar, and the few who are not vulgar are isolated when the many have a rallying point in the prince." Corners of the crowd chortling over his jokes, others screaming his balls in and Krickstein's out, Connors controlled the tempo and mood of an entire stadium. The boy from the boondocks was thoroughly in his element, and soon the match was dead even.

Connors reached 15-40 versus Krickstein's serve in the first game of the fifth set. Yelling towards his corner, Connors said, "He's going to have to pass me 60 times this set if he's going to win." But Krickstein fought and held.

Krickstein broke Connors at 2-3 and served at 4-2, 40-15. But again, Connors stormed forward and reached break point. After his approach was called long, Connors looked to Littlefield for an overrule and let fly. "You are an abortion," said Connors. "You are an abortion. Do you know that? . . . Get the fuck out of there." So often, Connors was above the law. Until he, Nastase and McEnroe emerged, there wasn't even a need for a code of penalties. In New York that year, Connors was the law. But despite holding three break points, even after 15 netrushes in that one game, Connors was unsuccessful. After eight deuces, Krickstein held for 5-2. The match was now four hours long.

With Krickstein serving at 5-3, 15-all, Connors came to net on a crosscourt forehand. Krickstein's pass was out by inches—an entire section of the crowd calling it wide.

The connection between Connors and the spectators was odd. He called it mutual love, but if so, it was love expressed in a manner I suppose you'd know best if you lived in the grime of New York and came from the streets of Belleville. It was a crude love, a love never seen before or since in tennis. "A toast, Jedediah," says Orson Welles to his embittered ex-best friend played by Joseph Cotten in *Citizen Kane*, "to love on my terms. Those are the only terms anybody ever knows, his own." No one in tennis devoured this concept better than Connors. His mother's love was a complex (or simple?) mix of conditional and unconditional. His father's love was nonexistent (Or was it? We'll never know). He knew most of all of the lonely love of Jones Park, a boy, a mother and a grandmother, walking one hundred yards on a muggy day for a drink of water. He knew of the days when crowds loved to hate him. Even when it all turned around and Connors became a venerated icon, he knew how fickle public opinion was, how easy it was to be cherished one day, forgotten the next. He thrived on being overlooked and, as I did in my own way, overturning that disregard into emotional capital. Months later, after Connors was resurrected once again into a national hero, a San Francisco broadcast journalist walked up to him and told Connors he was his favorite athlete. When Connors later asked me if I knew him, I mentioned how that same man had harshly criticized Connors after his '86 default in Key Biscayne and said how he'd never liked Connors. "You gotta love that, don't you?" replied Connors.

Don't count me out. I come from a small town in Illinois. You people have no idea where I'm from. Now let me show you.

Leave the disaffected decadence of Studio 54 and the prep school whining to McEnroe. Connors came to New York to kick ass. Connors' work ethic and drive was so profound it jarred the privileged fans in the seats, made them feel a speck of what he'd been through to get there, validated the struggles they thought personified New Yorkers' unstated belief that their beloved city's defining element was soot. McEnroe's game and persona, dominant and removed, rarified and subtle, was headed towards the limo, always at heart out to prove his superiority. Connors' game showed he was primed to walk the streets and dig out the rubble. So what if he was a momma's boy of a tennis player who'd earned more than $100,000 a year since he was 19? A myth is what people want to believe. Thanks to Connors, the myth was on display in vivid, fluorescent-yellowed glory. Beneath and beyond all the commerce and commotion, the tennis itself was painstakingly real. As Ava Gardner once said to Frank Sinatra, "you're only honest when you sing." By 1991, I'd loved Connors' act for half my life. He liked to say that at the Open that year he and his public were paying each other back for all the love they'd shared.

Yet as I watched Connors thrust his pelvis into the stands, it hardly seemed an act of love. Jimmy Connors wasn't simply making love to the crowd. He was fucking it, humping and thrusting his way into their hearts, minds and souls with both pleasure and pain, pleasure for his joy at playing great tennis, pain for all it had taken to make his way into the arena. For what did the public really know of that struggle anyway? Did they really care about the devotion and sacrifices Gloria and Two-Mom made? Walking up to Mozart, a fan told him, I'd give my life to play music like you. Said Mozart, *I did.*

And so, as the shadows swept over Louis Armstrong Stadium, Connors made yet one more charge at yet another opponent, supposedly because he wanted to, but perhaps also because he needed to. It was his nature. It was his nurture. High up in the press box, *Tennis Magazine's* Peter Bodo turned to Arthur Ashe and said, "So, Arthur, what's the bottom line? Is Jimmy Connors really just an asshole?" With trademark deliberation, Ashe finally concurred: "Yes, but he's my *favorite* asshole."

It was 5-3, 15-40. But Connors sprayed an approach, and when Krickstein passed him, the match was two points from the end. At deuce, to his credit, Krickstein did more than play not to lose. He ripped a forehand deep into Connors' forehand corner. All Connors could do was throw up a defensive lob. Here again, Krickstein's skills betrayed him. Three summers later, I'd spend a week with Pancho Segura. Every time he lobbed, he screamed, "Get back, keed! Get back behind the ball! You get back and then move forward into the ball. Get back!" But Krickstein didn't have a Segura in his corner. He didn't get back far enough. Unable to fully propel himself into the ball, he was awkwardly off-balance, and drove the smash long. "He missed it big," said Carillo. But Connors netted a forehand, and again Krickstein was two points away from the match.

At deuce, with a short ball to his backhand, logic called for Connors to approach down the line to Krickstein's weaker backhand. But Connors shifted gears, and drove the ball crosscourt for a winner. On the next point, again approaching crosscourt with his backhand, he struck a backhand volley winner. Connors was now 77 of 120 at the net. Connors and Krickstein traded holds. With Connors serving at 5-6, 30-30, he lunged for a volley. All Krickstein had to do was run forward and nudge the ball into the open court to reach match point. But again, his lack of skill in the transition and net area proved costly, and he pushed a forehand long. An overhead smash from Connors brought the match to a tiebreak.

As the crowd cheered—"those 20,000 sounded like 60,000," said Connors—Connors paused for breath, sat in the southeast corner and yelled into a courtside microphone: "This is what they paid for. This is what they want." The comment oozed commerce and cynicism. Was Connors angry that he'd primed the pump so much that he'd become a barking seal? Was he a tired performer slinging back one classic after another? Why "they" instead of "we"? No, "they" were "they," as they'd always been: different, separate from Connors, but now, as was the case since that night in '78 when he'd told New York how much he'd liked them, they were his flock, a mob that, if not exactly unruly, was something unique to tennis. Was all this commotion a betrayal of Belleville? Not necessarily, so long as you committed to the ball as Gloria commanded. Was it a vindication of the lessons learned in Beverly Hills? Absolutely, for this was "action" at its supreme apex, an iconic performer chewing it up and spitting it out. Was it what Riordan had in mind when he dubbed Connors "The One and Only"? Of course.

By now, Krickstein was out of his league. All he could hope for was that Connors would self-destruct. Connors went up 5-2. Connors served at 5-4 into the ad court. What was the play? Obviously, Connors wanted to attack. But better yet, he struck a perfect serve deep and wide into Krickstein's backhand corner that drew a long return. At match point, Connors served deep and down the middle. Few of his 136 netrushes this day were serve-volley points, but this time he moved forward and punched a crosscourt forehand volley to Krickstein's backhand. It was actually a rather tentative volley, and were it any time other than four hours and 40 minutes into the match, Krickstein might have felt relaxed enough to whip a topspin lob. But now both players were on auto-pilot. Krickstein went up the line. Connors read the pass like a book, angling the volley for an easy winner. The crowd screamed as it never had at a U.S. Open match. Thousands began to sing "Happy Birthday."

"This is a Connors miracle," Connors said moments later to CBS' Tim Ryan. Then he dashed into the arms of his entourage, received an IV and paced around the adjacent grandstand court while talking with reporter Mike Lupica. Said Carillo, "He knows how to throw a party."

In the quarters three days later, he played Haarhuis. Like Krickstein, Haarhuis bore a faint resemblance to a classic Connors foil: more adept at net than Krickstein, but tall, slow and lacking the firepower to overtake Connors. One win away from the final weekend—could he even win the tournament?—Connors started off tight, his forehand sailing, his feet sluggish. Haarhuis won the first set 6-4, broke Connors at 4-4 in the second, and soon reached 30-15—again likely two points away from an insurmountable lead. Haarhuis rocketed a serve deep to Connors forehand, but Connors reacted sharply, driving it so hard and deep crosscourt that Haarhuis' backhand was long. At 30-all, Haarhuis served and volleyed, striking a sharp wide serve—and Connors drove another sharp return down-the-line laser, a near-winner. Break point to get back on serve. The next point would outlive Connors.

Haarhuis took Connors' return and drove a deep backhand approach down the line. From far behind his court, Connors threw up a lob. Haarhuis pounded another smash, and again Connors hoisted a backhand lob. He was nearly touching the back fence. And Haarhuis, stubbornly, did not let the lob bounce. He pounded a third smash into Connors' backhand corner. And again, another lob. Now, on the fourth try, Haarhuis went after Connors' forehand. Another lob. The smashes, never deep, began to lose pace. This one was weak enough for Connors to lace a crosscourt forehand. Haarhuis lunged at the backhand volley. Instantly seeing a vulnerable opponent, Connors charged forward and passed Haarhuis up the line. The crowd was on its feet. They knew instantly they'd seen one of the greatest points in tennis history. Connors thrust his hips. It took a while, but he went on to win the next three sets, 7-6, 6-4, 6-2, a kind of present on the night of Patti's 40th birthday. For the 14th time in 17 years, Connors was in the semis.

On the final Saturday, the day where Connors had been 13 previous times, another Jim extinguished him. Courier was too good, his powerful forehand and solid backhand never giving Connors a chance to take charge with racket or emotions. "Nobody's leaving, Jimbo!" shouted a fan late in the third set. A few minutes earlier, though, Connors turned to a group courtside and said, "I guess this is the final frontier." After Courier won 6-3, 6-3, 6-2, he told Connors he was "unbelievable" and admitted he too was ambivalent about having to do his job at the expense of everyone's joy. "How can you *not* like what Jimmy is doing?" asked Courier. "He's great for the game."

In the scheme of Connors' career accomplishments, it was a run that meant nothing. Connors could have lost that opening match to Patrick McEnroe 6-0, 6-0, 6-0 and his genius would remain unassailable. From another view, it was a run that meant everything. Versus McEnroe, a night for the ages. Versus Krickstein, an unforgettable birthday in a long life of U.S. Open celebrations. Versus Haarhuis, just one point was one career. It was a grand coda, a summation of 20 years of great tennis, like the second side of the Beatles' *Abbey Road*, a final medley of great tunes in a sport starved for heroes. Connors was particularly pleased his children witnessed his resurrection and ascension. Son Brett was four when Connors last won a Slam. Daughter Aubree wasn't even born. Now, at age six, she noticed her friends commenting on her father. Connors, the man who told me so often he didn't care what people thought of him, was pleased when Aubree said, "Daddy, you're famous." But Connors would also say all he had done was play tennis the way he'd been taught: small steps, compact strokes, point to point, with fingers and racket. "Except for the point, the still point," wrote T.S. Eliot, "There would be no dance, and there is only the dance." Connors had proven a man of his word, returning and rocking New York as he'd declared to me in that cab a year prior. He'd made his point, and of course, it was an exclamation point.

Connors once again was news. A supermarket clerk who admitted she knew nothing about tennis asked me, "What's the deal with Jimmy Connors?" For the eighth and final time (more than any tennis player), he was on the cover of *Sports Illustrated*, the headline duplicating my 1985 *Tennis Week* story: "The People's Choice." TV, radio and print devoted more hours and inches to Connors than they had in years, virtually all of it positive (though a few noted how Connors was reinforced more for being a child than an adult). Having announced he was planning a full schedule in '92, Connors knew tournament directors and exhibition promoters would come knocking. There were dozens of endorsement offers. And, one of my sources in the Connors camp told me, a possible book deal.

My heart raced.

"Jimmy's talking with a bunch of publishers," he said. "They're looking to get one of those big ghostwriters, like the one who wrote Lee Iacocca's book. That was a best-seller, did you know that?"

My heart sank.

I said none of what was on my mind. Did I know that? Did I know that? Did I fucking know that? Wasn't one of the skills I'd mastered in nearly a decade in public relations the ability to ghostwrite? Do you think I'd be as motivated to compose a speech or article for a Fortune 500 executive if not for Connors? Do you think I hadn't devoted myself to the study of biographies as diligently as Connors had to his groundstrokes? Was Connors, the man who made his speech to me about loyalty, about to cast me aside? Where were these ghostwriters a year ago? How familiar were any with the subtleties of Connors' matches versus McEnroe and Borg? Did a mercenary ghostwriter understand what it meant for Connors to play what he called "a woman's game inside a man's body"? Did he know that much more than a river separated Belleville from St. Louis? Did he understand what it meant to grind out a match? How familiar was a ghostwriter with the nuances of Connors' life not just when he was winning, but in those odd periods of '73, '76, '78 and '81?

These ghostwriters knew nothing of tennis. Which, I came to see, was precisely why Connors was likely drawn to them—all the better to dictate the agenda on his own terms. I knew too much for my own good, was too armed with questions about low forehands, lawsuits and limos. Connors' success of '91 turned my asset into a liability. As these thoughts raced through my mind—*jilted*—I vowed to cool down and wait a week before I called Connors.

As usual, whenever I spoke to Connors he was kind. I like to think he valued my loyalty, but in the fall of 1991, there were other values on his mind. He told me he was just back from a series of lucrative exhibitions with Lendl in Brazil. He asked how things were with me, and again, if I was playing much tennis. "Business as usual," I joked. "And speaking of business, any thoughts on the book idea we talked about?" He told me he indeed was talking to publishers, and that they wanted to give him "Schwartzkopf-level" money for it (the general who'd led America to victory in Operation Desert Storm was paid millions for his autobiography). At no point did Connors tell me what he thought of my proposal or that he wanted to work with me. But he did confess that the publishers wanted him to write a book that "blew the lid" on pro tennis. They wanted him to tell tales of bedroom romps with Evert, parties with Gerulaitis.

"And what did you tell them?" I asked.

"Look, Joel, you probably know me as well as any writer, so you can imagine what I told them. I told them they could jump in the lake. There was no way I want to write a book like that."

"But you can write a book any way you want."

"No, no, I don't want to do it right now."

Literature, said the poet Ezra Pound, is news that stays news. This was the kind of book Connors and I had discussed in 1990. But now, in 1991, back in business, Connors was focused less on enduring art and more on maximum commerce. Publishers who a year ago might have paid a modest sum for Connors' soulful memoir now saw him as a cash cow. The man of 1990 was now given reinforcement for being the child he'd been for so long. It was hard to blame him for resisting me. How stupid was I to think Connors wanted to occupy my world of thought when he was getting so much action? With money the measure of his value, Connors was primed at the end of 1991 to play tennis and generate revenue with much more ease than if he was to sit on a couch and let me pepper him with questions of pain and sacrifice, defeat and anguish, women, children and father figures. Who can blame a man for doing what he does well in front of thousands for big money rather than do something unfamiliar with one other person? Were I in his place, I doubt if I'd have done it any differently.

A year later, a Connors book surfaced. *Don't Count Yourself Out: Staying Fit After 35* was an expedient how-to book "co-authored" by Connors with a doctor. It featured a series of charts so complicated I doubt Connors understood or even read them. Where, I wanted to ask him, was the tennis? Why had you let yourself be virtually indistinguishable from fitness guru Richard Simmons or Olympian Bruce Jenner? Maybe that was the point. When we first discussed the book, Connors wanted to get away from tennis, but with nowhere to run to in the fall of '90, all he saw was his palpable past. Now, in the wake of his '91 run, he had a place that welcomed him. Connors' future lay in the ether of celebrity.

In February 1992, Connors arrived for a tournament in San Francisco. Where previously he'd traveled to the Bay Area alone or with his affable friend, John Heller, this time he was accompanied by an old friend from Belleville, Bill Lelly, a gruff, chilly bodyguard. A month later, Connors was surprised to see me at a tournament in Indian Wells, California. "Getting out there more, son, aren't you?" he asked. When I asked Connors if he'd talk to me for stories I was writing on Gonzalez and Newcombe, he joked, "You won't be able to print anything I tell you." He declined to say anything.

As I wrote in a notebook the morning after Connors' first-round match in San Francisco, "Lelly's presence tells me there's something up with Jimbo, some need to guard himself against the crush." Whereas all through the previous decade, Connors often invited me to the locker, no such request came at these tournaments. When down, such as in '86 and '90, he valued loyalty. Now it was different. "Seeing all the hype," I wrote, "all the attention, all the push of crowds, makes me feel like Jimmy Connors is in many ways beyond me."

11

All By Myself

ugust 22, 1992 was a breathtakingly clear and warm Saturday
afternoon in the San Francisco Bay Area. I had just finished
two sets of tennis. Having lost the first, I came back to win the
second in a tiebreak. The next morning I was scheduled to play at 9 a.m.

I loved these summer weekends of tennis, relished the chance to put
aside work and dash after balls in corners, run forward for volleys,
lunge after service returns and then drive home, a mix of sweat and
fatigue. The U.S. Open was a week away. Though it wasn't likely that
Connors would repeat his '91 effort—his '92 results thus far were
negligible—who knew what might happen?

In Los Angeles, my father was in the hospital, recovering nicely from
prostate cancer surgery. We spoke the day before his operation. I
thanked him for the tape he sent me of Connors' recent three-set loss
in the quarterfinals of the LA tournament. We talked about my work
at the public relations firm and its engagement and boredom. "That's
kind of how life goes, doesn't it?" he said. I wished him well on the
operation. We looked forward to October when I planned a trip to LA
and we'd play a few sets of doubles.

That Saturday evening I called my father at 8:30 p.m. at the hospital.
An attendant told me he was in the bathroom. I decided to call him
the next day. Thirty minutes later, I went to sleep.

At 10:30 the phone rang. It was my mother. "Daddy died," she said.
In his sleep, of a heart attack, at 9:17. He was 66.

Six months earlier my mother sent me an envelope filled with
dozens of photos of our family. The vast majority was from the time
before Ken's illness. As my mind reeled over my father's death, I looked
through the photographs, as if I could touch the past and reclaim his

242

life. There was our father, Ken and I, his arms on each of our shoulders in the ocean off Carmel in 1965. This was the trip where he decided we should move to California. There were my mother and father during their first year of marriage nearly 40 years ago. There were dozens of photos of Ken and I prior to his illness. There was me in my king's outfit, football helmet, tennis clothes, prom tuxedo, college graduation gown. And there were a few of Ken and I from more recent years, Ken in random states of order and disorder, me usually in tennis clothes.

The next afternoon, I walked the grounds of Hillside Mortuary with my uncle. I wrote an obituary and a eulogy. Exerting executive power, I decreed that contributions go in my father's name to the National Alliance for the Mentally Ill. I called friends with the news. Some were supportive, and vowed to attend the funeral or reception. Others, no doubt fearful of mortality, were remote. My mother and I drove to Ken's board-and-care facility to tell him the news. "How does that make you feel, Ken?" asked my mother. "Empty," he said.

Two years earlier, at my sibling support group, I broke out in tears with fears and anger of how Ken's illness had exacted its toll on my family, most of all on my father. I was convinced that if he died, it would be because his heart was broken by the tragedy of his first-born. One year for his birthday, I gave my father a book of tennis pointers. "Except for Ken," he said, "the only things I have to worry about in my life are in that book." My father liked to recite a comment his father made back in the Depression: "If you don't laugh, you cry." He and my mother refused to be defeated by Ken's illness. Compartmentalizing it was a survival strategy, likely even more necessary for them than for me.

During the week Joan and I spent in Los Angeles, when we weren't with my mother, or Ken, or at the funeral, or at the reception, or sifting through family photos, I turned through the pages of back issues of *World Tennis* that lay in a closet. Naturally, I lingered on the photos and stories about Jimmy Connors. Maybe there was a message in them, or an escape, or something just to comfort me. There was nothing specific, just page after page of tennis, photos of Connors striking backhands and stories of his matches and controversies.

The day Joan and I flew home, I saw two brothers linger near the baggage claim area. The younger one lingered closely to the spinning carousel, touching the metal panels as they circled one after another. The older brother grabbed him kindly by the shoulders and suggested he move back a few feet. Instantly I thought of Ken and myself. The whole world looked vulnerable.

One week after my father's funeral, on Wednesday, September 2, the U.S. Open threw an on-court 40th birthday celebration for Connors prior to his first-round match. A large cake was wheeled onto the court. It was a grand celebration of Connors' life, and given his advanced age in tennis terms, a charming public eulogy. Soon enough it would be time for Connors to move on too. I burst into tears. I don't even know what I was crying for—the loss of my father, Connors' imminent fade-out, Ken's pain and what it meant for my family, my feelings in all of this. Nice as it was to see Connors whip his thoroughly-intimidated opponent, the next round was far more treacherous: Ivan Lendl, a man Connors last beat nearly eight years ago.

Joan suggested we enjoy the match with a Friday night pizza. Shortly into my second slice, Connors won the first set, 6-3. Playing every point with the fury of a man knowing it might be his last, Connors dashed forward for volleys and pounded groundstrokes into corners. He admitted afterwards his plan was to hit no more than five balls a point. When he broke serve early in the second set, his hitting partner, John Lloyd, told a courtside interviewer he was confident Jimmy could run out the match.

I knew better. At this stage in their careers, Lendl was far fitter and hit harder than Connors. Fitness also made Lendl more patient. In short order, he established control. The sequence of points was numbing. As in the glory days of the early '80s, Connors drove his backhand to Lendl's forehand. But as the decade wore on, Connors' decline coincided with Lendl's ascent, and that made all the difference on virtually every point. Lendl's forehand was better now, adept at drives and smart loopers that frustrated Connors. Lendl had also learned how to chip his backhand low to Connors' forehand. And most of all, Lendl's nerves and footwork were stronger. He won the second set, 6-3, the third 6-2. By the fourth, Connors was exhausted. Lendl won it, 6-0. Miffed as I was, my tears were allocated for far more significant matters than a tennis match. This wasn't 1986. I felt no need to take Connors' loss out on the court. Though Connors afterwards castigated Lendl for merely "bunting" the ball, even his anger seemed more of a caricature. After the requiem of '91, Connors needed nothing more from the U.S. Open. It was his last Grand Slam match.

Two days later, my mother, Ken and I visited our father's grave. We selected a headstone and went to eat. All my life, whenever our family went anywhere, my father drove. My father dead, my hero defeated, now I was the one behind the wheel.

12

Citizen Connors

The match was over. I was beaten. There, on the pages of *Tennis Week* in the fall of 1998, was a one-paragraph notice that sent a dagger to my heart. A biography of Jimmy Connors was due out shortly. The authors were two people I'd never heard of. How could that be? Instantly I had to devour this book. But it was already past 4:00 in California. The East Coast-based publisher was closed for the day. That night I tossed and turned. Who were these authors? Had Connors cooperated with them? I thought he didn't want a book. If they'd written it without Connors' help, who else spoke to them? Was there a new angle they'd unearthed? Time with Gloria? And most of all, why not me?

The next morning I called the publisher at 6:15 a.m. Pacific time. The company's representative said that the authors were new, a husband-wife team with "personal experience with Connors." What? This was even worse. If there were dozens of potential biographers, what writer had more proximity to Connors than I had? Why had he told me I knew him better than any writer? I had to have the book instantly. I gave the rep my Federal Express number. That afternoon I played tennis and roller-coastered between angry, focused attacks and bitter, frustrated errors.

Once the book arrived, I saw a chapter, "Jimmy Connors … The Legend and Me." What the hell was this? I was relieved to see the authors' only personal connection to Connors came from television. They'd never met him.

The book read like a series of magazine articles. It was obvious no interviews were conducted. But as I read one chapter after another, various quotes, concepts and statistical arrangements seemed familiar. Then again, I was such a ravenous reader of all related to Connors that all the stories ran together.

But when I came to the summer of 1978, an entire section on Connors rang exceptionally loud. The sentences, ideas and paragraphs sounded like Frank Deford's *Sports Illustrated* profile, "Raised By Women To Conquer Men." Comparing the book with Deford's story, I saw the authors had merely altered several verb tenses. Unbelievable.

I knew Deford from working with him the previous summer at HBO. "I thought you'd want to know," I told him, "that you've been plagiarized." He asked me to send him the book.

After the *Sports Illustrated* legal team reviewed the book, it found dozens of examples of plagiarism, comprising the vast majority of the text. The publisher was offered two choices: face a lawsuit for millions or immediately withdraw the book from circulation. Not eager for bankruptcy, the publisher chose the latter.

I have never met the couple who wrote this book. But somewhere, in some living room, I wonder if they sit with a stack of books, their covers torn off (a publishing protocol that signifies a destroyed work as surely as a smashed sculpture), wondering how their Connors biography was annihilated.

If I couldn't have Connors, no one could.

To explain where I stood with Connors by 1998, a quick look back to my infancy. I was a late walker. While other children such as Ken fell, picked themselves up and soon walked, I was more pensive. Once the landscape was scoped out, I was ready to move forward. Without a single fall, I transitioned from the crawl to the walk. Ambitious as I've been, I've often needed a kick in the butt. Tell me to play a tennis match versus Player X and I'll be neutral. Tell me Player X thinks I'm no good and, like Connors, I foam at the mouth.

My father's death widened the emotional gap between my job and my desires. Having always been drawn to the odd symmetries of history and numbers, I noted that I was 32 and he'd died at 66. The next year I'd be half his age, and how far had I advanced? Was I just going to go day to day, a middle manager directing accounts? Added to this I thought of Ken's loss, and the gift of survival I'd been given. Here was Ken, barely able to take care of himself. But I was the one with full health. Why take the future for granted? Public relations agency life provided me with many skills I'd use forever. But it occupied my head, not my heart. Through the winter of 1992-'93, I wondered how to make a mix of tennis, journalism and consulting viable.

Then my employers made it easy for me. For nearly a decade, I'd worked in a variety of product areas, ranging across food, travel, gaso-line, computers and more. Now, as nearby Silicon Valley accelerated into the '90s, my firm wanted to focus strictly on high technology accounts. As a senior associate, I was asked to either make a complete commitment to this world or leave. Much as I'd always been unin-volved with the various inanimate objects of the companies I'd coun-seled, consumer products like food and beverages were wrapped in a cultural context I enjoyed. For a wine cooler, for example, I created a video that showed off various periods of American history and their representative beverage, such as the Old South and the mint julep, the '20s and bathtub gin and, of course, the '80s and the wine cooler.

But technology struck me as sterile. After receiving my boss' ulti-matum, I said nothing for three weeks. I really wanted to leave, but lacked the guts to say so. Finally, I was summoned and dispatched. It was kind, with a fair severance package. Quickly I made a list of 50 people I could contact for work. By the next day, I was ghostwriting articles for a former client's CEO. A week later, I completed a creden-tial request for the 1993 U.S. Open. Connors was no longer coming to New York. Now it was my turn.

Instantly I felt I had the right to weigh in on tennis' great players. I'd sniffed Connors' fumes for years, so why not Agassi, Sampras and Becker? I began to cultivate relationships with editors, sending them ideas while building a network of agents, coaches, sponsors, tour offi-cials, parents, ex-players and players. In many ways, journalism is like tennis in that it is an individual endeavor, largely (but not entirely) merit-based. There are no others to boss around or hide behind. Like tennis players, each writer follows his own set of rituals and plays his own game. When in pursuit of a story, he's either moving forward or in retreat.

Invariably, there were more chances to write about Connors. When Connors launched his own 35-and-over tour in 1993, I soon gener-ated an assignment with a travel magazine and contacted Connors' public relations person to arrange an interview.

"Your request for time with Jimmy," he told me, "was turned down."

What? No way.

Never having called Connors to request an interview, I phoned him.

"How's everything, son?"

"I'm having a bitch of a time promoting your tour."

"You're kidding."

Two days later, the tour official said to come to an event at Pebble Beach for my interview with Connors. So what if right now Jimbo didn't want me as his ghostwriter? So long as Connors was willing to talk with me, I felt confident it would eventually lead to a major work. I'd read enough about the art of biography to know it wasn't always necessary to have a subject's cooperation. The reason *The New Yorker*'s portraits were called "profiles" was because the subject was viewed from the side, the writer interviewing as many people besides him or her as possible. In many cases, a lack of participation left the writer unshackled. Besides, if Connors was my object of desire, wouldn't Connors himself advise me to pursue that passion to its fullest?

For two years, in the spring of 1995 and '96, I wrote lengthy stories about Connors' tour at various venues. Connors gave me hours of interview time, ranging from the new tour to aspects of his career and thoughts on everyone from his grandmother to his rivals to his daughter. Even his gruff valet, Bill Lelly, warmed up. On June 21, 1996, at Pebble Beach, I couldn't help but tell Connors it was my birthday. "Lunch is on me," he said, requesting Lelly fetch hot dogs for the three of us from a nearby stand. A helpful Lelly asked if I preferred ketchup or mustard (it is amazing how the planets align when the sun is shining).

"What do you want for your birthday?" Connors asked me in between bites.

"How about a wild card into the next tournament?"

The three of us laughed.

Lelly, knowing I was about to interview Connors, made a suggestion. "Why don't you just make it up, Joel?" he asked. "You know everything about Jimmy anyway, so you probably know what he's going to say before he says it."

Connors and I that day walked across the Monterey Peninsula for three hours. True as Lelly's comment may have been, I hankered for that 15 percent that was unfamiliar, whether it was a random comment about Davis Cup to reflections on Gloria or an oblique reference to O.J. Simpson. "So how come I'm not a hero?" asked Connors. "I don't do drugs. I didn't kill anyone. But people don't want to remember anyone from tennis. You spill your guts out for 20 years, and who remembers any of it?" When Connors spoke like that, the flame of collaboration, dimmed in recent years, flickered.

Another time I played in a Pro-Am, partnered with McEnroe, versus Connors. I struck a half-volley. Connors moved across the court and struck a ball that grazed my head. Mocking Connors' trademark gesture, I wagged my right index finger at him. "That is war," I yelled. "I always told you it was a war," he yelled back.

In a way, it was fortunate I'd become a full-time tennis journalist when my favorite player was now more iconic golden oldie than cantankerous contemporary. Were Connors an active player, I'd be forced possibly to take complicated stands on issues related to his behavior and losses. Now, as he paraded around Pebble Beach, he was strictly a nostalgia act, Frank Sinatra in his dotage, the sounds of Rod Stewart singing "Forever Young" echoing through the banquet hall as highlights flickered across a screen.

Borg, Vilas, even McEnroe—all paled to a grand entrance or exit from Connors. "Jimmy, Jimmy!" screamed a group of 40 to 70-some-thing women at the Pebble Beach event. It was always the older women who clustered around him first, the enthused ones who cher-ished Connors less as a sex symbol and more for his everlasting spunk and charm.

"How's everything, ladies?" he asked a flock of 10.

"Would you sign my T-2000 racket cover?"

"You got it."

"Jimmy, I saw you in Boston in '73."

"Boy, that's when I could move."

"Jimmy, Doctor Robert bla bla from Decatur, Illinois, says hello."

"How is the good doctor?"

Gripping and grinning, joking and flirting, never more was Connors the grandson of a politician than in the early years of his senior tour. At a sponsor party one night, one of the guests was the astronaut Alan Shepard. "To see you, on the moon, walking with that golf club," said Connors, "man, that was something."

Meanwhile, in another corner of the same room, McEnroe, as much heir apparent to Connors on this tour as on the ATP in the late '70s, wrestled awkwardly to balance on-court warfare with off-court schmoozing. "It's like I was always following Jimmy," he told me one evening in Carmel. "He laid the path, and I was next, but he just kept staying around too."

I commenced an annual ritual. Every September 2, I called Connors to wish him a happy birthday from the grounds of the U.S. Open. He always said he wasn't watching, and would then ask who was in action.

"Well, there's this guy Philippoussis," I said.

"Who's that? What's he got?"

"Pretty big serve."

"Big serve? Is that all? What else has he got? How are his ground-strokes? How's his return? What's he like under pressure?"

One year I worked for CBS. On Connors' birthday, I was asked to write a feature on his relationship to the U.S. Open. As I shuttled back and forth through videotapes, back through the '70s, on into the '80s and '90s, I felt a wave of delight, euphoria and a tinge of melancholy. There was the '76 final on the day of Ken's break. There were the '82 and '83 finals versus Lendl that my father taped. There was that tearful loss to Todd Witsken. There in every frame was Connors, those small, squeaky steps, those splendid clean drives, that over-the-top desire. There was Connors' final Open match, 13 days after my father's death. There was my life, cascading in front of me through the tale of one man and one city. And now I was getting paid to write about it for a national TV audience. In a muggy, cramped TV truck, on a sticky vinyl chair with a notepad in my arm and a producer eager for copy, I wanted to step back and cry. When I made the birthday call, I told Connors I'd been writing about him. "Well, I hope you didn't say something too bad about me," he joked. "No, no, not at all," I said.

At least not that time. For by then, I'd crossed into new territory with Connors.

A player is eligible for entry into the International Tennis Hall of Fame five years after his last match in a Grand Slam. In late 1997, knowing Connors was set for induction in 1998, I convinced *Tennis Magazine* to let me write a story about Connors for publication just prior to the July ceremony honoring him in Newport, Rhode Island. Certain as always that he'd talk with me, I intended to assess his legacy, compare him with the game's all-time greats and issue the laudatory comments that typically accompany this honor.

Then Connors made news as only he could.

First there was the matter of his eligibility. Since he was still playing on his tour, Connors didn't think the time for his induction was right. Tony Trabert, a prominent Hall of Fame committee chair, explained that what mattered was that Connors was no longer playing ATP events. At last, after much discussion, Connors agreed to be inducted.

Then there were concerns that Connors wasn't planning to attend the ceremony. Apparently there was a scheduling conflict with one of his tour's events. Once that hurdle was cleared, Connors' induction was announced. But he remained exceptionally withdrawn. Outside of issuing a perfunctory set of quotes, officials from his tour and the Hall of Fame failed to get him to conduct interviews. Hall of Fame officials were baffled and worried.

There was no doubt in my mind that even if Connors had no time for other journalists, he'd speak with me. But when I called him, and even when a friend of his intervened on my behalf, Connors was elusive.

I faced an ethical quandary. On the one hand, I craved Connors' appreciation of my insights into his life and tennis. But no longer was I a full-time executive dabbling in tennis, waiting my call to be summoned into Jimbo's army. My journalistic credibility demanded I dissect the Connors story as I saw it rather than be an apologist for my subject's shortcomings (and make no mistake, the complicated nature of the relationship between author and subject demands a mix of throwing and pulling punches). Even if Connors at this point in his life favored the pristine lawns or Pebble Beach, he knew I was prepared to dive into tennis' boondocks.

My piece was titled, "The Reluctant Inductee." As I wrote, "The sad news for tennis fans is that Connors is approaching Newport with the exact opposite kind of passion he's always brought to his tennis." The story explained how Connors was "inspiring and obnoxious," pointing out Connors' various charms and contradictions.

His ex-fiancee provided exceptionally keen insights. "Jimmy doesn't like to be fussed over," said Evert. "Beneath all that bravado is someone who's actually rather sensitive and very private." This much we knew, but as she had demonstrated in '79 following their twin losses to McEnroe and Austin at the U.S. Open, Evert's capacity for introspection cast a keen light on Connors. "That weekend at the Hall of Fame is unbelievably emotional," she told me. "In some ways it's a last hurrah, the time when you've got to forget about tennis and get on with your life. Maybe there's something about letting go that's hard for Jimmy." Maybe? Other sources close to Connors were vague, exceptionally eager to speak off-the-record lest they incur Jimbo's wrath. Had Connors spoken to me, I might have learned what the honor meant to him. Instead, with no thoughts forthcoming, I speculated, based on his ambivalent actions, concluding that, "It's hard to believe this warrior who vowed that he'd follow an opponent to the ends of the Earth wants to tank his entrance into tennis history."

I learned later that Connors was livid when he saw the piece, that he had every intention of developing and delivering a first-rate speech. Connors, an associate of his told me, wanted to set the record straight rather than let others—like me—tell the world how he felt.

When that day came, he was true to his word. With Patti, Brett,

Aubree and Gloria watching, the Mayor of New York spoke as a wise King. "I love everything about this game," he said. "The work, the grind, the dedication, the competition, the sacrifice—but I didn't look at this as work. It was my pleasure . . . that is something that came from the heart—and I wasn't afraid to show you . . . all through my career, I wanted to bring the real sports fan into tennis, so tennis would be on the same level as baseball, basketball, football. And I was willing to do whatever possible to make this happen." Less than 15 minutes long, the speech mirrored Connors' tennis: well-prepared, efficient, impassioned. A year later, McEnroe was inducted and gave a rambling, unprepared monologue nearly triple the length, at one point randomly thanking people he wasn't sure were even in the audience.

In the fall of 1960, Norman Mailer wrote a profile in *Esquire* (then a highly-influential magazine) of John Kennedy titled "Superman Comes to the Supermarket." When Kennedy won by the narrowest popular vote margin in history, Mailer believed his story was one of the 50 deciding factors. Aping Mailer, I believe that my story was one of the 50 reasons for Connors' supreme effort at Newport. Even if he hated what I wrote, even if a Jimbo friend told me it was a "Waterloo" for our relationship, it accomplished one of my goals: getting Jimmy Connors to take history seriously. For all of us counterpunchers, a kick in the butt is helpful. For so long he helped me turn thought into action; I was delighted I'd motivated him enough to turn action into thought.

Which begs the question I wanted to originally ask in that story: How seriously does history take Jimmy Connors? So lengthy was his career that it was possible to assess Connors' impact and resonance even while he was playing. All through the late '80s, as Connors aged, as McEnroe teetered, many wondered who would emerge as the next great American champion.

Soon enough, by the early '90s, Andre Agassi, Michael Chang, Jim Courier and Pete Sampras all earned Grand Slams. Each in his own peculiar way bore the stamp of Jimbo. In Agassi's case, it was his ability to strike the ball early and oppress opponents with his groundstrokes like Connors. His Vegas-bred charisma also made him aware that he was not just an athlete, but an entertainer. Yet, while significantly more gifted than Connors at ballstriking, Agassi initially lacked Connors' talents as a versatile tactician and competitor. Not until age 29 did Agassi start to realize his potential, credited largely to an arduous physical fitness regime that provided exceptional mental fortification. Connors, though, bad-mouthed Agassi, telling the world in 1999 how Agassi squandered his gifts for much of his career. Asked late in 2003 to assess Connors, Agassi politely demurred.

Chang's abundance of tenacity and ingenuity made it easy to compare him to Connors even if Chang was a much less powerful ballstriker than Connors ever was. As the sport advanced in the '80s and '90s, it was easy to forget that well into his 30s, Connors was the hardest hitter in tennis. Still, for much of the '90s, Connors felt the most affinity for Chang of these four, even if Chang never became number one and only earned a single Grand Slam. John McEnroe referred to Chang as "a poor man's Connors."

In the case of Courier, besides the unintentional phonetic connection, this Jim's bulldog-like qualities were evocative of Connors. But while Connors thrived on being the top dog, Courier found life as the hunted far harder than as the hunter. Despite winning four Slams by the time he was 22 in 1993, after that year he never reached another Slam final. He remained a formidable competitor for the balance of his career—most notably in that distinctly Connors-free event, Davis Cup—but never again came close to his early heights.

Which leads us to Pete Sampras, the player Connors denigrated discreetly in '90 and publicly a year later. In style and manner, these two were miles apart. Sampras' highly-refined serve-volley game, coupled with his exemplary sportsmanship, struck many as impersonal, devoid of what the uninformed consider charisma. But beneath this tranquility lay a supremely ambitious man, ravenous and eager to leave the biggest possible mark. Like Connors, Sampras was driven, monomaniacal in a way that distanced him from his peers, at once enigmatic, respected and feared. By the late '90s, even Connors noted, "I like the way he comes out day after day after day." Leave the lamentations to Agassi and McEnroe. Let them wallow in irony, reflection and ambiguity. Sampras and Connors were lasers.

Another area where Connors' influence is widespread is in the realm of emotion. Prior to his emergence, players never pumped their fists, raised their arms or thrust their bodies. Since Connors, virtually every player in tennis—even the allegedly taciturn Sampras—has his or her own highlight reel of physical gestures. It's often common for TV networks to summarize the flavor of a tournament with one Jimbonian pump after another.

If Connors' influence on the generation after him was significant and obvious, his stature among the all-time greats is not so easy to define. Like most sports save for baseball and golf, the criterion for evaluating excellence in tennis is constantly shifting. The game's structure in the pre-Open Era, for example, minimizes the achievements of such titans as Jack Kramer and Pancho Gonzalez, who between them won just five Grand Slam singles titles but are often ranked in the all-time top five by dint of their dominance on the unsung pro tours. On the other hand, the formidable Roy Emerson, winner of 12 Slam singles titles (second behind Sampras' 14), is not considered even a top tenner because greats such as Rod Laver and Ken Rosewall were absent during his glory years of the mid-'60s.

Connors won eight Grand Slam singles titles. The only players with more besides Sampras and Emerson are Laver and Borg (11 each) and Bill Tilden (10). Others tied with Connors are Agassi, Lendl, Rosewall and Fred Perry. Just behind him are eight others with seven each, the most notable being McEnroe, Newcombe and Mats Wilander.

No one in the Open Era won more tournaments than Connors' 109. Lendl is second with 94, trailed by McEnroe's 77, Sampras' 64 and Borg's 62. In an unofficial tally conducted in 1992, Laver ranks ahead of Connors with 142 titles as an amateur, pro and Open-era player.

But again, mere numbers fail to do justice to Connors or virtually any other tennis player. Many of Laver's titles were won in small pro events. Many of Connors' came on the lesser Riordan circuit. Moreover, one of the saddest aspects of tennis is that because it is such a small sport, it's intellectually undernourished. Whereas sports like baseball, football and basketball have large retinues of long-standing beat reporters and experts evaluating various eras, players and teams, tennis' lack of magnitude has left it begging for rigorous histories and assessments. In the vacuum, ex-players often step in and offer their judgments. Though valuable to a degree, these verdicts are invariably tainted by the highly-personal experience of having played a sport in a specific time rather than observed it across many epochs. This can be as short-sighted as asking William Westmoreland, leader of America's failed effort in Vietnam, to write the definitive book on the history of 20th century warfare. Dare he credit any opponent more than Ho Chi Minh? Add to this the exceptionally individualistic, combative nature of tennis, and the result is a constant flow of negativity. At least Jack Nicklaus is gracious enough to publicly praise Tiger Woods. Tennis differs. Once when I interviewed Don Budge, for example, within 15 minutes he downgraded the achievements and playing styles of Laver, Borg, Connors and Sampras. Were Joe DiMaggio to so harshly criticize Willie Mays and Barry Bonds, he would be massively countered by at least 10 writers in every big league city. Unfortunately, tennis simply isn't popular enough to have a full-time journalistic cadre, particularly in the United States. Its all-time greats have often become de facto historians and intellectual bullies, typically making the case for their peers and elders without giving much respect to more recent generations. As the saying goes, the golden age of sports ends when the athletes start getting younger than you.

Ex-pros often castigate Connors for his poor sportsmanship, emphasis on baseline play (a carryover from those days of Gloria's youth when only men were considered potent enough to be netrushers) and weak serve. One writer renowned as a major McEnroe apologist constantly points out how Connors failed to earn a title on European clay—but never mentions that McEnroe didn't either. Nor does the writer cite how Connors reached three straight U.S. Open finals on clay (albeit a faster version than the one used in Europe), including a win over Borg in '76.

But if playing style is a subjective evaluation factor, more telling factors such as dominance and longevity enhance Connors' place in tennis history. Throughout the Open Era, top players typically enjoyed approximately a decade of productive results at Grand Slams—by that, I mean the time from a player's first appearance in a Grand Slam final to his last. Connors' 15 finals (8-7) took place from 1974-'84. Equally impressive, throughout this entire time he was ranked among the top three in the world, a feat unmatched in the Open Era. Though I've already noted how he wasn't necessarily the best in the world when the computer ranked him that high in '75, '77 and '78, he was indeed number one at the end of '74, '76 and '82 (even if, in the latter year, the computer left him at two). Connors' three years concluding the year number one matches the Open-era accomplishments of Lendl, McEnroe, Borg and Newcombe (Sampras was the best a staggering six straight years).

Where Connors makes a uniquely compelling case for himself is in the last portion of his career. Productivity in a tennis player drops significantly past the age of 30, often leading rapidly to retirement. Sometimes the drop occurs even sooner. McEnroe, for example, reached only three Grand Slam semifinals past the age of 26 before quitting at 33 in 1992 (the same year Connors stopped at 40). Borg never even played a Grand Slam past the age of 25. Agassi has been extraordinary, winning five Slams past the age of 29. Ditto for Rosewall, who returned from an 11-year exile once the game went Open to win four Slams past age 33 (although two were at the weakened Australian Open). Connors won three Slams from age 29 to 31.

If you consider Connors' glory years—Slam wins and finals, top three in the world—the tennis equivalent of hitting .320 or better, then it's also helpful to note how many years past 30 where he hit .285 or better. From age 31 to 39, Connors reached the semifinals at 10 Grand Slam events. Only Rosewall and Agassi have performed so consistently at Slams so late in their careers. Interestingly, Connors, Rosewall and Agassi have each been compact, low-to-the-ground baseliners with superb service returns and exceptionally strong funda- mentals, ranging from the unsurpassed footwork of Connors and Rosewall to Agassi's extraordinary ballstriking skills. And as Courier once told me, "In tennis they can't pull you in and out of the game for a few minutes, or let you pitch just a few innings."

So where to rank Connors? He is certainly on tennis' "A" list of all- timers. But I would have to rank him slightly below the "A+" performers such as Sampras, Laver and Borg, each of whom posted better Slam results. Others such as Kramer, Gonzalez and Budge (the first man to win all four Slams in a year) were precluded from attaining the statistical heights of Connors, but in their own way were excep- tionally dominant too, as was Tilden. Connors ranks near them, perhaps a shade lower for any number of a few shortcomings that defined greatness in his own time, whether it be his abysmal Davis Cup record and his so-so (for him) efforts at Roland Garros. Then again, Kramer and Gonzalez's Roland Garros efforts were negligible, largely because the tournament was considered significantly less important than Wimbledon or Forest Hills. These evaluations are not easy.

Connors is increasingly crowded by the still-active Agassi and also rivaled by McEnroe and Lendl. But this debate is largely a function of terms. Do we compare players strictly in one match or over the course of a tournament, a given year or an entire career? What about the surface? For example, over the course of a long set of matches on fast indoor courts, polished netrushers like Kramer and Gonzalez were extremely formidable. Tilden and Budge made their rivals feel helpless. McEnroe at his best proved he was slightly better than Connors, but had far fewer .285 years. The somber Lendl comes closer to Connors in achievements than any Jimbo backer cares to admit and should not be penalized for his unwillingness to win friends and influence people à la Jimbo. Agassi's achievement of winning all four Slams is superb, but he's only finished the year ranked number one once. Still, for one match, on a neutral surface, it's hard to imagine Connors not finding a way to at least make it as competitive as possible against anyone in the sport's history. Yet the never-ending tournament between greats is only part of the story. The lesser-told tale in tennis is what makes a player a genius in his own time.

But as my history teachers taught me, our understanding of the past is flavored by the present. In the '90s, for example, with the character of American presidents strongly questioned, a number of books emphasizing the moral fiber of Abraham Lincoln, Harry Truman and the founding fathers became best-sellers. In a twist of that theme, as Winston Churchill said, "History will be kind to me, for I shall write it." And in tennis, no one has done a better job lobbying on his own behalf—not just as a player, but as an icon and venerated champion—than Connors' heir apparent, John McEnroe.

Their lives after tennis have gone in radically different directions. But their off-court journeys didn't start that way. As Connors' career faded in the '80s, he became a creature of Madison Avenue. His image graced dozens of advertisements, ranging from a candy bar, TV set, stockbroker, pain reliever, beverage, sneaker and more. He auditioned for the host job on his friend Merv Griffin's show, "Wheel of Fortune." He spent two years with NBC as an analyst for the French Open and Wimbledon. Connors also made intermittent efforts to mend fences with his lifelong rivals, often praising them in his press conferences and greeting them kindly at events. Playing a World Team Tennis match versus a team coached by Bob McKinley, Connors was in the middle of a comeback during a singles match. World Team Tennis permits substitutions, and as Connors changed sides, he glanced quickly at his old St. Louis foe and whispered under his breath, "Don't you dare even think about putting yourself in." As *Tennis'* Donna Doherty wrote in 1988, "he exudes a boyish charm that makes you forget the boorish days of his youth."

Witnessing Connors' transformation from detestable rogue to likable rascal, McEnroe said, "I could never be that phony." Throughout the late '80s and early '90s, McEnroe continually emphasized how much more there was to his life than tennis, implying that he possessed a far wider range of interests than a Midwestern rube like Connors who had devoted his life to a silly sport.

Then the whole picture tilted. While Connors launched his senior tour in 1993, McEnroe began his own transition. Having auditioned quite proficiently as a TV commentator during Connors' '91 run in New York, McEnroe rapidly became one of the sport's preeminent broadcast voices. The good news for McEnroe was that just as the sport's officials learned from Connors' example how to discipline (or at least attempt to discipline) a tempestuous talent, TV producers better understood what it took to have someone like McEnroe in the booth. During Connors' years at NBC, he was kept on a leash, told to report as early in the day as all other broadcasters to prepare for a long day behind the mike. Connors hated to sit through production meetings while being told to review notes, gather players for interviews and wait hours to come on the air. By the time McEnroe surfaced as an announcer for USA Network, his producers agreed to curtail his responsibilities and usually let him show up just before the first ball was struck.

McEnroe's emergence as a first-rate announcer kept him in the public eye much more than the senior tour did for Connors. Like his tennis, McEnroe's commentary was aggressive and quick-handed. Away from the sport, his forays into fields like art and music were the efforts of a rich dilettante. A colleague who saw him in concert told me his guitar sounded like a two-hour tirade at an umpire. It dawned on McEnroe that only in tennis was he ever going to be as venerated, to the point where he shocked everyone by spending more time at tournaments than he even had as a player. In time, similar to the way Connors had in his playing days, he smoothed out his bratty image, parlaying its shtick appeal everywhere from commercials to public appearances. Notably, though, when McEnroe had a chance to return to tennis in a serious and demanding role as captain of the Davis Cup team, he quit after just one season, unwilling to put in the hard work necessary to succeed. Instead, he retreated to his media celebrity role. In his quest for admiration, McEnroe will go virtually any place where he can command an audience. Though it's hard to believe a man who prides himself on authenticity would stoop so low as to host a prime-time game show called "The Chair," to his credit, in his own self-centered and peevish way, McEnroe's involvement in tennis reveals an enduring love for both the game and the tennis community.

Connors retreated. He entered tennis as an outsider, and he left it as an outsider. In his mind, he'd earned his share of recognition on the court, squeezing every drop of public admiration from thousands of fans and even more millions on television. Despite several late-career runs, the back half of McEnroe's career had far fewer of the long victory laps Connors ran for at least a decade. Though both players exhibited their share of paranoia on-court (doses of it help players at all levels so long as they're willing to admit it), Connors was raised to be far more leery of people than McEnroe. As Gloria used to put it, "They're out to get you, Jimmy." The more refined McEnroe family was raised to attend fine schools and assimilate into the world. Nike may have once dressed McEnroe in the clothes of James Dean from *Rebel Without A Cause*, but at heart he was groomed to be an insider. From the outset of his career, Connors, older than McEnroe, was like

Brando, a man bred for exile. Or better yet, McEnroe resembles Donald Trump, a privileged New Yorker ready to exploit his vanity for fame and fortune. Connors is akin to Howard Hughes, a venerated and eccentric icon who enjoyed his time in Las Vegas and preferred to sit alone with his millions.

At the 2000 Wimbledon, McEnroe proudly took his place in line with a troupe of champions invited for yet another special parade. Even the reclusive Borg returned to Centre Court for the first time since his final loss to McEnroe 19 years earlier, kissing the lawn. Connors failed to RSVP. When ESPN's "SportsCentury" commenced a laudatory hour-long Connors profile, he declined to be interviewed. As the International Tennis Hall of Fame planned its 50th anniversary in July 2004, all 68 living members were invited to attend the celebration. By February 2004, 75 percent said yes, including McEnroe and Evert. A few begged off for health reasons. Connors had yet to respond, but the thinking among all in the sport was that his presence would be a major surprise.

Since the mid-'80s, Connors has lived near Santa Barbara, California, a precious, wealthy community 90 miles from Los Angeles that prides itself on its strict building codes. Connors' biggest passion is golf, where he plays an 8-handicap, righthanded game with the same intensity he brought to his tennis. Hockey great Wayne Gretzky, an occasional Jimbo golf partner, once told me he'd never met anyone more competitive than Connors. Over the 2003 holiday season, Connors was spotted walking into a pro shop near Santa Barbara with a driver he'd just broken in two pieces. He also likes being the notable tennis star at a golf event, and once greeted a former ATP player who showed up at a Pro-Am with a hostile inquiry: "What are *you* doing here?"

As was the case with Howard Hughes in his twilight atop Las Vegas, word emanates of Connors making his share of phone calls and initiating intermittent contact with his personal network. For a time, one of Connors' best cronies was Evert's ex-husband, John Lloyd. Another pal was ex-pro Eddie Dibbs, a Connors pal since the junior days who's the quintessential street-wise sidekick. Others circle in and out of Connors' orbit, uncertain if the lion in winter is content or bored, at peace or primed for some sort of battle, even if now it's only with words. In friendship, all say how hard it is to know the man, emphasizing how Connors keeps them at a distance and lives his life strictly on his own terms. In business, he is considered a notorious deal-breaker, a man who at the last minute will demand an outrageous sum of money and therefore capsize an opportunity, whether for the good of himself, a colleague, a corporation or even a non-profit organization that wishes to honor him. But then, without any need for recognition, he'll extend kindness, as with the Gerulaitis family following Vitas' sudden death in 1994. Not prone to initiate contact with many people, Connors made numerous calls and visited Gerulaitis' mother and sister in the wake of that tragedy, including covering all expenses to fly and host them for Thanksgiving that year. When another friend was stricken with a brain tumor, Connors paid thousands of dollars in medical bills.

Connors still plays tennis, most frequently against a backboard that's not inside the confines of a swanky country club, but at a public park near a freeway. It was a sign to me that Connors had indeed come full circle. Virtually anyone who has ever played first hits a ball against a backboard. Gloria was fond of calling herself a human backboard for her boy (an interesting notion, to pulverize balls as hard as possible at your mother), and she remains her son's best source for advice. Recently, Connors was playing so much golf that he felt a bit uncertain about his tennis backhand. Instantly he called Gloria, who reminded him that unlike golf, where the club is swung in a semi-loop down and up through the ball, she'd taught him to hit straight through the ball, to get the racket right behind it and swing through the hearts of those rich kids across the river.

"I did it my way," Connors loved to say. As Mike Lupica noted when Connors was just 28, he has been like Sinatra, up and down and over and out. He became champion in the most democratic and individual of sports, taking the game and the law into his hands like no one else. Yet there was also a price, a barrier Connors erected between past and future that he refused to examine or tear down. One way to examine Connors' exile was to say that, unlike McEnroe, once he'd hung up his racket, he so respected the authenticity of his craft that he refused to turn it into a marketable commodity. Another point of view was that Connors was so conflicted about what it took to become a champion—that very racket an instrument of death—that he turned his anguish and possible guilt into savage contempt for the sport he claimed to love.

Fame had come and gone and could come again if Connors wished to play the game on terms he knew were silly and so different than the meritocracy of a tennis match. Fortune he possessed in abundance. But friends? The day of his Hall of Fame induction, Connors said, "I was always a loner. But for me to be standing here today alone is not right." But maybe in the end, isolation was precisely what he wanted. Tennis gave and tennis took. Does a retired soldier truly wish to recount tales of killings? Yet can anything ever match the genuine qualities of Connors' on-court killer instinct? In its singular, democratic genius, his feet, his strokes, his fervor, tennis in Connors' hands was so pure it hurt—perhaps him most of all. As Alexis de Tocqueville wrote in *Democracy in America*, "Thus not only does democracy make every man forget his ancestors, but it hides his descendants and separates his contemporaries from him; it throws him back forever upon himself alone and threatens in the end to confine him entirely within the solitude of his own heart."

To steal Connors' lingo, he and I still had unfinished business. Since the inflammatory '98 Hall of Fame story, we'd spoken on the phone several times. He was no different than before, cordial, chatty, skating across various topics, primarily superficial. We'd come no further, really, than that cab ride in '90, and so, if you looked at life like Charles Darwin or Gloria Connors, since we weren't moving forward, we were probably in retreat. It hardly mattered. Connors' history and the meaning of tennis continued to fascinate me. Every time I watched or played a match, every moment I encountered a Connors' rival who explained him to me was another stitch in the tapestry.

Our first face-to-face contact in three years came in September 2000. I wondered how he'd treat me. But I also wanted to set the record straight.

He was on a court with Borg. I sat inconspicuously in a corner and watched. As much as I loved it in the present, my mind reeled back to the past. More than 20 years since their classics, the traces of Borg's speed and Connors' precision entranced me. After a half-hour, Connors took a break and saw me.

"Hey, how the hell are you, son? Stick around and watch." Five minutes later, Connors hit a trademark running backhand. Turning to me, he said, "Not bad for an old man, huh?" Business as usual. At least for him.

After it was over, as Connors walked to his rental car and we made small talk, I brought up the story and told him that I wrote it as I saw it, and hoped he wasn't still angry.

"Angry? Why would anyone say I was angry? Who said that?"

I divulged my source.

"*Him*? What the hell does he know? Christ, Joel, you've known me long enough to know I don't give a shit what anyone writes about me. You wrote it as you saw it." Then he paused, and added, "But sometimes what you think is the story isn't always the story. See you tomorrow."

As I watched Connors drive off, a wave of physical and mental sensations washed over me. My body felt flush. What the hell was that? If indeed Connors didn't care what people wrote, why make such a cryptic comment about "the story"? Why was Connors so eager to discredit someone who claimed to be his close friend? Who was Jimmy Connors but, simply, at that moment, a creature of the moment settling a two-bit score with an elliptical wisecrack?

An epiphany struck. Connors as a person hardly meant anything to me. Yes, indeed, the tennis was real, and so, at times, were many of the moments we'd shared. But my desire for any connection was an illusion, a dream of a bond willed into existence by me. There were occasions I'd reached him with words. But the words that to me constituted action were to him merely thoughts, floating in the air with as much duration as, well, hot dog wrappers. If Connors indeed ever wanted to tell his story, he wanted a pliant craftsman, not a creature in his own making who wanted to dig deeper and deeper. All along, I'd chased him, chomped to tell the tale of Connors. He hadn't really been the subject of my pursuit anyway. It was my own story, my own life on and off the tennis court, that I was chasing all these years. I felt like Dorothy in *The Wizard of Oz*, when the good witch of the north tells her she had the answer in her little ruby slippers all along.

What was Connors but the avatar, the embodiment of a motivational illusion, summoning me not towards him (history), but myself? Just as Connors' affinity with crowds was narcissism masquerading as community, equally one-way was my dream (myth?) that becoming his appointed writer (ghost!) was a tactic for bridging the gap on my own loneliness. So what if I thought Connors saved my life? What did he care anyway? During one of my up-down LA trips, I saw Ken, who due to years of neglect had lost all the teeth he'd shown so brightly that day his braces came off. I cried when I told that to Joan. The next day I interviewed an Oscar winner for a magazine and discussed a TV project with a cable channel. It was impossible for me not to feel blessed, relieved and guilty over the contrast between my life and Ken's.

Surely I didn't want to plague Connors with my dread of where Ken had been and how I would cope with him in the years to come. Yet I was the only one who saw the link between these two men, both flesh and blood, one literal, the other a talisman. The link was so clear that day in Stanford. Long before Ken got sick, he constantly urged me to be tough. His subsequent alienation from himself ignited me to grasp my own identity like a dog chews a bone. Connors' tennis gave me a model, but what was a model but a point of departure, not conclusion? In their own ways, Ken and Connors each beckoned me into life's arena, insisting through their own victories and defeats that I face life's sober and powerful truth. Why do you love tennis, I once asked Connors. "You're out there by yourself, your whole destiny is in your hands," he said. "That's how life should be." He was right. The loneliness of life, democracy and tennis—to me, Connors made it all transcendental, mainly because I was ready to accept his gifts and recast them. All I had to do was click my heels. *In your own way, in your own time.*

But Connors' mark on me remained, as deep and pointed as the two toothmarks left by a vampire on the jugular. His blood was in mine, and would run through my veins until I drew my last breath.

Twenty-two years ago, exactly half my life ago, an hour into our first interview, I asked Connors for his thoughts on retirement. "There's no fade away for me," he said. "I do it, I do it right and I do it right now. And when I can't do it right any longer, it will be time for somebody else to do it right. It will be time for me to go. There aren't going to be any tears when I go, not from me or the other side of the net."

Don't bet on it, Jimbo.

Epilogue:
A Note on
Jimmy Connors'
Participation

It wouldn't be true to the spirit of Jimmy Connors if I didn't try to talk with him for this book. After 20 years, though, I've completed what I'd call the undergraduate degree of interviews with him. Notebooks and tape recorders, file folders and memories, are filled with Connors' reflections on his tennis, personality, rivals, various matches and more. For this book, I wanted the graduate school interview.

At the 2003 U.S. Open, Connors was inducted into the USTA's new "Court of Champions," honoring great players and their contribution to the U.S. Championships. Making his first public appearance in New York since 1992, Connors stood alongside Billie Jean King, Rod Laver and Chris Evert. He chatted with his ex-fiancee, enjoying the kind of flirtatious, cozy banter they'd exchanged all through their romance, break-up and married lives. Watching Connors in his snappy blazer and Evert in her hot pink pantsuit, it was remarkable how far they had come since their reign as tennis' King and Queen. As a couple they were smart enough to see they had too much in common for their own good. But they remained deeply connected in ways unlike any pair of athletes in history. Where else but in tennis could two champions from the same era understand each other's journey so well without competing with one another—and nearly marry? Unable to integrate too many people in his life, Connors has been able to maintain amicable ties with Evert and each of their respective spouses.

Of more personal interest to me than Connors-Evert was the series of videos produced honoring each inductee. I was intimately involved in the development and writing of all of them. I saw Connors shortly before the ceremony, and when I told him that I'd written all the pieces, he said, "Good effort." Then I told him what his was about, playing back the U.S. Open theme he'd told me 20 years earlier. "Yours," I said, "could be called 'business as usual.'" Said Connors, "I like the sound of that." After the video aired, he gave a fine speech. I'm told he was emotionally moved by the entire ceremony. I'm also told he was angry it wasn't televised.

Three weeks later, I called Connors to tell him about this book. As always, he was friendly, but he was also firm. "Don't write a book about me, son," he said, "don't write a book."

I told him it was too late, that the ship was off the dock and I was deep in the thick of explaining what he meant to me, why he was so important to tennis, how it was vital to make sure the world understood his story. Simply put, I was buttering him up, doing what I could to stay in the point without giving him so much pace that he'd instantly hang up.

"I'm out of tennis," said Connors. "I've got nothing to do with the sport anymore."

When I mentioned my fascination with his days back in the juniors, his response struck me as inadvertently revealing. "Manker Patten?" he asked. "That's the wrong way, the wrong side of me. That's the back side. I don't want to look back. I'm looking forward." Why was it the wrong side? Then he added, "I'm through with tennis. Unless I come back."

What? "Well," he said, "you never know." I suspect, though, that if Connors did decide to return and talk with anyone it would be a soft-ball-throwing person like Katie Couric, Bob Costas or David Letterman—the kind of uninformed, thigh-rubbing celebrity who'd simultaneously stroke Connors' ego and reinforce Jimmy's belief that interviews were pure blarney. *I just gave 110 percent, just like my mother—my only coach—taught me.* Connors knew I wanted more. What was the cost-gain ratio of your mother serving as drill sergeant? What about Segura? More, more, always more. Then he said that while he didn't want to talk with me today, his mind was always subject to change. I got him to agree to talk with me in two weeks.

Meanwhile, for months before, during and after I contacted Connors, I felt his gravitational pull. The vast majority of witnesses to his life were not only engaged, they were often more impassioned about Connors than their own careers and lives, as if he'd touched the flame longer and possessed a power they lacked. I've even sensed this awe for Connors emanating from John McEnroe. Others were skittish. Close rivals, friends, agents and other intimates (it's hard to call them Connors' friends since even they scoff at that kind of connection) who looked me right in the eye and vowed to talk were hesitant to go on the record lest they incur Connors' wrath. But then, like a cat letting out yarn from a ball, they'd share various snippets from matches, or interactions in hotels, at parties and practice courts.

Let me make this clear: I doubt if Connors at any point since we've known each other has ever told anyone not to talk with me. But I also know how oddly his life has mixed commerce and controversy. He's touched dozens in this sport in their wallets and their hearts. But the inherent curiosity of a journalist represents something more than a business partner, something less than an intimate. An interviewer is like a tennis player in that one of his best weapons is the possibility of doubt. Repeatedly, I told everyone—including Connors—my sole interest was tennis. I wasn't concerned with his affairs in romance or business. My passion was inside the lines. But I think I also knew enough about Connors—and after 20 years of asking about him, enough people in tennis knew how deep my knowledge and curiosity went—that they were worried that I was on his trail sharply enough to deploy any puzzle piece.

In our second conversation about this book, Connors listened carefully to the concept. "Your story," he said, "that could be of interest. But not me. They only want smut from me."

Several sources have told me Connors was jealous of the success of John McEnroe's book, which leaped to number one on *The New York Times'* best-seller list. One major reason for its popularity was McEnroe's discussion of sex and drugs. As in 1991, I told Connors he could tell his story any way he wanted. Again he declined. "Tennis wants to know me but it doesn't want to know me," said Connors. Is introspection too painful or, perhaps, does Connors lack the capacity or vocabulary to even explain what it took? Trained to kill, a retired assassin is a man addled by inner turmoil. Trained to win, he only wants a book that will generate the results that have taken over for match victories: raw dollars.

"You'll have to do it on your own," Connors said to me. "But I'll tell you this. I'll be the first one to buy it."

I told him he wouldn't have to buy it.

"I'll buy it, son, I'll buy it. Good luck to you, son."

For a moment, I felt that connection of humanity I'd seen in him all the way back to the time I'd approached him at UCLA in 1976, and in the parking lot of Tower Records, and in all the interviews since. Two weeks earlier he'd told me to stop. Now he was basically saying, *do as you will*. One-on-one, moment-to-moment, point-to-point, Jimmy Connors was willing to touch me. I wanted to believe he trusted me at least an inch. So often, he'd let me glimpse a bit more closely the same connection he'd made with more spectators than anyone in tennis history. It reminded me of the long look he and Panatta gave one another after their spectacular match at the '78 Open. You may bludgeon away at an opponent for hours, but together you also make something too. You create tennis. But was Connors connecting with others or merely drawing back into himself? As far as buying this book goes, was he telling the truth? Or just yanking my chain to retain my vote? Against all my desires, I suspect I'll never know.

Bibliography

BOOKS

Ashe, Arthur, with Frank Deford. *Portrait in Motion*. City: Hougton-Mifflin, 1975.

Ashe, Arthur, with Arnold Rampersad. *Days of Grace*. New York: Knopf, 1993.

ATP. Annual Media Guides, 1981–1993.

Baltzell, Digby. *Sporting Gentlemen: Men's Tennis from the Age of Honor to the Cult of the Superstar*. New York: Free Press, 1995.

Barrett, John, editor. *World of Tennis*. Annual media guide, 1972–1992 editions.

Bartlett, Michael; and Bob Gillen, eds. *The Tennis Book*. New York: Arbor House, 1982.

Bell, Marty. *Carnival at Forest Hills*. New York: Random House, 1975.

Berry, Eliot. *Tough Draw: The Path To Tennis Glory*. New York: Henry Holt, 1992.

Bodo, Peter. *Inside Tennis: A Season on the Pro Tour*. New York: Dell, 1979.

Bodo, Peter. *The Courts of Babylon*. New York: Macmillan, 1995.

Borg, Bjorn, with Gene Scott. *My Life and Game*. New York: Simon and Schuster, 1980.

Carr, Edward Hallett. *What is History?* New York: Random House, 1961.

Collins, Bud. *Total Tennis: The Ultimate Tennis Encyclopedia*. Toronto: SPORTClassic Books, 2003.

Collins, Bud. *My Life with the Pros*. New York: E.P. Dutton, 1990.

Connors, Jimmy, with Robert J. LaMarche. *How To Play Tougher Tennis*. Trumbull, CT: Golf/Digest Publications, 1986.

Connors, Jimmy, with Neil Gordon. *Don't Count Yourself Out: Staying Fit After 35*. New York: Hyperion, 1992.

Epstein, Joseph. *Ambition: The Secret Passion*. New York: Penguin, 1980.

Fitzgerald, F. Scott. *The Great Gatsby*. New York: Charles Scribner's Sons, 1925.

Gottesman, Ronald; Francis Murphy, Laurence Holland, Hershel Parker, David Kalstone, William Pritchard, eds. *The Norton Anthology of American Literature*. New York: W.W. Norton, 1979.

Evans, Richard. *Nasty: Ilie Nastase vs. Tennis*. Briarcliff Manor, NY: Stein and Day, 1981.

Evans, Richard. *McEnroe: A Rage for Perfection*. New York: Simon & Schuster, 1982.

Evans, Richard. *McEnroe: Taming The Talent*. New York: The Stephen Greene Press, 1990.

Evert, Chris, with Neil Amdur. *Chrissie: My Own Story*. New York: Simon and Schuster, 1982.

Exley, Frederick. *A Fan's Notes*. New York: Washington Square Press, 1977.

Flink, Steve. *The Greatest Tennis Matches of the Twentieth Century*. Danbury, CT: Rutledge Books, 1999.

Fox, Allen, with Richard Evans. *If I'm the Better Player, Why Can't I Win?* Norwalk, CT: Tennis Magazine, 1979.

Hegel, Georg Wilhelm Friedrich. *Lectures on the Philosophy of World History.* New York: Cambridge University Press, 1975.

Laver, Rod and Collins, Bud, eds. *Rod Laver's Tennis Digest: New Second Edition.* Northfield, Illinois: Digest Books, 1975.

McEnroe, John, with James Kaplan. *You Cannot Be Serious.* New York: Putnam, 2002.

McPhee, John. *Levels of the Game.* New York: Farrar, Straus & Giroux, 1969.

Mewshaw, Michael. *Short Circuit.* New York: Atheneum, 1983.

Neugeboren, Jay. *Imagining Robert: My Brother, Madness and Survival.* New York: Morrow, 1997.

Newcombe, John. *Newk.* Sydney: Pan Macmillan Australia, 2002.

Schickel, Richard. *The World of Tennis.* New York: Random House, 1975.

Secunda, Victoria. *When Madness Comes Home.* New York: Hyperion, 1997.

Segura, Pancho, with Gladys Heldman. *Pancho Segura's Championship Strategy.* New York: McGraw-Hill, 1976.

Trabert, Tony, with Gerald Secor Couzens. *Trabert on Tennis.* Chicago: Contemporary Books, 1990.

Wind, Herbert Warren. *Game, Set and Match: The Tennis Boom of the 1960s and 70s.* New York: Dutton, 1979.

Zimman, H.O. USTA Annual Yearbooks, 1970-1992.

ARTICLES

Amdur, Neil. "The Heart of the Matter." *World Tennis,* May 1986; "Jimbo Sounds Off." *World Tennis,* December 1986; "Rock of Ages." *World Tennis,* September 1987.

Anderson, Dave. "Davis Cup Détente." *The New York Times,* September 7, 1975.

Bellamy, Rex. "Is There A New Jimmy Connors?" *World Tennis,* March 1976.

Bodo, Peter. "Is Bill Riordan Really Such A Villain?" *Tennis,* July 1975; "Forest Hills '76—The Year The Crowd Took Over." *Tennis,* November 1976; Wimbledon coverage. *Tennis,* September 1977; "Forest Hills '77—How A Tennis Era Ended." *Tennis,* November 1977; "Have You Noticed? Jimmy Connors Has Changed." *Tennis,* May 1978; "Can Jimmy Connors Come Back?" *Tennis,* September 1981; "Jimmy Connors: What It Means to be No. 1 Again." *Tennis,* February 1983.

Byrne, Bridget. "Jimmy Connors Superstar." *Tennis West,* January 1974.

Collins, Bud. "My Ad." *World Tennis,* October 1973.

Connors, Jimmy. "Hail and Farewell to the T-2000." *Tennis,* November 1984.

Cunningham, Kim. "He's Sitting Pretty." *World Tennis,* December 1982; "Three's Company." *World Tennis,* July 1984; "Hanging On." *World Tennis,* October 1985.

Darrah, Jack. Report on rising juniors. *World Tennis,* October 1967.

Deford, Frank. "Raised by Women to Conquer Men." *Sports Illustrated,* August 28, 1978; "Jumpin' Jimmyny." *Sports Illustrated,* July 12, 1982; "He Got Down and Did It." *Sports Illustrated,* September 19, 1983.

Doherty, Donna. "Jimmy Connors at 35: More Candid Than Ever." *Tennis*, March 1988.

Evans, Richard. "Connors Shines The Big Apple." *World Tennis*, March 1978; "Mowing and Blowing at the Meadow." *World Tennis*, November 1978.

Feinstein, John. "Never Say Die." *World Tennis*, May 1989.

Flink, Steve. "An Interview with Jimmy Connors." *World Tennis*, November, 1974; "Make Room For Daddy." *World Tennis*, May 1980; "He's a Two-Timer Now." *World Tennis*, August 1982; "Connors Saves His Best for Last." *World Tennis*, October, 1982; "Snarling For Dollars." *World Tennis*, September 1983; "Is Connors All Washed Up?" *World Tennis*, May 1985.

Gray, David. "Yes, Virginia, There is a New Jimmy Connors." *World Tennis*, April, 1976.

Henderson, Doug. "My Life with Jimbo." *World Tennis*, August and September, 1985.

Jares, Joe. "Battle of the Ages." *Sports Illustrated*, September 16, 1974; "A Two-Armed Bandit Hits the Jackpot." *Sports Illustrated*, February 10, 1975; "Jackpot for Jimbo." *Sports Illustrated*, May 5, 1975.

Kirkpatrick, Curry. "Jimbo Comes on Strong." *Sports Illustrated*, March 4, 1974; "Wimbledon Was Never Better." *Sports Illustrated*, July 11, 1977; "He Mowed Borg Down." *Sports Illustrated*, September 10, 1978; "He Lit Up The Joint." *Sports Illustrated*, September 20, 1982; "Take A Lesson, Andre." *Sports Illustrated,* September 9, 1991; "Open and Shut." *Sports Illustrated*, September 16, 1991.

Lorge, Barry. "Connors-Newcombe Grudge Match at Australia." *Tennis*, March 1975; "The Greening of Jimmy Connors." *World Tennis*, November 1976; "Jimmy Connors: Star-Spangled Hero or Ugly American?" *World Tennis*, January 1979.

Lupica, Mike. "Has The Champagne Gone Flat For Jimmy Connors?" *World Tennis*, January 1978; "The Best and the Baddest." *World Tennis*, February 1981.

McKelvie, Roy. "Wimbledon 1972." *Tennis World*, August 1972.

Segell, Michael "Jimmy Connors: The Games He Plays." *Rolling Stone*, September 4, 1980.

Tarshis, Barry. "What You Can Learn from the Connors-Laver Match." *Tennis*, April 1975.

Tennis Illustrated. Assorted articles.

Tennis Week. Assorted articles.

Tennis West. Assorted articles.

World Tennis. Assorted articles.

Index